The Making and Unmaking of Whiteness

The Making and Unmaking of Whiteness

Edited by Birgit Brander Rasmussen,
Eric Klinenberg, Irene J. Nexica, and Matt Wray

DUKE UNIVERSITY PRESS

Durham & London 2001

© 2001 Duke University Press
All rights reserved
Printed in the United States of
America on acid-free paper ∞
Designed by Amy Ruth Buchanan
Typeset in Scala by Keystone
Typesetting, Inc.
Library of Congress Cataloging-
in-Publication Data appear on
the last printed page of this book.

Contents

Acknowledgments vii

Introduction 1 *Birgit Brander Rasmussen, Eric Klinenberg,*
Irene J. Nexica, and Matt Wray

Universal Freckle, or How I Learned to Be White 25
Dalton Conley

"The Souls of White Folks" 43
Mab Segrest

The Mirage of an Unmarked Whiteness 72
Ruth Frankenberg

White Racial Projects 97
Howard Winant

The "Morphing" Properties of Whiteness 113
Troy Duster

"White Devils" Talk Back: What Antiracists
Can Learn from Whites in Detroit 138
John Hartigan Jr.

Transnational Configurations of Desire:
The Nation and its White Closets 167
Jasbir Kaur Puar

Perfidious Albion: Whiteness and the
International Imagination 184
Vron Ware

The New Liberalism in America:
Identity Politics in the "Vital Center" 214
  Eric Lott

How Gay Stays White and What Kind
of White It Stays 234
  Allan Bérubé

(E)racism: Emerging Practices
of Antiracist Organizations 266
  Michael Omi

Moving from Guilt to Action: Antiracist
Organizing and the Concept of "Whiteness"
for Activism and the Academy 294
  William Aal

Bibliography 311

Contributors 333

Index 337

Acknowledgments

First of all, the Editorial Collective would like to thank all those who participated in and attended the Making and Unmaking of Whiteness conference in April 1997. We also thank the many activists who contacted us before and during the conference with helpful advice and suggestions and who forwarded the conference announcement to so many people outside academia. In addition, we would like to gratefully acknowledge the financial support of the University of California Humanities Research Institute, the Department of Comparative Ethnic Studies, the UC Berkeley Office of the Dean of Social Sciences, the Graduate Assembly, the Townsend Center for the Humanities, the Department of African American Studies, and many other departments too numerous to list here. Special thanks go out to Pamela Perry, Kellie Stoddart, members of the Critical Studies in Whiteness Working Group and the many volunteers who helped us organize the conference; Margo Adair for stepping in and facilitating the last day's session with little notice; and José David Saldívar and Michael Omi, faculty sponsors for the conference.

Jillian Sandell played a key role in writing the introduction and editing this book. She was unable to continue her participation in our collective, but her influence on both the conference and this anthology remains strong. We are grateful for her contributions.

Our collective thanks also go out to Monica McCormick, Abdul JanMohamed, and Mike Davis for expressing early interest in this book project and for providing sage advice on the route from conference to anthology. And big thanks to Katie Courtland, Justin Faerber, Nancy Zibman, and to our editor Ken Wissoker for his calm patience and unflagging support of this project from the moment we signed a contract with Duke University Press to the delivery of the final manuscript.

Birgit Brander Rasmussen: I am grateful to all those who teach me in formal and informal ways. Michael Omi put the first book on whiteness in my hands. I thank him and Jose Saldivar, Saidiya Hartman, Michael Rogin, and Abdul JanMohamed for years of inspiration, encouragement, and mentorship. Ned Blackhawk has always been a great friend, colleague, and mentor. My family is a never-ending source of love and support—*dette er til jeres aere*. I would also like to acknowledge the support of the Danish Research Academy. I dedicate my efforts on this project to those in Denmark who struggle against racism in all its old and new forms.

Eric Klinenberg would like to thank Mike Rogin and Loïc Wacquant for orienting him in the fields of research on race and Kate Zaloom, Kimberly McClain DaCosta, and Rachael Stryker for encouraging him to move beyond the obstacles in the terrain.

Irene J. Nexica thanks Naeema Fox, MJC, the Spice Girls, the Oakland YMCA, Elaine Manuele, friends far and near, and hip-hop for helping maintain inspiration, integrity, balance, and good humor. Big-time gratitude goes to Susana Loza, Justin Remais, Cici Ambrosio, Priscilla Hung, Nicky Bird, and Justin Smith for their help in clarifying theory and practices.

Matt Wray would like to thank José David Saldívar, Michael Rogin, and Michael Omi for their intellectual guidance and support. He also extends warm thanks to Jill Gurvey, Sean Heron, and Bill Mosca for their friendship and affection over the years.

Birgit Brander Rasmussen,
Eric Klinenberg, Irene J. Nexica,
and Matt Wray

Introduction

What is Whiteness?

This book comes at a moment when questions about the status and project of whiteness studies need consideration. Is whiteness a useful category of analysis? Does it help explain or illuminate ethnoracial differentiation, division, and domination? Is whiteness a useful category for political action? What, if any, significance does it have for organizers and political officials? How does whiteness figure into various racial vocabularies? Does looking closely at whiteness help to sharpen or does it obscure the analysis of race? Does studying whiteness further marginalize the experiences of groups long left out of the historical record? In other words, is "critical whiteness studies" the Trojan horse through which the study and perspective of whites will be recentered in studies of race and ethnicity?[1]

In the last several years there has been a proliferation of thinking and writing about whiteness.[2] A combination of factors has led to this profusion of scholarly activity, and continued publishing in the field is one sign that scholars have yet to resolve the many issues to which they helped call attention. What roles do multiculturalism, the rise of identity politics, and the "declining white majority" of certain key states and urban areas play in this scenario? Equally important, what does discomfort about the emergence of whiteness as a topic of debate signal about the nature or limits of the inquiry as it currently exists?[3]

One of the problems with studying whiteness is that no one who does it has an easy time determining what authors and texts should be included in the inquiry. Indeed, as an editorial collective we had many contentious and lively debates about this and were not always able to agree on what exactly constitutes an appropriate intellectual genealogy for critical whiteness studies. Furthermore, what became clear from our heated—and sometimes uncomfortable—discussions was that as a group we did not necessarily share a unified political or intellectual goal. Instead, as one might expect with a group of graduate students with different disciplinary backgrounds and viewpoints, we found that these differences sometimes precluded consensus. While the irreconcilable nature of our differences was often discouraging to us as a collective, it also encouraged us to try to include in this book a range of (sometimes conflicting) perspectives in order to register a sense of the diversity of political and intellectual projects at work within the amorphous project we are referring to as critical whiteness studies.

Despite the recent spate of publications, it is worth reiterating that the study of whiteness in the United States is not a new phenomenon. Intellectuals, writers, and artists of color have long studied, in Langston Hughes's memorable phrase, "the ways of White folks." As Toni Morrison noted in *Playing in the Dark,* for African Americans knowing and sensing the demands, needs, and (often unspoken) desires of whites have been essential elements of physical and cultural survival and success in a society dominated by white elites.[4] More recently, David Roediger has published an anthology of essays and excerpts that document the histories of African American perspectives on whiteness;[5] similar anthologies could be collected to represent the perspectives of other ethnoracial groups.

Recognizing this legacy contextualizes contemporary analyses of whiteness.[6] As it emerges, critical whiteness studies owes an important debt to earlier work on identity and domination by groups and authors long marginalized in academic study. Increasing demands for recognition have been accompanied by some degree of institutionalization of programs designed to create multicultural educational curricula. In the United States, for example, one achievement of institutionalized academic programs such as ethnic studies or women's studies has been to challenge university communities to address the histories of subjugated people, including accounts of struggle and dissent.[7]

While the emergence of critical whiteness studies is probably a historical effect of the complicated identity politics within and outside the university, the effects it will have on social and cultural analysis remain unclear. Perhaps one of the most familiar versions of critical whiteness studies is the research into "white skin privilege"—analyses of the many ways in which whiteness both signifies and underwrites various kinds of social, political, and economic advantages in the United States and elsewhere. An abundance of qualitative and quantitatively grounded research has documented the scope of white skin privilege and explains the social and cultural mechanisms that produce and reproduce it. In the United States, there is considerable evidence that to be white is to be the beneficiary of numerous advantages in the process of finding and keeping a job, buying a house, getting a first-rate education, staying healthy, and receiving more favorable treatment from the police and the courts.[8] For many, if not all, scholars of critical whiteness studies, the social reality of white skin privilege is now an underlying research assumption, a point of departure for investigations into how it was established and how it is maintained.

Even so, scholarship on whiteness has taken off on a number of divergent and sometimes contradictory trajectories. Some scholars seek to document and explain the historical and emergent forms of racial stratification, making visible the relative positions and practices of both the dominant and the dominated groups. Other scholars focus on more ontological questions about being white in societies where everyday experiences and conditions are lived through race. Yet another group of analysts is interested in the symbolic meanings of whiteness and questions about how those meanings shape relations of power. Expanding their inquiries beyond a particular national setting, many of these scholars have taken up questions about how whiteness circulates as an axis of power and identity around the world. Finally, another group of writers and activists, including those known as the neo-abolitionists, argue for eliminating whiteness altogether. For them, the ultimate goal of whiteness studies must be to eliminate the conditions of its own existence. These various approaches to the study of whiteness entail distinct and sometimes conflicting political and disciplinary possibilities, some of which we will attempt to tease out in the section on definitions. First, though, we want to discuss the intellectual and political context out of which this anthology emerged.

Whiteness and the Politics of Race

Several productive tensions energized those of us involved in organizing the 1997 University of California at Berkeley conference called the Making and Unmaking of Whiteness, from which this anthology

emerged.[9] Although the conference, the first major academic forum
to assess the state of research on whiteness, quickly became a national
event, the gathering was born of two distinctly local factors. First, the
political and social climate in California regarding race and immigration took a reactionary and conservative turn in the early and middle
1990s. Second, an informal study group of Berkeley graduate students began to review and assess the emergence of a wide variety of
writings on whiteness. To situate the articles collected here in the
context in which they were initially delivered, we want to briefly discuss the debates over the politics of race in California and explain why
we think such a public examination of whiteness could contribute new
perspectives.

In 1994 California voters passed Proposition 187, a particularly
punitive initiative aimed at "illegal immigrants." This legislation,
which denied medical and educational benefits and services to undocumented workers and their children and helped to make apparent
the ethnic and racial fault lines that were dividing the state, passed
by a wide margin at the ballot box. As our reading group began to
take shape in early 1996, Californians became embroiled in another
heated debate concerning matters of race, resources, and redistribution—this time over Proposition 209, the so-called California Civil
Rights Initiative—which essentially sought to end affirmative action
programs throughout all state agencies. For us, as students and teachers, the referendum hit close to home. It not only threatened to reduce
the work and educational opportunities for disadvantaged and disproportionately poor African American and Latino residents; it also
threatened to undermine the diversity that had made the University of
California such a dynamic and exciting educational institution. As a
state-run entity, the entire public higher education system in California, including our own Berkeley campus, would be forced to dismantle many of the programs designed to promote the admission and
retention of qualified and historically underrepresented students if
the proposition passed.[10] Students from poor and largely black and
Latino neighborhoods disproportionately attend high schools without
the Advanced Placement (AP) classes that enable students to achieve a
grade point average (GPA) higher than 4.0 (AP grades are inflated by
one full grade point). Structurally unable to compete with students
from high schools where AP classes make it possible to attain GPAS
above 4.0, students in these schools have little chance of gaining

admission to UC campuses such as Berkeley and Los Angeles, where the average G PA of admitted students has long been above 4.0. Affirmative action helped to correct for this and other structural inequities in the educational system.

As the participants in the Critical Studies in Whiteness reading group looked closely at the debate in California surrounding Proposition 209, we noticed that there was little space in the political rhetoric of the campaign for discussing the impact of white privileges and the interests that George Lipsitz has called "the possessive investment in whiteness."[11] Through its appropriation of the term "civil rights," Proposition 209 deceptively drew upon the moral language of the collectivism of the African American struggle for civil rights, even though its actual content was one of stark individualism. The language of the Proposition 209 campaign relied heavily on notions of "merit," as advocates of the bill called for a "level playing field," demanded "color-blindness" in admissions and hiring decisions, and charged that "reverse discrimination" had narrowed the opportunity structures available to whites while simultaneously degrading people of color. This language is resonant with other strains in U.S. political rhetoric used by pro–Proposition 209 forces to appeal to the white males who had voted for Proposition 187 in such large numbers.[12] Proponents of Proposition 209 drew on the moral language of the African American struggle for social justice even as they violated its core principles concerning the promotion of equal opportunities. One of the ironies of the political debate was that ultimately both sides of the issue would quote the same passages from Martin Luther King's "I have a dream" speech as ideological support for their positions.

According to conservative leaders such as Ward Connerly, who became the major spokesperson for the bill, white women and people of color who stood to gain from affirmative action programs were actually victims of another kind. Connerly and his allies argued that affirmative action programs injured their intended beneficiaries because the policies placed them in educational and vocational environments for which they were not adequately prepared, thereby setting them up for failure. Moreover, proponents of Proposition 209 argued that policies giving special preferences to white women and underrepresented people of color made it impossible for members of these groups to respect themselves or feel confident with their abilities and accomplishments. The stigma of being an "affirmative action baby,"

Connerly and his comrades claimed, overrode whatever benefits the policy offered.

Focus-group testing revealed that although white voters generally favored some form of "affirmative action," they opposed "racial preferences." Pro–Proposition 209 campaigners promoted (and many journalists quickly adopted) the latter term as a purportedly neutral, shorthand term for the complexities of extant affirmative action programs. Without a coherent framework for establishing the consequences of ethnoracially organized inequalities that created better life chances for most of California's white population, advocates for 209 could argue that working- and middle-class white men were in fact the victims of an unfair system of preferences. As Cheryl Harris has argued, because of this skillful discursive legerdemain, public debate over the proposition was framed as a question of whether or not individual (code for white) rights should be subordinate to group (code for people of color) rights.[13]

Interestingly, given this "white-as victim" theme, the social and political power of whiteness was repeatedly used as a threat in this campaign. The image of "angry white men"—the men supposedly left behind as women and people of color advanced—was called upon in many debates over affirmative action and made occasional appearances in campaign advertisements and journalistic stories. This figure was both a sign of the putative loser of affirmative action programs and an implicit suggestion that white men around the state were seething with outrage, perhaps even preparing to use violence to defend their interests. Identifying men who were angry and increasingly unhappy, the term signified and promoted a white backlash against civil rights gains of the 1960s. It served as an effective means of configuring people of color (and, to a lesser extent, white women) as an oppressive group and angry white men as a group who could, would, and should revolt.[14]

In November of 1996 Californians voted in favor of Proposition 209 by a healthy margin, effectively abolishing affirmative action programs in state agencies and institutions. In the first years that it was in effect the number of black and Latino students admitted and enrolled in the flagship University of California campuses at Berkeley and Los Angeles plummeted, particularly in the law and medical schools. Since then, Connerly and other California leaders have moved their campaign to end affirmative action programs to other states and have *privilege is passed down too!*

made plans to enter national politics. Furthermore, several states have followed California's lead and passed legislation similar to Proposition 209. A number of state university systems have dismantled their affirmative action programs in favor of other admissions policies.[15] But at the time of this writing the capacity of these programs to maintain diverse campuses remains in question.

As in California, political debates about affirmative action in other states have largely taken place without a language that juxtaposes white skin privilege against the "white-as-victim" rhetoric. Public debates rarely focused on the relationship between white ethnoracial status and access to good neighborhoods, schools, health care, and even to property and wealth. Despite the establishment in 1998 by President Clinton of a "national conversation on race," a public inquiry into the legal codes and social mechanisms that create and maintain racial inequality in the United States remains elusive, as does an open conversation about the benefits that whiteness still affords. The fundamental question of how educational institutions and employers should measure merit in a racially stratified society remains at the center of contemporary racial politics. Can research on whiteness help to balance this debate? Or is accounting for the possessive investment in whiteness and the consistent dividends it pays destined to be a merely academic undertaking?

merit + race

Defining Whiteness

As these recent debates over resources and opportunities in California make clear, it is important to be critically attentive to the language used to make claims about race and race-based privilege. The shift from "affirmative action" to "racial preferences" was more than a linguistic shift, it also reinforced a political consolidation of previously disparate groups of white and conservative people of color voters. In this campaign it became clear that monolithic notions of whiteness not only oversimplified the issues and did a disservice to the ways in which race intersected with other axes of social power and inequality— they also hampered the ability of those struggling to maintain affirmative action to mount an effective political countercampaign.

power

Definitions of whiteness, as many contributors to this book argue, will always be dynamic and context-specific. This is why the work of explaining what happened to the groups who "became white" but who

whiteness → flexible

did not profit from it is becoming a more important part of the study of whiteness. For example, the question of how whites themselves are internally differentiated, how the same white skin that has facilitated the integration, assimilation, and enrichment of some does not guarantee that others—such as poor whites and queer whites—might not also experience deprivation, stigmatization, and subjugation.[16] Scholars of "multiraciality" have helped to show how race is simultaneously connected to and disconnected from bodies and narratives about bodies, especially when those bodies can "pass" for white. Moreover, scholars of sexuality and difference, such as Cherríe Moraga, have argued that lesbian or gay whiteness does not guarantee, nor does it entirely abrogate, access to white skin privilege.[17]

There is an inherent definitional slipperiness and instability to whiteness, just as there is with all categories of race.[18] Like any other racial label, whiteness does not exist as a credible biological property. But it is a social construction with real effects that has become a powerful organizing principle around the world. It is not always clear what we mean when we refer to race or whiteness because both empirical and theoretical accounts define them inconsistently or not at all. In practice, this means that readers and audiences are left to apply their own conceptions of race to every analysis they confront. But the multiple definitions of race that people draw on—what we might identify as "folk," "analytical," and "bureaucratic" definitions—acquire different and sometimes contradictory meanings.[19]

Some popular discourses, for example, might conceive of race as a set of physical or physiological traits, perhaps rooted in a collective belief in a group-specific genetic structure. Whiteness, in this terminology, might be partially or even primarily conceived of as pale skin. In other popular discourses, race might be perceived as a set of behavioral characteristics: performing well in school or playing hockey or golf could be considered ways of "acting white."[20] Acting white can also correlate to a more general assumption of social power and a sense of entitlement. Terms like "oreo," "banana," "apple," and "coconut" are examples of what might be called "folk theories" of race that borrow but also depart from purely biological notions of race and attempt to name the disjunctions between skin color, lived experience, desire, and social status.[21] To make matters even more complicated, whiteness travels across national borders in contingent ways, and the same white body can be lived differently in various locations as intersections of race and gender flux. In her work on Thailand's sex trade, Annette Hamilton suggests that *farang* (foreign white-skinned) men in Thailand assume and enact those traits of masculinity that are increasingly not "at home" in the West. Specifically, even if poor and underprivileged by Western standards, *farang* men can go to Thailand and meet native women with whom they can participate in what Hamilton refers to as "the conventional Western masculinist imaginary," living out sexist—and sometimes misogynistic—versions of white masculinity in ways that make them feel paradoxically more "at home" in the East.[22]

What we are referring to as folk conceptions of race rarely correspond with state-based, bureaucratic versions of race. The U.S. Census, for example, defines whites and blacks as racial groups, but American Indians and Hispanics as cultural groups. Bureaucratic racial categories constitute the legal bases for official counts and accounts of particular populations, formally classifying and sorting groups into political as well as social units. As scholars in critical race studies have shown, bureaucratic and legal categories of race have been central in organizing state policies concerning rights, resources, and citizenship, particularly in the American context.

Analytic conceptions of race are likely to differ from both bureaucratic and folk notions, even though they emerge in relation to them. Most contemporary social scientists, for example, view race as a social but not a scientific fact, a mark that is sometimes written on the body but rooted in culture, not biology. Other scholars refuse to recognize race altogether, claiming that if race is not a scientific fact then it has no real meaning.[23] Definitions of whiteness, some of which are discussed below, suffer from the tendency to slip between these various conceptions of race or simply leave their theoretical foundations unstated.

While the project of refining (or rejecting) a workable concept of race is too broad and complicated to take up in this introduction, advancing the debate over definitions of whiteness is an integral part of the work that many authors in this volume do here. In the section that follows, we chart some of the ways in which researchers in critical whiteness studies have attempted to define whiteness as both a category of analysis and a mode of lived experience. There are many competing ways that whiteness can be viewed, analyzed, and critiqued, and the different points of reference offered here may help the reader create a fuller picture of the many configurations that whiteness takes in the growing body of literature. Some of us think that the conceptions of whiteness below are useful analytical and pedagogical tools, while others find them insufficient. As an editorial collective, we have argued among ourselves about how to theorize or define whiteness and have reached no consensus on the matter. Clearly each of the definitions that we discuss below, like all theoretical perspectives, has its own intellectual and political stakes.

WHITENESS IS INVISIBLE AND UNMARKED.
The idea that whites do not recognize or acknowledge their unearned racial privileges has become one of the most cited claims of critical whiteness studies.[24] In this line of thinking, whiteness operates by being "invisible," so ubiquitous and entrenched as to appear natural and normative. Here whiteness operates as the unmarked norm against which other identities are marked and racialized, the seemingly un-raced center of a racialized world. Therefore, while whiteness is invisible to whites it is hypervisible to people of color.

This assumption rests on two presuppositions. First, the "invisibility" of whiteness as a concept is predicated on an unknowing and unseeing white racial subject. Second, it posits a clear distinction between a group of white insiders who cannot recognize themselves for who they "really are" and nonwhite outsiders whose point of view affords them authentic insight. Neither of these presuppositions allows for the possibility that whites who are positioned differently in society may actually view or live whiteness quite differently. The claim also tends to privilege the viewpoint of whites, begging the important questions of how, when, and to whom whiteness becomes visible.

WHITENESS IS "EMPTY" AND WHITE IDENTITY
IS ESTABLISHED THROUGH APPROPRIATION.
This is another prominent theme in recent research, one that insists that whiteness as a category of identity has no "positive" content—that it is constituted solely by absence and appropriation. This position, which is perhaps most strongly associated with the work of the neo-abolitionists,[25] maintains that whiteness is defined solely by what it is not. Whiteness is then best understood as a lack of cultural distinctiveness and authenticity, one that leads to attempts by whites to fill in the blanks through acts of cultural appropriation or what bell

hooks has called "eating the other."[26] Similarly, Kobena Mercer has identified the tendency among white youth to perceive whiteness as empty, noting that by adopting markers of black self-empowerment such as dreadlocks or hip-hop fashion, white youth simultaneously displace whiteness and its historical connections to racial prejudice and discrimination.[27]

There are several limitations to the claim that whiteness is empty. First, the idea that whites have no culture suggests that the power of whiteness is in no way cultural. This would seem to rule out ap- *Culture* proaches to understanding how white hegemony is built through cultural praxis as well as inquiries into the symbolic dimensions of racial domination. Second, the idea that whiteness is nothing more than appropriation rests on the twin assumptions that cultures "belong" to racial groups and that there are clear and identifiable lines that separate and demarcate racialized peoples internally and externally. Recent *Hybridity* theories of hybridity and transculturation offer a direct challenge to these assumptions.[28] Finally, writings by neo-abolitionists rarely venture outside the familiar black/white dualism of U.S. racial relations, obscuring other forms of racial interaction from view. The emphasis in many of these writings on the inherently oppositional nature of "black culture" suggests an uncritical, romanticized view of blackness, one that privileges blackness as *the* authentically liberatory counterpoint to whiteness.

WHITENESS IS STRUCTURAL PRIVILEGE.

This claim is synonymous with the notion of white skin privilege we discuss above. Recent examples include one study that shows that young whites are up to four times more likely than equally qualified blacks to be given work in the service sector.[29] In the area of housing, Douglas Massey and Nancy Denton have shown how whiteness opens doors—quite literally—to homes in the most affluent neighborhoods in the country. Not only do real estate agents routinely select for whites when showing housing units in the best neighborhoods; banks also favor white applicants when awarding loans. Several decades of these now illegal (but still common) practices have helped to engineer patterns of spatial segregation by race and class.[30] Related to this is the fact that, because public schooling in the United States is funded *schools* largely through property taxes, students from wealthier white districts *taxes* attend well-funded schools. Thus they are granted many more resources in terms of teachers per student, books, computer access, and educational counseling, factors that are predictive of increased success in further education and greatly enhanced employment opportunities.[31] In the health care system, benefits are also distributed unevenly among racial groups. White Americans have lower general levels of morbidity and mortality than minoritized Americans.[32]

Many of these analyses, however, often fail to address the many social divisions within whiteness and among ethnoracial groups. Indeed, one of the blind spots of such research is an analysis of how class, race, and gender intersect to produce and mediate structural privilege; some of the inequalities that we recognize in terms of race— for example, levels of morbidity and mortality—are in fact better explained through differences in class and gender. Racial frames are certain ways of seeing, but also of not seeing, the nature of social division.

Claims about how whiteness functions in society sometimes obscure equally important questions about how different individuals understand, relate to, and negotiate whiteness as an identity and social position. In addition to studies of how whiteness enables forms of social control, how it affects distribution of power and resources, or how it generally operates to maintain the status quo, we must gain a better understanding of the creative and varied responses of individuals as they interact with each other and with social institutions.

WHITENESS IS VIOLENCE AND TERROR.

Bell hooks argues that one way in which whiteness has been experienced by those subordinated to its power is as an ever-present and overbearing source of dread for people of color.[33] White supremacy has been used to justify and rationalize the genocide, enslavement, lynching, and public humiliation of people of color for centuries.[34] Understanding whiteness primarily as violence and terror is associated with the view, discussed below, that whiteness is properly understood as the historical legacy of colonialism and imperialism.

The notion that whiteness is violence and terror challenges the idea that whiteness is invisible and unmarked. Acts of white supremacist violence stand out even to whites because they are often designed to instill terror through their visibility. Indeed, one of the central uses of white violence and terror is to make a display of white privilege and to assert the power to subjugate others.

WHITENESS IS THE INSTITUTIONALIZATION
OF EUROPEAN COLONIALISM.
Historians such as Edmund Morgan and Theodore Allen have argued
that contemporary conceptions of race and institutionalized racial inequality in the United States are rooted in histories of colonialism and
imperialism.[35] Notions of racial inferiority emerged to justify a social
structure organized around subjugation and exploitation and was
then elaborated by biologistic theories of inherent differences in the
nineteenth and twentieth centuries. Other scholars, informed by a
transnational and postcolonial perspective, have developed these ideas
to suggest that notions of race and class that informed each other as
social divisions inside Europe were transposed to and transformed by
colonialism.[36]

Recent work by M. Jacqui Alexander, Chandra Mohanty, and Robert
Young, among others, has problematized this discussion further by
tracing the dynamic whereby scholarship itself reproduces the privileged status of whiteness instituted by colonialism. Some postcolonial scholars have argued that Western theory and discourse itself has
been an example and instantiation of whiteness as colonialism.[37] Yet
others, such as Aijaz Ahmad, claim that this position reduces colonialism to a metaphor and as a consequence empties the term of its
political significance and utility.[38]

CRITICAL WHITENESS STUDIES IS AN ANTIRACIST PRACTICE.
This theme dominates a great deal of the activist-oriented literature on
whiteness and runs through much of the academic scholarship as
well.[39] Whiteness, it is argued, serves as a foundation for racial domination and inequality. Through careful study of how white privilege
has been historically constructed, we may find ways to dismantle it or
abolish it altogether, thereby destroying the entire system of racial
stratification.

Much of this literature dodges, however, the questions of what
exactly constitutes antiracism. As William Aal and Allan Bérubé argue, antiracist practice is often undermined by the desire of white
people to remain comfortable. If the imperative in a process is comfort
rather than transformation, the process fails to address the question of
who has the power to decide just what comfort is and what assumptions and structures it rests on. As we organized our conference and
researched this book, it became clear to us that many people are pro-

foundly uncomfortable with whiteness studies—but that discomfort stems from very different reasons.[40]

These themes at work in the research on whiteness—and there are others we have not discussed—make for an often confusing mix of theoretical starting points and research agendas. As we have said, the confusion is compounded when writers fail to make clear their theoretical assumptions about race and their definitions of whiteness. As new interest in researching white identity has grown, so have the many different ways of constructing whiteness as an object of knowledge and analysis. These various constructions of whiteness are sometimes in conflict and, when they are uncritically conjoined, can produce theoretical tensions and undermine effective political action.

The Essays

In bringing together the essays for this anthology, we faced a number of dilemmas. As a practical matter, we simply could not include all the fine essays from the conference; with over thirty-five participants, the resulting anthology would have been better suited as a doorstop than a useful classroom text. Thus, we had to be selective. Also, there were few activists and independent scholars at the conference. We first became aware of this as a problem after sending out announcements via email to a wide audience. Feedback from people doing critical whiteness studies outside the academy made it clear that they were excited to participate, and we were excited to have their participation. In our view, if critical whiteness studies remains separate from antiracist practice, it will likely produce scholarship that is divorced from any consideration of its political significance. While we had hoped to bring academics and activists into dialogue about the ways that public silences about white skin privilege and whiteness work to effectively maintain the benefits of whiteness, we were unprepared to meet and mediate the often divergent needs of activists, community leaders, and organizers.[41] We have featured more activist voices in this volume and have tried to critically address more activist-oriented concerns as well.

We begin with a personal narrative by sociologist Dalton Conley, followed by essays from activist-writer Mab Segrest and cultural critic

Ruth Frankenberg. All three essays explore how the idea of whiteness as an invisible social norm negatively affects the lives of those who inhabit places of racial privilege. In "Universal Freckle, or How I Learned to Be White," Conley describes the unusual education in race he received growing up as a white minority in the projects on Manhattan's Lower East Side. Weaving insights gleaned from his childhood experiences with those he has made in his analytical studies of race and inequality, Conley narrates his own natural experiment to trace the meanings and consequences of becoming white and middle-class.

In her essay, "'The Souls of White Folks,'" Segrest suggests that white people do pay a terrible spiritual price for living in a system of white supremacy. Looking into her own and other southern family histories, Segrest locates personal pain and addiction in a larger political context of exploitation and suggests that, in order to be effective, individual and collective therapy must be connected to activist practice. Finally, in "The Mirage of an Unmarked Whiteness," Frankenberg departs from her earlier, influential argument that whiteness is an unmarked category and instead claims that whiteness is by no means invisible to everyone. Those who insist on not seeing whiteness, Frankenberg argues, suffer from a kind of spiritual and social blindness.

A second set of essays by social scientists interrogates whiteness as a critical term for social analysis. In his essay, "White Racial Projects," Howard Winant introduces the term "global racial projects" and discusses the historical transformations of white identity politics in the latter half of the twentieth century. Winant deliberates on the status of whiteness as both identity and analytical concept and argues that only through a comparative sociological approach can we hope to understand the nature of whiteness. In "The 'Morphing' Properties of Whiteness," Troy Duster explores the vicissitudes of shifting racial and class identity, noting that whiteness can and often does exist in multiple states. Employing the metaphor of H_2O, he explains how whiteness can manifest itself as vapor, water, or ice, and he explores the kinds of theoretical and methodological quandaries this can create for researchers. Anthropologist John Hartigan Jr.'s essay draws on ethnographic fieldwork in Detroit, Michigan, to challenge the idea of whiteness as a monolithic or uniform site of social privilege. Hartigan's essay, "Interrogating the Souls of White Folks in Detroit: Notes from the Field on the Concept of Whiteness," describes his research among poor "hillbilly" whites in the urban core of a predominantly African American city.

The idea that whiteness as an identity can function to emblematize national belonging and help secure citizenship is central to the essays by cultural theorists Jasbir Kaur Puar, Vron Ware, and Eric Lott. As Puar argues in her essay, "Transnational Configurations of Desire," for many women of color, especially immigrants, "coming out" as a lesbian in the United States often means identifying with white culture and identifying with a certain identity of privilege. Puar unpacks the processes of racial and sexual identification and disidentification that accompany these crossings. In "Perfidious Albion," Vron Ware comments upon the efforts by a newly centrist Labour Party to realign "Englishness" and "Britishness" with whiteness and analyzes their mixed successes in this regard. Her critique of the racial politics of "Blairism" and her discussion of postwar immigration to the United Kingdom reveal how whiteness plays a central role in binding white subjects to the state. "The New Liberalism in America: Identity Politics in the 'Vital Center,'" Eric Lott's wide-ranging essay on cultural politics, explores the new political center in the United States. Citing a crisis in "white liberal boomer" masculinity, Lott takes to task many of the most prominent advocates for the new politics, noting that their rhetoric is designed to combat black nationalism through a renewed emphasis on the necessity of foregrounding class analysis over race.

We close with a trio of essays that seek to situate and analyze various efforts at antiracist organizing. In "How Gay Stays White," independent community historian Allan Bérubé traces the difficulties and quandaries of being antiracist in a racist society. Bérubé explores the convergence of racial and gender privilege with the identity politics of sexual minorities and offers a detailed postmortem of the racial politics of gay opposition to the "Don't Ask, Don't Tell" campaign against gays in the military. In "(E)racism," sociologist Michael Omi focuses on antiracist coalition work among communities of color in U.S. cities. Omi suggests that in the context of multicultural and multiracial urban settings, even where the population is primarily composed of African Americans and whites, using a black/white model of racism can limit rather than enable the kind of activist work such groups try to accomplish. This essay provides a model of the potentially synergistic conversation between critical whiteness studies and antiracist activism. Furthermore, Omi's essay instantiates our belief that the analysis of whiteness or of white privilege does not necessarily have to recenter white people.

In "Moving from Guilt to Action: Antiracist Organizing and the Concept of 'Whiteness' for Activism and the Academy," William Aal explains the places where critical studies in whiteness have been useful or useless for his work as an antiracist organizer for the Seattle-based organization Tools for Change. Drawing on interviews with other antiracist activists, Aal discusses the limits and possibilities presented by the academic discourse on whiteness. This essay challenges readers to imagine the potential of more cooperative efforts between scholars and activist communities.

Whether critical studies of whiteness will contribute to the project of understanding or unmaking racial hierarchies ultimately depends on how members of all communities interested in redrawing or erasing the color lines—authors, readers, students, activists, and those who are a little of each—learn to work with each other. The range of articles in this anthology reflects our collective sense of how daunting it is to consider "unmaking whiteness" and represents our conviction that a diverse group of people, strategies, and actions are necessary for this kind of work. At present, there are still far more questions than answers. Our hope is that this transdisciplinary collection will move us all a little closer to understanding what it is we talk about when we talk about "whiteness."

Notes

1 We use the term "critical whiteness studies," rather than the term "whiteness studies," to mark the explicitly analytical nature of this inquiry. This book, as well as the intellectual project of which it is a part, does not intend to celebrate or denigrate any particular group but rather aims to analyze the processes and mechanisms that organize various forms of racial stratification.

2 This anthology enters an increasingly crowded field of edited collections on whiteness. Among them are Richard Delgado and Jean Stefancic, eds., *Critical White Studies: Looking behind the Mirror* (Philadelphia: Temple University Press, 1997); Michelle Fine et al., eds., *Off White: Readings on Race, Power, and Society* (New York: Routledge, 1997); Ruth Frankenberg, ed., *Displacing Whiteness: Essays in Social and Cultural Criticism* (Durham:

Duke University Press, 1997); Mike Hill, ed., *Whiteness: A Critical Reader*
(New York: New York University Press, 1997); Joe L. Kinchloe et al., eds.,
White Reign: Deploying Whiteness in America (New York: St. Martin's,
1998).

3 For a careful consideration of these and other questions, see Robyn Wiegman, "Whiteness Studies and the Paradox of Particularity," *boundary 2* 25,
no. 3 (fall 1999): 115–50.

4 Toni Morrison, *Playing in the Dark: Whiteness in the Literary Imagination*
(Cambridge, Mass.: Harvard University Press, 1992).

5 David Roediger, *Black on White: Black Writers on What It Means to Be White*
(New York: Schocken, 1998). For a provocative analysis of African American autobiography and its theorization of white identity, see Crispin Sartwell, *Act Like You Know: African-American Autobiography and White Identity*
(Chicago: University of Chicago Press, 1998).

6 Although the recent academic attention to whiteness has been sparked
mainly by books and articles with "whiteness" or "white" in their titles,
numerous other texts, from many generations of scholars and writers,
have looked closely at the subject and contributed to the study of how the
dominant group exerts, maintains, and reproduces its position in a society
organized around racial hierarchies and domination. When we limit the
inquiry to those texts that announce their focus as "whiteness," we neglect
and render invisible relevant work by scholars who chose not to make
it the explicit center of their projects. For example, in the early 1970s
Adrienne Rich wrote important essays on the need for white Western
feminists to come to terms with their whiteness and to interrogate how
whiteness functions in the production of feminist theory, but she did so
without including the word "whiteness" in her title. See her collection of
essays *On Lies, Secrets, and Silence: Selected Prose* (New York: Norton, 1979).
See also Dorothy Allison, *Skin: Talking about Sex, Class, and Literature*
(Ithaca, N.Y.: Firebrand, 1994); Elly Bulkin, Minnie Bruce Pratt, and Barbara Smith, eds., *Yours in Struggle: Three Feminist Perspectives on Anti-
Semitism and Racism* (Ithaca, N.Y.: Firebrand, 1984); and Audre Lorde,
Sister/Outsider: Essay and Speeches (Freedom, Calif.: Crossing Press, 1984),
for examples of works by some of the many women of color, feminist, and
lesbian activists and writers who were publishing critiques of whiteness
long before the term "critical whiteness studies" was in circulation.

7 On the other hand, Loïc Wacquant argues that a danger of "group-based"
work that is generated in group-specific disciplinary structures is that it
tends to succumb to what he calls the logic of the trial, in which the
implicit or explicit goal of scholarly inquiry is to judge the merits of specific groups based on the normative standards of the inquirer. Wacquant
cautions that such projects often lack an analytic basis and therefore do not

advance theories of racial differentiation and domination. See Loïc J. D. Wacquant, "For an Analytics of Racial Domination," *Social Theory and Political Power* 11 (1997): 221–34.

8   While empirical findings of scientific studies about the historical evidence for and contemporary manifestations of white privilege may not give us a complete picture of white racial identity, they begin to indicate the extent of social advantages for whites in the United States. Among the most prominent of these studies from the 1990s are Tomás Almaguer, *Racial Fault Lines: The Historical Origins of White Supremacy in California* (Berkeley: University of California Press, 1994); Dalton Conley, *Being Black, Living in the Red: Race, Wealth, and Social Policy in America* (Berkeley: University of California Press, 1999); Ruth Frankenberg, *White Women, Race Matters: The Social Construction of Whiteness* (Minneapolis: University of Minnesota Press, 1993); Ian F. Haney López, *White by Law: The Legal Construction of Race* (New York: New York University Press, 1996); Douglas Massey and Nancy Denton, *American Apartheid: Segregation and the Making of the Underclass* (Cambridge: Harvard University Press, 1993); Mel Oliver and Thomas Shapiro, *Black Wealth/White Wealth: A New Perspective on Racial Inequality* (New York: Routledge, 1995); David R. Roediger, *The Wages of Whiteness: Race and the Making of the American Working Class* (New York: Verso, 1990); and Michael Tonry, *Malign Neglect: Race, Crime, and Punishment in America* (New York: Oxford University Press, 1995).

9   The organizers of the conference were seven graduate students: Birgit Brander Rasmussen (Comparative Ethnic Studies), Eric Klinenberg (Sociology), Irene Nexica (Comparative Ethnic Studies), Pamela Perry (Sociology), Jillian Sandell (English), Kellie Stoddart (Psychology), and Matt Wray (Comparative Ethnic Studies). The conference was hosted by the Department of Comparative Ethnic Studies at University of California, Berkeley, campus in April 1997 and received major funding from the University of California Humanities Research Institute. Those who presented papers or moderated at the conference were Norma Alarcón, Allan Bérubé, Roxanne Dunbar-Ortiz, Troy Duster, Michelle Fine, Shelley Fisher Fishkin, Ruth Frankenberg, Evelyn Nakano Glenn, Cheryl Harris, John Hartigan Jr., Saidiya Hartman, Patricia Penn Hilden, Mike Hill, Aida Hurtado, Noel Ignatiev, Caren Kaplan, Josh Kun, Eric Lott, Steve Martinot, Cameron McCarthy, Walter Benn Michaels, Annalee Newitz, Michael Omi, Sam Otter, Fred Pfeil, john powell, Jasbir Kaur Puar, David Roediger, Michael Rogin, José David Saldívar, Alexander Saxton, Nancy Scheper-Hughes, Mab Segrest, Richard Walker, David Wellman, Lois Weis, and Yvonne Yarbro-Bejarano.

10 Actually, within the University of California system (just one part of Cali-

fornia's three-tiered system of higher education) this was already a *fait accompli*. In the summer of 1995, the governing body of the University of California system, the Board of Regents, led by then-governor Pete Wilson in what was a transparent bid for Republican presidential candidacy, unilaterally eliminated affirmative action programs in hiring and admissions, despite widespread opposition from administrators, faculty, and students. Proposition 209 was designed to impact *all* state funded public agencies. See Robert Post and Michael Rogin, eds., *Race and Representation: Affirmative Action* (New York: Zone Books, 1998).

11 George Lipsitz, *The Possessive Investment in Whiteness: How White People Profit from Identity Politics* (Philadelphia: Temple University Press, 1998).

12 White men voted 63 to 37 percent in favor of Proposition 187. For this statistic and a thorough analysis of the Proposition 209 campaign, see Linda Chavez, *The Color Bind: California's Battle over Affirmative Action* (Berkeley: University of California Press, 1998). For an engaging critique of the history of the state initiative process in California, see Peter Schrag, *Paradise Lost: California's Experience, America's Future* (New York: New Press, 1998).

13 See Cheryl Harris, "Whiteness as Property," *Harvard Law Review* 106, no. 8 (June 1993): 1709–91.

14 At least one group, Angry White Men for Affirmative Action, led by Paul Rockwell, an Oakland librarian, sought to insert into public debate concrete examples of some of the racial and gender advantages held by white males and to expose the pro–Proposition 209 campaign's deceptive tactics. For essays on the political uses (and abuses) and social referents of the term "angry white men," see David Wellman, "Minstrel Shows, Affirmative Action Talk, and Angry White Men," in *Displacing Whiteness*, ed. Frankenberg, 211–22; and Matt Wray, "Angry White Men: Figuring Whiteness and Masculinity in Affirmative Action Debates," in *What, Then, Is White?* ed. Noel Ignatiev and Jacqueline Mimms (New York: Oxford University Press, forthcoming).

15 As of 1999, California guaranteed admission to one of the University of California campuses to the top 4 percent of every graduating high school class in the state; Texas admitted the top 10 percent; and Florida, the top 20 percent. There are other variations among these policies. Texas, for example, allows all admitted students to choose the campus they will attend, whereas California does not guarantee admission to the more selective schools.

16 See Ross Chambers, "The Unexamined," in *Whiteness: A Critical Reader*, ed. Mike Hill (New York: New York University Press, 1997), 187–203. For analyses of how being poor can confound and complicate the benefits of being white, see Neil Foley, *The White Scourge: Mexicans, Blacks and Poor*

Whites in Texas Cotton Culture (Berkeley: University of California Press, 1997); John Hartigan Jr., *Racial* Situations: *Class Predicaments of Whiteness in Detroit* (Princeton: Princeton University Press, 1999); and Matt Wray and Annalee Newitz, eds., *White Trash: Race and Class in America* (New York: Routledge, 1996).

17 Cherríe Moraga, "La Güera," in her book *Loving in the War Years* (Boston: South End Press, 1983).

18 This is not because deploying whiteness as an analytic category is a recent phenomenon. Eighty years ago W. E. B. Du Bois commented on the (then) recent "discovery of personal whiteness among the world's peoples," adding with sarcasm that at the same moment that white people notice their whiteness they simultaneously celebrate it but do not really define it. "The Souls of White Folks," in W. E. B. Du Bois, *Darkwater: Voices from Within the Veil* (New York: Harcourt, Brace, and Howe, 1920), 29–30.

19 For an explanation of the confusing barter between folk, bureaucratic, and analytical conceptions of race, see Wacquant, "For an Analytics."

20 See Signathia Fordham, *Blacked Out: Dilemmas of Race, Identity, and Success at Capital High* (Chicago: University of Chicago Press, 1996).

21 These terms are used to refer to African Americans, Asian Americans, Native Americans, and Latinos, who, because of their attitudes, practices, and/or social position, are considered to be "colored" on the outside, but "white" on the inside.

22 Annette Hamilton, "Primal Dream: Masculinism, Sin, and Salvation in Thailand's Sex Trade," in *Sites of Desire, Economies of Pleasure: Sexualities in Asia and the Pacific,* ed. Lenore Manderson and Margaret Jolly (Chicago: University of Chicago Press, 1997), 145–65. In her work on China, Louisa Schein argues that whiteness works differently for urban or coastal Chinese than it does for inland and rural Chinese, with whiteness (associated with cities) often signifying modernity and commodity culture and "color" (associated with rural China) signifying a lost or distant national identity. See Louisa Schein, "The Consumption of Color and the Politics of White Skin in Post-Mao China," *Social Text* 41 (winter 1994): 141–64.

23 See, for example, Walter Benn Michaels, "Autobiography of an Ex-White Man," in "The White Issue," *Transition* 73, 7, no. 1 (1998): 122–43.

24 Richard Dyer, "White," *Screen* 29, no. 4 (autumn 1988): 44–64. See also Frankenberg's *White Women, Race Matters,* in which she explores how whiteness was an invisible or unmarked category for her white female interviewees.

25 See, for example, Noel Ignatiev and John Garvey, eds., *Race Traitor* (New York: Routledge, 1996), and David Roediger, *Towards the Abolition of Whiteness: Essays on Race, Politics, and Working Class History* (New York: Verso, 1994). For a modified neo-abolitionist argument, see Vron Ware

and Les Back, *The Trouble with Whiteness* (Chicago: University of Chicago Press, forthcoming).

26 See bell hooks, "Eating the Other," in her *Black Looks: Race and Representation* (Boston: South End Press, 1992), 21–39. Roediger also argues along these lines, stating that "whiteness is not merely oppressive and false, it is nothing *but* oppressive and false." *Towards the Abolition of Whiteness*, 13. See also Dyer, "White."

27 Kobena Mercer analyzes this facet of white signification when he describes the ways that, for some whites, whiteness is both rendered transparent and given meaning by appropriating significations that are considered nonwhite. Mercer, *Welcome to the Jungle* (New York: Routledge, 1994), 339.

28 See, for example, Shelly Fisher Fishkin, "Interrogating 'Whiteness,' Complicating 'Blackness': Remapping American Culture, *American Quarterly* 47, no. 3 (1995): 428–66; and José David Saldívar, *Border Matters: Remapping American Cultural Studies* (Berkeley: University of California Press, 1997).

29 See Troy Duster, "Postindustrialism and Youth Unemployment: African Americans as Harbingers," in *Poverty, Inequality, and the Future of Social Policy*, ed. Katherine McFate et al. (New York: Sage, 1995).

30 See Massey and Denton, *American Apartheid*. For articles by Massey and Denton that go beyond black/white divides, see "Residential Segregation of Blacks, Hispanics, and Asians by Socio-Economic Status and Generation," *Social Science Quarterly* 69 (1988): 797–817; and "Trends in the Residential Segregation of Blacks, Hispanics, and Asians," *American Sociological Review* 52 (1987): 802–25.

31 See Jonathan Kozol, *Savage Inequalities: Children in America's Schools* (New York: Crown, 1991), and Cameron McCarthy and Warren Crichlow, eds., *Race, Identity, and Representation in Education* (New York: Routledge, 1993).

32 Nancy Krieger et al., "Racism, Sexism, and Social Class: Implications for Studies of Health, Disease, and Well-being," *American Journal of Preventive Medicine* 9 no. 6-suppl. (1993): 82–122. See also Andrew Hacker, *Two Nations: Black and White, Separate, Hostile, Unequal* (New York: Scribners, 1992).

33 In addition to bell hooks, "Representations of Whiteness" in *Black Looks*, see Richard Dyer, *White* (New York: Routledge, 1997); Mab Segrest, *Memoir of a Race Traitor* (Boston: South End Press, 1994); and Michael Novick, *White Lies, White Power: The Fight against White Supremacy and Reactionary Violence* (Monroe, Maine: Common Courage Press, 1995).

34 Because of this history, those who have important insights to offer about the nature of whiteness may be reluctant to speak on the issue or become identified with critical whiteness studies. In *Black Looks*, bell hooks argues that minority scholars in the United States have hesitated to describe their

discomfort and reveal their negative associations with whiteness, partly out of a fear of disquieting their readers and partly on account of the historic ways in which people of color have learned to pretend to be comfortable and safe with encounters with whiteness. Nonetheless, she says, there is a long-standing oral tradition among African Americans of studying and theorizing about whiteness, a folk knowledge necessary to survive in a white supremacist society.

35 See Edmund Morgan, *Slavery and Freedom: The Ordeal of Colonial Virginia* (New York: Norton, 1975), and Theodore W. Allen, *The Invention of the White Race*, 2 vols. (New York: Verso, 1994–97). Morgan is one of several scholars who detail the ways European attitudes and language of class characteristics were related to or transferred to race. See also Winthrop D. Jordan, *White over Black: American Attitudes toward the Negro, 1550–1812* (Baltimore: Penguin, 1968). Other scholars have argued that concepts like race existed in times and places prior to European colonialism and imperialism. See, for example, Frank Dikotter, *The Discourse of Race in Modern China* (Palo Alto: Stanford University Press, 1992).

36 See, for example, Ann Laura Stoler, *Race and the Education of Desire: Foucault's History of Sexuality and the Colonial Order of Things* (Durham: Duke University Press, 1995), and Anne McClintock, *Imperial Leather: Race, Gender and Sexuality in the Colonial Conquest* (New York: Routledge, 1995).

37 In *Colonial Desire: Hybridity in Theory, Culture and Race* (New York: Routledge, 1995), Robert Young argues that contemporary theory, often unwittingly, repeats the patterns through which culture and race were defined in the nineteenth century. See also M. Jacqui Alexander and Chandra Talpade Mohanty, eds., *Feminist Genealogies, Colonial Legacies, Democratic Futures* (New York: Routledge, 1997); Hortense Spillers, "Mama's Baby, Papa's Maybe: An American Grammar Book" *Diacritics* 15 (summer 1987): 65–81; and Gayatri Chakravorty Spivak, "French Feminisms in an International Frame" and "French Feminisms Revisited," in her *In Other Worlds: Essays in Cultural Politics* (New York: Routledge, 1995).

38 See Aijaz Ahmad, *In Theory: Classes, Nations, Literatures* (London: Verso, 1992).

39 For representative work, see Paul Kivel, *Uprooting Racism: How White People Can Work for Racial Justice* (Philadelphia: New Society Publishers, 1995); Judy Katz, *White Awareness: A Handbook for Anti-Racism Training* (Norman: University of Oklahoma Press, 1978); and Segrest, *Memoir of a Race Traitor*.

40 See Alistair Bonnett, "Constructions of Whiteness in European and American Anti-Racism," and Michel Wieviorka, "Is it so Difficult to be Anti-Racist?" in *Debating Cultural Hybridity: Multi-Cultural Identities and the*

Politics of Anti-Racism, ed. Pnina Werber and Tariq Modood (London: Zed Books, 1997).

41 For an attempt by the conference organizers at self-reflexive critique, see "Conference Report: The Making and Unmaking of Whiteness," in *Bad Subjects* 33 ⟨http://eserver.org/bs/33/whiteness.html⟩. For a critique of the conference based on activist concerns, see Cynthia Kaufman's article in the *Socialist Review* double issue " 'The Making and Unmaking of Whiteness': A Conference Report" (autumn 1997) [incorrectly published as vol. 26, nos. 3 & 4, 1996].

Universal Freckle, or How I Learned to Be White

I am not your typical middle-class white male. I am middle-class, despite the fact that my parents had no money; I am white, but I grew up in an inner city housing project where most everyone was black or Hispanic. I enjoyed a range of privileges that were denied my neighbors but that most Americans take for granted. In fact, my childhood was like a social science experiment: Find out what being middle-class really means by raising a kid from a "good" family in a "bad" neighborhood. Define whiteness by putting a light-skinned kid in the midst of a community of color. If the exception proves the rule, I'm that exception.

Ask any African American to list the adjectives that describe him, and he will most likely put black or African American at the top of the list. Ask someone of European descent the same question, and white will be far down on the list, if at all. Not so for me. I've studied whiteness the way I would a foreign language. I know its grammar, its parts of speech; I know the subtleties of its idioms, its vernacular words and phrases to which the native speaker has never given a second thought. For example, I had to learn that I was supposed to look white people in the eye when I spoke to them, that it didn't mean that I wanted to "throw down"—challenge them to a fight. I learned that snapping that someone's mother was so poor that she put a Big Mac on layaway was not taken with good humor. There's an old saying that you never really know your own language until you learn another. It's the same with race. In fact, race is nothing more than a language, a set of stories we tell ourselves to get through the world, to organize our reality. In learning this language of race, and thereby learning to be white, I was no different than European culture as a whole. Early modern conceptions of the white race—in fact of all races—stemmed from confrontation *with* and domination *of* peoples outside the European sphere. As the story goes, scientific theories of race arose in tandem with the ascent of colonialism. In 1684, François Bernier, a French physician who had traveled widely, published an article in a Parisian journal on the subject of human differences. "The geographers up until this point," he claimed, "have divided the world up only according to the different countries or regions." He then suggested a novel classification scheme based on the facial lineaments and bodily conformations of the peoples of the world. Bernier proceeded to divide the world's peoples into four categories: the Europeans, the Far Easterners, the blacks, and the Lapps. Native Americans he did not classify as a separate people or lump in any of his four groupings. Less than a century later, another Frenchman, George-Louis LeClerc Buffon, formally categorized the "races" of the world as part of a larger project of classifying all living species, published in the forty-four-volume *Histoire naturelle* (1749–1804). With the publication of these and related volumes, the modern European conception of race was born.

These early conceptions of race, however, were quite different than those commonly held today in the scientific community or by the public at large. Back then, racial differences were seen as a result of local climates and thus mutable—fluid both within and across generations. In fact, in 1787, the Reverend Mr. Samuel Stanhope Smith (president of the College of New Jersey—now Princeton University) wrote that dark skins could be considered a "universal freckle." Early modern racial theorists such as Smith believed that, over the course of several generations in a different climate, racial attributes would gradually change to adapt to local conditions. That is, northern peoples would get progressively darker, and darker peoples would loose their pigmentation with migration.[1]

Almost three centuries after Bernier carved up the world according to his schema of physical attributes, my white parents crossed over the contemporary equivalent of a racial border, moving into a nonprofit housing project on the Lower East Side of New York City. Compressed into the area of two city blocks, our housing complex had a population comparable to the town of Carbondale, Pennsylvania, where my mother had grown up before moving to New York. It was composed of mostly African American and Puerto Rican families; we were one of the few white households. What distinguished my family from our neighbors was not so much the color of our skin per se as it was how we had arrived at the buildings in which we lived out our lives. The essential difference was that we had some degree of choice about whether to live there or not. Our black and Hispanic neighbors, for the most part, did not. This difference was a whiteness lesson that I would not learn until much later, when I was deciding as an adult where in New York to live. As for my parents, my father was a painter, my mother a writer; in short, they had no money. But still, white poor people have choices in America that minorities do not enjoy. They could have lived in a white, working-class neighborhood in the outer boroughs or in New Jersey, for example. Our neighbors were not so lucky, however, being largely unwelcome elsewhere on account of the fact that they would probably lower property values because of the linkage between race and economics in our society.

That is, white neighborhoods are consistently worth more than black neighborhoods with similar housing stock. This pattern is maintained by the fact that when a white neighborhood just begins to integrate (usually somewhere around the 10 to 20 percent minority range) many of the white residents move out, fearing that the neighborhood will "tip" from white to black, depressing their housing values. Of course, this becomes a self-fulfilling prophecy. Property values drop since whites, who make up most of the demand for housing, sell in droves and flood the market.

Likewise, when whites move into a minority neighborhood with low housing values, prices start to climb, and these early, "pioneer" whites reap the profits. Through these waves of neighborhood succession, whites manage to squeeze dollars out of the symbolic advantage of their race. Though they were "pioneers," there was no such luck for my parents since the projects were not part of the private market and white "gentrification" would never take place there. That said, given their ostensible other options, I have often wondered why my parents made the choices they did in 1968. Whenever I ask them, they tell stories about having to move quickly because of a vendetta against my mother on the part of a burglar she had caught and prosecuted. But I think the real answer is somewhat along the lines of the reason white kids in the suburbs now buy more rap music than any other group: the mystique of the "ghetto,"[2] an attraction to the other that many middle-class individuals experience today. Such is the strange political economy of race in contemporary America. It is a political economy in which whites like my sister's husband, who grew up across the river in northern New Jersey, memorize rap lyrics and pine to be darker or at least to be called "white chocolate." It is a political economy where rap artists themselves brag at how "project" they are to sell records to these white teenagers. The essential rule of this racial-cultural system is that it is acceptable for whites to appropriate African American culture, but it is considered "passing" or being an "Uncle Tom" when blacks attempt to adopt white cultural practices in terms of modes of speech, dress, and so on. Though this gravitation toward blackness appears at first glance to be rooted in a romanticized kinship, its appeal is, in a counterintuitive way, a mechanism by which whites assert their cultural dominance, their right to tread on other people's cultural turf.

Back in 1968, long before the Sugar Hill Gang recorded the first, mass-marketed rap lyrics, my parents answered an advertisement in the tabloid *Daily News* soliciting applications for a newly minted housing complex not far from their tenement walk-up. An entire stretch of Manhattan, almost a mile long, from Fourteenth Street to well below Houston Street is lined with projects. As my parents strolled down Avenue D, every few blocks the brown-bricked projects changed in name and only slightly in style. The Jacob Riis houses melted into the Lillian Wald projects and then the Bernard Baruch houses, names that held little meaning for most of the residents who occupied them. Not only did the buildings look like each other, they looked exactly the same over the course of decades. Man landed on the moon; the Oil Shock of 1973 came; business cycles rolled by; but nothing about the projects gave any sign of societal change. There was never any new construction or renovation. And since they were brick, there was never even a new coat of paint. They constituted an unchanging monument to the social policy of their time.

The social texture of the neighborhood stood in stark contrast to the physical flavor. While the projects cast a stoic, oppressive shadow over Avenue D, the real street life was on the other side of the road, which was lined with dilapidated tenements. Many of the buildings were condemned or boarded up, often burned out for insurance money by the landlords themselves. However, almost every building that still functioned as a residence (and even some that did not) enjoyed an active storefront. Men sat in front of these bodegas and restaurants playing dominoes while children ran to and fro in front of them, their mothers sitting on the hoods of cars or standing, rocking infants on their hips. When it was hot, fire hydrants were opened by residents

and kids congregated around them, taking turns ducking into the forceful stream. Back then, the fire department had not yet issued caps with holes pricked into them to allow for moderate streams of water flow. So, instead, the city fought a constant battle with overheated residents. Every so often, a fireman showed up and turned off the water. This would last for only about half an hour or so, before someone with the special wrench turned the flow back on. To an outsider, the kids seemed to roam freely, but in reality everyone was watching everyone else's children; there was a degree of community-based social control that would not have been obvious to the casual observer. The same can be said for the traffic. Cars seemed to disobey most parking restrictions since traffic enforcement was a low priority in this neighborhood. Despite this lack of state control, cars flowed slowly but freely up and down the avenue, following their own logic much like the children; traffic jams were hardly ever a problem. Men washed their cars with soapy buckets of water that came from the same gushing hydrants the kids played in. Others kept all four doors and the trunk open to blast salsa music to the entire block. In short, during the summer months the entire neighborhood seemed to be partying all the time. During winter, the street life went a bit dormant, receding into the apartments that served as spores to preserve social relations until the next spring.

When my parents finally arrived to the advertised set of buildings, they appeared different from the other projects in the area. For one, they were yellow-bricked. Masryk Towers, as the place was called, had its own security force and its own grant from the government as part of the latest social science initiative to integrate the working class with the non–working class. Little did my mother know that the security guards did little to stop the violence that would parallel our lives—cops getting shot in the elevator, hostages being taken in the pharmacy, or girls getting raped in the stairwell. These future tragedies my mother could not foresee. At the time, she was impressed with the layout. Six buildings surrounded a central courtyard area. The central area of the project contained a series of three small playgrounds, roughly graded by age group, each hosting games of caps, ring-a-levio, Spalding baseball, and manhunt. The complex had trees and grass and its own ecosystem of wildlife that ranged from the tropical—huge cockroaches and water bugs—to the temperate, in the form of thick-furred squirrels. It was springtime—the trees were lush with white blossoms, and the grass was thick. To my mother, the grass seemed greener than any she had ever seen, but maybe that was only in contrast to the hot, glass-littered concrete that covered the rest of the neighborhood.

Despite the horrible reputation of the "inner city," high crime rates, pollution, and graffiti on every conceivable surface, my mother described our neighborhood as an idyllic landscape to raise children. We had the "ghetto penthouse"—as my sister and I liked to call living on the twenty-first, top floor, too young to realize the tastelessness of our monicker. We could see the hills of New Jersey out of one window and the farthest reaches of Queens from the other. If we didn't look straight down at all the burnt-out, boarded-up slums, we enjoyed a river-to-river view of the Manhattan skyline. The irony was that we had immovable bars bolted into the window jambs, obscuring the view. There was good reason for this. Once when we were away, my parents left a window open. A cat burglar tied the fire hose to the railing on the roof and swung into the kitchen window, proceeding to liquidate the entire house through the front door. Thinking we merely had to keep the windows shut and locked, we did the best we could to replace our television set and other semivaluable belongings. The next time we were gone he crashed through the window feet first and emptied out our apartment anew, leaving a trail of broken glass and blood to the front door. Finally, my parents had to invest in bars. They could only afford the cheapest kind. These least expensive window gates could not be opened or unlocked, and a prison-like barrier marred our river-to-river view.

Maybe to assuage her own sense of guilt for having raised my sister and me in a dangerous area (two of our close friends would be shot in the fourteen years we lived there), my mother constantly reminded us of how beautiful our surroundings were. "Look at the birds," she might say as she led us across the complex by a tightly gripped hand. "Ooh, there's a robin." I would refuse to look as she pointed out some brightly colored bird that stood out from the gray pigeons. She stood out as well, humming audibly as she strolled through the projects with her flowing dresses and her mismatched, brightly colored socks. She appreciated the colorful graffiti in the same way she liked the birds, for their purely aesthetic value. She appeared oblivious to the power dynamics behind race and class that came to dominate my conscious life. To her, race was about having Goya beans and exotic vegetables like yucca stocked in our supermarket. In other words, it was more like ethnicity in that it was about culture and lifestyle choices. Or maybe it was the case that she knew exactly what was going on in terms of power dynamics under the surface and her way of subverting this system was to ignore it, becoming a passive resister on the cultural front. If you don't pay attention to race, her logic might have gone, it will lose its power; it is socially constructed, after all. I can only speculate what my mother was thinking (or not thinking) back in the 1960s and 1970s; she herself does not give an account of her presentation of self to the neighborhood.

Like Bernier and (perhaps) my mother, I too, initially thought of my race as mutable and adaptable to the local conditions of the neighborhood. Actually, at first I was completely oblivious to the concept of race. In my desire to have a baby sister, I "kidnapped" the infant daughter of the leaders of a black separatist movement. How was I to know that the rules of endogamy pretty much precluded a brown-skinned baby from coming from my two white parents? To a toddler, size seems a lot more important than skin color in how the population is organized. Kids on big wheels were my peer group—regardless of complexion. Adults— white, black, other—constituted the alien race, the other. Race as we adults know it is something that has to be taught to us by parents, teachers, and society more generally. It is not something innately programmed into our minds by evolutionary psychology.

My sister, Alexandra, endured similar developmental lessons about the importance of race as a category. For Christmas one year at Alexandra's head start program, the black Santa Claus gave all the kids culturally appropriate GI Joe and Barbie dolls. As a result Alexandra was the only one to get a white Barbie. As soon as the other kids saw that Alexandra had a *real* Barbie, they stampeded her, begging, pleading, and demanding her to trade with them. Her first reaction was defensive, and she clutched the doll to her chest as girls and even boys tried to pry it from her.

"Black is beautiful!" the teachers screamed over the din of crying and yelling.

"We want Barbie!" the kids yelled back in unison, according to the teachers' explanation to my mother at the end of the day.

Finally, one kid pulled hard at her doll's legs and the toy broke in half. This girl was evidently satisfied that she had secured at least a piece of the Barbie and scurried off to a corner to dress up the half-doll. Eventually, my sister got the two halves back and willingly traded the doll for one in the African American style. I wonder if the teachers

Barbie
of consumerism
Branding style monopoly

took away the same lesson from the incident that I did. Namely, that it is not so easy to overcome the immense power of racial socialization. Here were very young children—as young as could possibly be "reeducated"—and they had already internalized a robust rank ordering of "real" and "other" of white Barbie and fake Barbie. This is the cultural power of whiteness writ large that never needs to speak its name explicitly (and is more powerful in its silence). It is the power structure that lurks beneath everything we do in our day-to-day lives, most often unknown to us all except when it erupts in incidents like this one.

My sister's next lesson about racial lines came when she was six years old and wanted to cornrow her hair like her friend Adoonie did. At first my mother resisted her demand, explaining that her hair wouldn't work in a cornrowed style but was beautiful in its own right. After many tears, my sister gave up on the dream of cornrowed hair. That is, until the next year when the movie 10 came out. At first all the little girls thought that its star, Bo Derek, was black on account of her tropical tan in the movie. Though everyone was too young to have actually gone to the R-rated film, that didn't stop all the girls with cornrows from wanting to grow them longer so that they, like Bo Derek, had the best of both worlds, long hair and tight braids along their scalp. Then one of the older girls told the group that Bo Derek was actually white.

The girls were confused, hurt, and betrayed by this revelation, as they would later be on learning that Madonna was also white. My sister, however, was joyous since this proved that she, too, could have the cornrows she had been denied because of her race. When she brought this piece of information to our mother, she had no choice but to relinquish and braid her hair as best as she could, putting in black, red, and orange African beads as my sister had requested. To no avail. The braids frayed, and the beads didn't stand out against her chestnut hair; rather, they looked like colored gnats or lice that had infested her scalp. My sister was not entirely satisfied with my mother's effort, but she wanted to show Adoonie, nonetheless, so she rushed out to the playground to find her.

"Yo, excuse me miss," an older girl said and laughed, "someone left some twine on your head."

"Is that some cornrows?" another asked, stopping from her jump-rope counting game. "Looks more like wheat to me."

"Oh snap," added a third girl, cracking up.

Alexandra started crying and ran back into the pitted brick building. When Adoonie found her upstairs, she tried to console her. "My
mother will do your braids for you if you like," she was petting my
sister's head as she spoke softly to her. "Won't that be nice, wouldn't
you like that?"

"Forget it," Alexandra said and started to unwind the cornrows that
had already begun to unbraid themselves as if they, too, didn't like how
the experiment had turned out. "I don't want the stupid cornrows.
They're stupid." This was the first time Alexandra remembered using
the value of her whiteness in the broader cultural marketplace—in this
case her hair type—to comfort herself. But, of course, it was by necessity a put-down of color, and at this comment Adoonie cried and ran
off. From then on, Alexandra only wanted long blond hair, straight as
could be. We were learning race, its uses and abuses. In this case, it
was the converse lesson of Barbie—namely, that it wasn't so easy to
cross racial boundaries even when you are of the white, dominant
group.

These messages of whiteness had begun to seep into us, making us
realize that race was not a universal freckle, that we would never quite
fit into our local community. For each of us, this realization took a few
years. For European history, it took almost a century after Bernier's
first article. In the nineteenth century, the idea that racial differences
were independent of climate and therefore immutable began to take
hold in the public and scientific imagination.

What paved the way for this new, evolutionary theory of race was
the downfall of Lamarckianism. Jean-Baptiste Lamarck thought that
adaptive or learned behaviors could be transmitted across generations. For example, if a generation of giraffes stretched its necks a little
further to reach the highest leaves, they would pass this advantage on
to the next generation, which could, in turn, build upon the longer
neck length as a base for further improvement. Darwin's theory of
natural selection shot this concept down by suggesting that evolution resulted not from the efforts of organisms to adapt and survive
but from random, beneficial mutations over a much longer time
frame. With the advent of Darwin's theory of evolution, the immediate
linkage of environment to racial difference had been severed, and
races could be seen as separate, immutably different lines of human
development.

In light of these epistemological changes, the prime debate became not whether nonwhite races were inferior or not, but rather whether the different races, in fact, constituted distinct species (monogenism versus polygenism). The foundation of this debate was the aforementioned conception of the separate origins of the different groups of humans. The more traditional religious adherents sided, ironically, with Charles Darwin, who effectively ended the debate, stating that though there was some variation between peoples of the world, it was on the whole small, and humans are, in fact, one species.[3]

While these nineteenth-century theorists looked to the past to define race, for me it was really more about the future. My whiteness was defined by my expectations, by the fact that I knew that being European American meant that my own personal life course would diverge radically from that of the kids around me. Societal and state institutions made sure this was so, and in this way reinforced these expectations. This is the essence of social structure: individual expectations that both reflect and reinforce the patterns of inequality already governing society—"expectations about expectations" in the words of systems theorist Niklas Luhmann.[4]

Middle-class, white "expectations about expectations" had already reared their head by first grade in the local public school. I was told that I did not "fit" into any of the classes and must arbitrarily pick between the Puerto Rican, black, or Chinese classrooms. While *Brown v. Board of Education* may have eliminated school-based segregation, evidently within-school segregation continued unabated, at least on the Lower East Side of Manhattan. Faced with such racially structured educational choices, my parents chose the African American class.

My first teacher, who was black herself, beat everyone except me. The other kids seemed to think that this was quite normal—and, in fact, their parents had requested the use of corporal punishment.

"Yo, your momma been on welfare so long," one of my fellow students whispered to me one day early that year, "her face's on food stamps." He gave a low five to the boy seated in front of him. When the teacher saw him, she demanded him to come to the front of the room immediately. He marched up slowly, staring at his sneakers, his face down and afro up as if it offered protection. It did not. She took his hands and whacked them three times with the thin edge of her ruler. I felt my body leap from the seat with each whack, as if the ruler were a lever, the end of which I was sitting on. My spine and head stayed still, and the rest of me moved upward. Then I blinked and twitched my cheeks. The kid receiving the blows did not flinch, yelp, or move in the least.

Each time a classmate would pass by my desk on the way back to his seat after having been beaten with a ruler, I would stare down, unable to look him in the eyes. At the same time, I would try to catch a glimpse of his bloodied knuckles where his brown skin had opened up through the white layer underneath to the scarlet flesh that I could identify with. While I felt intense guilt over my position of being the privileged other who wasn't hit, I slowly realized that the other kids didn't resent this fact. To everyone involved, teachers and students, it was quite "natural" that a black teacher would never cross the racial border to strike a white child. The use of corporal punishment was a cultural distinction, but the fact that an African American teacher wouldn't dare strike a white child while she would those of her own race is about race. Specifically, it's about fears of state retribution, about a tacit respect for certain privileges that undergird whiteness.

Here was my first taste of white rights, the same dynamic at work when, today, I confidently walk into a hospital without proper identification or into a private party uninvited or sit in a hotel lounge reading the paper without being questioned. In first grade, however, I felt guilty about it, so guilty that I developed a series of tics, blinks, and twitches to the point of becoming dysfunctional in school. My guilt was of a different genre than the general white angst felt by many liberals in America. It was in my face all the time, at school and at home in the neighborhood. I experienced constantly what most urban, middle-class Americans feel when a street person asking for change accosts them. I don't mean to imply that my classroom dynamic was the same in terms of the charity aspect, for instance, but rather just in the way it gets white people to become conscious of their privileged position, even if just for a split second on their way to work.

Eventually my parents switched me into the Chinese class. It was in this context that I began learning—albeit on an unconscious level—the difference between race and ethnicity. On the first day of the spring term, the teacher took roll, having each student stand up when his or her name was called. She announced that if we had a Chinese name, the next day she would tell us an equivalent in English. If we had an American name, she would perform the reverse service. The next morning she read off two names for each student.

"John," she said, "Jiang."

"Jiali," she read next, "Julie."

Then she got to me, "Dalton," she said, "Dalton," she repeated.

I was crushed. She announced that she could not find a translation of my name. Of course, at the time I didn't know that none of these name pairs were actual translations, that there was no straightforward way to convert names from a tonal, character-based language to our own. Nonetheless, to make me feel better she said my name once again in the second tone, so that it went up in pitch in the second syllable. She made the entire class repeat it in her Cantonese accent. They did. The kids chuckled to themselves, but their laughter did not have the same sharp edge that wounded me like that of the black kids from my previous class. It would have seemed absurd and impossible if the African American teacher had tried to take steps to better integrate me into that class. The jagged edge of race was about domination and struggles for power. It was also taken as something insurmountable.

The differences I experienced in the Chinese class were ones that seemed more tractable. Strange as it may seem given the vast cultural and linguistic ocean that separated these recent immigrants of first-generation Americans from me, fitting into the Chinese class appeared possible, if still difficult. The differences were cultural, firstly. The physical distinctions between us were not unnoticed, but they did seem trivial or epiphenomenal. When such culturally loaded physical differences verged into the realm of exploitation and exclusion, they entered the territory of race as we know it today. Twentieth-century racial theories have alternated between seeing racial divisions as wholly related to these cultural differences[5] (really more like ethnicity) or as related to some larger economic or territorial dynamic of oppression. These latter approaches are called class and nation paradigms of race, respectively.[6] The class paradigm sees race as constructed either by the elite to weaken the working class through cleavage or as a division created by a portion of the working class (whites) to drive up their wages by excluding many (black) workers from the labor market.[7] The nation paradigm is one that sees the early conflict over imperialist expansion and colonial domination as having continued into our modern era. Race is the byproduct of struggles among exclusive groups of peoples to dominate and exploit others. The same power dynamics that (literally) colored the era of imperialism have now been inculcated within the nation-state, developing into a dynamic of internal colonialism.[8] Regardless of which one (or more) of these accounts of race is correct, common to all of these theories is the rejection of early conceptions of race as a fundamental biological category—something that it took me quite a while to learn growing up (that is, once I had learned about the differences to begin with).[9]

For me, choice is central to this difference between race and ethnicity. Within certain (racial) constraints an individual can choose her ethnicity. The constraint that limits "ethnic options" is inequality. When one group enjoys a status advantage over another, it is in their interest to restrict membership, and the affiliational quality disappears—ethnicity becomes racialized. In other words, to the extent to which Italian identity and Irish identity enjoy the same level of status within American society, individuals of mixed national parentage can affiliate with one or both groups, even maintaining a fluid identity that changes depending on the advantageous cultural circumstances of the moment and the ability of the individual to subscribe to the cultural practices of the group.[10] In other words, I decide my ethnicity, but you decide my race.

For example, when I got older, I came to know a woman who was born in Korea to what we would call Korean parents. However, she was orphaned in the first month of her life. She was lucky enough to be adopted almost immediately by a wealthy couple who raised her in northern Italy. She never enjoyed the opportunity to learn the Korean language, to practice the social norms and customs that govern most social interactions in Korea or among Korean nationals living abroad, to understand Korean history, or to develop a taste for what we would call Korean cuisine. By contrast, having been raised in Italy, she speaks the official language of the *Repubblica Italiana* as her maternal tongue; she is quite proficient at cooking Italian cuisine and knows the wines of the region in which she was raised. When she became an adult, she moved to the United States. There she found that when she walked into a greengrocer in New York City, she was spoken to in Korean by the owners who, themselves, had migrated from that Pacific Rim country. She also found that African Americans and whites treated her differently, making assumptions about her based on her looks. In short, she found herself to be racially Asian while remaining ethnically Italian.[11]

The essential point of my friend's story is that ethnicity, as Mary Waters argues in her book *Ethnic Options,* is something about what we do, whom we choose to identify with/as. Race is imposed on us from the outside, based on how others choose to treat us within a power hierarchy. In fact, ethnicity is a luxury enjoyed by only certain groups of people. Many African Americans I knew growing up spoke of no national ancestry the way white kids talked about being Irish or German. They had race but no ethnicity. For most people of European ancestry, the reverse is true: being part of the white race is a default identity—one that does not play such a big role in their everyday lives. In fact, when I ask my students to list four or five attributes that describe them, Latinos and African Americans always put their race near the top of the list. Only once among hundreds has a white student listed his racial identity at all. Meanwhile, many of the whites I know wear their ethnic identities very prominently.

However, my racial identity as a white person is probably stronger than that of most people of European ancestry. In other words, I was definitely reminded that I was a *honky*, and I didn't forget it, either. Even though I never faced the level of harassment and violence that an African American might if he moved into a poor white neighborhood, my white racial identity was always with me growing up, a master status that defined who I was. That is, like being blind or having cancer, it overwhelmed all other attributes in defining how I was treated and marked in my day-to-day interactions. I imagine that this is not the case for most white Americans, at least those not living abroad.

But it is also true that in many ways I have felt little ethnic identity compared to most white people I know. Being part Hungarian Jew, part WASP, I probably should have been keenly aware of the important role of ethnicity within the white race, but given my particular geographic circumstances, these distinctions did not register with me—they were washed over and washed out by race.

I remember one particular time when I was oblivious to the meaning of ethnic ties. I had stolen candy from the local luncheonette run by a husband and a wife who were both Holocaust survivors. When I confessed my crime to my mother, she dragged me down to the store to pay, explain what I had done, and ask for their forgiveness. After I confessed the lady with the blue numbers tattooed into her arm broke out into a morality tale.

"Let me tell you a story," the woman said. I was praying that none of my *Las Piratas* little league teammates would walk in and see me there with my mother, see me actually talking to the luncheonette lady that everyone made fun of. "When I was a young girl in Germany in the concentration camp my family and I were being marched off to the gas chambers." She paused. I had heard about the Nazis before in school and from my mother.

"I was only a young girl of twelve," she recounted her time in Dachau, "But we had all heard about the showers and ovens, so we knew we were going to die. I had nothing to lose, so I ran up to one of the guards," she continued. "I looked him right in the eye and said, 'We all have to die some time, and it may be sooner for me than for you, but at least I'll be able to face my Jewish God when that time comes. What about you? Can you face your God?' Do you know vat he did?" she asked me. "Do you know vat this guard did?" She didn't wait for an answer. The Socratic part of this lesson was over. "He pulled me out of the line and saved my life. Everyone else in my family was killed. All my brothers and sisters and my parents, too." Now she was crying, as was I. "But I spoke up for my beliefs and God spared me." Then she turned to my mother. "It is because of this, I say, you have to raise them Jewish. You're raising him Jewish?"

"Why?" I interjected suddenly when I had worked through what I thought were the logical implications of her yarn, namely, that being Jewish generally led to execution. "Does she want us to all get killed?"

My mother gasped behind me and grabbed me by the ear, twisting the cartilage. She yanked on the ear and pulled me toward the door. "I apologize," she said to the woman as I wailed. "I'm so sorry. Please forgive us." Even through the visceral reality of my pain I thought it strange that my mother had asked for her forgiveness of *us,* when she had not done anything at all. This was the first time that it dawned on me that my words and actions spoke for more than just myself, that I was, in a sense, an ambassador for my family, for my ethnic group, in fact, for any group to which I belonged by virtue of birth or affiliation. It was my first glimmer of ethnic consciousness. Only later did I fully realize what lesson the woman was giving my mother and I with her story. It was the message that as ethnic Jews we were all part of one tribe (albeit tinted with religious overtones), that we were in some distant way kin to her, and that by virtue of this fact we have to stick together, that there would be strength and comfort in our numbers, even if they have dwindled. Still, it took me a while and several more gaffes like the one in the luncheonette to learn the culture of whiteness—that is, to accept the group membership that the luncheonette woman and others were offering me. Actually, I had to learn how to be several types of white ethnic, since my father's tribe (New England WASP) had its own rituals and code of conduct.

Whether or not I knew how to behave ethnically "white" was really immaterial to the more serious issue of race, however. I could never even know what my "roots" were, and yet my racial identity would (and did) provide me with a privileged position vis-à-vis the state and society more generally. Whiteness had already given me choices for my educational career. It also gave me choices about where to live, since I now reside about a mile or so away from where I grew up, but in an entirely different world, one in which property values are soaring along with the stock market. I choose to live in New York despite the fact that I work in Connecticut at an elite, predominantly white institution: Yale University.

I cannot help but see my two-hour commute as a metaphor for the dynamics of race and class in America. When I speed up the Merritt Parkway and feel a surge of acceleration in my gut, I experience an unparalleled rush of freedom. I could go anywhere, as long as I have some gas left in the tank. But if one were to pull back and take an aerial view of the ebbs and flows of traffic, something would change dramatically. From a helicopter, traffic flows seems absurdly constrained and rhythmically patterned. Masses of cars lunge and recoil according to some not-so-complicated algorithm. Pulling back even farther, we would notice that roads cover only a small portion of the earth's surface. From above, we don't appear to have much choice in where we are going or how fast we can get there, but that does not deny each driver's experience of freedom and agency. It's the same with race and class. When I look back on my life and that of my neighbors, I cannot say that it was racism that got my best friend shot or that sent another neighbor to prison for twenty-five years on a nonviolent drug charge. Nor can I conclude definitively that it was class that propelled me to the school district across town or got me off the hook when I burned down a friend's apartment. Rather, it could have been that I happened to change lanes just in the nick of time to avoid an accident or that a traffic cop happened not to see me when I pulled an illegal maneuver. But when I add up all these particular experiences, the invisible contours of inequality start to take form, like the clogged traffic arteries of I-95. At the same time, my life, like anyone's, is only a sample of one, hardly statistically generalizable.

When I arrive at Yale, I spend my nonteaching days running mathematical models on my laptop computer, in pursuit of that statistical certainty—trying to understand in some scientific way the leitmotif of race and class that has dominated my life. I have based the majority of my work on one particular interview study. It is a survey given to more or less the same set of 5,000 families each year for the last three decades. In fact, this data set and I are almost exactly the same age. So, when I develop a computer model to predict what conditions in 1969 led to educational success or economic security in the 1990s, I am perhaps driven by the misguided—but comforting—feeling that the answers to my own life and those of my neighbors are just one key punch away. But, of course, they never are. What is gained from numbers is lost in story.

Notes

1 Such a conception was intertwined with the more general notions of the Enlightenment. Enlightenment thinkers argued that all humans were created equally by God; such optimism extended to theories of race in the eighteenth century.

2 I use this term in quotes since, academically speaking, where we lived did not constitute a ghetto. First of all, there was a mix of minority groups. Many scholars think that the only type of ghetto in America is purely African American. Also, a ghetto requires a better seal-off from the larger society. Since we were there ourselves, the boundary was too porous to meet the strict definition of a ghetto. Finally, a ghetto needs to contain institutions that duplicate those in the mainstream society in order to function autonomously. However, many of the residents in my neighborhood worked in other areas of the city. Likewise, there was no informal banking or medical system as far as I knew.

3 For a discussion of this, see Thomas F. Gossett, *Race: The History of an Idea in America* (New York: Schocken, 1963).

4 Niklas Luhmann, *Trust and Power: Two Works,* trans. Gianfranco Poggi (New York and Chichester: Wiley 1979).

5 This approach is best embodied by the work of early Chicago School thinkers such as Horace Kallen, *Culture and Democracy in America* (New York: Boni and Liveright, 1924), and Robert E. Park, *The Collected Papers of Robert E. Park,* ed. Everett Hughes (Glencoe, Ill.: Free Press, 1950).

6 For a formal review, see Michael Omi and Howard Winant, *Racial Formation in the United States* (New York: Routledge, 1994). Of course, there are

many other approaches as well, but a thorough discussion is well beyond the scope of this chapter.

7   See, e.g., chapter 1 of William Julius Wilson, *The Declining Significance of Race* (Chicago: University of Chicago Press, 1978).

8   See, for example, Bob Blauner, *Racial Oppression in America* (New York: Harper and Row, 1972).

9   For a formal review of all these theories, see Omi and Winant, *Racial Formation*. There are many other approaches as well, but, again, a thorough discussion is well beyond the scope of this chapter.

10 For this argument, see, for example, Mary Waters, *Ethnic Options: Choosing Identities in America* (Berkeley: University of California Press, 1990).

11 In fact, I would later learn that physical distinctions may not even be necessary for a racial division to occur. For example, Japan has a minority group, called the Burakamin, that is physically indistinguishable from the rest of the population, yet they constitute a separate race. In our own society, molecular biology established DNA as the hereditary material and the development of electrophoresis, which measured protein differentiation, allowed scientists to measure and classify human genes. In tandem with these new theories, racial theory adopted the evolutionary paradigms of adaptation and genetic drift to legitimize population categories. As a result of this "scientific" discourse, today we are witnessing in the United States a cessation of the physical (phenotypic) basis for racial classification. Increasingly, molecular genetics are serving the legitimating role that physical appearance often did. Racial types are being classified on the basis of allele frequencies; see, for example, Troy Duster, *Backdoor to Eugenics* (London: Routledge, 1991). I have come to the tentative, personal conclusion that all that is necessary for a racial distinction is the perception of unique bloodlines (resulting from actual or perceived endogamy) in tandem with a power inequity. The ideal-type of ethnicity, then, is the perception of a common bloodline without the categorical power division.

"The Souls of White Folks"

"To deny the importance of subjectivity in the process of transforming the world and history is naive and simplistic. . . . Those who authentically commit themselves to the people must examine themselves constantly."
—Paulo Freire, *The Pedagogy of the Oppressed*

"What therapist would tell us to read history?" I asked at the beginning of my last book, *Memoir of a Race Traitor,* my attempt to describe seven years of anti-Klan and neo-Nazi organizing in North Carolina and to come to terms with my own history as a white person. Part of my project was to convey as compellingly and believably as possible the epidemic of racist and homophobic violence we confronted in North Carolina in the eighties. Another was to explore the conditions that created the violence and held it in place. If I wanted to lay out the economics of racism and its expression in all the institutions of the culture, I was also interested in probing its psychology. I wanted to study, borrowing W. E. B. Du Bois's term, "the souls of white folks"—assuming (as Malcolm X had difficulty doing for most of his life with regard to the "white devil") that we *have* souls, and beginning, inevitably, with my own.[1]

This part of the project was more than self-indulgence. Part of the mythology around racism is that it only affects people of color. Because racism normalizes whiteness and problematizes "color," we whites as "generic humans" escape scrutiny for our accountability as a group for creating racism and as individuals for challenging it. One response is to begin to problematize whiteness and calculate its wages. We can explain the advantages of being white in terms of not going to prison, becoming coaches of major sports, obtaining home mortgages, buying cheaper cars, dying less often from cancer, obtaining better jobs, and so forth. Such a calculus can almost be too convincing. Why should anyone give up such privilege?

What we miss in such an accounting is insight into the profound damage racism has done to us, as if we as a people could participate in such an inhuman set of practices and beliefs over five centuries of European hegemony and not be, in our own ways, devastated emotionally and spiritually. The business of therapy, both professional and self-help, has emerged in this century in the United States to deal with the psychological damage, which in a culture structured around scarcity and profit happens to people first in the context of our racist, sexist, and homophobic families. But these therapies are highly depoliticized. This failure of therapy to take into account the political causes of personal and family distress is another factor that insulates white people from realizing the damage we suffer from racism and therefore from realizing our own stake in changing racist systems for ourselves, as well as for people of color. We need to balance off calculations on the benefits of whiteness (and maleness and heterosexism and the drive for profits) with calculations of pain and loss for all people in this culture: for example, 60 million people suffering from alcoholism, the leading killer in the country; stress that contributes to heart disease and cancer; 50 percent of the population with eating disorders; 34 million adult women sexually abused.[2]

I want to be clear that I am not equating the damage done by racism to white people with the damage done to people of color: conflating victim with perpetrator. Over the five-hundred-year history of colonialism and imperialism, people of color have formed the superexploited labor pool that has allowed capitalism to reap its profits. This money has stayed, primarily, in the coffers of Europeans and their white descendants in the United States. White allies of people of color have often been targets of racism—of physical attacks, social ostracism, economic deprivation. But whites *as* whites have not been lynched, enslaved, had lands stolen, suffered forced relocation onto reservations, had reserved for us the most difficult labor at the lowest wage, been bombarded by dehumanizing messages and ideologies, and so on ad nauseam.

Bell hooks warns against the discussion I want to undertake about the damage of racism to white people. She is leery of whites constructing a "narrative of shared victimization" that "recenters whites" and obscures the "particular way racist domination impacts on the lives of marginalized [racial] groups." She prefers a solidarity "based on one's political and ethical understanding of racism and one's rejection of domination." But hooks allows that a white solidarity based on rejection of domination "does not have to negate collective awareness that a culture of domination does seek to fundamentally distort and pervert the psyches of all citizens or that this perversion is wounding."[3] It is this wounding psychic perversion that I am trying to address, without equating it with the effects of racist exploitation on people of color, some new strain of emotional "reverse discrimination." I can make these distinctions, I find, as a lesbian. I can see how homophobia and heterosexism distort heterosexual relationships in ways that are wounding, while also insisting that this pain not be used to recenter heterosexuality and obscure the fact that there is institutional power in heterosexism that falls violently and painfully on lesbians and gay men. The pain of dominance is always qualitatively different from the pain of subordination. But there is a pain, a psychic wound, to inhabiting and maintaining domination. Our acknowledging that emotional cost helps keep our white ethical/political solidarity from slipping over into a new form of paternalism.

I should also make clear that I do not assume that whiteness is monolithic. Its power as a constructed category has been its very historic malleability, under the flag of biological determinism. If whiteness is a signifier of power and condition of access in U.S. culture, then women are less white than men, gay people less white than straight people, poor people less white than rich people, Jews than Christians, and so forth. Over the centuries, people of various European nationalities have climbed into and sometimes fallen out of whiteness, the core of which has always been Anglo-Saxon, Protestant, propertied, and male (and now straight).

W. E. B. Du Bois was one of the first to explore the economic cost to white people of racism. In *Black Reconstruction in America, 1860–1880,* originally published in 1935, he wrote:

> Indeed, the plight of the white working class throughout the world today is directly traceable to Negro slavery in America, on which modern commerce and industry was founded, and which persisted to threaten free labor until it was partially overthrown in 1863. The resulting color caste founded and retained by capitalism was adopted, forwarded and approved by white labor, and resulted in subordination of colored labor to white profits the world over. Thus the majority of the world's laborers, by the insis-

tence of white labor, became the basis of a system of industry which ruined democracy and showed its perfect fruit in World War and Depression.[4]

For a modicum of economic privilege and a dollop of racial superiority—what Du Bois called the "psychological wage" of being white—white workers gave up class solidarity that could have created better working conditions for all races. But Du Bois also recognizes that the loss here is as much psychological, or spiritual, as it is material: "[The white worker] began to want, not comfort for all men but power over other men. . . . He did not love humanity and he hated niggers."[5] In gaining power, whites lose "comfort" of the nonmaterial kind: ease, well-being, consolation, help, solace, and relief. In acquiring hatred, whites lose feelings and practices of love.

I am interested here, then, in exploring further what we whites give up as human beings in "love of humanity" to a racist system. I am interested in psyche as human soul, spirit, or mind. The subject here is racist consciousness, which I want to theorize a bit via slave apologists, slave narratives, Sigmund Freud, Herbert Marcuse, and my own experiences as a white southerner, living my lifetime in a region still shaped by slavery. I believe that in the United States we have not been able to have a clear conversation about our emotional pain. Instead, we have alternative discourses that get to part of the dynamic but obfuscate the sources of pain in historical imbalances of power. This essay is an attempt to close the gap between the personal and the political, between the intimate and the public, the emotional and the historical.

A Rock Feels No Pain

These considerations of the personal cost of exploitative systems are not abstract questions for me. My search for answers began inevitably in my own family's pain. Before exploring the more theoretical implications of the questions I am asking, I want to share with you how these issues have arisen in my own life. For it is from my own life that my questions, and my tentative answers, emerge. To talk about "the souls of white people" without talking about myself as white, myself as soul, would be more hypocritical than I could endure. I elaborated much of this autobiographical material in *Memoir of a Race Traitor*, but am seeking to explore and extend it here.

My mother was chronically ill and addicted to prescription drugs, from which she died a slow and painful death; my father withdrew for years into silence; my brother and sister and I were left to fend for ourselves amid our mother's periodic bouts of illness. During these times my mother (who was lively and loving when she was feeling good) withdrew almost completely from us physically and emotionally, or left home indefinitely for the latest cure—which all that was left of her grandfather's capital allowed her to do. My legacy was a deep sense of pessimism, a distrust for the world in which I found myself, a chronic sense of guilt and responsibility for whatever I must have done to make her sick, and a need to maintain semblances of control amid the turmoil. One of my technologies of anesthesia was eating. Food became both nurture and narcotic. After a heavy dinner of roast beef and potatoes and vegetables laced with lard, I could sleep off "family time" on Sunday afternoons up in my room or in front of the TV. Or I would go on summer-long diets, starving myself.

Raised in a segregationist family in Alabama, I had an increasing sense of alienation and difference throughout my adolescence: a growing disquiet about my mother's mental health, an increasing dismay over white racism literally exploding all around me, and a fear that I was somehow different in a way that would keep me from ever finding or giving love. I read voraciously, trying to understand what was happening to my world and to find some larger version of it; but I also intellectualized most of my feelings, which were increasingly complicated by a lesbian adolescence for which I had no language. I attended college at a small liberal arts school forty miles from home, although I had longed to get out of the state. In Montgomery, where the bus boycotts had launched the civil rights movement a decade before, the black freedom and antiwar movements of the late sixties passed me by. If I had joined the protest movements of the times, I might have focused my anger and acquired more hope. Instead, in 1971 I headed off to graduate school in North Carolina, running as much from the racism as the homophobia. I had a strong conviction that if I stayed in Alabama, I could not live. But I came up to North Carolina to graduate school with an incoherent rage—a rebel without a cause.

In grad school, I experienced periodic bouts of depression; I felt as if I were boxing blindfolded with a giant who would occasionally floor me. Pat, my first woman lover, would sing Simon and Garfunkel, saying that it described me: "I have my books and my poetry to protect me; I am shielded in my armor. Safe within my room, silent in my tomb, I touch no one and no one touches me. I am a rock. I am an island. A rock feels no pain. And an island never cries." Crises in my closeted relationship with Pat took me to group therapy in my mid-twenties. Two psychiatry residents introduced me to the concept that I could think about my feelings in ways that made me less at the mercy of my more destructive ones, to begin to align mind and heart. I went back to therapy a couple more times—to couples counseling in that first relationship and then in my second long-term relationship, with Barbara, which has lasted now for eighteen years. One thing I came to understand is how often I played out my relationship with my mother in other relationships, holding my breath for disaster; or I became my father, withdrawing into silence. This fear, this silence, this pain: in their thickness they were surely more than one generation old?

In *Memoir of a Race Traitor,* I searched for the interfaces between my (white) subjective life and history. I found them repeatedly. I had known that part of my mother's sadness came from having lost her father, whom she idolized, when she was three. He died of influenza in 1918, in part because he was in poor health from having caught malaria when he went off as a young man to fight in the Spanish-American War. He was an engineer, a traveler, an adventurer—and caught his second case of malaria from an expedition up some Central American river when he was in Panama working on the canal. I had never considered his relationship to his own father, Judge James Cobb, who came sharply into focus for me in the process of writing: Confederate officer; Democratic Judge, who threw Republican Reconstruction officials into the chain gang; then Congressman, until he was kicked out of Congress for voter fraud against an insurgent inter-racial Populist movement in 1894. Before he died, he helped to redraft the Alabama constitution to bring in Jim Crow. And, I know from my mother's stories, he beat his children, including my grandfather Ben—who perhaps left home for war and adventure to flee this rigid father.

My father's sister shared with me the story of their grandfather, also a Civil War veteran, who had died in the public insane asylum about the time Judge Cobb was reworking the state constitution. Charles Segrest's family had committed him when he began imagining that men were shooting at him from trees and was inclined to return fire. Charles had fought as a foot soldier in the Carolinas and Virginia, then walked all the way to Alabama at the end of the war. His psychic break seemed liked post-traumatic stress disorder, now more familiar to us from Vietnam vets. My aunt explained the stigma under which she and my father had grown up, having a certified crazy person in the family. I began to understand my father's silence more. What I saw was at the root of both my parents' pain: in a very real sense, it originated in my families' involvements in racist wars and their aftermath, racist peace.

Political struggle, like therapy, has been a source of healing in my life. If I was using therapy to pursue more emotional balance, I was also, on a parallel track, increasingly politicized. Coming out as a lesbian in 1976–77 was the first step in my politicization, and it opened me up creatively. I began writing seriously and joined a collective doing lesbian feminist cultural work. This soon led me to antiracist activism within the lesbian and gay community. In 1983 I left both a closeted teaching job and what was beginning to feel like ghettoization within the lesbian community. I began organizing against a growing neo-Nazi movement and climate in North Carolina with many other people, a majority of them heterosexual African Americans. I increasingly focused my anger outward in organizing for "social change": change of the homophobic world that had so isolated me and of the racism that had dismayed me with its violent fury as a child and an adolescent. I had an instinctive sense that the forces of race and class that white Alabamians had acted out so flagrantly were the same forces that, interacting with a misogynist world, were still destroying my mother's health. Her body was in a process of slow deterioration, an organ at a time, a process that left me anxious, fearful, and bereft. Something was killing my mother. I would locate and slay that dragon: revolution as both therapy and revenge.

Therapy also provided part of the framework by which I understood my antifascist organizing. The acquittal of Klansmen and neo-Nazis for the murders of anti-Klan demonstrators in Greensboro in 1979 had opened a floodgate of white supremacist organizing and racist violence. The neo-Nazi White Patriot Party was organizing all over the state, running candidates for public office (free publicity for the most racist propaganda), and marching its battalion, first one hundred, then three and four hundred strong, through little towns across the state. We began to show links between members of the White Patriot Party and The Order, a white terrorist organization in the West. We were doing our best to sound the alarm, but the resistance was incredible. The epidemic of cross burnings across the state were "pranks" or "isolated incidents," according to reports in county newspapers. Patriot leader Glenn Miller's boasts of building up a white Christian army to take back the South—a violation of the state's paramilitary laws—was merely "free speech," although it was accompanied by increasing acts of racist violence. I kept telling reporters: this man is confessing to a crime (breaking the state's paramilitary laws). What we kept running into felt like the massive denial I had experienced in my family as an adolescent, when most of the whites I knew had refused to acknowledge the reality, much less the moral significance, of the violent white resistance to black freedom movements. "Denial" was also a concept popular in Twelve-Step programs, which for a while I also attended: that is, people in denial about their addictions. I began to formulate a metaphysics of genocide: people don't need to respond to what they can pretend they do not know, and they don't know what they can't feel.

In 1985, I became coordinator of North Carolinians Against Racist and Religious Violence, and I immersed myself in anti-Klan organizing in communities all across North Carolina. The work had its own urgencies, to which I added my own. In a growing climate of violence, I worked myself to exhaustion. I brought all my old anxiety of abandonment by my mother into play with my new anxieties about Klan violence; all my old pessimism and fatalism into a new fear of growing fascism; my old rage at my mother's pain into my new anger at the pain experienced by the people I was working with, many of whom had lost loved ones in moments of searing violence. But putting these feelings into an organizing context helped me to become more conscious of them. It gave me a context to resolve old conflicts. In the short term, it broke me down; I got sick for several months and couldn't seem to get well. We were working on multiple murders in two different counties, and in neither locale did justice prevail. In spite of early victories, the depth of racism and homophobia in these environments was beyond our capacity to change. But, difficult and messy as the process was, I broke down in a way I needed. I studied the shards and began to reassemble them. I saw that things would get even worse before they would get better in my lifetime. But my reaction should not be one of pessimism and despair, but of love and hope. From the shards, the fragments, the pieces, this question of soul began to emerge. What happens, in white supremacist culture, to the souls of white folks?

The Anesthesia of Power

My own experience of the effects of racism, then, begins inevitably in the South. Our regional black-white experience of racism is not the only racial experience in the United States, of course, but it is one of the prototypical ones. "Next to the case of the black race within our bosom, that of the red on our borders is the problem baffling to the policy of the country," former President James Madison explained in 1826. And, as Du Bois argued, "Negro slavery" formed the basis for class relations in modern commerce and industry the world over. The southern white plantation experience of the "black race in our bosom" can give us language for the intimate experience of racism in the United States, as captured both in "slave narratives" (the liberation stories of slaves who escaped the South) and slave apologists (the white southern writers who generated defenses of slavery in the thirty years before the Civil War, when slavery as an institution was under the complex set of challenges that eventually brought it down). The apologists were much more frank about claiming racism than we are today, when much of racial language is coded but racism is still entrenched. The "playing field" of five hundred years is supposedly evened by two civil rights laws; U.S. culture is now "color blind"; and the primary form of discrimination is "reverse discrimination" experienced by white men. Reading the unapologetic apologists for slavery can give us insight into the enduring effects of racism on white consciousness shaped within the family.

On southern plantations, this family was quite a mess. The white father/master/owner was married to a white woman, who bore his white children. But he also raped the African women who were his slaves and who also bore his children. The white children inherited their darker siblings, whom they never acknowledged as kin. (The claim that Thomas Jefferson fathered children by Sally Hemings, an African woman whom he owned as a slave, has been supported by

DNA analysis.) The white women got the rap for frigidity, the African woman for promiscuity, a split that justified the white father's rape. When the white father wanted to, he could sell off the black portion of his family and send them "down the river," breaking the hearts of African parents and children alike.

The Narrative of the Life of Frederick Douglass, An American Slave plunges the reader immediately into the identity confusions inherent in the plantation family:

> The whisper that my master was my father, may or may not be true; and, true or false, it is of but little consequence to my pur-pose whilst the fact remains, in all its glaring odiousness, that slaveholders have ordained, and by law established, that the chil-dren of slave women shall in all cases follow the condition of their mothers; and this is done too obviously to administer to their own lusts, and make a gratification of their wicked desires profitable as well as pleasurable; for by this cunning arrangement, the slave-holder, in cases not a few, sustains to his slaves the double relation of master and father . . .
>
> The master is frequently compelled to sell this class of his slaves, out of deference to the feelings of his white wife; and, cruel as the deed may strike any one to be, for a man to sell his own children to human flesh-mongers, it is often the dictate of human-ity for him to do so; for, unless he does this, he must not only whip them himself, but must stand by and see one white son tie up his brother, of but few shades darker complexion than himself, and ply the gory lash to his naked back.[6]

Remarkable in Douglass's explanation of the effects of the "double relation of master and father" is the mirror, the effect of the "double relation of slave and son." Douglass explains in the early section of his narrative that "the whisper that my master was my father, may or may not be true."[7] In the passage cited, responsibility for the beating is displaced onto the white mistress, with the father "compelled" to sell his slave children, or else the father as master who "must" whip them or watch his sons do the same. Douglass must give the father/master either no agency or no humanity, and it is the agency that goes. Doug-lass describes his master's beating of his aunt Hester—we assume his mother's sister—because she had been keeping company with an African, Ned Roberts. Douglass makes clear the sadistic, sexualized nature of the whipping:

> Before he commenced whipping aunt Hester, he took her into the kitchen, and stripped her from neck to waist, leaving her neck, shoulders, and back, entirely naked. He then told her to cross her hands . . . "Now you d——d b——h, I'll learn you how to disobey my orders!" . . . The louder she screamed, the harder he whipped; and where the blood ran fastest, there he whipped longest. He would whip her to make her scream, and whip her to make her hush; and not until overcome by fatigue, would he cease to swing the blood-clotted cowskin.[8]

Douglass called this event "the blood-stained gate, the entrance to the hell of slavery, through which I was about to pass"—a vaginal passage that inclined him to identify with the white manhood of his father against his African mother, even as he challenged the institution of slavery that held them both in thrall.

What happens to white emotional life in such an environment? Is there anything left from all of this that white folks can call a "soul"? Douglass gives a terrifying description of the way that the near total control over African bodies that white men had on southern plantations created depraved white people capable of great atrocities. Henry Hughes, a slave apologist writing in 1854, gave some insight into the soul-destroying dynamic of the plantation. He wrote of what he called the "Orderer's esthetic" and its implications for human relationships: "But the esthetic system is both positive and negative. It is not for the production of pleasure only. It is for the prevention of pain. It is both eunesthetic and anesthetic. Warrenteeism [his euphemism for slavery] as it is, is essentially anesthetic. It systematically eliminates bodily pain. It actualizes comfort for all."[9] Such accounts as Douglass's of his master's beating of Hester show how completely Hughes encodes the masters' point of view in his analysis of slavery as a system that "eliminates bodily pain." Clearly, it does not eliminate pain in bodies of Africans, who are not considered fully human. Rather, it intensifies pain beyond endurance. But what does it do to white bodies? What is this "anesthetic esthetic" that Hughes articulates?

Although aesthetics is that branch of philosophy that deals with judgments concerning beauty, it comes from *aisthēsis*, "to perceive."

Anesthesia adds the prefix *a(n)*, signifying a blocked perception translated as "insensibility . . . the loss of sensation without a loss of consciousness." Sensation is "a perception associated with stimulation of
a sense organ or with a specific bodily condition" connected with "the
faculty to feel or perceive."[10] Sensation, then, begins in impulses from
eyes, ears, nose, tongue, skin, central nervous system—as the brain
"perceives" or interprets them. These sensations also have associated
feelings—localized somatically in the chest and metaphorically in the
"heart." Consciousness, then, is an amalgam of sensation, perception
about those sensations that become thought and the emotions that
respond to them. The particular anesthesia of slavery seems to block
the feeling from consciousness, leaving a more abstracted "reason."[11]
Necessary to the slave system was the masters' blocked sensation of its
pain, an aesthetic that left him insensible not only to the fellow human
beings he enslaved but also to the testimony of his senses.

The Civil War diaries of Mary Boykin Chesnut provide an additional gloss, from a white woman's (slave mistress's) point of view, on
Hughes's notion of the soul-destroying anesthesia necessary for the
maintenance of power. The contradictory position of "woman" and
"mistress" made Chesnut more vulnerable to feeling the pain of domination and gave her the space to articulate her contradictory status.
Mary Chesnut's husband served in Confederate president Jefferson
Davis's cabinet during the Civil War, and she enjoyed her status and
vehemently supported the Confederate cause. Yet her diary in places
makes analogies between the condition of women and of slaves. She
felt the schisms in her culture more than many white upper-class
women of her day, making her both observer and site of struggle for
the forces contending within southern slave society in its penultimate
moment. She describes a "tragedy" she observed on the auction block:

> A mad woman taken from her husband and children. Of course
> she was mad, or she would not have given her grief words in that
> public place. Her keepers were along. What she said was rational
> enough, pathetic, at times heart-rending. It excited me so I quietly
> took opium. It enables me to retain every particle of mind or sense
> or brains I have, and so quiets my nerves that I can calmly reason
> and take rational views of things otherwise maddening.[12]

In this remarkable passage, we arrive again at the anesthetic of
slavery. The African woman in her reasonable grief gives voice to

her pain, and Chesnut's perception of her situation rends the white woman's heart, arousing dangerous sensation and feeling—"excitement"—which she immediately blocks quite literally by opium in a "systematic elimination of bodily pain." She loses "sensation without the loss of consciousness," and her quieted nerves leave her with a distracted rationality—the ability to "take rational views of things otherwise maddening." This process also distorts the body's feedback system to let us know that something is dangerously awry. "Poor women, poor slaves": Mary Chesnut only articulated what Hughes and others explained more dispassionately: "All other people in the State, who are not sovereign people, are subsovereign. To this class belong women, minors, criminals, lunatics and idiots, aliens and all others unqualified or disqualified"[13] (not to mention how it might make a person lunatic or criminal to be constantly "unqualified or disqualified").

These passages, which describe and defend the institution of chattel slavery around which much of what we call racism evolved on this continent, suggest that there is not only a psychology but also a physiology of racism: it encodes itself in our "consciousness" through our central nervous system. Its energy enters our energy, which also is our sexual energy. Its spirit enters our body. That thing that it partially displaces when it does so is what I am calling "soul."

Is the blunted white consciousness described in Chesnut and Hughes only a white upper-class southern phenomenon? (As Du Bois points out, in the antebellum South there were five million white people who held no slaves, and an oligarchy of 8,000 among the two million slaveholders.)[14] I do not think so. Rather, in their frank charting of the psychology of mastery in the South in the mid-nineteenth century, Douglass, Hughes and Chesnut articulate a process basic to racist consciousness and to the generic consciousness of domination. As Hughes explained, "In any order there are two classes. These are the, (1) Ordered or Superordinates, and the, (2), Orderees or Subordinates. This, of necessity."[15]

I find it helpful to read southern accounts of slavery (theoretical and personal, black and white) against a European equivalent: Hegel's analysis of "Lordship and Bondage" in *The Phenomenology of Mind*, published in 1807. Hegel makes a chilling distinction between two modes of consciousness, which are always in relationships of dominance and subordination: "The one is independent, and its essential nature is to be for itself; the other is dependent, and its essence is life or existence for another. The former is the Master, or Lord, the latter the Bondsman."[16] However, the Master is dependent on his subordinate for his self-existence, giving the Bondsman more chance of "real and true independence"—an independence that does not come, in Hegel's worldview, from insurrection but rather from continued subordination.[17]

For Hegel, this is the essential nature of human consciousness, not a result of colonialism (which in one hundred years would result in Europe's controlling 80 percent of the globe) or patriarchy. For my purposes, Hegel's passage is useful precisely as a description of what happens to consciousness under systems of domination—of "Orderer and Orderee," in the words of my slave apologist. Hegel calls this struggle a "trial by death," a process by which the two selves "cancel their consciousness which had its place in this alien element of natural existence . . . and are sublated as terms or extremes."[18] The Master holds the Bondsman in thrall in obvious ways, as "the power controlling the state of existence. . . . In other words he gets the enjoyment." (Just so for Hughes: southern slavery "eliminates bodily pain" and "maximizes pleasure for all." Simone de Beauvoir attributes to this passage in Hegel the origin of discourses on Otherness.[19] But if Hegel (typically European and typically male, I am arguing) had not had the sense of "natural existence" as an "alien element," might he have been able to imagine relationships of mutuality and reciprocity and communities built not on exclusion but inclusion?

A Lost Sense of Eternity

Segue to Sigmund Freud, another cartographer of modern European (male) consciousness. In *Civilization and Its Discontents* Freud described the emotional void about and from which he theorized. Freud published *Civilization and Its Discontents* (1930) in the last stage of his theorizing, when he was extending the insights of psychoanalysis developed over four decades into other spheres of human endeavor— at the end of his "long road from cerebral anatomy and cerebral physiology, by way of psychopathology to his new form of psychology (metapsychology)."[20] He was expanding the theoretical core—on the interpretation of dreams as access to the "unconscious" in *On the Psychopathology of Everyday Life* (1904) and *The Interpretation of Dreams*

(1900) and the fuller evocation of sexuality as libido in *Three Essays on Sexuality* (1905) and *Introductory Lectures on Psychoanalysis* (1916–17). He had first begun his critique of religion in *Totem and Taboo* (1913) and would end it in *Moses and Monotheism* (1939).

Freud begins *Civilization and Its Discontents* by citing a poet friend who had responded to Freud's debunking of religion in *Future of an Illusion* (1927). This friend explained what he saw as the "true source of religion" as a "sensation of eternity, of something limitless, unbounded." This "oceanic feeling" connected a person to the world in an "indissoluble bond, of being one with the external world as a whole." Freud confesses, "I cannot discover this oceanic feeling in myself. It is not easy to deal scientifically with feelings. One can attempt to describe their physiological signs. Where this is not possible—and I am afraid that the oceanic feeling too will defy this kind of characterization—nothing remains but to fall back on the ideational context which is most readily associated with the feeling. . . . From my own experience I could not convince myself of the primary nature of such feeling."[21] Where Mary Chesnut frankly resorts to opium to contain her feelings, Freud (who had his own cocaine problem) resorts to psychoanalysis to justify the absence of his, "attempting to discover a psycho-analytic explanation of such a feeling."

I bring Freud perhaps simplistically into this discussion on the souls of white folks because in 1930 he was a Jew who had been charting the European psyche for three decades, as it edged toward fascism (a particularly European form of virulent racism). I also bring this particular passage in because in it his poet friend points us to how this complex consciousness (sensation, emotion, and thought) has a spiritual dimension, the point of psyche where mind becomes soul, or animating spirit, within and beyond. Its emotional content leads us beyond ourselves to "a feeling of an indissoluble bond, of being one with the external world as a whole." Remarkably in the opening to *Civilization and Its Discontents,* Freud reveals the stunted nature of his own consciousness, from and with which he charts "human" consciousness in his psychoanalytic narratives of id, ego, and superego, oedipal development, and so forth. Freud's lack of a sense of 'indissoluble bond, of being one with the external world as a whole," leaves him with what Hegel called an "alien existence" that underlies the will to mastery.

What happens to lost sensations and feelings? Much of his life,

Freud worked at answering this question. His terms for what I have called "sensation" are "sense," "sensation," "principle," and "instinct," the last of which he defines as "the source of a state of excitation within the body."[22] He ultimately collapsed all instincts into two categories: sexual instincts and death instincts. In *Civilization and Its Discontents*, one of his last formulations, Freud described the dynamic whereby sexual instinct, or desire, is antithetical to (Western) civilization. "It is impossible to overlook the extent to which civilization is built upon a renunciation of instinct." Isolated individuals enter community "by a sacrifice of their instincts [to a rule of law] . . . which leaves no one . . . at the mercy of brute force." He variously classifies the processes of renunciation or sacrifice, such as repression, suppression, sublimation, and dissociation. By implication, this is a Western (European) process. It is "white folks" who do it. He writes: "Civilization behaves towards sexuality as a people or a stratum of its population does which has subjected another to its exploitation. Fear of a revolt by the suppressed elements drives it to stricter precautionary measures. A high-water mark in such a development has been reached in our Western European civilization."[23] Herbert Marcuse in *Eros and Civilization* paraphrases Freud:

> Free gratification of man's instinctual needs is incompatible with civilized society: renunciation and delay in satisfaction are the prerequisites of progress. Happiness must be subordinated to the discipline of work as full-time occupation, to the discipline of monogamic reproduction, to the established system of law and order. The methodical sacrifice of libido, its rigidly enforced deflection to socially useful activities and expressions, *is* culture.[24]

By Freud's formulation, instinctual gratification, revolt, and freedom lie outside European culture, which is constituted to repress them. He observes that the human "desire for freedom may be their revolt against some existing injustice" that springs "from the remains of their original personality, which is still untamed by civilization and may thus become the basis in them of hostility to civilization." Here Freud draws on Darwin to code civilization as European, with the original "untamed" personality coming from the more "primitive" cultures that Europe subdued: civilization and its discontents, sublimation and prior instinct, recapitulate the relationship between colonizer and colonized. Repression of instinctual feelings, like the conquest of "primitive" cultures, made inevitable what Freud called the "return of the repressed," a kind of psychic revolution congruent with national independence movements then active in Asia, Latin America, and Africa.[25]

Herbert Marcuse in *Eros and Civilization* was the first to specify that the European "civilization" that suppressed instinct is or was the civilization of industrial capitalism. "Behind the reality principle lies the fundamental fact of Ananke or scarcity (*Lebensnot*), which means that the struggle for existence takes place in a world too poor for the satisfaction of human needs without constant restraint, renunciation, delay" by some for others. The "brute fact of scarcity" is a consequence of a "specific organization of scarcity" under capitalism that makes renunciation of instinct and desire necessary in order for workers to be able to carry out all the alienated labor required of them.[26]

The affective void from which feelings and perceptions have been blocked in oneself and cast onto Others is the psychological space from which whiteness and maleness have been mobilized throughout their histories. What happens in the space between Hegel's dominating self and dominated other, between Hughes's Orderer and Orderee, was what Freud called "projection." And the result of such projection is a high state of unconsciousness: in Hughes's terms, anesthesia, a stripping away from fuller consciousness of strata of perception.[27] This void both justifies racist exploitation (by projecting onto the exploited all the cast-off fearsome and evil feelings of the exploiter—Freud's projection) and holds it in place (the exploiter cannot then feel the violence of his acts, because he cannot feel—Hughes's anesthesia).

Within U.S. culture, various therapeutic movements since Freud have begun to reveal the extent to which exploitative relationships have cost us personally, familially, and socially. They have elaborated the cost of our anesthesia; of how the emotional void, once vacated, is filled again and again with destructive and compulsive thoughts, feelings, and habits. In the past twenty years, also, the Right has made use of what Lawrence Grossberg calls "affective epidemics"—around drugs, the family, nationalism, and so forth: "Questions of fact and representation become secondary to the articulation of people's emotional fears and hopes. This partly explains the new conservatism's 'ideological' successes: they have been able to control specific vectors without having to confront the demands of policy and public action.

Similarly they have been able to construct issues with enormous public passion . . . without leaving any space for public engagement."[28]
Or, as Marcuse put it, "The era tends to be totalitarian even where it
has not produced totalitarian states."[29] Promisekeepers, the Christian
"men's movement," mass in football stadiums, hold one another, and
weep—and make blood promises to regain dominion over the family
for the one race.

Toward the Thirteenth Step

What would it mean to open up therapeutic discourses and practices
more fully to their political implications? To begin to answer that
question, I want to look at two pervasive mental health movements
based in discourses on "addiction" and on "dysfunctional families."

The Twelve-Step Program, originating in the 1930s and 1940s
in response to an epidemic of alcoholism, has proliferated into a
variety of Twelve-Step programs, in which addiction has become a
characteristic of the central problems of the culture. The World Health
Organization defines addiction as "a pathological relationship to any
mood-altering experience that has life-damaging consequences." Mary
Chesnut blocked painful feelings with opium. Freud describes a very
similar process:

> The most interesting methods of averting suffering are those
> which seek to influence our own organism. In the last analysis, all
> suffering is nothing else than sensation; it only exists in so far as
> we feel it, and we only feel it in consequence of certain ways in
> which our organism is regulated. The crudest, but also the most
> effective among these methods of influence is the chemical one—
> intoxication. I do not think that anyone completely understands
> its mechanism, but it is a fact that there are foreign substances
> which, when present in the blood or tissues, directly cause us
> pleasurable sensations; and they also so alter the conditions gov-
> erning our sensibility that we become incapable of receiving un-
> pleasurable impulses. The two effects not only occur simulta-
> neously, but seem to be intimately bound up with each other.[30]

"Averting suffering" by chemical means or compulsive processes is
the emotional basis of addiction. Within the "recovery movement,"

problematic addictions range from heroin and alcohol to shopping and too much of the wrong kinds of love.

Entering into a Twelve-Step program was inevitable for me, given that my mother's issue was addiction, and I had, still, an issue with food, and given the growing presence of "recovery" programs in the lesbian community. With the other folks in my Overeaters Anonymous group—95 percent women of various sizes, many of whom I would consider downright skinny—I would close each meeting with the Serenity Prayer: "God, give me the serenity to accept the things I cannot change, the courage to change the things I can, and the wisdom to know the difference." But I could never quite get it right: "God give me the courage to change the things I cannot change" was my shorthanded version. I got as far as the first nine steps. Through the first three steps, I admitted that my problem with eating was out of my control, that its solution was beyond me, and that I could turn to a "higher power" for help ("HP," in the shorthand of many of the women in the group, although that always made me think of "horse power," water-skiing behind an Evinrude motor).

Steps four through nine involved taking a fearless and searching moral inventory, sharing it with God and another person, and making amends. At first I resisted, since over-responsibility was one of my patterns. But I came to see that this process helped to undercut my sense of victimhood; there were aspects of the emotional and interpersonal conflicts in which I found myself to which I contributed. If I could at least change my own part of the interaction, I could perhaps shift the relationship in a more positive way. Practicing acknowledging the times when I made particular mistakes so I could move on (rather than always being guilty for everything) was also helpful. I taught in a minimum security prison for six months, and most of the young black men who were my students went from my GED class to Twelve-Step programs—both of which on hot days were preferable to the road gang.

Twelve-step discussions rightly recognize, I think, that addictions are behavior patterns used to control feelings of pain or depression or hopelessness or rage. But why are we so miserable in the first place, and where did we get the encouragement to deal with this unhappiness and emotional disorder through substance abuse? Those questions lie beyond the scope of the Twelve Steps. They take us into a history of racist, sexist capitalism.[31] As Elayne Rapping argues in *The Culture of Recovery*: "That these [addictive] behaviors, in today's world, do indeed reflect the growing self-destructiveness of people trying desperately to keep up and succeed in a competitive, market-driven world is masked in public discourse by the idea that 'addictive disorders' are genetically—not socially—engendered."[32]

Attending Overeaters Anonymous and reading about racism, I picked up the connection between addiction and capitalism first when C. L. R. James explained how Europeans developing a taste for coffee and cocoa had finally made African slavery profitable. The sugar that went into both drinks came from sugar plantations in the Caribbean, and the addictive qualities of sugar, cocoa, and caffeine created enough of a market that the huge losses in the slave trade (which is to say, all the Africans who died in the Middle Passage) could be offset by the new, addictive demand for sugar. The "triangle trade" from Africa to New England to the Caribbean also had at its center sugar and rum, other addictive substances. The cash crop for slave plantations in North Carolina was tobacco—which also fueled the growth of Durham, my hometown, by robber tobacco baron James B. Duke. Duke liked to brag that he "taught the world to smoke." One of the first companies to use modern marketing techniques, American Tobacco sent free cigarettes into the desert of North Africa, or gave them away on the streets of Asian cities, or handed packs to immigrants coming off the boats in the United States. Duke understood too that an addictive demand would allow him to run up his supply. Expanding capitalism had built addiction into the whole culture, starting with slavery.

In the week that I finished this essay, the Raleigh *News and Observer* carried a story originally run in the *San Jose Mercury* detailing the steps by which the Central Intelligence Agency helped the Nicaraguan contras sell crack cocaine very cheaply to gangs in Los Angeles to fund their war against the Sandinistas, and how this diabolical scheme introduced crack to this country, a substance so addictive that people would murder for it, destroying untold lives and devastating American cities. There is only so much Twelve-Stepping can do in the face of racist, genocidal government schemes that create addiction for profit and control.

The Twelve Steps gave me a set of emotional guidelines that, when I applied them, could indeed help, in the words of the program, restore my personal emotional life to sanity. But I felt some equally deep need to help restore to sanity the life of my culture. As far as amends go, how do humans "make amends" for slavery, or genocide—especially when the Eleventh Tradition taught us that the Twelve-Step Program "has no opinion on outside issues; hence . . . ought never to be drawn into controversy"? Would folks in "the Program" have a different attitude toward affirmative action, say, if they thought politically about amends and saw their own emotional investment in a restored cultural sanity? Also, serenity was not an emotional state with which I had much affinity, righteously pissed off as I felt at most forms of authority. And why was this called the "Serenity Prayer," anyway? Why emphasize acceptance of what could not be changed? Why not the "Wisdom Prayer"? Or even better, the "Courage Prayer?" What space is there for divine discontent? What if my "spiritual awakening" in the Twelfth Step included liberation theology? Might not there be some Thirteenth Step, such as "eliminate racism, sexism, homophobia, and capitalism?"

The "Dysfunctional Family" Becomes Redundant

Another therapeutic discourse that obfuscates the source of emotional pain is the discourse on dysfunctional families, which emerged in part from Twelve-Step programs and in part from the rediscovery of incest in the evolution of both feminism and therapy (a discovery that Freud soon suppressed with his oedipal theory and his theory of female hysteria, his own most flagrant projection, according to Jeffrey Masson).[33] These therapies also elaborate on Freud. John Bradshaw is one of the popularizers of this "family therapy" that addresses "dysfunction." Bradshaw traces his psychotherapeutic lineage back to R. D. Laing, the existentialist psychotherapist who suggested the theory of family systems, elaborated on by Milton Erickson, Gregory Bateson, Carl Whitaker, and Virginia Satif, among others. Freud observed that suffering "exists in so far as we feel it." Both discussions of addiction and of dysfunctional families acknowledge that suffering exists in relationships (or systems) and that one person's denial augments another person's pain in a family (or, I would add, a social) system. Feelings will out.

According to Bradshaw, a "functional family" is one in which each person gets to have her own thoughts, feel her own feelings, express her own ideas and creativity. The alternative—so common as to make "dysfunctional family" redundant—was "enmeshment": everybody glommed on to each other, undifferentiated, the kind of togetherness that leaves us ultimately alone. According to Bradshaw, children in dysfunctional families suffer from abuse, abandonment, or neglect, and they learn behaviors in response to environments where to various degrees alcoholism, drug addiction, incest, battering, and sexual abuse are rampant: in other words, the typical American family of the past several decades.[34]

Bradshaw traces the "crisis in society" to a "crisis in the family," and he sees the family as that context that sets the rules about what it means to be human. He argues that these rules ("poisonous pedagogies") are abusive and shaming and that shame is soul-murdering. Shame occurs primarily through parental abandonment of children, triggered by behavior ranging from physically leaving a child, to not providing for its needs, to sexual abuse, to enforced secret-keeping. In this abandonment, the child is forced to take care of the parents, rather than the reverse. The child cannot bear to admit how badly the parent is doing, so he forms a "fantasy bond," deifying the parent and taking on the blame himself. "For a child at this stage to realize the inadequacies of parents would produce unbearable anxiety." The ego defends itself through a number of numbing processes: idealization, denial, repression, and dissociation. The child projects her own split and false self onto others and adopts a rigid mask. This shame is then passed on to another generation when the former child has children. Bradshaw traces the origins of "poisonous pedagogy" to the shift from the agricultural to the factory system 150 years ago, when fathers became absent and mothers bonded too closely with children.

What the dysfunctional family discourse does not do is point to sexism, racism, classism, or homophobia as a source of the sadness or anger that overwhelms people or as a source of the cultural system that then gives them no expression for those feelings other than denial or oblivion. To talk about a shift from the agricultural to the factory system, which absented fathers, is to talk about industrial capitalism. To talk about authoritarian systems by which fathers operate as gods is to talk about sexism or patriarchy. What more dysfunctional family might there be than the southern plantation family as described by Frederick Douglass? What bigger "boundary violations" than slavery or the genocide of indigenous people?

Bradshaw uses Hitler as the ultimate example of the destructive effects of poisonous pedagogy, tracing Nazism to authoritarian and abusive family systems in Germany and to Hitler's emotional and physical abuse as a child. That's a good enough point—as far as it goes. But what about centuries of racist practices and ideologies as they landed on Jews in the form of anti-Semitism? What about the German insistence on expansion and militarism consistent with imperialism? It's all right to psychologize history, as Bradshaw does, if we at the same time historicize psychology.[35]

What, then, is the cost to white people of racism? Perhaps now we can more accurately make the assessment, recognizing that racism implicates systems of oppression based on gender and class, on patriarchy, capitalism, and heterosexism:

Racism costs us intimacy.

Racism costs us our affective lives.

Racism costs us authenticity.

Racism costs us our sense of connection to other humans and the natural world.

Racism costs us our spiritual selves: "a feeling of an indissoluble bond, of being one with the external world as a whole," as Freud's poet friend tried to explain.

Out of Slavery

Of course, not only white people pay this cost. And not only Orderers do. Frederick Douglass knew that he too paid the cost of his affective life to slavery when he, like many other slave infants, was separated from his mother, an abandonment over which she had absolutely no control: "For what this separation has done, I do not know, unless it be to hinder the development of the child's affection toward its mother, and to blunt and destroy the natural affection of the mother for the child."[36] Douglass never saw his mother "by the light of day." Four or five times, she walked the twelve miles to see him after her day's work. "Never having enjoyed, to any considerable extent, her soothing presence, her tender and watchful care, I received the tidings of her death with much the same emotions I should have probably felt at the death of a stranger."

Douglass's narrative tells the story of "how a man was made a slave and how a slave was made a man" through a process of many years of reclaiming the oceanic feeling of connection. Ironically, this life of feeling was also all around him in his fellow slaves, singing their way through the woods, their spirituals "revealing at once the highest joy and the deepest sadness . . . a tale of woe . . . tones loud, long, and deep." Douglass learns "the pathway from slavery to freedom" when his master forces his mistress to stop teaching him to read because "it would forever unfit him to be a slave." Poor white children in his neighborhood teach him the alphabet, and they "express for [him] the liveliest sympathy." He begins to abhor slavery so much that he wishes himself dead, until he learns the word "abolition," the light "breaking in on [him] by degrees." He realizes his strong attachment to his young white friends when he is sent back to the country from Baltimore. Back on the plantation, he falls under Covey, the slave breaker, and is whipped severely over a period of months, broken in "body, soul and spirit." He runs away to ask his master for mercy and is refused. On the way back, he is befriended by Sandy, a slave with a free wife. Sandy gives him a magical root that "would render it impossible for Mr. Covey, or any other white man, to whip me." Sandy's solidarity and his medicine prove powerful, and the next time Covey attacks, Douglass fights back, beating the white man soundly. Covey never beats him again. Defending himself gives Douglass self-confidence and a determination to be free. By appropriating violence and the ability to inflict pain, Douglass contradicts the anesthetic aesthetic that slavery "actualizes comfort for all [white men]." By defending himself, finally, when being beaten, perhaps he breaks his psychic identification with the white master/father and reclaims some identification with the black mother/slave, which augments his capacity for feeling. Until this point, Douglass has carried the burden of a white masculinity; by using the violence of slavery against itself, he claims a revolutionary Black masculinity.[37]

He is sent back again to Baltimore, where he teaches other "dear fellow slaves" to read in a Sabbath school at the house of a "free colored man": "I loved them with a love stronger than anything I have experienced since. . . . I believe we would have died for each other. We never undertook to do anything, of any importance, without a mutual consultation. We never moved separately. We were one; and as much so by our tempers and dispositions, as by the mutual hardship to which we were necessarily subjected as slaves."[38] Paradoxically, the "number of warm-hearted friends in Baltimore—"friends that [he] loved more than life"—make his final escape both "painful beyond expression" and finally possible. Douglass can escape the slave South when he has completed the making of the slave into not so much a "man" as a human, by reclaiming his capacity to feel and love (including to love his African self enough to defend himself from white violence).

What does Frederick Douglass's reclamation of his own humanity and his "love of humanity" have to teach white people? Well, for one thing, he responded to his "family dysfunction" first by escaping, then by changing the structures that created the dysfunction. Douglass's narrative is part of his attack on the slave system that created his and many others' misery. And Frederick Douglass (with the help of a few other people) *abolished slavery* by such efforts. Perhaps if we are really to "systematically eliminate bodily pain" of family dysfunction, as Hughes would have us do, we should systematically eliminate racism, homophobia, sexism, and capitalism. As Marcuse explained in the preface to *Eros and Civilization,* "Private disorder reflects more directly than before the disorder of the whole, and the cure of personal disorder depends more directly than before on the cure of the general disorder."[39]

We can see in Douglass's narratives the evolution of radical subjectivity that Brazilian Paulo Freire called *conscientizaçao,* which involved a praxis of action and reflection. This "critical thinking . . . perceives reality as process, as transformation, rather than as static entity . . . [and] does not separate itself from action, but constantly immerses itself in temporality without fear of the risks involved." Thus Douglass learns to act, and reflect, and act, and reflect, until he has gained a fuller humanity for himself and his culture.

So I am not arguing for the elimination of therapeutic spaces such as counseling or twelve-step programs. I am arguing for politicizing them, using those reflective spaces to generate clearer actions, and taking those actions back to absorb their full emotional and intellectual and spiritual impact on our consciousness, and so on until we die. Nor is this consciousness only critical *thinking,* as Freire terms it, but, as we have seen, a thick soup of thought, feeling, and sensation, much of which may not always be grounded in self-awareness. Such a dialogue requires an intense faith in humanity, in the "power to make and remake, to create and re-create, faith in [the] vocation to be more fully human." It also requires some ability to negotiate this question of white people's souls.

Mary Chesnut's pain, felt in response to the black woman on the auction block, was her spontaneous biological and spiritual reaction to another human's exploitation and grief, the reassuring mark of her humanity. Then she chose opium. The Grimké sisters, white southern women of Chesnut's generation, made another choice: abolitionism. The active engagement with real structures, with (in Freire's terms) "reality as transformation," not only alleviates future suffering; it is itself therapeutic, because it brings us as humans back to our birthright of "love of humanity" and an "oceanic feeling" of connection, with ourselves, with one another, and with the animate world. It brings us to the moment when, or the place where, the fact of love surpasses the fact of death, and we are restored our lost sense of eternity.

Notes

1 My project in *Memoir of a Race Traitor* (Boston: South End, 1994) of breaking down the boundaries between the personal and the historical was being pursued also by Catherine McClintock in *Imperial Leather: Race, Gender and Sexuality in the Colonial Contest*, published a year later (New York: Routledge, 1995). She wrote: "In the chapters that follow, I propose the development of a *situated psychoanalysis*—a culturally contextualized psychoanalysis that is simultaneously a psychoanalytically informed history. . . . In sum, *Imperial Leather* is written with the conviction that psychoanalysis and material history are mutually necessary for a strategic engagement with unstable power" (72, 73).

2 John Bradshaw, *Bradshaw on: The Family* (Deerfield Beach, Fla.: Health Communications, 1988), 7–8.

3 bell hooks, *Killing Rage/Ending Racism* (New York: Holt, 1995), 152–53.

4 W. E. B. Du Bois, *Black Reconstruction in America, 1860–1880* (New York: Atheneum, 1979), 30; see David Roediger, *The Wages of Whiteness: Race and the Making of the American Working Class* (New York: Verso, 1991), as he presses "why the white working class settles for being white."

5 Du Bois, *The World and Africa: An Inquiry into the Part Which Africa Has Played in World History* (New York: International Publishers, 1965), 18–21; quoted in Roediger, *Wages of Whiteness*, 6.

6 Frederick Douglass, *The Narrative of the Life of Frederick Douglass, an American Slave*, ed. Houston Baker Jr. (New York: Penguin, 1982), 49–50.

7 Ibid., 49.

8 Ibid., 52, 51.

9 Henry Hughes, "Treatise on Sociology," in *The Ideology of Slavery: Proslav-*

ery Thought in the Antebellum South, 1830–1860, ed. Drew Gilpin Faust (Baton Rouge: Louisiana State University Press, 1981), 256.

10 *Merriam-Webster's Collegiate Dictionary*, 10th ed., s.vv. "aesthetics," "anesthesia."

11 Perhaps here we have the formula for fascist intelligence that justifies genocidal practices in the name of the superior intelligence of a master race, an intelligence seemingly devoid of human empathy or compassion. See Richard J. Hernnstein and Charles Murray's *The Bell Curve* (New York: Free Press, 1994), for its implications.

12 Mary Chesnut, *A Diary from Dixie*, ed. Ben Ames Williams (Cambridge, Mass.: Harvard University Press, 1980), 25–26.

13 Hughes, "Treatise," 258.

14 Du Bois, *Black Reconstruction*, 26.

15 Hughes, "Treatise," 243.

16 G. W. F. Hegel, *The Phenomenology of Mind*, trans. J. B. Baillie (New York: Harper and Row, 1967), 231, 234.

17 Ibid., 235–37.

18 Ibid., 233.

19 Simone de Beauvoir, *The Second Sex*, trans. H. M. Parshley (New York: Vintage, 1953), xx. "Things become clear, on the contrary, if following Hegel we find in consciousness itself a fundamental hostility toward every other consciousness; the subject can be posed only in being opposed—he sets himself up as the essential, as opposed to the other, the inessential, object."

20 Hans Kung, *Freud and the Problem of God* (New Haven: Yale University Press, 1979), 27.

21 Sigmund Freud, *Civilization and Its Discontents*, trans. and ed. James Strachey (New York: Norton, 1989), 10–11.

22 Freud, *New Introductory Lectures on Psychoanalysis*, trans. and ed. James Strachey (New York: Norton, 1965), chapter 4.

23 Freud, *Discontents*, 60.

24 Herbert Marcuse, *Eros and Civilization: A Philosophical Inquiry into Freud* (Boston: Beacon Press, 1966), 3.

25 Marianna Torgovnick in *Gone Primitive: Savage Intellects, Modern Lives* (Chicago: University of Chicago Press, 1991), and McClintock in *Imperial Leather* have a similar reading of this passage of *Civilization and Its Discontents*. For Torgovnick, Freud's ambivalence toward his position as a Jew in Vienna as Europe edged toward fascism heightened his ambivalence toward the primitive, a characteristic attributed to Jews by Nazi anti-Semitism. But he was not able to reject his identification with power as "civilized": "Given the material he had to work with, Freud might have arrived at a radical critique of the very idea of 'hierarchy' and 'mastery' in

the political contexts of the late twenties and thirties. . . . Instead, Freud continued to lay siege to the top level of power" (201). She agrees that there is much at stake in Freud's rejection of the "oceanic" but focuses her questions on a critique of gender, rather than on race and colonization, as I am suggesting: "He never fully considers the questions invited by his opening meditation on the oceanic. If there is a state of mind, and potentially a state of culture, that could be derived from the original relationship of our bodies to the bodies of our mothers, what differences in father-centered psychoanalytic theories would follow? What differences in the relation of men and women to the physical world would follow? What political consequences would follow? Might these provide a form of 'civilization' with fewer 'discontents'?" (208). McClintock draws on Kristeva's explanation of abjection as a process by which "in order to become social the self has to expunge certain elements that society deems impure. . . . The abject is everything that the subject seeks to expunge in order to become social" (71). She continues in a vein similar to mine: "Abject peoples are those whom industrial imperialism rejects but cannot do without: slaves, prostitutes, the colonized, domestic workers, the insane, the unemployed, and so on" (72).

26 Marcuse, *Eros* 35–36.

27 Psychoanalysis was Freud's brave attempt to heal the breach marked in Hegel between dominating self and dominated other. With Freud this dynamic had become in his later theory an internal drama: ego caught in the middle between dominant superego and repressed id.

28 Lawrence Grossberg, *We Gotta Get Out of This Place: Popular Conservatism and Postmodern Culture* (New York: Routledge, 1992), 292.

29 Marcuse, *Eros,* xxvii.

30 Freud, *Discontents,* 27.

31 Elayne Rapping in *The Culture of Recovery: Making Sense of the Self-Help Movement in Women's Lives* (Boston: Beacon Press, 1996) makes a more extreme form of this argument:

Why are we in need of so many, more powerful crutches to get through a day of life in America? I believe the reason is not "addictive personalities" today any more than it was alcohol during the days of Prohibition. But we can "come to believe" that addictive personalities do cause our distress, personal and social. If we can further "come to believe" that our compulsive attraction to food, shopping, or abusive mates is rooted in diseases and allergies, which can be sometimes, partly, controlled by a spiritual, confessional group process which can be extended and enforced throughout society, we are on the road to a massive system of social control—from church basements to prison wards—in which actual social problems are made invisible and things, somehow, keep getting worse. My long months of visiting and interviewing those who maintain this now vast system of institutions and policies based upon 12-Step thinking and practice—an empire of medical/religious/health professionals and entrepreneurs now so massive and influential as to boggle the mind—convinced me we are well on our way down that road. (80).

See also Fernando Ortiz, *Cuban Counterpoint: Tobacco and Sugar*, trans. Harriet de Onis (Durham: Duke University Press, 1995), originally published in 1947.

32 Rapping, *Culture of Recovery*, 69.

33 Jeffrey M. Masson, *The Assault on Truth: Freud's Suppression of the Seduction Theory* (New York: Farrar, Straus and Giroux, 1992).

34 Bradshaw, *On the Family*, 7–8.

35 McClintock and I are on the same track here. She calls for a *"situated psychoanalysis*—a culturally contextualized psychoanalysis that is simultaneously a psychoanalytically informed history"* (see note 1 above). I am arguing not so much for a reform of psychoanalysis but for a way to popularize the understanding of the emotional and spiritual cost of racism to white people and more generally of oppressive systems to those who perpetuate them.

36 Douglass, *Narrative*, 48.

37 Cynthia Willet, "The master-slave dialectic, Hegel versus Douglass," in *Subjugation and Bondage: Critical Essays on Slavery and Social Philosophy*, ed. Tommy L. Lott (Lanham: Rowman and Littlefield, 1988), 151–70.

38 Douglass, *Narrative*, 121–22.

39 Marcuse, *Eros*, xxvii.

Handwritten margin note at top: Language of Capitalism — rugged individual = "white immigrant"

Ruth Frankenberg

Handwritten margin note: PM

The Mirage of an Unmarked Whiteness

Handwritten left margin note: what is the social context in which race is constructed?

Scholars of race, especially those of us who are poststructuralist and/ or social constructionist in orientation, frequently emphasize as a ground rule of our discussions that race is a term that is in actuality by no means self-evident, by no means "real" in the positivist sense of that term. To draw on one example, Paul Gilroy, in his now classic study of the history of racism in Britain, emphasizes that " 'Race' has to be socially and politically constructed and elaborate ideological work is done to secure and maintain the different forms of 'racialization' which have characterized capitalist development. Recognizing this makes it all the more important to compare and evaluate the different historical situations in which 'race' has become politically pertinent."[1]

Handwritten left margin note: race as a process

One should note that Gilroy consistently places "race" in quotation marks, the better to remind his audience of its unreality, its instability. This does not, however, mean that Gilroy disputes the potency of race as an organizing framework in the relations of oppression and exploitation.[2] This emphasis on race as process rather than thing has from the start been critical to my understanding of race and, within that, of whiteness.[3] In a similar vein, Becky Thompson and Sangeeta Tyagi begin their collection of essays engaging contemporary racism through autobiography by emphasizing that "[r]ace is about *everything*—historical, political, personal—and race is about *nothing*—a construct, an invention that has changed dramatically over time and historical circumstance."[4] Race, then, emerges as an awful—make that awe-ful—fiction, arguably the most violent fiction in human history. I say "arguably" because gender and enforced heterosexuality tie with "race" for first place. (Class and nation are two of the other key axes in relation to which race, gender, and sexuality are organized.)

One challenge in the critical examination of whiteness is thus to hold onto the unreality of race while adhering tenaciously to the recognition of its all-too-real effects. The critical examination of race, racism, and whiteness requires a particular kind of vigilance, breadth of vision, and refusal of "either-or" thinking. Like Gilroy, Thompson and Tyagi, and others, I have also previously argued that race be analyzed as a constellation of processes and practices rather than as a bounded entity and have foregrounded the need for attention to history, process, change.[5] Race, as a social construct, is transformable, malleable. *flexible* But also, given their foundation in historical process, racisms are demonstrably firmly rooted *in* that process. Race is in fact anything but presentist in its character. (By "presentist," I mean focused in and emergent from the present historical moment.) Indeed, racist discourses have recourse all too often to that which is tried and (un)true—or perhaps "*tired* and (un)true," which turns out to be only one letter different. The terrorist Muslim; the asexual Asian man; his always-sexually-available female counterpart; the inherently dangerous young African American man; the overly fertile African American *racist types* woman, Native American woman, Chicana or Mexicana, are all-too-familiar tropes.[6] Stereotypes would be banal were they not so lethal, so apt to wound physically, emotionally, spiritually. The difficulty then becomes how to notice change when it happens and how to recognize stasis and continuity.

Meanwhile, where was whiteness in this mercifully brief list of sad old stereotypes? An obvious, simple answer to this question would be to propose that it is invisible, or unmarked, as usual. However, it is all too easy to universalize the particular, to repeat the gestures of hegemony, when examining race. Hence the claim that "whiteness is invisible" is often made as though representative of a timeless certitude. For one of the truisms about whiteness with which scholarly critics of whiteness frequently operate at the present time is the idea that whiteness is an unmarked category.[7] It is indeed one with which I myself worked for a number of years. The more one scrutinizes it, however, the more the notion of whiteness as unmarked norm is revealed to be a mirage or indeed, to put it even more strongly, a white delusion. The next interesting question is, then, what is the nature, the character, and the origin of this delusion, and when and how does its opposite, the marking of whiteness come about? In fact, it seems to me that the making and marking of whiteness needs to be accounted for before one can begin to understand its occasional, partial, and temporary *un*marking in the late twentieth century.

In fact, whiteness is in a continual state of being dressed and undressed, of marking and cloaking. It has been so since the time when the term was first used racially, partway through half a millennium of European imperializing travel through, settlement in, and expropriation from the Americas, Africa, parts of Asia, Australia, and the Pacific region. I will not, here, detail the enormously various and complicated processes by means of which colonization became a specifically *racial* project.[8] Such work has been done elsewhere and deserves far more space and attention than I can offer it here.[9] I will, though, note several of the results of that history especially pertinent to this discussion.

First, it is critical to remember in examining the term "whiteness" that in the context of colonization, the constructs identified as "people(s)," "nations," "cultures," and "races" became complexly interwoven. This is why, in the present, they continue to bleed into one another in racist terms, with "American" apt to be taken to mean "white," for example. Second, we must remind ourselves that the term "race" was a relative latecomer on the linguistic scene,[10] as was the name "white," and that indeed both terms were birthed by imperialism. It is not the case, then, that the previously neutral word "race" was "corrupted" by colonialism. Likewise, it is not true that a somehow benign notion of "whiteness" was then made malignant by the march of history. Neither construct existed *prior* to colonialism. This makes utterly misplaced, entirely falsely premised, the idea of a "return" to racial innocence. Equally impractical is the attempt to carve out spaces within the terrain of whiteness unspoiled by the relations of colonialism. For that matter, the same is true of the terms blackness, Asianness, Nativeness, Chicana/o-Latina/o-ness, and so on. In short, we are all immersed in the waters of history, and those waters are pretty murky.

Third, we must note that, like the word "race" and like "racial names" (whiteness, blackness, and so on), the words "culture," "nation," and "people(s)" continue to be organized by hierarchical ranking systems dating back to the very beginning of the western European colonial project. In the colonial context, the naming of "cultures" and "peoples" was very much linked to naming and marking out a host of Others as beings deemed lesser than the "national" Selves who sought to dominate them. Further, those Others were named in terms that justified, at least in the minds of marauding nations, the legitimacy of colonization. In this context it is hardly surprising that "white" emerges as barely marked, again if only from the standpoints of white people themselves. And it is also not surprising that part of the project of naming whiteness would result in a sequence something like the following: appear, self-name, violate, plunder, appropriate, and become apparently invisible. Or was that invincible? Mercifully, not so. This system of naming and evasion might even have worked, but for the fact that the colonized were watching closely throughout, but for the reality of differences within whiteness and resultant boundary disputes for entry into the category, and but for the existence of some people of all races with alert minds, hearts, and spirits.

process of Colonialism

Fourth and linked to all of the above, "whiteness" is positioned asymmetrically in relation to all other racial and cultural terms, again for reasons whose origins are colonial. Whiteness, or white people, I suggest, have through history mainly named themselves in order to say "I am not that Other." Whiteness is, while as relational as its others, less clearly marked except, ironically in terms of its not-Otherness. As I, and colleagues, have argued elsewhere, there are times when whiteness seems to mean only a defiant shout of "I am not that Other!"[11] This indeed is why, to the chagrin of some white people, it becomes extraordinarily difficult for white people to name whiteness, and why whiteness has a habit—annoying for those who are trying to name it— of sliding into class and nationality all the time.[12] Indeed, it is for the same reason that even words like "humanity" and "Man" (uppercase "M") are very easily elided into whiteness, thus giving it the appearance of being unbounded.

Class

Having sketched in some of the historical context for the concept of whiteness, we may now move to a discussion of its meaning in the contemporary United States.

I begin this part of the essay with one contribution to the marking of whiteness. The following eight-point definition of whiteness is one that, rather than seeking to name it in cultural terms, indicates its location in societies that are (using Stuart Hall's terminology) "structured in dominance."[13] This definition has been evolving over the last decade of my work on the subject, and it will, I am sure, continue to alter, both as my own consciousness changes and as the conditions and practice of whiteness are (no doubt for better *and* worse) also transformed:

1. Whiteness is a location of structural advantage in societies structured in racial dominance.
2. Whiteness is a "standpoint," a location from which to see selves, others, and national and global orders.
3. Whiteness is a site of elaboration of a range of cultural practices and identities, often unmarked and unnamed, or named as national or "normative" rather than specifiably racial.
4. Whiteness is often renamed or displaced within ethnic or class namings.
5. Inclusion within the category "white" is often a matter of contestation, and in different times and places some kinds of whiteness are boundary markers of the category itself.
6. Whiteness as a site of privilege is not absolute but rather crosscut by a range of other axes of relative advantage or subordination; these do not erase or render irrelevant race privilege, but rather inflect or modify it.
7. Whiteness is a product of history, and is a relational category. Like other racial locations, it has no inherent but only socially constructed meanings. As such, whiteness's meanings are complexly layered and variable locally and translocally; also, whiteness's meanings may appear simultaneously malleable and intractable.
8. The relationality and socially constructed character of whiteness does not, it must be emphasized, mean that this and other racial locations are unreal in their material and discursive effects.

Suddenly, the notion that whiteness might be invisible seems bizarre in the extreme. More shocking than the recognition of whiteness's existence is the idea that it is ever *not* seen. I suggest that it is only to the extent that particular kinds of racially supremacist hegemony are ever achieved that whiteness can come anywhere near to invisibility. And even here, a considerable number of qualifications must be made. The canny critic will of course always qualify her use of the term "hegemony" by noting the inevitable instability, the inherent ineffectuality, of any ideological system. But when one contemplates the degree to which populations are ever fully compelled by arguments for the normativity and neutrality of whiteness, one wonders whether these particular strands within hegemony are less stable than others. The question already posed in this essay—"to whom is whiteness invisible?"—is germane here, and I will return to it. As noted, it is safe to suggest that whiteness remains quite visible to men and women of color even when "cultural micro-climates" make it possible for the concept to disappear into false universality from the purview of some white people.

Meanwhile, I am struck by the extraordinary ease with which (especially white) individuals can slide from awareness of whiteness to the lack thereof and, related to that slippage, from race-consciousness to unconsciousness and from antiracism to racism, whether from year to year, situation to situation, or sentence to sentence. My own history, for example, is marked by a shift from unconsciousness both of my whiteness and of my own enmeshment in racism to an awakening to them. This trajectory also shapes the life-paths of many comrades with whom I share race, class, gender, and nationality.[14] But my awakening is never complete. Although the initial transformation was one of major earthquake proportions, there is always room for another aftershock, always need for further awakening. White antiracism is, perhaps, a stance requiring lifelong vigilance.

To work through an example of this phenomenon, I was intrigued and "(after)shocked" once again in opening David Roediger's introduction to his collection *Black on White: Black Writers on What It Means to Be White*.[15] In it, Roediger comes ironically close to replaying the very erasure that his collection seeks to confront and challenge. (I examine this text in detail, not because of any disrespect for the author but rather for the opposite reason: one can learn most by looking at the work of a master craftsperson and asking what still needs to be improved. David Roediger is, to my mind, one of the finest contemporary white critics of whiteness.[16]) Roediger opens the book by inviting his readers to "Consider a slave on the auction block, awaiting sale": "Imagine the slave being seen, indeed examined, by the potential bidders. Imagine what she felt. Imagine her trembling and crying, breaking down, even fighting back. Such attempts to imagine looking in on the auction block and to empathize with those for sale have found a hard-won place in the mainstream of American culture. But little prepares us to see her as looking out, as studying the bidders."[17] Roediger's opening lines are chilling. His depiction of the enslaved woman generated the very horror in my white mind that, appropriately, the author sought to achieve. Next, the reminder of the woman's own seeing eyes, her gaze on whiteness, proffered a very timely moment of jarring to my white consciousness. If one is white, one cannot, it seems, be reminded too often that the person conceived as Other in one's own psyche is not only a suffering being but also a thinking subject. As Roediger points out, the latter move is crucial and without it, he implies, empathy is partial at best.[18] Yet, as Roediger continues, it is as though the blinders fall back over his own eyes. Who is or are the group designated "us" in his next sentence when he notes that "little prepares us to see her as looking out, as studying the bidders"? Here it seems that an all-white readership is envisaged for Roediger's text. Otherwise, one would not dare to generalize about the unpreparedness of the audience for the intelligence, the consciousness of the enslaved woman.

One must situate Roediger's paragraph in a set of narrative conventions whose long histories extend far beyond the United States.[19] The depiction of the oppressed or wounded Other as suffering body first and seeing mind second is central to a history of the enlistment of ostensibly wiser, more conscious, more civilized, whiter Selves. It travels from records of colonial officials and missionaries at the funeral pyres of *satis* committed in India[20] all the way to advertisements for Third World–focused charitable organizations in today's Sunday newspapers. In this schema, the injured Other is also wrested from context, typified or genericized rather than enabled to retain her or his particularity.[21] The enslaved woman of Roediger's text did not, after all, land on the auction block from Mars but rather after a horrendous journey across the Atlantic or perhaps after birth and early years on one or more plantations. She might indeed have been moved to tears and have been shivering with cold, fear, or rage on a particular day. Or she might have been in a state of near-catatonia. Or something else. I cannot and should not, of course, speculate about the state of mind and heart of any particular woman. But I do wish to note that Roediger's portrayal emerges from and contributes to a certain kind of "suffering female victim" genre that owes much to nineteenth-century European efforts toward a civilizing mission—of Indian women coerced into committing *sati*, of enslaved Africans, of English prostitutes, and so on. It should perhaps be emphasized that this is not, by any means, to deny or dismiss the reality of the suffering of a woman on the auction block. Rather, I wish to point out the degree to which a white gaze is reinstated even as efforts are made to displace it.

The hierarchization of mind, emotion, and body derived from Platonic thought has marked the racialized rankings of peoples and cultures from colonial times down to the present and has also been closely associated with a hierarchical division of masculine and feminine. Here, the difficulty of asserting the status of the woman as victim and simultaneously as thinking subject becomes comprehensible. It is in this context that recognition of the enslaved woman's intelligence and consciousness can only arrive in the text as a supplement. The semantic range of the words "trembling," "crying," and "breaking down" are significant: while all three are likely responses to finding oneself placed on the auction block, each connotes, particularly from a white (masculinist?) purview, an almost inescapable frailty and/or fragility and possibly youthfulness as well. Likewise, within this framework it is the case that crying and trembling in the face of her fate could in no way be seen as "rational" but rather must be conceived as entirely separate from her status as "one who looks."

There is more to be uncovered here about the text fragment, about exactly how it is that "we," white people, are made unready to recognize that we are not the only ones who see. There are many ways in which the terms of Roediger's conjuring of the woman on the slave auction block speaks to us about how, even in avowedly liberatory voices, one may find a very complex interweaving of racism, colonialism, patriarchy, and the history of European consciousness. Roediger's own discourse mirrors that of the slaveholder in repeated reference to the woman *as a slave* (an inherent quality) rather than, as for example, a person who *is enslaved* (her situation in that moment). One could go further in this regard and suggest that Roediger's imagined ordering of the woman's priorities and conception of her situation reflects that of the buyer and seller rather than that of the woman herself. In her own terms, is she "awaiting sale," or is she perhaps awaiting another step in her enforced movement from one location to the next?

One can, then, learn much about whiteness from asking how white people depict people of color. None of this is to say that Roediger is mistaken in summoning up this kind of description. However, it *is* to suggest that in doing so more self-consciously, in historicizing his depiction, Roediger would have offered the reader deeper insight into the context and form of whites' interpellations by these modes of description. For as Roediger says, enlistment into a liberal pity for the suffering Other is a paltry step forward. Moreover, it is one that keeps intact the Self-Other binary and offers no insight into the Self's self-designated authority and sanctity.

The same "now you see it, now you don't" pattern continues on in these early pages. For myself, even scanning the contents pages of Roediger's collection had the potency to disrupt and destabilize some of the certitudes of white discourse with which I am all too familiar. To take only three authors and titles—"Ethiop" William J. Wilson, "What shall we do with the white people?" (1860); George S. Schuyler, "Our White Folks" (1927); and Cheryl Harris, "Whiteness as Property" (1993)—a reversal or inversion is clear in each instance. Wilson identifies and marks whites as the problem that needs to be fixed. Schuyler mocks the patronage of white southern middle-class pretensions to "own" and "know" African Americans. Finally, Harris's title complicates the term "property," urging one to ask how and when blackness and whiteness might be bought, sold, counted on, or cashed in. All of this is made manifest, then, without even entering the book beyond page three.

Yet, on page four, when Roediger writes, "few Americans have ever considered the idea that African Americans are extremely knowledgeable about whites and whiteness,"[22] the structure of the sentence seems to erase the presence of any U.S. residents who are not white. In effect, I suggest, it once again normativizes whiteness. (There is another occlusion here, that of conflating "United States," the country, with "America," the continent.) Which Americans would not have considered this possibility? Chinese Americans perhaps? But think of Maxine Hong Kingston's depiction of white ghosts in *The Woman Warrior* and *China Men*.[23] Native Americans? I will always remember an incident in Louise Erdrich's novel, *Love Medicine*. A young man recalls that for unknown reasons a teacher had taught him *Moby-Dick* for each of his four years in high school: "This led to another famous misunderstanding. 'You're always reading that book,' my mother said once. 'What's in it?' 'The story of the great white whale' [the narrator explains]. She could not believe it. After a while she said, 'What do they got to wail about, those whites?'"[24] What is, I think, interesting here is the simultaneity of whites' visibility to some and the tenaciousness of their capacity to disappear, discursively, for others.

Thus far, I have pointed to the entanglement of the notion of whiteness in colonial history, and the enormous challenge one faces when one tries to disentangle the white gaze from that history. As I have also demonstrated, the efforts of white people, even antiracist ones, are all too easily entrapped within the webs of a gaze and consciousness one might conveniently name, as a shorthand, white.

As I said earlier, one of the more frequently expressed ideas about whiteness in recent times is its invisibility—an invisibility that, as I have also stated above, must be immediately specified by the question "to whom?" But what else can be said here? How else might one specify what lies beneath this façade? What are some of the means by which the "invisibility of whiteness" is achieved? Here, I have been discussing the phenomenon of unselfconscious performance of whiteness, of whiteness not "seeing itself seeing," whiteness falsely claiming transparency.

The phrase "the invisibility of whiteness" refers in part to moments when whiteness does not speak its own name. At those times, as I noted, whiteness may simply assume its own normativity. It may also refer to those times when neutrality or normativity is claimed for some kinds of whiteness, with whiteness frequently simultaneously linked to nationality. Such claims often also demonstrate the possibility of fissuring within whiteness. Drawing on my own research interviews with white women, I find the following comment from Helen Standish, born in 1950, illustrative here: "The way I was brought up was to think that everyone who was the same as me were Americans and the other people were of such-and-such descent."[25]

It is also crucial to contemplate just how recently many explicit namings of whiteness went underground in the United States. It was only in 1967, for example, that the criminalization of marriage across racial lines was successfully challenged in the U.S. Supreme Court.[26] Just a few years before that, the notion of "separate but equal education" (the "equal" part in any case a fiction) was declared unconstitutional.[27] It was only around the same time that signs labeling the entrances to public and commercial facilities "For Whites Only" were made illegal. I need not, I think, belabor the point that in all three cases means have been found to evade the banning of these practices.

> for us it was inverted

my localised environment

And when, in the 1980s, I was undertaking research with U.S. white women, those above forty could remember the use of phrases such as "I can do what I want—I'm young, white and twenty-one" and "That's very white [civilized] of you." All of this is only to remark on the explicit uses of the term "white" in public culture. Of course the term "white" and the self-consciousness of self as white were and still are very comfortably in use in private culture and in the public discourse of white supremacists.

yes

This, I think, implies several things. First, a certain naïveté, possibly middle-class and definitely presentist, marks the assertion of the invisibility of whiteness. Second, a kind of literalism (at times intentionally obfuscatory) marks assertions that whiteness is invisible. Thirdly, it is necessary to widen our interpretation of the word "whiteness" to examine its coconstitution with nationality, class, ethnicity, and culture. We must, for example, attend to the nation/class/ethnicity/race-based namings of people and groups that may turn out to be about whiteness. Also, if we are to be adequate critics of whiteness, we must become as educated about the history of colonialism, worldwide, as we are trying to become about the history of racism in the United States.

One irony of writing about whiteness's invisibility is that the late 1990s have witnessed intense debate over whiteness in academia, in the media, in classrooms, and in many private worlds. That debate continues, of course. The challenge then becomes one of asking *what* is being said about whiteness, whether what is being said has more liberatory or more retrogressive implications, and from whence came the present upsurge of discourse about it.

Let us take the last question first. Here, one can argue that through most of this century within the United States and elsewhere, greater attention to whiteness has correlated with, and in fact followed on from, movements led by communities of color for the enhancement of civil, economic, and political rights across race lines and/or movements for the transformation of public culture to reflect recognitions, assertions, reclamations, and critiques of cultural terrain. But in the United States, at the start of the twenty-first century, things are slightly different. For we see whiteness reasserted by white people and also whiteness under critical scrutiny by a range of people including whites. Both are taking place in tandem with the reentrenchment of preexisting racisms. Increased pressures against legal and illegal immigrants, efforts to abolish bilingual education, and wide-ranging anti-affirmative legislation are some examples here. It is also striking that whiteness is under examination by white people from, as it were, all directions. Thus white critics of whiteness are speaking forcefully, even as other white people are trying to "hold the line" and refuse any criticism of, encroachments on, or challenges to white turf or territory, whether cultural, economic, or political.

We can further subdivide these issues. Easiest to name are the "roots" of progressive and/or critical engagements with whiteness. They follow directly from the work of the last several decades to transform public culture and to materially alter the racialized inequities that mark U.S. society. It is thus no accident that, here, work by whites against race dominance melds very easily into activity that is more multiracial in scope. Activists have sought to alter the hierarchies of leadership and rights in workplaces and political groups, as well as to revise assumptions about "correct" dress, language, and style in such places. These changes are frequently inseparable from efforts to challenge sexism and also at times homophobia in the public sphere.

The now wide-ranging intellectual engagement with whiteness is signaled in many recent collections and monographs on whiteness,[28] with these enabled by and adding to the earlier scholarship of sociologists, historians, legal theorists, film and literary critics, and interdisciplinarians of various stripes.[29] Foci have included some of those already discussed in this essay and more: critiquing false universals in the spheres of gender, class, nationality, and canon formation; remarking on cultural practices previously labeled "national" rather than "white"; naming and reclaiming from the shadows forms of whiteness hitherto deemed unworthy of study because of their marginality, low status, or even shamefulness.

If there are goals common to most critical work on whiteness, they are, perhaps, the effort to find a way through and out of the historical legacy of whiteness and the commitment to retaining a strong connection between attention to whiteness and a broader antiracism. And there is also a struggle over hegemony: the quest for a means of drawing a large enough proportion of white people into the making of a new, more equitable multiracial common sense.

Throughout this work, a concern has dogged scholarship on whiteness: fear that the very process of critical engagement will in fact serve

white Scholarship

to do the opposite of what is hoped, by recentering whiteness rather than putting it in a new place in our (whose?) collective racial consciousness. As Michael Apple puts it, "such a process can serve the chilling function of simply saying, 'but enough about you, let me tell you about me.'"[30] Involving as it does close and detailed attention to whiteness, this worry about scholarship on whiteness is very reasonable.

A related concern is the tendency, especially in print media and television, for the making of easy analogies between new curricular and scholarly work on whiteness, on the one hand, and ethnic studies, on the other. I and other critics of whiteness have found ourselves trying to correct this false analogy on many occasions.[31] Another effect of the slide from discussions of work on "the critical study of whiteness" to "whiteness studies" is an erroneous interpretation of the critical study of whiteness as linked to white supremacist activity. This is something I myself experienced when undertaking research for my first book, *White Women, Race Matters*.[32] The organizers of the first national conference on critical whiteness studies, The Making and Unmaking of Whiteness, in April 1997 also encountered this problem. After they released a brief announcement of the conference, they were inundated by calls from the media; some who called expected to hear about a white supremacist meeting of some kind.[33] As I have argued elsewhere, there are many good reasons to engage critically in the study of whiteness.[34] Still, an ambivalence about the goals of work on whiteness and a hunger to redeem whiteness and to parallel it with other racial/ethnic locations are at times evident even in context of work by "diversity educators" ostensibly focused on progressive social change.[35]

Meanwhile, the efforts of other white people are caught up in the forging of an altogether more retrogressive interpretation of the historical moment, one that mistakes several decades of *talk about* the need for racial equity, with the *actual achievement* of that goal. Thus whites (and a small minority of people of color, among them notably Ward Connerly and Clarence Thomas) speak as though we now *do* live in a meritocracy. It is claimed that we now *do* operate on an even playing field—as opposed to some people simply having expressed the belief that that would be a fine thing to achieve someday. As we know, much political capital has been made out of this kind of "virtual

merit

history-writing" by conservatives. It has indeed been successful to the point of shaping the middle ground.

We witness, as a result, a new set of false presumptions about whiteness and about race relations, including the following:

1. White people were once the oppressors but are no longer because of the economic and cultural transformations brought about by the civil rights movement.

2. The gains of civil rights have now created the possibility, if not yet the actuality, of racial equality, and there is now an ever-present danger of "overcorrecting" past inequality and placing whites in danger of victimization.

3. The government does not yet quite understand that white people are now an oppressed group, so that government is increasingly antiwhite.

4. White people can and should now benefit from civil rights discourse, using concepts like "reverse racism," "uneven playing field," and "race-blind" to help ameliorate their own predicament.

5. Many people of color are still angry. This must be because: (a) they have not yet woken up to the new reality but are stuck in history, (b) they are simply inherently angry people, or (c) they hate white people out of habit.

6. Many white people are angry. This is because things have gone too far, and whites are now victims of a history not of their own making.

Let me repeat, these are a set of *false* presumptions about whiteness and race in the United States (and it may not be paranoid to state that I will sue anyone who uses them out of context!)[36] They present a nightmarish picture—the ideas listed and the recognition that many people believe them, if not in whole cloth, at least in some part. And if we were to imagine for a moment that this is an exaggeration, we might contemplate the context for the Oklahoma City Federal Government Building bombing of April 1995. We might also think about the "angry white men" so ably discussed by David Wellman among others,[37] and the even more disturbing epidemic of angry white boys and young men participating in the burning of black churches and the murder of their schoolmates around the country.[38]

It is within the sheltering frames of this extremism that new norma-tivities about race, racism, and whiteness are located. Whether this is a *new* racist common (non)sense—or simply an old one having been re-habilitated and brought from the right flank into the center of the field—is arguable. As the saying goes, "The more things change, the more they stay the same." And yet if nothing else, we see whiteness made visible once again to more white people. Further, as we witness the presence of a new/old racist common (non)sense now in place, but this time alongside a flourishing community of critics of whiteness, we have the opportunity to plunder hegemony and seek to counter it. This is therefore a very potent moment in the history of whiteness.

Dateline: Washington, D.C., August 2000. The next question is what are we to do with this moment in the history of whiteness? What are we already doing with it? Is there a singular we of white folks or of whiteness? Is there a clear separation between those white people "for" and those white people against racism? More germane to the topic of this paper, is there a distinct boundary between those who see whiteness and those to whom it is invisible? Or rather, are the bound-aries blurry? And lastly, when whiteness is seen, just what is it that is seen?

I will not presume to answer these questions on a large scale. Rather I will situate my concluding comments in relation to one site, the 95th Annual Meeting of the American Sociological Association, which took place in Washington, D.C., 12–16 August 2000. At these meetings I was intrigued by the reiteration of many of the themes discussed in the earlier parts of this paper, as well as by the very new *and* the very repetitive news about whiteness.

Things have moved. Whiteness was not discursively invisible at the ASA meetings, nor was it unmarked. It is a clear sign of the remaking of racial formation in the United States that whiteness is now a topic on the agenda at the ASA. At this five-day gathering—one that like other national (or in effect, transnational) meetings oriented around particular fields and disciplines, was dizzying in the sheer quantitative enormity of panels, sessions, and discussions that it incorporated—there was, as the program demonstrated, a session on whiteness every single day.[39]

Moreover, some of the key aspirations of many critics of whiteness were being met, at least on this occasion. First, whiteness was *not* named in ways that sought to reestablish its dominance nor its centrality, but rather in ways that sought to problematize both. Second, and related to the first point, whiteness was seen *as* a problem—as an entity, an identity, and an identification still poorly understood and, from the purview of some of those scholars whose presentations I heard, one in urgent need of revision. Third, while I was not able to attend all of the sessions engaging whiteness, on no occasion did I encounter the kind of "paralleling" of the study of whiteness with that of other racial-ethnic groups that some scholars have dreaded and that much media coverage focused on in the mid-1990s. Rather, the effort to examine whiteness was seen as inextricably a part of, but also *not the same as,* the process of focusing on other namings and other groupings within contemporary United States racial formation. It is worth noting that the ASA Section on Racial and Ethnic Minorities in Sociology sponsored several of the sessions dealing with whiteness. But this was not, presumably, because whites are viewed as a racial minority nor as an ethnic one, but rather because it is clear that the study of whiteness is pertinent to the study of racial formation.

Reviewing the conference program is interesting inasmuch as it demonstrates how and where whiteness was situated in the eyes of those commenting on it. A refereed roundtable discussion sponsored by the ASA Section on Racial and Ethnic Minorities in Sociology, titled simply "Whiteness," underscores the actuality that whiteness now *does* exist conceptually in the eyes of the scholarly world. (This is not self-evident, by the way—as recently as 1998 I needed to debate and explain at great length the meaning of that word while seeking university approval for a graduate course, "Interdisciplinary Approaches to the Critical Study of Whiteness.")

Session titles like "Talking with Whites about Race" and "Race Relations and the Changing Meaning of Whiteness" make clear that whiteness is seen to be about race. On one level this idea appears so obvious as not to be worth mentioning. But let us remember the starting point of this paper, an examination of how, when, and why whiteness has disappeared from the racial radar screen, with whites exempt (in the views of some people) from definition as a racial category. Session titles such as "Racial Privilege: The View from Above," "Whiteness: Current Research and Activism on Racial Privilege," and *white privilege*

"White Privilege in Democratic Society" push the envelope further: whiteness exists, it has something to do with race, and it is in particular connected with racial privilege.[40]

As noted, in this conference program whiteness is situated racially. It is also linked to the democratic project with the session titled "White Privilege in Democratic Society." From a slightly different angle, white privilege was situated in relation to the notion of dominance via a special session "The Sociology of the Superordinate: Masculinity, Heterosexuality, Whiteness." Again, while it was not explicitly named, one might assume that whiteness was in play in a session on "Social Movements: Right-Wing Movements" that included the paper, "Explaining Variation in Levels of Patriot and Militia Mobilization."[41]

In sum, we learn from the ASA conference program that whiteness exists, that it is a racial(ized) term, and that it must be examined in relation to dominance. We learn from the titles of sessions that a group called "white people" exists (here borrowing from Marx) not just *in* itself but also *for* itself, hence the possibility of a session titled "Talking with Whites about Race." Lastly we learn that whiteness is not necessarily deemed static (as evident from a session called "The Changing Meaning of Whiteness"). One might even suggest, then, that W. E. B. Du Bois would have been pleased to see whiteness conceived conceptually as a "problem." Indeed, as scholars detailed new ethnographic and interview-based research, it became clear that not only did sociologists view whiteness as a space riven with problems, but so also did many white interviewees.

Needless to say, however, things were not simply an occasion for celebration as the above might suggest. In the following pages I will comment on just two sessions, "Race Relations and the Changing Meaning of Whiteness,"[42] and "Racial Privilege: The View from Above."[43] It was clear that the statement, "whiteness is a problematic space" had radically different meanings for authors and white subjects. The papers in these sessions detailed the results of very recent data collection. (Two papers, that of Richard Zweigenhaft, discussing research on African American professionals, and my own, which was not directly based on new research, will not be discussed here.)

What I do here is to draw out the patterns and themes that struck me as I listened, whether from platform or audience, to these five papers. I must emphasize that I comment on these papers as an outsider who has not had the opportunity to read the larger projects-in-progress from which each was drawn. I must also clarify that while I am in no way attempting a revisionist reading of these works, I am aware that at times I commit the offense of reordering, and certainly that of reducing the range of each author's analysis. That being said, as a listener I was struck by what they taught, individually and collectively, about the current status of whiteness.

The first extraordinarily striking feature was the degree to which the five papers on whiteness paralleled one another in terms of their findings, in ways that did not seem to be disrupted by class, gender, or region. Research from Detroit, Atlanta, Appalachia, New York State, and elsewhere in the United States brought news of white interviewees' conviction that racial formation was, at this time in history, unfair to people like themselves. If affirmative action was deemed axiomatic of that injustice, African Americans and, on occasion, Latinos were seen as the groups that received ill-gotten gains from that system. In contrast, Asian Americans were seen to be like whites in two ways—first as immigrants and second, as hard workers striving to achieve in the United States of America.

Time and again papers detailed white interviewees' sense that, while "history" had perhaps dealt an unfair hand to racial and ethnic "minorities" (borrowing here the terminology favored by some interviewees themselves), history *was* history, period. For many of these white interviewees, that "history" was over, and if people of color continued to fare badly, this was possibly thanks to their own lack of effort. Here the term "history" is, of necessity, placed in quotation marks. For as the authors of these papers made clear, that term stood in for an amorphous "past" filled with some sufferers (who should now learn to stand on their own feet), and a few beneficiaries (who had in fact worked very hard to achieve their hard-won gains). As far as these papers suggested, research subjects did not have a sense of the structural forces and multiple processes in play throughout this space that I am calling "history." Rather, bad luck, and hard work to overcome that bad luck, were the twin motors of human advancement that seemed to rule the day in the minds of white interviewees. In this context, Monica McDermott's encounters with poor whites who were ashamed of their current positionings in a working class, primarily Black, Atlanta neighborhood made some kind of sense.[44] For when these white research subjects felt ashamed of their failure to thrive economically *despite their whiteness*, one sees their recognition that whiteness is somehow connected to power and privilege, albeit in a way that cries out for rearticulation in relation to class, region, and local economics.

This shame in fact speaks to a second theme that ran through the papers: a kind of "now-you-see-it, now-you-don't" articulation of whiteness and its relationships to power and privilege on the part of white interviewees. These white folks knew they were white, at least enough to be aware of themselves as non-beneficiaries of post-Civil Rights gains like affirmative action, and as the kinds of Americans who had arrived and thrived by means of hard work and no "handouts." Yet ambivalence about that knowledge crosscut these five papers. Moreover, white people's equivocation about their whiteness was dramatized in their discourse. Literal equivocation as stammering, hesitation, and verbal backtracking in response to questions about interviewees' relationships with people of color was present in so many papers that it can only be read as a sign of the nature of whiteness at this moment in U.S. history, and I suggest that this sign might be taken literally. We might view it as signaling hegemony in crisis, the repressed returning. Further, this kind of prevarication perhaps also indicates that at least some white interviewees sensed a call (from whom is not clear) that they should act, live, and behave in racial formation in ways different from those in which they were willing or able to do. (Instances of prevarication and hesitation arose in relation to questions about parental attitudes to children's interracial dating; parents' desire to place children in monoracial schools; and views on history, justice, and injustice.)

In 1993, in the context of my own research with white U.S. women, I argued that many white U.S. citizens' sense of race might be named "color- and power-evasive."[45] Refusing the naturalizing implications of the more commonly used term, "colorblind," I noted that many white men and women are both aware and striving *not* to be aware of the racialization of their daily lives and subjectivities. I contrasted color- and power-evasiveness with a "race cognizance" that does name the racialization of daily life and subjecthood. The latter, I emphasized, draws upon the "characterizations of race difference (including awareness of structural and institutional inequity. . . .) that emerged out of civil rights and later movements for the cultural and economic empowerment of people of color from the late 1950s to the present day."[46] Finally, I argued that both modalities emerge from and must be differentiated from the essentialist racism that was and is the discursive bedrock of racialization in the United States.[47] I argued that all three of these modes of seeing—essentialist racism, color- and power-evasiveness, and race cognizance—circulated in the United States of the 1980s and early 1990s, but that color- and power-evasiveness was dominant at that time. Lastly, and perhaps too optimistically, I implied that moves toward race cognizance on the part of white people could only correlate with a move toward greater antiracist consciousness.

However, something a little different seems to be present in the United States at the start of the twenty-first century, if the papers just discussed are to be interpreted in the way that I have just proposed. On one level white people were more conscious of themselves as white and more conscious of themselves as living and acting in a racialized world. But in these interviews, race consciousness did *not* correlate with antiracism. Rather, what I witnessed as I listened to these accounts was neither race cognizance nor color- and power-evasiveness, but rather a hybrid of the two, that which one might name *"power-evasive race cognizance."* As stated above, moves toward a progressive race cognizance among white U.S. citizens may be explained by reference to the period of civil rights struggle. Likewise the emergence of "power-evasive race consciousness" can undoubtedly be understood by reference to the efforts to *undo* civil rights gains that gathered force through the late 1980s and continued through the 1990s. And there is an ironic way in which essentialism and non-essentialism coexist here: No longer do white people have recourse only to claims about the inherent inferiority of people of color in seeking to explain (away) inequity. It is now possible to make two claims simultaneously. One is that African Americans and Latinos do not need the "handouts" of affirmative action because they are perfectly capable of achieving without help. The second is that when African Americans and Latinos do succeed alongside whites, this is not because of their own efforts and talents, but rather because of unfair assistance.

Thus all three discursive repertoires circulate in the United States, in forms rearranged but hardly changed. It is also still the case that the United States continues to grapple for better *and* worse, with its roots, which is to say, with the racism upon which this nation was founded. In this context white residents of the United States continue to move in ever-decreasing circles around the notions of race, difference, justice, and entitlement, variously and simultaneously demonstrating several things. The first of these is an increasing attention to whiteness as such, together with the recognition of the white self as a racialized subject. The second is an attachment to a sense of white entitlement and/or a struggle to comprehend and seek means of challenging this attachment. The third is a recognition of the continuing presence of racial injustice, racial dystopia, and racial(ized) distress and discomfort in a range of forms (however defined and diagnosed).

All of this was signaled by the considerable analysis of whiteness at the ASA (undertaken mainly although not only by white scholars); by white interviewees' depictions of self and other; and by the discursive and semantic difficulties interviewees faced as they tried to put forward arguments about white entitlement. Lastly, lest it appear that a distinction is being made here between progressive white scholars on one hand and retrogressive white interviewees on the other, it should not be forgotten that although not named in these two panels, whites' efforts to cultivate progressive race consciousness *are* still underway in the United States.[48]

Is the unmarkedness of whiteness a mirage? Certainly. Has whiteness become more marked at the start of a new millennium? Yes, it would seem to be the case. But what one learns forcefully here is that the marking and unmarking of whiteness is not the only challenge that faces those of us striving to achieve a race cognizance that will correlate with antiracism.

Notes

I thank Lata Mani for her careful and astute commentary on this paper, as well as members of the Making and Unmaking of Whiteness editorial group for their careful reading and comments.

1 Paul Gilroy, *There Ain't No Black in the Union Jack* (London: Hutchinson, 1987), 38.

2 Ibid.

3 Ruth Frankenberg, *White Women, Race Matters: The Social Construction of Whiteness* (Minneapolis: University of Minnesota Press, 1993), 11 and elsewhere.

4 Becky Thompson and Sangeeta Tyagi, "Storytelling as Social Conscience: The Power of Autobiography," in *Names We Call Home: Autobiography on Racial Identity*, ed. Thompson and Tyagi (New York: Routledge, 1996), ix.

5 Frankenberg, *White Women*, 11–18; 236–37.

6 Ruth Frankenberg, "Introduction: Local Whitenesses, Localizing White-

ness," in *Displacing Whiteness: Essays in Social and Cultural Criticism,* ed. Frankenberg (Durham: Duke University Press, 1997), 11–15; Ruth Frankenberg and Lata Mani, "Crosscurrents, Crosstalk: Race, 'Postcoloniality' and the Politics of Location," *Cultural Studies* 7 no. 2 (May 1993): 292–310.

7 An early and influential articulation of this idea is to be found in Richard Dyer's article, "White," *Screen* 29 no. 4 (autumn 1988): 44–64.

8 For the concept of "racial project," see Michael Omi and Howard Winant, *Racial Formation in the United States: From the 1960s to the 1990s* (New York: Routledge, 1994), 55–56.

9 See, for example, Theodore W. Allen, *The Invention of the White Race,* vol. 1, *Racial Oppression and Social Control* (London: Verso, 1994); Tomás Almaguer, *Racial Faultlines: The Historical Origins of White Supremacy in California* (Berkeley: University of California Press, 1994); James Campbell and James Oakes, "The Invention of Race: Rereading *White over Black,*" in *Critical White Studies: Looking behind the Mirror,* ed. Richard Delgado and Jean Stefancic (Philadelphia: Temple University Press, 1997), 145–51; George M. Fredrickson, *White Supremacy: A Comparative Study in American and South African History* (Oxford: Oxford University Press, 1981); David Theo Goldberg, *Racist Culture: Philosophy and the Politics of Meaning* (Oxford, Eng., and Cambridge, Mass.: Blackwell, 1993); Reginald Horsman, *Race and Manifest Destiny: The Origins of American Racial Anglo-Saxonism* (Cambridge, Mass.: Harvard University Press, 1981); Robert Miles, *Racism* (London: Routledge, 1989).

10 Horsman, *Race and Manifest Destiny,* esp. 10–24, 98–115.

11 Ruth Frankenberg, " 'When We Are Capable of Stopping, We Begin to See': Being White, Seeing Whiteness," in *Names We Call Home,* ed. Thompson and Tyagi, 7; Phil Cohen, "Labouring Under Whiteness," in *Displacing Whiteness,* ed. Frankenberg, 244–82.

12 Frankenberg, "Whiteness and Americanness," in *Race,* ed. Steven Gregory and Roger Sanjek (New Brunswick, N.J.: Rutgers University Press, 1994), 62–77.

13 Stuart Hall, "Race, Articulation and Societies Structured in Dominance," in UNESCO, *Sociological Theories: Race and Colonialism* (Paris: UNESCO Press, 1980), 305–45.

14 Ruth Frankenberg, " 'When We Are Capable of Stopping,'" 3–17; Becky Thompson, "Time-Traveling and Border-Crossing: Reflections on White Identity," in *Names We Call Home,* ed. Thompson and Tyagi, 93–110.

15 David R. Roediger, *Black on White: Black Writers on What It Means to Be White* (New York: Schocken, 1998).

16 See also David R. Roediger, *Towards the Abolition of Whiteness: Essays on*

Race, Politics and Working Class History (London: Verso, 1994), and *The Wages of Whiteness: Race and the Making of the American Working Class* (London: Verso, 1991).

17 Roediger, *Black on White*, 3.

18 Ibid., 3–4.

19 I am indebted to Lata Mani for this insight, for our conversations about this part of the paper, and for her analysis of the complex and ambivalent discourses that framed colonial representations of *sati* (widow-burning) in nineteenth-century India. Lata Mani, *Contentious Traditions: The Debate on Sati in Colonial India* (Berkeley: University of California Press, 1998).

20 Ibid., chap. 5.

21 Ibid.

22 Roediger, *Black on White*, 4.

23 Maxine Hong Kingston, *The Woman Warrior* (New York: Vintage, 1976), and *China Men* (New York: Ballantine, 1981).

24 Louise Erdrich, *Love Medicine,* new and expanded version (New York: HarperCollins, 1993), 124–25.

25 Frankenberg, *White Women*, 198.

26 *Loving v Virginia*, 338 US 1 (1967).

27 *Brown v Board of Education*, 347 US 483 (1954).

28 In addition to texts named in notes above, see among others, Michelle Fine et al., eds., *Off White: Readings on Race, Power and Society* (New York: Routledge, 1997); Matt Wray and Annalee Newitz, eds., *White Trash: Race and Class in America* (New York: Routledge, 1997); John Hartigan Jr., *Racial Situations: Class Predicaments of Whiteness in Detroit* (Princeton: Princeton University Press, 1999); Grace Elizabeth Hale, *Making Whiteness: The Culture of Segregation in the South, 1890–1940* (New York: Pantheon, 1998).

29 In addition to texts named in notes above, see among others Bob Blauner, *Black Lives, White Lives: Three Decades of Race Relations in America* (Berkeley: University of California Press, 1989); Toni Morrison, *Playing in the Dark: Whiteness and the Literary Imagination* (New York: Vintage, 1993); David T. Wellman, *Portraits of White Racism*, 2d ed. (Cambridge: Cambridge University Press, 1993).

30 Michael Apple, "Foreword," in *White Reign: Learning and Deploying Whiteness in America*, ed. Joe L. Kincheloe et al. (New York: St. Martin's, 1999), xi.

31 See, for example, remarks by Ruth Frankenberg and Matt Wray on the KCSM-TV program *A Higher Education*, for the segment on "White Studies," 6 May 1998.

32 Frankenberg, *White Women*, 33.

33 Annalee Newitz and Matt Wray on *A Higher Education,* "White Studies," KCSM-TV, 6 May 1998.

34 Frankenberg, "Introduction: Local Whitenesses," 1–2; Frankenberg, "Whiteness and Americanness," 62.

35 Frankenberg, "Introduction: Local Whitenesses," 18–20.

36 "Anti-Gay Use of Research Angers Boston Doctor," *San Francisco Chronicle,* 4 August 1998, states, "Criticizing a national anti-gay advertising campaign that draws on his research, a Boston doctor accused conservative religious groups yesterday of distorting his work to support their own theory: that homosexuality can be 'healed.'"

37 David Wellman, "Minstrel Shows, Affirmative Action Talk and Angry White Men: Making Racial Otherness in the 1990s," in *Displacing Whiteness,* ed. Frankenberg, 311–32.

38 For an interview with Timothy Welch, one of two young white Klansmen currently serving jail time for setting fire to an African American community's church in Manning, South Carolina, in June 1995, see the film *Forgotten Fires,* directed by Michael Chandler (1998); Welch is no longer a klan member. See also "Two Boys Found Guilty in Arkansas School Shooting," *Reuters Limited,* 12 August 1998.

39 *Program, 95th Annual Meetings of the American Sociological Association,* Washington, D.C.: American Sociological Association, 12–16 August 2000.

40 For the record, it should be noted that "Race Privilege: The View from Above" also included a paper titled "Are There Blacks in the White Establishment? Another Look."

41 Nella K. Van Dyke and Sarah A. Soule, "Explaining Variation in Levels of Patriot and Militia Mobilization," 95th Annual Meetings of the American Sociological Association, Washington, D.C., August 16, 2000.

42 "Race Relations and the Changing Meaning of Whiteness," panel, 95th Annual Meetings of the American Sociological Association, Washington, D.C., August 13, 2000; papers presented: Charles A. Gallagher, "White Stories: Race Relations According to the Dominant Group," Amanda E. Lewis, "Some Are More Equal than Others: Whiteness and Colorblind Ideology at the Dawn of the 21st Century," Monica McDermott, "Whiteness as Perceived Stigma: Identity Construction among Disadvantaged Whites."

43 "Racial Privilege: The View From Above," panel, 95th Annual Meetings of the American Sociological Association, Washington, D.C., August 14, 2000; papers presented: Eduardo Bonilla-Silva, "Poor Whites Are Not the Only 'Racists' in America: An Analysis of the Racial Views of Upper Class Whites in Detroit," Ruth Frankenberg, "Contexts and Attachments: Re-

flections on the Psyche of Whiteness," Richard L. Zweigenhaft, "Are There Blacks in the White Establishment? Another Look," Rhonda F. Levine, "What White Men Think About Race."

44 Again, I am aware here that I am offering only a reduced rendition of McDermott's argument.

45 Ruth Frankenberg, *White Women, Race Matters: The Social Construction of Whiteness* (Minneapolis: University of Minnesota Press, 1993), 14–15.

46 Frankenberg, 140.

47 Frankenberg, 138–140.

48 In this regard, see for example, Jennifer Eichstedt, "White Identities in the Struggle for Racial Justice," paper presented at the 95th American Sociological Association Annual Meeting, Washington, D.C., August 16, 2000; Ellen K. Scott, "Creating Partnerships for Change: Alliances and Betrayals in the Racial Politics of Two Feminist Organizations" in *Gender & Society* 12: 4, 400–423, 1998; "From Race Cognizance to Racism Cognizance: Dilemmas in Anti-Racist Activism," in Kathleen Blee and France Winddance Twine, eds. *Feminism and Anti-Racism: International Struggles for Justice*, New York: New York University Press, forthcoming; and Ellen K. Scott, "Feminists Working Across Racial Divides: The Politics of Race in a Battered Women's Shelter and a Rape Crisis Center," Dissertation, Department of Sociology, University of California, Davis. See also Becky Thompson, *A Promise and a Way of Life. White anti-racist activism*, Minneapolis: University of Minnesota Press, 2001.

White Racial Projects

Uncertainty about whiteness, anxiety about the meaning of white identity, is nothing new. As Toni Morrison has pointed out, this anxiety is central to American literature.[1] Racist thought, indeed, is laced with fears about the integrity, the purity, and the putative "dangers" whiteness encounters in the modern world: think of the founding documents of eugenics; think of the legislation required to institutionalize slavery or to restrict citizenship rights along racial lines. Indeed, U.S. racism can be understood as a continuing struggle to allay fears about the instability of whiteness, as a number of creative historians have begun to show in recent years.[2]

Nothing new there. What is new is a different kind of uncertainty about whiteness, coming not from those who wish to preserve it, who seek to defend racial hierarchy and inequality, but rather from those who wish to overcome it, to transcend it, to forget it, or to abolish it. The new uncertainty and anxiety about whiteness is very different from the old varieties that were visible in eugenics, that can still be seen in *The Bell Curve,* and in a thousand other places. This is post–World War II post–civil rights anxiety.

Our newfound attention to whiteness must be understood as a product of both the accomplishments and the containment of the postwar movements of racially defined minorities, especially the black movement. It should be seen, too, in light of the partial, contradictory, and inadequate racial reform policies enacted during the 1960s. It consists of a series of uncertain and conflictual responses by movement veterans—conservative, liberal, and radical—to present-day uncertainties: about what race means, about what an egalitarian and social justice–oriented racial politics would look like, and about the continuing significance of race.

In what follows I first make some comments on the emerging

"new racial order," to set anxieties about whiteness in a broader context. Then I summarize the concept of racial projects developed by Michael Omi and myself in our work on racial formation, for this notion of "projects" is central to my purposes here.[3] Next, I critically analyze what I take to be the three crucial white racial projects that have developed in the post–civil rights era: the neoconservative, liberal, and new abolitionist projects. Although I make no secret about my sympathy with the radical side of that spectrum, I conclude with some criticisms of all three of these reactions to the post–civil rights contradictions of whiteness. My questions are inflected by Du Boisian allegiances: they center on the hazards of calls for the abolition of whiteness, no matter what political origins they may have. I suggest that efforts to *deconstruct* whiteness are more practical and more promising than attempts to abolish it.

The New Racial Order

We are living through a profound upheaval in the meaning of race, the emergence of perhaps the most contradictory and unsettling racial formation that has ever existed. In a sentence: the past half century or so has been the first time since the dawn of modernity, since the rise of capitalism and the knitting together of the globe in one unified "system," that white supremacy has been called seriously into question on a world-historical scale.[4]

This profound transformation in the global logic of race began with the end of World War II. After the war, a worldwide range of sociopolitical mutations took place, many of which had tremendous racial meaning. These included an acceleration of the U.S. black movement, of course, but we should see the movement's rise as part of a global process that also involved many other insurgent phenomena: an upsurge of anticolonial pressures springing from the liberation of numerous countries from Axis occupation (and these countries' consequent reluctance to embrace anew the Allied colonialists of the past); a massive need to reintegrate former soldiers who had become used to bearing arms and who had been politically tempered by wide-ranging international experience; a celebratory atmosphere surrounding the global victory of democracy over the horrors and the racisms of the Nazis and the Japanese; the onset of new global competition between the "free world" and the Soviet Union, that is, the Cold

War. All these factors (and others too numerous to list) contributed to the problematization of the traditional, racialized forms of rule which had, *mutatis mutandis,* shaped the world order in crucial ways for half a millennium or so.[5]

These new, more progressive racial tendencies intensified from the war's end to about 1970. They resulted in the formal decolonization—often only as the result of ferocious armed struggles—of the great European imperial holdings in Africa, the Caribbean, Asia, and the Pacific. They challenged, sometimes successfully and sometimes not, the neocolonial arrangements put into place by the new worldwide hegemonic power, the United States, which had sought to impose a new (let us call it "northern") order after the old European powers had been compelled to lower their flags.

They set in motion other, deeply related tendencies as well, for example enormous waves of migration. The old empires "struck back" as former colonial subjects—East and West Indians, Caribeños, Maghrebi and sub-Saharans, Filipinos and Moluccans, Koreans and Chinese—set off in unprecedented numbers for the northern metropolises, often locating themselves in the heart of their former "mother countries," indeed often recruited as *gastarbeiter*.[6] As a result, the face of Europe was forever changed, Yamato supremacy in Japan was for the first time challenged, and the United States became a far more urbanized and multiracial country than it had ever been before.

So, since World War II, and particularly since the 1960s, *the world has undergone a profound shift in the global logic of race* or, in Michael Omi's and my terms, in *racial formation*. This shift was the most significant challenge to global white supremacy that had been mounted since the rise of Europe half a millennium earlier. Yet, world-shaking as it was, it could not dislodge, but only somewhat weaken, that ferocious tradition of white supremacist world rule.

During this postwar period, as had been foretold by many—W. E. B. Du Bois and Gunnar Myrdal among others—there was widespread U.S. mobilization against white supremacy. As a result, not only because of the rise of the black freedom movement, but also because of these tremendous international shifts, there occurred a partial reform of the racial state and of racial attitudes. Many types of discrimination that had previously been virtually taken for granted were regulated, if hardly entirely eliminated. Though obviously none of these changes heralded the definitive end of white supremacy, they did portend the rise of a new U.S. racial order, consonant with the global changes I have discussed. They signaled that from now on, what survived of the legacy of centuries of relatively unquestioned *herrenvolk* democracy would have to coexist with the partial and problematic antiracism generated by the movement and its allies. This is the continuing situation in which we find ourselves today: a contradictory one in terms of racial politics. To paraphrase Antonio Gramsci: the old refuses to die, and the new cannot be born. Hence many morbid symptoms appear.

So in what ways are these recent developments important in reshaping the meaning of whiteness? In lots of ways, actually.

This peculiar state of racial affairs in the contemporary world is (to use a Du Boisian concept) *dualistic*. The old white supremacy has been challenged, wounded, and changed. A new, countervailing framework has emerged, after centuries of lonely and isolated gestation in many varied settings, and has gained considerable ground. Reforms have occurred; massive populations have moved; democracy is at least widely espoused in racial matters. Yet white supremacy, though perhaps weakened, remains. It may even have gained some new strength, paradoxically enough, from the very racial reforms that it was forced to initiate. At a minimum, tremendous tensions have emerged between the "new racial order" and the old one, whose white supremacy was taken for granted.

One of these tensions concerns the contemporary significance of whiteness. In such an unusual world-historical moment, it is not surprising that whiteness and white identity have come in for some serious scrutiny. A contentious batch of *white racial projects* has arisen; the debate between them is about what white supremacy will mean in the future.

Racial Projects

In racial formation theory, racial projects link significations or representations of race, on the one hand, with social structural manifestations of racial hierarchy or dominance, on the other. Racial formation is a permanent process in which historically situated projects interact.[7] In the clash and conflict, as well as the accommodation and overlap of these projects, human bodies and consciousness, as well as social institutions and structures, are represented and organized. Conversely, when organizations, institutions, or state agencies advocate or resist a certain racial policy or practice, when they mobilize politically along racial lines, they necessarily engage in racial signification, at least implicitly and sometimes explicitly.

In any given historical context, racial signification and racial structuration are ineluctably linked. To represent, interpret, or signify upon race, then, to assign meaning to it, is to locate it in social structural terms. It is the connection between culture and structure, which is at the core of the racial formation process, that gives racial projects their coherence and unity. In the process of developing and institutionalizing racial policies and practices, in the articulation and socialization of racial meanings, various racial projects confront each other and undergo conflict and synthesis. This is the way racial formation occurs. Because racial formation is the articulation of culture and structure, signification and social organization, it is necessarily a political process. Without going into all the theoretical implications of this perspective here, it suffices to note that this perspective has connections to Gramscian theory and some species of left "post-" perspectives (notably that of Michel Foucault). It also draws on important sociological sources, particularly the antiracist pragmatism of Herbert Blumer and certain approaches to "micro-macro" linkage issues.[8]

Rearticulating the Meaning and Politics of Whiteness

Using this approach, we can understand the various arguments about whiteness; they are racial projects at play. We can distinguish, for example, between white racial projects that represent race as an intractable biological difference (certain neofascist positions, for example), and those that understand it as a sociohistorical construct. For present purposes, I want to focus on those projects that view race and whiteness as social, not biological distinctions. In other work, I have considered the survival of traditional, explicit white supremacist projects, which usually (though not always) invoke biologistic racial logic.[9] Here, though, I am concerned with projects that have reinterpreted or rearticulated the meaning of whiteness, and race in general, in the post–civil rights era.

The very "success"—partial and problematic, but nonetheless real— of the antiracist movement in the postwar United States, raised thorny political and intellectual problems for its sympathizers, who themselves occupied a range of positions on the ideological map. These problems were complicated by the fact that the movement's "success" occurred in the context of the massive global reconfiguration I have already mentioned. Thus one's position vis-à-vis the movement and vis-à-vis the reformist racial policies enacted in the 1960s had important implications: on the left-right spectrum, in terms of U.S. interventionism in the "Third World," and in respect to dawning issues of "personal politics," to name but a few themes. The anxieties caused by the upsurge and containment of the struggle against racism, in short, precipitated widespread political crises and realignments across much of the political spectrum, for people of every ideological and racial "hue," so to speak. A crisis over white identity, anxiety over the meaning of whiteness, was widespread and much debated.[10] It is no surprise, then, that a reevaluation of the meaning of whiteness emerged as part of a fierce effort to come up with a post–civil rights era concept of race.

I turn now to three such efforts: the neoconservative, liberal, and new abolitionist racial projects. All of these projects were developed by movement sympathizers: moderates, centrists, and radicals. While they overlap in some respects (and thus should be seen as only schematically, ideal-typically distinct), each project offers an alternative interpretation of the meaning of race, and thus of the post–civil rights era significance of whiteness.

NEOCONSERVATISM

Neoconservatism inherited the most "moderate" and incrementalist tendencies that emerged from the civil rights movement. Already in the mid-1960s academics were decrying the tendency toward "positive discrimination" as too extreme, too threatening to whites whose favor, they thought, would be necessary for the success of racial reform.[11] By the mid-1970s, an influential work argued that efforts to overcome patterns of discrimination would generate a "white ethnic political reaction."[12]

Neoconservatism can thus be seen as an attempt to spell out the limits of the black movement's legitimacy. It attempted to frame the new, post–civil rights meaning of race as a type of ethnicity, a largely cultural difference. A series of assimilationist arguments directed at blacks—for example, Irving Kristol's "The Negro of Today Is Like the Immigrant of Yesterday"—sought to instruct both blacks and whites on the changing dynamics of racial identity.

The neoconservative project was not just an academic ideology but also a nascent grassroots one. Ordinary whites adopted a more prosaic version of the same "moderate" stance that Nathan Glazer, Kristol, and fellow neoconservatives were at pains to theorize. Unable and unwilling in the aftermath of the civil rights era to espouse white supremacy, they simultaneously reacted to perceived threats to their racially privileged status. Unable and unwilling to sympathize with the more radical successors to the movement, which after the mid-1960s had lost faith in the ideal of integration, many whites came to support a conservative and individualistic form of egalitarianism, thus upholding a supposedly "colorblind" (but actually deeply race-conscious) position.[13]

The neoconservative project eventually consolidated as a strategy to conserve white advantages through denial of racial difference. It opened up the political space that has by now become familiar in terms of the critique of "reverse racism," "race-thinking," and "racial preferences of any kind." Neoconservatism thus sought to synthesize the legacy of centuries of racial hierarchy with the egalitarian and democratic norms of the black movement.

Although beset with contradictions and riddled with bad faith, the neoconservative project was quite successful where it counted most: in appealing to white voters. Obviously, a racial politics that could present itself as consistent with Dr. King's dream, " . . . that my four little children will be judged, not by the color of their skin, but by the content of their character," was far more subtle, far more politically effective, than open or coded appeals to white racial fears.

LIBERALISM

The hallmark of the neoconservative project has been its insistence that, beyond the proscription of explicit racial discrimination, every invocation of "race-thinking" was suspect. It goes without saying that in the absence of a serious movement for racial justice and equality, in the current atmosphere of assaults on affirmative action and similar programs of 1960s provenance, a great deal of political expedience remains in this view today. But where does it leave our understanding of the meaning of race? How does it handle the status of whiteness? These are questions that partisans of the neoconservative project preferred to avoid.

Not so the advocates of the liberal project. Here the struggle is to develop an alternative approach, both to the neoconservative effort to view race as a subset of ethnicity and to radical projects of various kinds. From the liberal standpoint, the race concept is itself flawed beyond repair, and the problematic nature of white identity is but an extension of the incoherence of the race concept itself.

Probably the most vocal academic proponent of the view that the idea of race itself must be discarded is literary critic Walter Benn Michaels. In a recent series of articles, Michaels has questioned not only biologistic concepts of race but also social constructionist ones.[14] If racial distinctions do not exist in nature, Michaels argues, then they can only be hypothesized to be social. Yet if they are social, they would have to do with certain practices, certain actions, that could be carried out by anyone, regardless of their racial identity. In fact, if race is a social construct, racial identity could be chosen or refused at will. But this doesn't work either, Michaels says. "Passing" for white, for example, or refusing whiteness—to pick some of many possible examples— is not possible: "[F]or a black person to pass for white is for that person to conceal whatever it is in his or her body that identifies her (sic) as being black. But since it is possible to pass only because that thing is already invisible, passing is therefore less a matter of hiding something than of refusing or failing to acknowledge something."[15] A tell- tale essence remains—a biological residue that cannot be disavowed.

Hence Michaels's dilemma: "Either race is the sort of thing that makes rejecting your racial identity just a kind of passing; or passing becomes impossible and there is no such thing as racial identity."[16] Since race cannot be understood as either biological or social, nature or nurture, timeless essence or sociohistorical fact, it must be seen as illusory, an epochal mistake(!). "We cannot think of race as a social fact, like slavery or . . . class," says Michaels.[17]

It is rather difficult to deal with this argument in a short space; in other work I have tried to show why race should be seen neither as "objective" nor as "illusory."[18] Certainly Emile Durkheim or Herbert Blumer, not to mention W. E. B. Du Bois, would have a field day demolishing Michaels's premises about what a "social fact" is and to what extent race qualifies for this designation. Critical race theorists such as Richard Delgado, Cheryl Harris, or Kimberlé Crenshaw, con- sidering Michaels's argument from a legal standpoint, would view with puzzlement and dismay the idea that race is a "mistake." It hardly seems necessary to say the following, but one must: entrenched in the

Constitution, elaborated through centuries of legislation and jurisprudence, embedded in economic life, language, art, taste, and mores, in short, a ubiquitous dimension of U.S. society, race is obstinately resistant to the sort of dismissal that Michaels proposes.

But I do not wish to cast any more aspersions on Michaels. Here I shall focus on a more limited agenda, discussing the liberal racial project of which Michaels's confusion is but a part.

What is the relationship between the discovery that race is a "mistake" and the crisis of post–civil rights racial politics? Already in 1964, Lyndon Johnson famously wondered whether in signing the Civil Rights Act he was turning the South over to the Republicans. By the late 1960s, with the "southern strategy" in place, Dr. King dead, and "black power" (brown power, red power, yellow power) seemingly entrenched in the movement, liberals who had supported the movement in its civil rights days found themselves excluded and lacking in political alternatives. For some—black and white (and brown, yellow, and red)—the answer was neoconservatism. Others turned to the left. But for those who sought to follow a middle course, commitment to an "equal opportunity" program seemed a feasible alternative. As David Plotke has suggested, the "equal opportunity" strategy sought to frame a limited commitment to the civil rights agenda, eschewing both the abandonment of egalitarianism visible among the neoconservatives (consider the popular joke of that time: "A neoconservative is a liberal who has been mugged") and the "equality of result"/group rights position of the left. It seemed to give a progressive racial spin to individualism.[19]

The liberal racial project flowed in general from this orientation. While not denying the importance of race *tout court,* while not opposing "transitional measures" or "dialogues" aimed at undoing the legacy of centuries of racial subordination, it also sought, for pragmatic political reasons, to avoid commitment to racial redistribution. Most significant for this essay's concerns, it attempted to diminish, and eventually to eliminate, the significance of race in affecting, and especially in constraining, the "life-chances" of racially defined minority group members.

What did this mean for whites and whiteness? To an important degree, as Plotke argues, this strategy resulted from liberal efforts to maintain white voters' loyalties.[20] Such exertions became necessary in the atmosphere of backlash that began with the "southern strategy"—

or with Johnson's trepidations in 1964—and continues today through anti–affirmative action initiatives.[21]

Looked at negatively, this strategy amounts to a soft version of the color-blindness position associated with neoconservatism. Seen more positively, it is an effort to frame racial egalitarianism incrementally enough that large numbers of whites will sign on to the effort to get "beyond race." In order to do this, the liberal project must strenuously resist any concept of whiteness that equates it with preservation of "a sense of group position," much less with the maintenance of racial privilege.[22] Michaels's idea that race is a "mistake" thus attempts to provide a theoretical rationale for the liberal quest to reduce the significance of race, without embracing the "reverse racism" approach of the neoconservatives. As such, it is but one of many attempts to preserve the allegiance of whites to a centrist racial politics.[23]

NEW ABOLITIONISM

Emphasis on white privilege is, of course, the central component of the new abolitionist position, which derives from new left roots. The argument here is that whiteness is a strictly negative category, empty of all content save its distantiation from "color," its refusal of "non-whiteness": "It is not merely that whiteness is oppressive and false; it is that whiteness is *nothing but* oppressive and false. . . . It is the empty and terrifying attempt to build an identity based on what one isn't and on whom one can hold back."[24]

As befits its birth in the new left, the core message of the new abolitionist project is the imperative of repudiation of white identity and white privilege, the requirement that "the lie of whiteness" be exposed. This rejection of whiteness on the part of those who benefit from it, this "new abolitionism," it is argued, is a precondition for the establishment of substantive racial equality and social justice—or, more properly, socialism—in the United States. Whites must become "race traitors," as the journal of the new abolitionist project calls itself. Its motto: "Treason to whiteness is loyalty to humanity."

It is easy to sympathize with this analysis, at least up to a point. It too is a response to the black movement, which in the U.S. context at least served as the point of origin for all the "new social movements" as well as for the much-reviled "politics of identity." The movement taught the valuable lesson that politics went "all the way down." That is, meaningful efforts to achieve greater social justice could not tolerate a public/private or a collective/individual distinction. Trying to change society meant trying to change one's own life. The formula "the personal is political," commonly associated with feminism, had its early origins among the militants of the civil rights movement.

Well and good. But is whiteness so flimsy that it can be repudiated by a mere act of political will—or even by widespread and repeated acts aimed at rejecting white privilege? I think not. Whites may not have a discrete, "positive" content to their racial identities, but whiteness certainly has meaning, an "overdetermined" political and cultural meaning to be sure. Whiteness no doubt has much to do with priv- ilege in the sense of socioeconomic status but it also involves religious affiliation, ideologies of individualism, opportunity, citizenship, na- tionalism, and so forth. Like any other complex of beliefs and prac- tices, "whiteness" is embedded in a highly articulated social structure and system of significations; while it is valuable to deconstruct it, and important to challenge the system of racial privilege that sustains it, the idea that whiteness can be abolished seems quite utopian, almost Sorelian.

Furthermore, whiteness is a relational concept, unintelligible with- out reference to nonwhiteness—note how this is true even of Roe- diger's formulation about "build[ing] an identity based on what one isn't." The abolition of whiteness is unthinkable without the eradica- tion of the concept of race itself, an outcome as undesirable as it is impossible.[25]

Where This Critique Leads Us, and Leaves Us

Abolishing whiteness is one thing; *deconstruction* of whiteness is quite another. Whiteness can be deconstructed; it can be reinterpreted. It was never "pure," never *only* the "absence of color." Long before there was whiteness, there was hybridization, with its contradictory mixture of opprobrium and longing for "the other."[26] While there can be no doubt about the underlying concepts of status and privilege that shape whiteness, neither can it be understood as "merely" privilege.

But deconstruction differs from abolition. I take the deconstruction of whiteness to be the practicable core of the new abolitionism. I understand deconstructing whiteness to mean rethinking and chang- ing ideas about white identity and reorienting the practices conse- quent upon these ideas. Deconstructing whiteness can begin relatively easily, in the messy present, with the recognition that whiteness already contains substantial nonwhite elements. Cannot antiracists dispense with the "one-drop rule," the defense of racial purity, the abhorrence of hybridity? To be sure, these are not easy tasks, not matters to be talked away in a few sophisticated (or sophistic) articles à la Michaels. They suggest some of the strategies, the ideas and actions, that can realistically be demanded of whites. Nor are all the practical ideas of the "race traitor" school to be dismissed: without denying one's white identity, one can certainly oppose and interrupt racist activity or speech, for example.[27]

Such activity and awareness demand thought and discipline. They hark back to Du Boisian concepts: of the inevitable duality of racialized experience, of the "conservation" of races, of the pitfalls and pities of the "psychological wage" that racism offers to whites.[28] It demands recognition of the centrality of the enormous contributions that racially defined minorities have made to U.S. society and culture. Think of American music and dance and poetry, think of the very language Americans speak. Think, too, of the oceans of labor sunk into this soil by people of every color, whose origins span every continent, every modern historical epoch. Think, finally, of what it means to acknowledge that the half-millennium of domination of the globe by Europe and its U.S. inheritors is the historical context in which racial concepts of human difference have attained their present, and still relatively unquestioned, foundational status.[29]

All this whites must come to know not only as ideas but also as practical reason, as instrumental knowledge, whose yield is profound social reorganization. Yet, compelling as such knowledge would be, it does not entail the abolition of whiteness or the end of the race concept. Instead it poses once more, as profoundly as ever before, the possibilities of human variability, pluralism, self-determination, and democracy.

Notes

1 See Toni Morrison, *Playing in the Dark: Whiteness and the Literary Imagination* (Cambridge, Mass.: Harvard University Press, 1992).

2 For eugenics, see Madison Grant, *The Passing of a Great Race, or The Racial History of European History* (New York: Scribners, 1916). On slavery and citizenship, see Edmund Morgan, *American Slavery, American Freedom:*

The Ordeal of Colonial Virginia (New York: Norton, 1975) and Rogers M. Smith, *Civic Ideals: Conflicting Visions of Citizenship in U.S. History* (New Haven: Yale University Press, 1997). For historical work on the instability of whiteness, see David Roediger, *The Wages of Whiteness: Race and the Making of the American Working Class* (New York: Verso, 1991), and Alexander Saxton, *The Rise and Fall of the White Republic: Class Politics and Mass Culture in Nineteenth-Century America* (New York: Verso, 1990).

3   See Michael Omi and Howard Winant, *Racial Formation in the United States: From the 1960s to the 1990s*, 2d ed. (New York: Routledge, 1994).

4   I do not use the term "world-historical" casually: the crisis of racial meanings, I suggest, is not confined within the United States, but a global phenomenon. Although in this essay I confine myself to the United States, in other comparative work I seek to place the contemporary racial upheaval in a global context. See Howard Winant, *Racial Conditions: Politics, Theory, Comparisons* (Minneapolis: University of Minnesota Press, 1994).

5   Of course, opposition to racial hierarchy has always existed, for wherever there is oppression there is resistance. There had even been some important "rehearsals" for the massive critique of white supremacy that consolidated after World War II: notably the Haitian revolution and its hemisphere-wide influences and the tide of abolitionism that engulfed both sides of the Atlantic for most of the nineteenth century. But important as these precedents were, they did not congeal as coherent, global critiques of racism. On the Haitian revolution, see C. L. R. James, *The Black Jacobins: Toussaint L'Ouverture and the San Domingo Revolution*, 2d ed., rev. (New York: Vintage, 1989). On abolitionism, see Robin Blackburn, *The Overthrow of Colonial Slavery, 1776–1848* (London: Verso, 1988) and *The Making of New World Slavery: From the Baroque to the Modern, 1492– 1800* (London, Verso, 1997).

6   See Aristide Zolberg, "The Next Waves: Migration Theory for a Changing World," *International Migration Review* 23 no. 3 (1989): and John Solomos and John Wrench, eds., *Racism and Migration in Western Europe* (Providence, R.I.: Berg, 1993), 403–30.

7   What is wrong with "solving" the race "problem"? Why shouldn't we try to "get beyond" race? While a full account of the complexities of race remains far beyond our reach, such objectives are either foolish or dangerous or both. Is it not rather disingenuous to contemplate "getting beyond" race when in almost every corner of the globe, dark skin still correlates with inequality? Since when has it been possible to make large-scale conflicts "go away"? What other major forms of human difference have been transcended recently? Class? Gender? Nationality? When we look with any degree of seriousness at the "problem" of race, we must recognize that it is

not about to go away, not about to be "solved." See Winant, *Racial Conditions*, xii.

8 Herbert Blumer, "Race Prejudice as a Sense of Group Position," *Pacific Sociological Review* 1, no. 1 (spring 1958): 3–7, and Herbert Blumer and Troy Duster, "Theories of Race and Social Action," in UNESCO, *Sociological Theories: Race and Colonialism* (Paris: UNESCO, 1980), 211–238. See also Randall Collins, "Interaction Ritual Chains, Power, and Property: The Micro-Macro Connection as an Empirically Based Sociological Problem," in Jeffrey Alexander et al., eds., *The Micro-Macro Link* (Berkeley: University of California Press, 1987), 193–206.

9 Howard Winant, "Behind Blue Eyes: Whiteness and Contemporary U.S. Racial Politics," *New Left Review* 225 (September–October 1997): 73–88.

10 For just a few manifestations of this crisis, see, among many others, such iconic writings as James Baldwin, "White Man's Guilt," in *The Price of the Ticket* (New York: St. Martin's, 1985); Norman Mailer, *The White Negro* (San Francisco: City Lights, 1957); and Norman Podhoretz, "My Negro Problem-and Ours," in Mark Gerson and James Q. Wilson, eds., *The Essential Neoconservative Reader* (New York: Addison-Wesley, 1997), 5–22. For SNCC's decision in May 1966 to expel its white participants, see Clayborne Carson, *In Struggle: SNCC and the Black Awakening of the 1960s* (Cambridge, Mass.: Harvard University Press, 1981). See also Bayard Rustin, "From Protest to Politics," *Commentary* 39 (February 1964): 25–31; and Roy Wilkins's denunciation of black power as "the father of hatred and the mother of violence" in Robert Allen, *Black Awakening in Capitalist America: An Analytic History* (New York: Anchor, 1970), 129ff.

11 See Milton M. Gordon, *Assimilation in American Life: The Role of Race, Religion, and National Origins* (New York: Oxford University Press, 1964).

12 Nathan Glazer, *Affirmative Discrimination: Ethnic Inequality and Public Policy*, 2d ed. (New York: Basic, 1978).

13 Glazer has recently abandoned his racial neoconservatism for a more centrist view, closer to what I call a liberal racial project (see below). Nathan Glazer, *We Are All Multiculturalists Now* (Cambridge, Mass.: Harvard University Press, 1998). See also James Traub, "Nathan Glazer Changes His Mind, Again," *New York Times Magazine*, 28 June 1998, 23–26.

14 See Walter Benn Michaels, "Race Into Culture: A Critical Genealogy of Cultural Identity," *Critical Inquiry* 18, no. 4 (summer 1992): 655–85; "Posthistoricism: The End of the End of History," *Transition* 70, no. 6, 2 (1996): 4–19; and "Autobiography of an Ex-White Man: Why Race is Not a Social Construction," *Transition* 73, no. 7, 1 (1998): 122–43.

15 Michaels, "Autobiography," 129.

16 Ibid., 125–28.

17 Ibid., 125.

18 Winant, *Racial Conditions.*
19 David Plotke, "Democratic Breakup," unpublished manuscript.
20 See Plotke. For a variety of expressions of this idea, see William Julius Wilson, *The Declining Significance of Race: Blacks and Changing American Institutions,* 2d ed. (Chicago: University of Chicago Press, 1980); Thomas Byrne Edsall and Mary Edsall, *Chain Reaction: The Impact of Race, Rights, and Taxes on American Politics,* rev. ed. (New York: Norton, 1992); and Paul M. Sniderman and Thomas Piazza, *The Scar of Race* (Cambridge, Mass.: Harvard University Press, 1993).
21 See Stephen Steinberg, *Turning Back: The Retreat from Racial Justice in American Thought and Policy* (Boston: Beacon, 1995).
22 See Blumer, "Race Prejudice."
23 Other toilers in this vineyard include William Julius Wilson, "The Right Message," *New York Times,* 17 March 1992; Michael Lind, *The Next American Nation: The New Nationalism and the Fourth American Revolution* (New York: Free Press, 1995); and Todd Gitlin, *The Twilight of Common Dreams: Why America Is Wracked by Culture Wars* (New York: Holt, 1995).
24 Roediger, *The Wages of Whiteness,* 13 (Roediger's emphasis).
25 Why "impossible"? First off, see Omi and Winant, *Racial Formation.* Then, consider once more the social structural embeddedness of race: "[R]ace is a condition of individual and collective identity, a permanent, though tremendously flexible, element of social structure. Race is a means of knowing and organizing the social world; it is subject to continual contestation and reinterpretation, but it is no more likely to disappear than other forms of human inequality and difference. Of course, racial inequality can be lessened, racial difference can be respected, but in no sense would such changes, though obviously desirable, get us 'beyond' race." See Winant, *Racial Conditions,* xii.

   Why "undesirable"? Because race is not simply the product of racism, of centuries of exploitation, exclusion, and domination, of the denial of freedom and even identity. No, it is also the product of centuries of *resistance* to racism, of determined refusal to accept racial oppression, and of wildly imaginative efforts to *create* identity. Moreover, from these undertakings in self-invention and resistance developed not only the peoples whom we now designate by the term "of color," but also in significant measure our general concepts of freedom and democracy. So there is much to honor, much to preserve, in the concept of race. Beyond that, to deny the significance of race in the modern world must be seen as willful blindness: it would be as absurd as repudiating, say, the importance of religion. Would even an atheist question the significance of religion in shaping history and society? Would she claim that since religious faith is "objectively" without basis we should have done with it?

These are, of course, questions far too big to be adequately addressed here. I merely hope to suggest some general contours for a more sophisticated understanding of the meaning of race than those we are often offered in this day and age.

26 See Eric Lott, *Love and Theft: Blackface Minstrelsy and the American Working Class* (New York: Oxford University Press, 1993) and Roediger, *The Wages of Whiteness*. "Hybridity" is itself a somewhat suspect term, also in need of deconstruction, for it implies the melding of discrete and differentiated variants. See Robert Young, *Colonial Desire: Hybridity in Theory, Culture, and Race* (New York: Routledge, 1995).

27 For a good primer on white antiracist practice, see Paul Kivel, *Uprooting Racism: How White People Can Work for Racial Justice* (Philadelphia: New Society Publishers, 1996).

28 Du Bois's concept of racial dualism has received extensive analysis. For my views, see Howard Winant, "Racial Dualism at Century's End," in Wahneema Lubiano, ed., *The House That Race Built* (New York: Random House, 1996), 87–115. Du Bois's concept of racial "conservation" merits attention because it theorizes racial dualism in a world-historical sense: equality and difference, as well as inclusion and particularity, Du Bois argues, must be simultaneously pursued. W. E. B. Du Bois, "The Conservation of Races" in David Levering Lewis, ed., *W. E. B. Du Bois: A Reader* (New York: Holt, 1995). In disagreement with Appiah's simplistic reading of this essay, I suggest it retains great validity for today and successfully preserves an emancipatory concept of race. See Kwame Anthony Appiah, *In My Father's House: Africa in the Philosophy of Culture* (New York: Oxford University Press, 1992). On Du Bois's notion of the psychological wage, see his *Black Reconstruction in America: An Essay toward a History of the Part Which Black Folk Played in the Attempt to Reconstruct Democracy in America, 1860–1880* (New York: Atheneum, 1977), originally published in 1935.

29 In this brief paragraph I can only hint at a few of the main themes of Du Bois's mighty analysis of race on the American and the world-historical stage. While Du Bois has an unparalleled perception of the range of white delusions and atrocities, even at the heights of his indictment he does not propose the abolition of whiteness. See, for example, "The Souls of White Folk," originally published in 1920, in David Levering Lewis, ed., *W. E. B. Du Bois: A Reader* (New York: Henry Holt, 1995).

Troy Duster

The "Morphing" Properties of Whiteness

In discussions of race and the recent rediscovery of the American pre-occupation with whiteness, it is possible to isolate two overarching but sharply conflicting frameworks that run at cross-purposes. On the one hand, there are those who portray race and whiteness as fluid, continually reflecting emergent and contingent features of social life, emphasizing the relational and ever-changing character of race. On the other hand, it is not difficult to identify historians, writers, and social analysts who have emphasized the deeply embedded, structural, hard, enduring, solid-state features of race and racism, sustained throughout three centuries even as they have acknowledged the occasional shifting boundaries of who gets included in the category "white."

Race as Arbitrary and Whimsical versus
Race as Structural and Enduring

If we take even a casual excursion through the last few centuries of racial classification, there is overwhelming evidence on the side of those who have argued that race is arbitrary, shifting, and often *biologically* and *sociologically* inconsistent, contradictory, and simple-minded. The rule that one drop of black blood makes one black is the easy mark along a full continuum of mind-boggling, ludicrous taxonomies.[1] "Passing" and incoherent "miscegenation laws" and slave-owner/slave offspring do more than simply dot the landscape with the mine-fields of this topic. This continuum extends well into the present period, in which we find more and more people asserting a mixed-race identity. Since the classification of race is arbitrary and often whimsical (for example, one drop of blood), accepting the idea that race is something identifiable with fixed borders that could be crossed and thus "mixed"—while others are "not mixed"—is supplanting one multitiered fiction with another. At the biochemical level of blood types and hematology, at the neurological level of neurotransmission patterns, at the level of cell function—at all these levels, we are all "mixed" by any taxonomy or measure of allele frequency of large population groups.[2] It would seem that we must "score one" for the side that sees the superficiality and artificiality of race.

Other Voices

Yet there is another set of very compelling voices (present in other papers in this volume) emphasizing how race, or in this case whiteness and its attendant privilege, is deeply embedded in the routine structures of economic and political life. From ordinary service at Denny's Restaurants, to far greater access to bank loans to simple peaceful, *police-event–free* driving—all these things have come unreflectively with the territory of being white.[3] One does not give up racial privilege, neither in the United States nor in South Africa, by simply denying that it exists. Whites who have come to a point where they acknowledge their racial privilege are in a difficult circumstance morally because they cannot just shed that privilege with a simple assertion of denial.

So who is right? One side sees race as ever-changing. The other side sees enduring race privilege. Oddly, both sides are correct. Or, at least, both sides have an important handle on an elementary truth about race. But *empirically,* one could easily ask, if these two positions are poles apart, how can both be correct about race? How can race be both structural and embedded yet superficial, arbitrary, and whimsical—shifting with times and circumstances?

The best way to communicate how this is possible is to employ an analogy—to *water* or, more precisely, H_2O. While water is a fluid state, at certain contingent moments, under thirty-two degrees, it is transformed into a solid state—ice. This is an easy binary formulation. But things get more complicated, because when H_2O, at still another contingent moment boils, it begins to vaporize or evaporate. And now the coup de grâce of the analogy of H_2O to race: H_2O in its vapor state can condense, come back and transform into water, and then freeze and hit you in its solid state as an ice block; what you thought had evaporated into the thin air can return in a form that is decidedly and consequentially real. In short, H_2O is to serve now as more than just my analogy to race—and, in this context, whiteness. Race, like H_2O, can take many forms, but unlike H_2O it can transform itself in a nanosecond. It takes time for ice to boil or for vapor to condense and freeze, but race can be *simultaneously* Janus-faced and multifac(et)ed—and also produce a singularly dominant social hierarchy. Indeed, if we make the fundamental mistake of reifying any one of those states as more real than another, we will lose basic insights into the nature and character of racial stratification in America. So it depends on when a picture is taken in this sequence and on who takes the picture as to whether race is best understood as fluid or solid or vapor—or has evaporated into a temporally locatable nonexistence, a color-blind fragment in time and space.

If We Are All One Race, How Could There Be "Whiteness" in Its Solid State?

A consortium of leading scientists across the disciplines from biology to physical anthropology issued a "Revised UNESCO Statement on Race" in 1995. This is a definitive declaration that summarizes eleven central issues and concludes that in terms of "scientific" discourse there is no such thing as a "race" that has any scientific utility, at least in the biological sciences: "[T]he same scientific groups that developed the biological concept over the last century have now concluded that its use for characterizing human populations is so flawed that it is no longer a scientifically valid concept. In fact, the statement makes clear that the biological concept of race as applied to humans has no legitimate place in biological science."[4] By the mid-1970s, it had become abundantly clear that there is more genetic variation within the most current common socially used categories of race than between these categories.[5] The consensus is newly formed. For example, in the early part of this century, scientists in several countries tried to link up a study of the major blood groups in the ABO system to racial and ethnic groups.[6] Since researchers knew that blood type B was more common in certain ethnic and racial groups—which they believed to be more inclined to criminality and mental illness—this was often a thinly disguised form of racism.[7] They kept running up against a brick wall.

It is not difficult to understand why they persisted. Humans are symbol-bearing creatures who give meaning to their experiences and to their symbolic worlds. The UNESCO statement of the 1990s is ultimately about the problem of the difference between first-order constructs in science and second-order constructs. Some fifty years ago, Felix Kaufmann made a crucial distinction that throws some light on the controversy.[8] Kaufmann was not addressing whether or not there could be a science of race. Rather, he noted that there are different kinds of issues, methodologies, and theories that are generated by what could be called first-order constructs in the physical and natural sciences versus second-order constructs. For the physical and natural sciences, the naming of objects for investigation and inquiry, for conceptualizing and finding empirical regularities, is in the hands of the scientists and their scientific peers. Thus, for example, the nomenclature for quarks or neurons, genes or chromosomes, nitrogen or sulfides, and so on all reside with the scientist qua scientist in his/her role as the creator of first-order constructs.

This is quite different from the task of the observer, analyst, or scientist of human social behavior. Humans live in a pre-interpreted social world: they grow up, from infancy, in a world that has pre-assigned categories and names for those categories, which were in turn provided by fellow commonsense actors, not by "scientists." Persons live in the world that is pre-interpreted for them, and their continual task is to try to navigate, negotiate, and make sense of that world. The task of the social scientist is therefore quite distinct from that of the natural scientist. While the latter can rely on first-order constructs, the former must construct a set of categories based on the pre-interpreted world of commonsense actors. The central problem is that "race" is now, and has been since 1735, both a first- and second-order construct. This was the year that Linnaeus published *Systema Naturae,* in which he revealed a four-part classification scheme of the human races that has residues still today.

We now turn to the matter of whether race can be studied scientifically. If we mean by that, is there a consensus among the natural scientists about race as a first-order construct, then the answer since about 1970 is categorically no. The UNESCO statement summarizes why this is so at every level that is significant to the biological functioning of the organism, with two exceptions. We have already noted that scientific research on first-order constructs about race as a biological category in science in the last four decades has revealed over and over again that there is greater genetic heterogeneity within rather than between major racial groupings. One of the two exceptions has to do with the fact that the gene frequencies, as demonstrated in the use of specific polymorphic markers, occur more frequently in certain populations than in others.[9] But this distribution of allele frequencies, though occasionally overlapping with racial groupings, is definitely not only a racially defined issue. For example, northern Europeans have greater concentrations of cystic fibrosis than southern Europeans, and both are categorized as "Caucasians." Moreover, southern Europeans have higher rates of beta-thalassemia than northern Europeans—but, even more to the point, sickle-cell anemia is found in greater concentration in Orchomenus, Greece, than among African Americans.[10] While clinical geneticists are quite familiar with these wide patterns of variations between and among persons who appear phenotypically to be of a certain "race," when an African American with cystic fibrosis shows up at a cystic fibrosis clinic, there is as much consternation about this person's possibly being in the wrong place. When a white person with sickle-cell anemia appears in a sickle-cell clinic, there is often explicit speculation that this person is "passing" and is *really* black.[11]

Thus, the "commonsense" question of whether someone is black or white or Asian is frequently difficult to pin down at the margins—but residents of the United States have been acting as if this were self-evident. The allocation of such resources as loans to build houses has been based on such casual visual cues as whether one "appears to be" white or black. Over time, with the patterned distribution of loans, the racialized shape of suburbs and inner cities began to look "quite real"—solidifying into a solid state of racial boundary maintenance—all the while a kind of second-order construct.

Race, Law, and Second-Order Constructs

Three acts were passed by the U.S. Congress in 1934–35 that would seal the accumulation of wealth into white households for the next half-century. There is some new scholarship emerging reexamining the role of race in explaining U.S. domestic policy for the last half-century.[12]

The new work is fascinating in that it points out the systematic, integrated character of policies of the federal government that will surprise most Americans who grew up reading high school civics books that trumpeted the race-neutral character of Franklin Roosevelt's New Deal government policies. For example, Jill Quadagno notes that while there is some truth to the claim that the New Deal was designed to provide a "floor of protection for the industrial working class," it was the brokered compromises over the New Deal that simultaneously "reinforced racial segregation through social welfare programs, labor policy, and housing policy." How, and why?

In 1935 Roosevelt had put together a fragile coalition of northern industrial workers and southern whites still engaged in a primarily agrarian economic order. Blacks were a vital part of that agrarian system, but they could not vote in the South. Thus Roosevelt did not need to even try to court what was not there: the black southern vote. During this period, more than three-quarters of the black population still lived in the South. Most of them sharecropped and were tied to the plantation economy at poverty-level wages. Those who were not sharecroppers were engaged in day labor—with most of these employed at $2.00 per 100 pounds of cotton. This translated to $2.00 per day for a strong worker.[13]

Black women worked as maids, making $2.00 per week on average. White southerners in control of key positions in Congress explicitly voiced fears that any federal programs that would put money directly into the pockets of blacks would undermine the very infrastructure of this plantation economy. As chairs of the powerful committees of the House and Senate, they blocked any attempt to change the agrarian system that indentured black sharecroppers. Because of this opposition, which is documented in memoranda between Congress and the White House, Roosevelt compromised, and agricultural workers and servants were excluded from the Social Security Act of 1935. The exclusion of agricultural workers and house servants appears in retrospect to have been race-neutral. At the time, however, *the key actors said they would block all Social Security legislation if it included blacks.*

Similarly, the Wagner Act of 1935, labeled in some circles as the Magna Carta of labor, was on closer inspection the Magna Carta of white labor.[14] The original version, which permitted the organization of industrial labor and legalized collective bargaining, *prohibited racial discrimination.* But the American Federation of Labor and the same constellation of white southerners who controlled the key committees of Congress fought it, and the final version permitted racial exclusion. Because the racial exclusion language was applied to closed shops, blacks were blocked by law from challenging the barriers to entry into the newly protected labor unions and securing the right to collective bargaining.[15]

Finally, in 1937 Congress passed the National Housing Act, which sealed the fate of America's cities, creating the social policy and economic basis for sustained and exacerbated racial segregation. While many commentators have blamed "white flight" for the creation of ghettos and barrios, it was actually this heavily coded racial policy of the federal government of the United States that created white enclaves in the suburbs. In 1939 the Federal Housing Authority's *Underwriting Manual* guidelines for granting housing loans explicitly used race as the single most important criterion. The following passage is from Section 937 of the FHA manual that covered the period in question: "If a neighborhood is to retain stability, it is necessary that properties shall be continued to be occupied by the same social and *racial* classes."[16]

On this basis, for the next thirty years, whites were able to get housing loans at 3 to 5 percent, while blacks were routinely denied such loans. For example, of 350,000 new homes built in northern California between 1946 and 1960 with FHA support, *fewer than 100 went to blacks.* That same pattern holds for the whole state, and for the nation as well. Between 1935 and 1950, eleven million homes were built in the United States with federal assistance, and Charles Abrams has documented well his assertion that "discrimination against Negroes was a condition of federal assistance." The official code of ethics of the National Association of Real Estate Boards not only barred its members from selling houses across the racial divide but put teeth behind its code. In a 1943 brochure titled *Fundamentals of Real Estate Practice,* the association outlined grounds for expulsion of realtors who violated race-based sales and then went on to state explicitly what constituted problematic behavior:

> The prospective buyer might be a bootlegger who would cause considerable annoyance to his neighbors, a madame who had a number of Call Girls on her string, a gangster, who wants a screen for his activities by living in a better neighborhood, a colored man

> of means who was giving his children a college education and
> thought they were entitled to live among whites . . . No matter
> what the motive or character of the would-be purchaser, if the deal
> would instigate a form of blight, then certainly the well-meaning
> broker must work against its consummation.

The urban redevelopment programs sponsored by the federal government under the National Housing Act of 1949 also served to undermine the financial solidity of the black community. The alignment of
corridors in the major cities was chosen so that the freeways almost
universally cut through core areas of black settlements, while connect-
ing the white suburbs to the central business districts of the cities. As a
direct result of these programs, many urban black areas lost their
neighborhood shopping districts of successful small businesses. This
was soon followed by empirically demonstrable race-conscious systematic mortgage "redlining," which had a downward-spiraling effect
on the economic vitality of scores of black communities.[17]

It should now be clear that the assertion of a fact—that median
family net worth of individuals in the United States who are socially
designed as "white" is $43,279, while the median family net worth of
individuals in the United States who are socially designated as "black"
is $4,169—is a matter that can be determined to be true or false by the
systematic collection of empirical data, and either replicated or re-
futed. In other words, it can be investigated scientifically, without
reference to blood groups, the relationship between genotype and
phenotype, or the likelihood that one group is more at risk for cystic
fibrosis while the other is more at risk for sickle-cell anemia.

To definitively assert that at the blood group level, or at the level of
the modulatory environment for neurotransmission in the brain,
there are no real racial differences (read biological) is to reify a particular version of the biological sciences as *science*. This would ignore the
capacity of scientific inquiry to apprehend the social reality of the ten-
to-one economic advantage of coming from a white household in
America versus coming from a black household. Although loan al-
locations based on crude phenotypical versions of racial differences
are second-order constructs, the ten-to-one ratio by "race" noted above
is subject to scientific investigation as well. It can be challenged or
proven false or replicated over and over again. Nonetheless, patterned
social behavior associated with "race" leads to a confusion about the

role of genetics and the way in which the analyst peers through the prism of heritability at the direction of the causal arrow. Richard Herrnstein and Charles Murray, James Wilson and Richard Herrnstein, Arthur Jensen, and a wide band of other claimants with no training in genetics make the commonsense mistake of treating race as a biological construct, then reading back through social patterns (scoring on a test; rate of incarceration) to make inferences about the biological underpinnings of social patterns.[18] For example, Herrnstein and Murray posit the dominance of genetics in explaining IQ, concluding that "the genetic component of IQ" is 60 per cent. Then, taking IQ as the independent variable, the authors extend this analysis to the genetic explanation of social achievement or failure, so that unemployment, crime, and social standing are "explained" by IQ.[19] Despite a heavy reliance on the genetic explanation of intelligence as measured by test scores, the basic data from the molecular genetics revolution of the last three decades are completely absent.

Herrnstein and Murray posit that genetics plays an important, even dominant role in IQ, proposing that it is a whopping 60 percent of g, a statistical measure assumed to be related to "general intelligence." Neither Herrnstein (a psychologist) nor Murray (a political scientist) demonstrates sufficient knowledge of contemporary developments in the human biosciences to be aware of a fundamental problem in attributing g to genetics. Even single-gene determined phenotypical expressions such as Huntington's disease, beta-thalassemia, and sickle-cell anemia exhibit a wide range of clinical manifestations. For multifactorial conditions—of which, incontestably, we must include the evolving thought processes of the brain—the interaction between nutrition, cellular development, and neurological sequencing has been firmly established. Developments of the last decade reveal a remarkable feedback loop between the brain and the "experience" of an environment. We now can demonstrate that a single neuron displays a variety of activity patterns and will switch between them, depending on the modulatory environment.[20] Anyone aware of current developments in cognitive science knows that a one-way deterministic notion of the firing of the neurotransmitters and subsequent behavior is a deeply reductionist fallacy. Thus to assign to "genetics" a ballpark figure of any kind, without regard to these well-known interaction effects, is to display a profound ignorance of the last three decades of developments in molecular biology and the neurosciences, most especially since Herrnstein and Murray posit genetics (60 percent) as the most powerful explanatory variable.

The inverse of the attempt to get at a biological construct of race is the assertion, by those committed to a class analysis, that class rather than race is ultimately the master stratifying practice in technologically advanced industrial and postindustrial societies. But that is also open to empirical investigation. Both the biological construct and the class construct are attempts at first-order conceptions, and, as such, they appear on the surface to be more scientific. Yet, there is a fundamental error in the logic of inquiry here. As we have seen, when those who make bank loan decisions do so with their own sets of symbolic strategies—*and those practices are routinized*—the stratified outcomes are a compelling site for *scientific* investigation.

The debate about whether race or class is "more real" as a stratifying practice can be better understood by reexamining how the issue is framed. What is it about class that makes it more real than race—save for the empirical fact that more people employ it (or do not) as a way of sorting social, political, and economic relations? The power of apartheid in South Africa and Jim Crow in the United States demonstrates that such facts are as much located in the practices of actors as in the "objective" relations of workers to capital. The answer is that, objectively speaking, class relations are governed by just such an attempt at a first-order construct: the connections to the workplace. But during apartheid (and even after, there is evidence to believe), whites have had greater access to scarce resources than blacks. This is an "objective" reality of a stratifying practice, no less because it is a second-order construct employed by those acting in the world. Rather, during apartheid, it was even definitively a pattern with notable and obvious replicability (i.e., as a stratifying practice).

The trouble with expertise about race is that once we write books and articles about it, we capture some part of it for a particular understanding. We then become committed to that singular version of it, and often become defensive and aggressive in our defense of our "turf" of a particular rendering.[21] But if scholars and researchers have trouble, lay persons have at least as hard a time holding simultaneously conflicting imagery about the multiple realities of race in America. And so I am going to tell a story about my own youth, when I came to understand the contingent character of race and whiteness and how people can make strategic use of it.

Race in its Fluid State: A Personal Tale

When I attended college many years ago at Northwestern University, I was one of six black undergraduates on a campus of over seven thousand students. Northwestern is just outside Chicago, something of the midwestern equivalent of Stanford in that it draws heavily from the upper middle-class of the Chicago region. And so it follows that it would be very unlikely that my particular phenotype would be expressed at Northwestern.

While I was there, I came to know Jack Doyle, a fellow student who was from an Irish working-class background. Gruff in manner and tough in appearance, Doyle was also something of a standout in that world. He and I became close friends, and we have sustained that friendship long beyond our collegiate careers. After our college days, and over the years, we would often get together whenever I returned to Chicago. A dozen or so years later, after I got my Ph.D. and was teaching at Berkeley, I returned to Chicago, visiting my mother for a week. One evening, I gave Jack a call, and he came over on this particular hot August night to join me for a beer. Around eleven o'clock at night, my mother came home from a neighborhood meeting and said she forgot to get food for the next day's breakfast. She asked if I would drive her around to the store on Sixty-third, just off Cottage Grove. So I said, "Of course," and we got in the car and drove around to the store. Jack Doyle joined us, so there we were—the three of us. We parked on Sixty-third Street, and, while Jack and I sat in the car, my mother went in to the store to get the groceries. I noticed that police cars occasionally would circle, but that was nothing new to me.

After about the third or fourth time around, however, three big, tough-looking, white police officers jumped out, one with gun drawn, and said to us, "Get out of that car." So we got out. They bent us over the hood of the car and frisked us, and then they said to me, "What are you doing here?" But before I could answer, they turned to my friend, "And what are *you* doing here?" Remember, this is an all-black area of Chicago.

And he said, "I've come to visit my friend." One of the police officers said, "Your friend from where?" "Northwestern," I replied. He said, "Northwestern? You're college boys?" Then with sardonic disbelief dripping from the question, he asked, "Okay, college boys— what did you study?" We told them. We were not very convincing because one of them said, quite agitatedly, "I asked you, 'What are you doing here on a Saturday night parked in front of a grocery store?'" Sometimes the truth will not set you free. I told the truth: "I'm waiting for my mother." That's when I saw his billy club. He lifted it slowly, deliberately, and I had the experience of all of this happening as if in slow-motion—as in a baseball pitcher's exaggerated wind-up before the delivery. And all the while he was saying, "You're a real wise ass—" Then, all of a sudden, the voice from the heavens parts the thick hot August night air. It is my mother's voice booming with authority: "Officer, what's going on here?"

In that one moment, perhaps even a nanosecond, I understood the fluid and contingent and Janus-faced character of race. I saw it happen with my own eyes. With his arm in midair, this tough white cop turned officer-of-the-law and literally turned and tipped his hat to my mother and said, "Madam, we're here to serve and protect you." Yes. A remarkable capacity for transmogrification or, perhaps better, *morphing*. He went from solid state to fluid state. He transformed himself from "an occupying force of domination" into someone there "to protect a woman citizen" from a suspicious character—from the sort of person like me who waits out in front of grocery stores casing the joint "'round midnight." Back in the 1960s there were two competing versions of the police. One version said, "*The police are a force to serve and protect you.*" Bumper stickers with that slogan were pasted on cars all over the country. Contrarily, there was another set of bumper stickers, disproportionately seen in the black communities of the nation, which read, "*The police are an occupation force.*" In America, depending more on your race than anything else, you will routinely see this issue of police "occupation" or "service" through one lens or the other.

The concept of race has that complexity. Writers Noel Ignatiev, John Garvey, and David Roediger have discussed "the abolition of whiteness."[22] That is not a bad idea, depending on context and historical circumstances. However, it might not be a good idea either. That is, what would you say if suddenly after forty-eight to fifty years of apartheid, in which whites had begun to collect and accumulate lots of wealth—land—they suddenly turned around and said, "Let's abolish whiteness—now we're all individuals. Apartheid is over, so we'll all start from scratch. Let's have no group designation by color."

To many, this sounds like hollow rhetoric, more like the ideology of privilege in behalf of the accumulation of more privilege of those who take the position that one cannot simply decontextualize or ahistoricize the notion of race.

As the extreme case, let us take the current situation in South Africa. Whites spent the last half century (1947–93) creating and implementing laws that permitted themselves, as whites, to accumulate wealth and land and power, to have access to universities and corporate boardrooms, to have wages five to ten times that of black workers doing the same labor. Blacks had to carry identification cards in order to move out of legally enforced residences in squalid all-black townships and villages, where there was no running water, no sewage drainage, and underfunded and poor schools.[23] Then, in 1993, after forty-five years of official apartheid, white monopoly on access to good jobs and good education suddenly came to a *legal* end—but not before whites had accumulated more than ten times the wealth of blacks.

The new president, a black man imprisoned for twenty-seven of those years because of his opposition to apartheid, issued guidelines for trying to redress some of those past grievances. He and his cabinet would call for a plan of "affirmative action" to redress the following situation: In 1992, when the writing was on the wall and apartheid's days were numbered, the corporate managers at Telkom, South Africa's national telephone company, did a quick review of the racial composition of its corporate structure, an organization with more than 58,000 employees. In late 1993, they found one more black manager than many expected—that is, they found one. By the second half of 1995, Telkom employed eighty-three black managers and since then has embarked on an aggressive affirmative action program to recruit and hire more.

Would it then be imaginable that some groups of whites would step forward and cry foul? They already have. More than 5,000 white workers threatened to strike to protest the new policy.[24] The rhetoric regarding why affirmative action is morally wrong is rich in irony. "It's reverse discrimination," complained A. C. van Wyk, spokesman for the Mine Workers Union of South Africa, a union that still bars blacks from membership!

To illustrate the further abuses of the extraordinary manipulation of power through language, critics of affirmative action programs in South Africa that would place blacks in positions held exclusively by whites for the last half-century are now dubbing affirmative action "neo-apartheid." *The banner under which this all flies is fairness to the individual!*

Now let us imagine an even more unlikely circumstance in which a group with 2,000 years of historic privilege, that has accumulated wealth and power as a consequence of havng been part of a group, then suddenly turns around and says, "From now on, we are only individuals." This might be the caste system of India. For more than 2,000 years, certain groups had access to literacy—indeed, were required by the caste system to be literate. And, by contrast, other groups were channeled into occupations that required differing skills, training, and education. Finally, some in this system were "outcastes"—literally outside the system and therefore "untouchable." If one inside the system touched one from the wrong category, ritual cleansing had to occur in order to rid oneself of the pollution created by this contact.

Ironically, the apartheid system in South Africa was officially beginning (1948) just one year after the caste system ended officially, formally and legally. But just because the laws ended the caste system, 2,000 years of habit, pattern, ideology, *and privilege* could not be brought to a sudden halt. The caste system prohibited the lowest castes from drawing water from the same wells or from walking down the same paths; and, most relevant to today's debates about individual fairness, the children were forbidden to go to schools—any schools.[25]

The government of India embarked on a program to redress these past exclusionary policies, and much later that policy would be renamed affirmative action. Scheduled castes were to be provided with at least 12.5 percent of vacancies in government positions where there was to be open recruitment across the nation.[26] Not only were places in the workforce set aside for occupancy by members of the scheduled castes; places in universities and in law schools were also set aside for formerly disenfranchised groups. In 1961, after a review of the situation, the figure was raised from 12.5 to 15 percent set-asides.[27] By 1990 the government actually set aside more than twenty percent of jobs that it controls for the scheduled castes and scheduled tribes. It would be difficult to guess what the Brahmans argued. They called the plan "reverse discrimination" and said that it would hurt their chances of finding work after graduation.[28] They argued that to use any group criterion would not be fair to those individual Brahmans who had studied hard and gotten better grades than students from the lower castes. No matter that the Brahmans were the group required to be literate so that they could avail themselves of the sacred books. No matter. After all those centuries of accumulation of cultural capital that came directly from membership in a group category, many of them took to the streets to demonstrate and riot, arguing that the caste system was dead and gone . . . that from now on, they were only individuals . . . that, in short, only individuals without any significant remnants of caste privilege remained in India. Suddenly, after more than 2,000 years of the caste system, and familial access routes to privilege afforded to individuals because of their membership in a group, now nothing remained but *objective* grade-point averages.

Both the Brahmans and the white South Africans who oppose policies to partially redress gross injustices that favored their group can retreat to a comfortable position of personal nonculpability: since "I didn't personally discriminate against anybody, I can't be blamed for apartheid (or caste stratification), and so I should not be penalized for something I didn't do." And with that marvelously simple sleight-of-hand, Brahmans in India and white South Africans can wash their hands of any taint of privilege that they experience for having been born to a position of enormous social and economic advantage. Indeed, since there are only individuals, and individual responsibility and individual entitlement are the only currency in the contemporary discourse about race policies and affirmative action policies—not having had a personal hand in the oppression of others makes one innocent. The mere fact that one is from a group that has accumulated wealth at a ratio of more than ten to one over the capital of another group is rendered irrelevant by the legerdemain of invoking individual fairness. We are all individuals, but we are also simultaneously members of families, nation-states, racial and/or ethnically designated groups, and sometimes religious groups. "Fairness to the individual" must always have a social and historical context; when that context is ignored, it is a cheap political trick in the service of the ideology of those in power.

In the United States significant wage and salary differences between the races persist, with blacks earning anywhere from about two-thirds to three-quarters of what whites obtain in wages and salaries.[29] Since this gap has narrowed somewhat over the last three decades, analysts who wish to portray the situation as one of a slow improvement inevitably focus on these figures. *However, focusing merely on wages and salary differences obscures a critical measure of wealth: net worth.* Wages and salaries are dependent on employment, and in the current economic situation of the United States there is far less job security than in previous periods. A combination of massive downsizing and layoffs, along with seasonal and part-time employment, characterizes much of the contemporary work setting. Different spheres of work are more likely to employ whites than blacks. For example, blacks are more likely to be employed in the public sector, the focus of systemic and often effective attacks by conservatives for the last decade and a half. All of this means that wages and salaries are not the most secure measures by which to assess the likelihood of sustained socioeconomic improvement and long-term wealth.

At the end of the more than 2,000 years of the official caste system of India, caste law was struck down in the late 1940s, and "all of a sudden" all Indians had equal "formal" legal status. And, of course, what happened was predictable: those groups that had accumulated privilege based on the accumulation of all those years would turn around and say, "We're only individuals." Such a framing of the problem is transparently in the service of the perpetuation of privilege and power. The deck, in short, is stacked when, after systematic accumulation of wealth based on group membership, laws are suddenly passed that have the surface appearance of applying to all. It brings to life Anatole France's famous line, "The law, in its majestic neutrality, forbids both rich and poor from sleeping under bridges at night, begging and stealing bread."

In a society that is racially stratified, the claim that individualistic universalism is the best way to end race or racism—that we should all become color-blind—is itself a not so subtle denial that race has produced deeply consequential structural privilege. But, of course, all whites are not equally privileged. Many do not experience material privilege, and they certainly do not feel it.

Race in its Solid State

Why study whiteness at this historical moment? What has happened in the last twenty, thirty years in America to generate a remarkable surge of interest in this topic? Several developments help explain it, but one important element is a demographic shift in the urban landscape.

In the last twenty-five years, cities in the United States have undergone the greatest racial transformation of their entire history. In the 1970s almost every major metropolitan area—certainly the top twelve—were primarily white ("Anglo" by those classifications). By 1990, however, the census revealed that of those top twelve, ten now had majority "minority" populations. Indeed, in some jurisdictions, most notably Los Angeles, the ratio had gone from 75 percent white to about 37 percent white. In New York City we witnessed a similar kind of transformation, and that shift was occurring all over the country.

During this period, the white population—especially in urban America—began to experience its "whiteness." It began to feel marked by "race," and, once marked, there's something to observe, to study, and to account for. The need to deny "white flight to the suburbs" and the need to simultaneously deny the accumulation of wealth are reminiscent of the way elites of India and whites in postapartheid South Africa now face their worlds "as individuals." Yet most white Americans find it very hard to swallow that one should even mention these three countries in the same breath. Indeed, they are often offended.

In *Black Wealth, White Wealth,* Melvin L. Oliver and Thomas M. Shapiro show that net worth either entitles or precludes one from getting a loan to buy a home. The median net worth across the racial divides has been relatively stable over time. As noted earlier, the median net worth of white families in America is $43,279. For African Americans, median net worth is $4,169. To put it another way, whites in the United States have ten times the median wealth of African Americans. The metaphorical fluidity of race becomes a kind of frozen brick of ice when we understand and acknowledge that net worth is the primary measure of access to bank loans—whether for purchasing a house, starting up a business, purchasing a car, or getting the means to go to college or medical or law school. From this perspective, the bland figure of "net worth" has deeply structural consequences.

Whiteness and the Black-White Model of Race Relations

Another theme in this volume is that the black-white dialogue or paradigm dominates any discussion of race in America—to the near exclusion of a more complex set of relationships that must develop when there are a number of other racial and ethnic groups. We are inclined to rehearse and replay the same old duet—or pas de deux, if one prefers the dance metaphor. But if it is the dance, then it has more often than not been the *danse macabre* in white and black. But when there are only two parties in a "race relationship," then part of how one of the parties knows its own racial identity and boundaries is by knowing that "it" is not "the other"!

Especially in California there is certainly something deeply resonant to the critique that the black-white dialogue misses much of what is important about how "whiteness" plays itself out in different situations. The institution of slavery, which was mainly about white-black relations, frames much of the early part of the country's understandings of race. This occurred alongside the genocidal extermination of Native Americans. Once that was settled (that is, the effective extermination of Native Americans, their confinement to reservations, or their "assimilation"), slavery was the dominant institutional arrangement that shaped our legal structures.

At the Making and Unmaking of Whiteness conference, one of the audience participants said, "This is 1997. This is California. And California is clearly a place where one can be attentive to this multifaceted feature of race in America. Why not more representation of these issues on the various panels and in the many papers?" It is possible to defend the organizers. It is certainly true that we would have had a fuller portraiture of "whiteness" if we had talked more about the state and federally mandated exclusion of the Chinese at the turn of the last century. Or the discussions might well have incorporated a parallel discussion of the Japanese Gentleman's Agreement during this same period. And finally, in the middle of this century, of course, Japanese Americans were forced into concentration camps during World War II. But whenever there is a decision to include a finite number of topics in the short space of two or three days, there are always tough choices of what to emphasize.

There are very strong empirical and theoretical reasons for bringing into this black-white duet more the notion of the third party, the trio, and then the quartet and whatever number there are on the dance floor. Once we change the number, the dance has to change, too. And California has seen a new political alignment based on its peculiar configuration of ethnic and racial groups.[30]

Once we take a closer look at how whiteness gets configured and then reconfigured when there are more than two or three or four groups, the theoretical insights of looking at "whiteness construction as a process" will be more fully illuminated. Remarking on the historically situated, contingent, fluid character of whiteness, Ron Takaki has reported on how Armenians "became white" in the first part of this century in California. This in turn helps explain why Armenians could get housing loans—that is, build equity and gain later leverage to positions of power (like governor of the state). Ian Haney Lopez chronicles the same kind of emergent development of Armenian transformation into whiteness—with case law.[31]

Some of the students who organized this conference have been involved directly in the study of whiteness as a relationship, and that is where the most promising work is likely to develop. We cannot study whiteness in any meaningful way unless or until one sees it as a relational phenomenon. Pamela Perry has completed research in two high schools, taking a look at how white students in a multiethnic environment deal with issues of identity around their whiteness. Because it is California, she describes and analyzes how new Asian immigrants are having to deal creatively with a prefabricated and binary world dominated by notions of whiteness and blackness. Perry chronicles an emergent configuration at the "borderlands," where many of these students are making complex choices—but moving back and forth, navigating "multiple identities," and giving new meaning and substance to the fluidity of ethnicity and race.[32]

Perry reports that some of these Asian American high school students (often second-generation immigrants), chose to adopt a version of the dress style, the language style, and the consumer style of blacks. Others choose the style of suburban whites. In the "borderlands" there will be other developments—not simply this notion that there is a black or white style and the conflict that ensues.[33] Rather, there will be emergent phenomena that will reshape how people think about their whiteness, their Asian-ness, their Latino-ness, their blackness, their American-ness.

Some of our best research is being done, I think, by writers attentive to the borderlands, addressing and analyzing the contingent, fluid character of whiteness: *how the nature and shape of "whiteness" can change nature and shape (morph!) and yet remain structurally privileged.* Here, the cultural studies critique is most powerful and most able to inform us about what I call the "fluid and evaporating state" of race.[34] But we should not be fooled into the belief that fluidity substitutes for structure. This is simply a matter of when you take the picture. Recall that vapor can condense; and once back in a fluid state, it can freeze. So it is a fundamental mistake to think that, because we have seen this evaporating condition with our own eyes, it is gone forever and that the use of race will no longer be a powerful stratifying practice in America.

For all the brimming insights of cultural studies around race, a strong caveat is in order. There is a tendency to see *only fluidity* or at least to so emphasize fluidity that one lacks the capacity to see enduring structure. Well, my story about Jack Doyle and the Chicago police says that under certain conditions, things can change dramatically, in the moment, if only momentarily.

I want to end with another story. I was reminded of it by David Roediger, who has written that blacks have been studying whites for a long time and thus have a particular set of insights about "whiteness" that the current vogue of new studies would do well to mine. Indeed, African Americans have been engaged in white studies for at least three centuries. It is a necessity, if one is without formal power, to be attentive and especially alert to power relationships.

I have been a member of the National Advisory Commission for the Human Genome Project's ethical-legal-social issues program. Consequently, I had the occasion to attend meetings at Cold Springs Harbor, New York. As at Northwestern University many years ago, I am often one of a very few African Americans present in a scholarly setting.

The site is in a somewhat remote location—a long distance from New York City—and there is no easy public transportation. One deplanes at JFK Airport, and typically one takes a waiting limousine. I get off the plane, go out to the curb, and find this big, stylish limousine indeed waiting for me. The driver is working-class white male by appearance. He greets me with a kind of heartiness and takes my bags, says, "Cold Spring Harbor, sir?" I say, "Yes," and hop in.

But we can't quite get out onto the main exit because of all the traffic, and the person who is sort of directing traffic and guiding things is not very official-looking. He is wearing street clothes and about thirty-five-years-old. This is an African American male, and his gestures and his movements are, to put it mildly, unorthodox. He gives the strong impression that he is self-appointed to this task. The driver of the limousine is waiting patiently to be told when it is okay to move. (To give the story the proper frame, I would say that this particular person directing traffic was being quite creative and sometimes not very responsible.)

On two occasions, he appears to wave my driver on, then quickly changes his mind and says, "Oops!" Finally, he definitively tells my driver, "Pull out right now!" Then another car seems to come from out of nowhere and nearly bends our fender, and my driver says, "Dumb nigger!"

There are about twelve seconds of silence. I do not break it. Finally, he says, "I'm sorry. I'm terribly sorry," and begins to mumble something. I say, "I understand." And for a moment his shoulders seem to relax, and then I say, "I understand how you must feel in this situation." The rest of the ride was in total silence. Ice. What had evaporated and transformed into choreographed class relations had recondensed into race relations.

Notes

1   The pencil-test is only the latest methodology for precision that I discovered recently on a trip to South Africa. During the apartheid era, only "coloureds" could work in Capetown. So whether one was classified as black or coloured had important consequences for one's livelihood. Thus, some "blacks" would apply to have their status changed from black to coloured. The apartheid regime devised a pencil test to make the classification definitive. Applicants were told to place a pencil in their hair. If, when they were told to "shake their head," the pencil fell out, they were classified as "coloured"—but they remained black if the pencil was not easily dislodged by a shaking motion.

2   Alleles are different versions of one gene. For example, while the "generic gene" will instruct the proteins and cells to make an eye, a particular allele variation may produce a blue or brown or grayish-green eye. The same for epicanthic fold (or lack of it) over the eye, hair texture, skin color, and a wide band of human physiognomy. When researchers try to make guesses about which group a person belongs to, they look at variation at several different spots, usually six or seven. What is being assessed is the frequency of genetic variation at a particular spot in the DNA in each population. They are not necessarily looking at genes they may instead be looking at genetic variation in noncoding DNA. Occasionally, these researchers find a locus where one of the populations being observed and measured has, let's call them for example, alleles H, I, and J and another population has alleles H, I, and K. We know that there are alleles that are found

primarily among subpopulations of North American Indians. When comparing a group of North American Indians with a group of Finnish people,
one might find a single allele that was present in some Indians but in no
Finns (or it's at such a low frequency in the Finns that it is rarely, if ever,
seen). However, it is important to note and reiterate again and again that
this does not mean that all North American Indians, even in this sub-
population, will have that allele. See Stephen Molnar, *Human Variation:
Races, Types, and Ethnic Groups,* 3d ed. (Englewood Cliffs, N.J.: Prentice-
Hall, 1992).

3   The perils of "driving while black" have made it into the houses of several
state legislatures already. In California, the state assembly considered such
a bill in 1998. At the federal level, in March 1999 Attorney General Janet
Reno called for an investigation of "profiling" possible suspects by using
race.

4   See S. H. Katz, "Is Race a Legitimate Concept for Science?" in *The AAPA
Revised Statement on Race: A Brief Analysis and Commentary* (Philadelphia:
University of Pennsylvania, 1995).

5   In addition to Molnar, *Human Variation,* see Anthony P. Polednak, *Racial
and Ethnic Differences in Disease* (New York: Oxford University Press,
1969); A. H. Bittles and D. F. Roberts, eds., *Minority Populations: Genetics,
Demography and Health* (London: Macmillan, 1992); Malcolm Chapman,
ed., *Social and Biological Aspects of Ethnicity* (New York: Oxford University
Press, 1993); and Pat Shipman, *The Evolution of Racism: Human Differences
and the Use and Abuse of Science* (New York: Simon and Schuster, 1994).

6   For the discussion in this paragraph and for the references to the German
literature that are cited below, I am indebted to William H. Schneider, a
historian at the University of Indiana.

7   For examples, see Max Gundel, "Einige Beobachtungen bei der Rassenbiologischen Durchforschung Schleswig-Holsteins," *Klinische Wochenschrift* 5 (1926): 1186, and G. A. Schusterov, "Isohaemoagglutinierende
Eigenschaften des Menschlichen Blutes nach den Ergebnissen einer Untersuchung an Straflingen des Reformatoriums (Arbeitshauses) zu Omsk,"
Moskovskii Meditsinksii Jurnal 1 (1927): 1–6.

8   First published in 1944, Felix Kaufmann's *Methodology of the Social Sciences* (New York: Humanities Press, 1958) was one of the key works that
was later developed into a more systematic rendition of the problem of
first and second order constructs by Alfred Schutz, "Common Sense and
Scientific Interpretation of Human Action," in Maurice Natanson, ed.,
Collected Papers I: The Problem of Social Reality (The Hague: Martinus
Nijhoff, 1973), 3–47.

9   Molnar, *Human Variation,* 72–79.

10 Troy Duster, *Backdoor to Eugenics* (New York: Routledge, 1990), 89–92.

11 See Melbourne Tapper, *In the Blood: Sickle Cell Anemia and the Politics of Race* (Philadelphia: University of Pennsylvania Press, 1999).

12 I refer primarily to Jill Quadagno, *The Color of Welfare* (New York: Oxford University Press, 1994); Douglas Massey and Nancy Denton, *American Apartheid: Segregation and the Making of the Underclass* (Cambridge, Mass.: Harvard University Press, 1993); and Kenneth O'Reilly, *Nixon's Piano: Presidents and Racial Politics from Washington to Clinton* (New York: Free Press, 1995). There were, of course, earlier analysts who described parts of the picture. For example, Charles Abrams, writing in the 1950s and 1960s, had documented how the Federal Housing Authority's policies were explicitly racist. See his essay "The Housing Problem and the Negro" in *The Negro American,* ed. T. Parsons and K. Clark (Boston: Houghton Mifflin, 1966), 512–24.

13 Quadagno, *Color of Welfare,* 21.

14 The CIO was far more receptive to blacks than the AFL, but complete racial exclusionary practices in many CIO locals continued well into the 1970s.

15 Quadagno, *Color of Welfare,* 23.

16 Quoted in Abrams, "The Housing Problem and the Negro," 523.

17 Literally, those authorized to make loans at banks would draw on a map a red line around a black community, and no one inside that red line could get a loan. Until 1949 the FHA also encouraged the use of restrictive covenants banning African Americans from given neighborhoods and refused to insure mortgages in integrated neighborhoods. Thanks to the FHA, no bank would insure loans in the ghetto, and few African Americans could live outside it. See Quadagno, *Color of Welfare* 24–25, and Massey and Denton, *American Apartheid.*

18 See Richard J. Herrnstein and Charles Murray, *The Bell Curve: Intelligence and Class Structure in American Life* (New York: Free Press, 1994); James Q. Wilson and Richard Herrnstein, *Crime and Human Nature* (New York: Simon and Schuster, 1985); and Arthur R. Jensen, "How Much Can We Boost IQ and Scholastic Achievement?" *Harvard Educational Review* (winter 1969): 1–123.

19 Herrnstein and Murray, *Bell Curve,* 105.

20 Ronald M. Harris-Warrick and Eve Marder, "Modulation of Neural Networks for Behavior," *Annual Review of Neuroscience* 14 (1991): 41.

21 Many of my colleagues will recognize the phenomenon that I am describing. Over coffee, over dinner, we will hear a textured version of the complexity of what we know about race. But the very next day, from the public stage, we hear (and speak of) a more singular and unidimensional characterization of scholarly work and empirical results of research.

22 Noel Ignatiev and John Garvey, eds., *Race Traitor* (New York: Routledge, 1996), and David R. Roediger, *Towards the Abolition of Whiteness: Essays on Race, Politics, and Working Class History* (New York: Verso, 1994).

23 In fact, black miners in South Africa, during apartheid, worked for one-tenth the wage of white workers. For more on wage differentials, see George M. Fredrickson, *Black Liberation: A Comparative History of Black Ideologies in the United States and South Africa* (New York: Oxford University Press, 1995).

24 Bob Drogin, "South Africa's Hot Issue—Affirmative Action," *San Francisco Chronicle*, 22 August 1995.

25 Frederick G. Bailey, *Tribe, Caste and Nation: A Study of Political Activity and Political Change in Highland Orissa* (Manchester: Manchester University Press, 1960).

26 The term "scheduled caste" was first used by the Simon Commission and then embodied in the Government of India Act of 1935. Until this time, the term "untouchables" was used. Gandhi renamed these groups "Harijans," but many resented and rejected the name. After 1938, the word "Harijan" was officially replaced by the government with the term "scheduled castes," which has been in place as the formal term ever since. Of course, in the population at large, the terms "Harijan" and "untouchables" are in various locations still used. See B. D. Purohit and S. D. Purohit, *Handbook of Reservation for Scheduled Castes and Scheduled Tribes, on the Matters concerning Employment, Education, and Election* (New Delhi: Jainsons Publications, 1990).

27 There was an exemption for jobs classified as scientific and technical. While this classification has been the source of some contention as to which jobs apply, it is not a matter that bears substantially on the current attack on affirmative action in India. See Purohit and Purohit, *Handbook*, and *Brochure on Reservation for Scheduled Castes, Scheduled Tribes, and other Categories of Backward Classes in Services and Posts* (Bangalore, India: Department of Personnel and Administrative Reforms, Government of Karnataka, 1987).

28 "Students in India Riot over Favored-Job Plan for Backward Castes," *Oakland Tribune*, 25 August 1990.

29 Melvin L. Oliver and Thomas M. Shapiro, *Black Wealth/White Wealth: A New Perspective on Racial Inequality* (New York: Routledge, 1995).

30 It has permitted, for example, the manipulation of sentiment around matters of ethnicity and race that one could not even have thought about forty years ago. Asians, after all, are now 10 percent of the population in California; blacks are 7.5 percent; Latinos, upward of 27 or 28 percent. In that kind of mix, where African Americans are number four among the four "groups," the politics changes sharply. In my view, that is why California

was selected as the major site of the attack on affirmative action. It was seen by the Republican Party as a wonderfully propitious circumstance. This is a position that is explored more extensively in my article "Individual Fairness, Group Preferences, and the California Strategy," in Robert Post and Michael Rogin, eds., *Race and Representation: Affirmative Action* (New York: Zone Books, 1998); originally published in *Representations* 55 (summer 1996): 41–58.

31 Ronald T. Takaki, *Strangers from a Different Shore: A History of Asian Americans* (Boston: Little, Brown, 1989), and Ian F. Haney López, *White by Law: The Legal Construction of Race* (New York: New York University Press, 1996).

32 Pamela Perry, "Beginning to See the White" (Ph.D. diss., University of California, Berkeley, 1998).

33 Thomas Kochman, *Black and White Styles in Conflict* (Chicago: University of Chicago Press, 1981).

34 See George Lipsitz, *The Possessive Investment in Whiteness: How White People Profit from Identity Politics* (Philadelphia: Temple University Press, 1998).

John Hartigan Jr.

"White Devils" Talk Back: What Antiracists Can Learn from Whites in Detroit

The study of whiteness is developing a critical momentum both within and outside academia; this is perhaps made clearest in the oft-expressed anxiety that "white studies" will soon become ensconced as something of a scholarly cottage industry. This ominous possibility features a scenario of well-established (white) academics consuming limited resources to maintain a circuit of self-aggrandizing conferences and publications.[1] The specter of "white studies" frames substantive concerns about the co-opting of activist impulses and marginalized voices that have tenuously combined to make whiteness a subject of serious analysis and deconstruction. But I think it also unfortunately preempts a necessary assessment of various apparent uncertainties over how whiteness can and should be studied. Questions about audience (academic or activist), subjects (what ethics govern their treatment), methods (which disciplinary tactics are most effective), theories (whose and how many), as well as an overdue accounting of the class biases animating antiracist activists and theorists (why are working-class and poor whites disproportionately subject to analysis?), constitute an agenda so unwieldy that concerns over the institutionalization of the various projects that fall under the cover of "studying whiteness" seem a bit overstated.

I am more concerned by a consensus emerging from the disparate projects taking white people as their subject of study, one that ratifies whiteness as a clearly delineated ideological object. That is, I think the problem is more the developing sense of confidence that we know what it is we are studying. This confidence masks a host of assumptions about "proper" (class) conduct in the public sphere, the operation of power in civic conflicts, and the absolute nature of the hegemonic status of white people in this country. The political and ethical imperatives that compelled us to objectify the cogent but occulted forces shaping the terrain of racial inequality have been adequately served to date; now some reflection is warranted on what has been overlooked, distorted, and disregarded in the process.

I was provoked to engage in such reflections during the course of conducting ethnographic fieldwork in Detroit, Michigan. The conditions of whites in this city—a mere 22 percent of the population in a city that is 77 percent black—are so diverse that I was unable to discern a common unifying ideology among them, such as whiteness. Indeed, the widely trumpeted assertion that whiteness is an unmarked and normative identity often seemed laughable in Detroit. The lives of white Detroiters disrupt as much as they confirm generalizations about whiteness and its operation, maintenance, and reproduction. Which is not to say that their distinct situations discount an overarching attention to whiteness as a position of power and privilege; rather, the ludicrousness of rendering them as a homogeneous subject prompts a consideration of how the specificity of these whites' lives can be accounted for in conjunction with an understanding of why and how whiteness matters.

Rather than simply reiterating my findings, this essay pursues two objectives in relation to my fieldwork in Detroit.[2] The first is to discuss epistemological and methodological issues raised by applying an ethnographic perspective to the subject of whiteness; the second is to relate particular insights I garnered from observing white Detroiters grappling with the significance of race in their daily lives, within their neighborhoods and the city at large. These two discussions derive from a recognition that racial identities are locally constituted, following place-specific dynamics that are informed by class positions.[3] And they each are linked in a more general assertion that the racial thinking and actions of white people needs to be analyzed in relation to generic conceptions of "race," rather than via a studious delineation of whiteness (as opposed to blackness) as a unique cultural construction.[4] In the course of providing a glimpse into the lives of white Detroiters, this essay develops a rumination on how their situations provide a basis for examining more abstract issues, such as the contentious matter of the linkages between class and race.

My fieldwork in Detroit deployed a comparative class perspective on whites in three neighborhoods. I based my study in an underclass neighborhood near the city's downtown, where well over half of the predominantly white residents lived below the poverty line. I contextualized this setting by additionally studying an adjacent area neighborhood that was debatably undergoing gentrification and a middle- and working-class community bordering one of Detroit's suburbs. Both of these communities were also predominantly white. I was interested in how class shapes the way whites identify racially. I found whites' perceptions and projections of racial identity and difference contoured by the class-specific concerns active in each neighborhood and that intraracial distinctions among whites, according to issues of class belonging and status, informed their judgments of when situations, exchanges, or conflicts were "racial." But I also observed that in these settings whites are subject to the ambiguities, misperceptions, and confusions that generally constitute "racial" conditions. This is not to suggest that these whites endure the *same* kinds of inequality and disadvantages as their black neighbors or African Americans generally. But this situation does neatly frame the way the significance of race in this country is mutating rapidly, responding in divergent manners to unique regional and local transformations. The terrain where these transformations are most tangible—and where the political perils of this tricky matter are most effectively rendered and negotiated—is the realm of everyday life, a setting that the ethnographic approach brings most sharply into view.

Ethnography privileges an attention to everyday life and to peoples' efforts—often inchoate, contradictory, and ambivalent—to interpret the flux of experience and the stratifying social forms that constitute their existence. In the form of means for generating "data" from stories, gossip, and conversations, as well as modes for observing the interplay of spatial arrangements and social interactions, ritual codification or contestation of collective meanings and symbols, and the implicit or unconscious forms for maintaining and naturalizing social order, methods of ethnography have begun to migrate productively to other academic disciplines. As well, some of these have been adopted by antiracist activists as effective means of objectifying the occulted operation of racist judgments and racialist thinking among whites.[5] But key presumptions guiding anthropologists' uses of ethnography have not accompanied these methods in their disparate migrations. Most critical of these is the recognition that the specificity of people's lives exceeds what can be generally posited about their conditions;

indeed, the particulars of everyday life in locales are the basis for revising and rethinking theoretical generalizations about society and humanity. Culture is fashioned in response to local conditions; its content often contested or debated, by heterogeneous collectives. This view of culture quickly dissolves when academics wield such grand abstractions as "race" and "class."

Over the course of my fieldwork in Detroit, I moved away from regarding class in terms of abstract formulations—either as "relations to the means of production" or status and stratification—and began to recognize it as a pervading texture of daily life, patterning distinctions that shape people's thoughts, comments, and actions.[6] As well, in analyzing these settings, I came to see class as a set of expectations or assumptions, predetermined positions for explaining and under-standing the actions of whites—indeed, delimiting in advance who could properly be subjected to this form of social analysis. Given the limits of this essay, I will only develop this point in relation to one of the three sites: the middle- and working-class neighborhood, Warren-dale. Emphasizing this site allows me to convey in detail the class biases that inform the discussion of race and social commentary on racial conflicts, as well as to depict how class textures the terrain that whites inhabit, grounding their perceptions of how race matters, both to themselves and to peoples of color. My purpose here is not to argue that class is more fundamental than race; rather, I aim to convey the classed assumptions that contour the recognition of what counts as "racial" in social discourse in the United States. These assumptions are most evident in the economy of examples that brings images of "racists" to middle-class white Americans.

Why are the most familiar and oft-used images of white racists drawn from the working class or the lives of poor whites? Is this because these people are more racist than other whites, or is it, rather, that most whites are comforted by the notion that racism is located in the lower economic orders? Both possibilities highlight the near con-stant linkage between "ignorance" and racism, an association that continues to limit the recognition by middle-class whites—who regard themselves as more sophisticated in their thoughts, deeds, and gen-eral comportment—of the racism and privileges of race that animate their daily lives. The most commonly circulated media representa-tions of white racism are accompanied by a fairly invariable set of adjectives ("mean," "brutal," "ugly," and "villainous acts")[7] that suggest a class sensibility or aesthetic at work in whites' consciousness of racism. Middle-class decorum is offended by racists perhaps as much because their offenses rupture social etiquette—being "angry" and "loud" (that is, vulgar)—as it is by the evidence of intolerance and racial bias. Since racial inequality is perpetuated in this country precisely in the realms that poor and working-class whites have little control over—housing, access to medical care and higher education, and employment—it is necessary to question why the pool of collective imagery of racists is disproportionately drawn from the lower white social ranks. One way to begin is by listening closely to the comments of working-class whites who have been caught up in such objectification, as were whites in the Warrendale neighborhood of Detroit.

In addition to my interest in developing a comparative perspective on class communities, I was drawn to interview residents in Warrendale because of a dispute that broke out there in the summer of 1992, when the Detroit Board of Education decided to reopen a previously closed school building (formerly Leslie Elementary) in this 80 percent white community. The school was renamed the Malcolm X Academy and featured an Afrocentric curriculum. Whites in this neighborhood were furious over this move for a number of reasons: some had repeatedly inquired about getting the school reopened because of overcrowding at George Washington Carver (the remaining area elementary school) and had been informed that the Detroit Public Schools did not have available funds to reopen that school; many residents were upset about the Academy's name and were concerned that the curriculum promoted race hatred; others were furious over the lack of input asked of residents on the matter, or the fact that they had not been informed regarding the school board's plans; then there were people who were deeply disturbed at the thought of black children being bused into the neighborhood. Some white residents expressed a fear that the Academy would lead to a rise in crime in the area. This cluster of concerns, however, was easily reduced to sound bites and stock footage of loud whites expressing fear or anger toward black children.

Media coverage transformed this array of concerns into a spectacle of white racism, one that greatly shocked Detroiters. The formal elements of the controversy were simple and sparse: an informational meeting hosted by the superintendent of the Detroit Public Schools, which turned rancorous; then a series of small demonstrations around the Academy organized alternately by opponents or supporters of the school. The Academy opened without incident and operated for two years in Warrendale, eventually moving to another location, in part because school officials alleged that a pattern of vandalism against the building was being perpetrated by unknown assailants. It never amounted to a serious political battle, partly because there was never a broad-based, unifying protest by Warrendale residents, but also because the board of education was in complete control of the process. But journalists and editors remained interested because residents were so animated in their objections to the school and its Afrocentric curriculum. Talk show hosts Sally Jessie Raphael, Jerry Springer, and Montel Williams were also drawn to this spectacle that briefly blipped across the fleeting news consciousness of the nation.[8] White opponents of the Academy initially regarded the media as their only means for articulating a position in this dispute, but they soon recognized that their statements only amounted to evidence of white racism, edited to fit the interests of this coverage.

The comments that were reported all revolved around a tight core of racial concern and fear. White supporters and opponents of the Academy alike grew increasingly frustrated at their inability to control the mediums through which they were objectified and their interests reduced to caricatures. Supporters unsuccessfully tried to draw media coverage for their rallies against racism held outside of the school; these events were apparently not considered as newsworthy as potentially violent "racist" protests. While opponents of the school complained to me about being portrayed as racists, they were more distressed that the array of issues generated in this controversy were so incessantly distilled as being all and only about race. Whites in Warrendale were upset not simply about how they were depicted or how their neighborhood was portrayed, but because of the severely delimited means by which complicated social and cultural issues involving race were rendered through the media.

Their frustrations were as multilayered as the forms of mediation delimiting the coverage of the controversy over the Malcolm X Academy to a simple narrative of white racism. The coverage of this conflict deployed two interpretive frames: one editorial and the other explanatory. The first derived from a tendency by commentators to render whites' statements as "really" or entirely about race. This framing was prompted, in part, by a series of signs that trigger such reductive assessments, elements that seemed to be transparent indicators of "racism," such as the emotional intensity of residents and their "blue-collar" trappings and mannerisms. However, this reductive process also reflected the inevitable distortions of editing techniques required to generate a highly time-sensitive commodity (news) for the widest possible dissemination and consumption. I raise this matter, though, because it bears an interesting correspondence with the way academics and antiracist activists generally regard or analyze the comments of working-class whites—with a conviction that they conceal or contain racists sentiments, which must be rendered or drawn out clearly for all to see.

The second feature, the invocation of an explanatory frame, seemed to stem from assumptions about the state of race relations in the country at large. Much like academics who stress historical determination in explaining the operation of whiteness, commentators on the Malcolm X Academy controversy emphasized the precedent of such conflicts in other white working-class communities to make sense of Warrendale. They decided that the points of resonance with historical defenses of white neighborhoods were more telling than the novel aspects of this dispute, such as the claim by white opponents that the board of education was attempting to "resegregate" black children, subjecting them to a "separatist" curriculum. White residents commonly criticized the incessant comparisons drawn in the media between Warrendale and Little Rock, Arkansas, or other "blue-collar" communities where fierce contests over race and schools exploded. Generally, news commentary regarded this case as a primitive white backlash to black incursions into a white neighborhood. The story of the neighborhood's "racism" was conveyed through a form of temporal othering or distancing, similar to that described by Johannes Fabian in *Time and the Other*—opponents of the school were regarded as hold-outs from a time long past. This analysis, though, misses what is undeniably contemporary about such protests and disruptions, particularly in Detroit. Most notably, this was not a contest over integration or desegregation; rather, it was a clash that revealed the drastic disjuncture between two sets of assumptions: those held by black city and school officials in a system where 88 percent of the students are black and those held by whites in a neighborhood precariously perched between the city's crumbling core and the wealthy white suburbs. Whites in Warrendale maintained ambivalent and at times contradictory understandings of race and racial matters; the ambiguity of their positions, though, were usually effaced by the interests of observers in making this racial situation "fit" the historical precedent of radical white defense of neighborhoods and schools.[9]

What opponents of the Academy could never quite manage to speak about was the fact of their racialness, which formed a signifying background that surmounted the nuances of their "personal opinions" or "experiences." As whites upset over a black school in their predominantly white neighborhood, they found their actions, comments, and emotions read immediately as racially significant. Their class position encouraged this reading. In their talk, bodies, and perceptions, these whites evidenced a fairly obvious class conditioning: their articulations were not sophisticated, nor, largely, were they adept at manipulating the supposedly neutral apparatuses of bureaucratic power and political office.[10] They looked uncomfortable and spoke awkwardly on television, and their comments resonated with a historical continuum of "blue-collar" racism.[11] It was hard for observers to believe that the intense emotion generated by these frustrations was not racial in nature, that it was not spawned by a seething core of racial hatred and anxiety. Rather than serving as an index of their relative lack of power in this situation, their emotions—distilled into ugly images on the evening news—stigmatized these whites, both in the city at large and within Warrendale.

These whites encountered an overdetermined discursive terrain when they tried to speak about these matters; their concerns, already emotionally laden and resonating with historical images of violent defenses of white supremacy, were authoritatively rendered as "racist" by the calm, objective voices of black school officials. Interestingly, the comments by black representatives of the Academy or the board of education achieved a racially unmarked status.[12] While opponents of the Academy tried to turn reporters' and residents' attention to the Afrocentric curriculum and the explicit stress it laid on racial identity, the "blackness" of the school and those associated with it remained literally unremarkable. More than just a reflection of the social and political order in Detroit, this was also a reflection of the professional status and authoritative positions of blacks involved with the Malcolm X Academy. Just as important, too, was their ability to speak apart from any attachment to place and maintain an air of cool bureaucratic authority. It was this link with place—presented in the media by images of aluminum-sided tract housing and fervent residents worried over "crime" and "property values"—that demonstrated and delimited the significance of race; this link was carefully honed through editing and citation techniques that disturbed local white supporters of the school as much as its opponents.[13] When I talked with them about the Malcolm X Academy, they consistently turned to discussing the limits that seemed to operate on what they could say and what people could hear them saying.

These residents became astute readers of the mediated attention that used their neighborhood to convey a traditional story about race to an audience of metropolitan viewers. They particularly noticed how the "obvious" significance of their racialness supported a truncated attention to the way other predominantly white neighborhoods, either in Detroit or its suburbs, managed to stay "white." Warrendale was characterized in some media accounts as a "white enclave." Residents were upset by this designation and regarded it as a charge that their neighborhood was defensively segregated. In response, they pointed to the fact that blacks had been moving into Warrendale over the last decade and that the area was quietly but steadily integrating, despite appearances linked to protests over the Academy. They also perceptively challenged the way the significance of whiteness only seemed apparent in an interracial clash. They chastised editors over their inattention to the suburbs—areas that one resident characterized as "whiter than we are"—where residential segregation worked more subtly but more emphatically, where schools could remain predominantly white without drawing any attention to their maintenance of sharp racial boundaries. Warrendale whites were as bitter about the ability of suburban whites to elude such objectification as they were about the Academy. One white, who asserted that "the media is dominated by very liberal whites who live in the suburbs," articulately summarized this sense of bitterness: "What I resent about them is their racial hypocrisy. Here they are, living out in their lily-white suburbs, trying to find racists in Detroit. What they love to see is a kind of confirmation of who the white racists are. They love to expose their white racist brothers. But they can't find a racist person in their own neighborhood."

Opponents of the Academy were the keenest critics of the media; some kept scrapbooks of news clippings or videotaped television news stories that in the course of our interviews they used to criticize their objectifications. As they talked with me about their engagement in this controversy, they tried to discern how their multifaceted concerns and nuanced sensibilities regarding race were washed out in the rendering process that reduced them to brute "racists." They disputed the opening of the Malcolm X Academy for a variety of reasons, but they were commonly linked by having children in the Detroit Public Schools system. As well, many had attended Detroit schools in the late 1960s or 1970s, a period of intense violence as the student population shifted from majority-white to majority-black; they did not want their children to be caught in a repetition of their racial ordeals.[14] This sensibility placed them at a remove from older residents, many retired from jobs in auto plants or with the city. They were even further distanced from white neighbors by the circuits they traveled in as they challenged the propriety of the Afrocentric curriculum the Detroit Public Schools administration was planning to infuse on a system-wide basis. As they attended school board meetings—hearing the hiss of "white devil" from the audience when they tried to raise issues about the curriculum—listened to the "black talk shows" on the radio as guests and experts explained theories linking concentrations of melanin to black cultural and intellectual superiority, or read about plans for establishing the separatist, black nation that at least one school board member had openly advocated, they were left stammering, unable to convey to whites or blacks their interests and concerns in this matter.[15] The emotions generated by this predicament were intense and obvious, even though the intriguing social features were not; indeed, the significance of their emotional state (as a sure indicator of racist motivation) obliterated any attention to these particulars.

White opponents' emotionality stemmed from frustrations over the implicit class and racial contours to their discursive interpellation in this controversy. While for most observers this emotionality read as transparent signifiers of "white racism," opponents contextualized their emotional outbursts either as products of media manipulations or as signifying a broader set of concerns than pure racial motivation, such as their concerns over their children's place in the city's changing institutions.

Diana—a white woman with two children and a husband who worked as a machinist—pointed to an image of a Warrendale resident that had become part of the opening sequence of a local television news program. She was explaining how upset she and her neighbors were when antiracists from across the city began demonstrating at the school.

Diana: Like Sue, when she went after that lady when the pick-eting was going on. They keep showing her, Sue. She was screaming at that woman. They were holding a rally, an antiracism rally. And Sue, "It's not about racism!" And they, this woman kept baiting her and baiting her, until Sue just went nuts and the cameras went on, and here's this *screaming woman* [rage in Diana's own voice], you know, and that keeps being shown.

JH: What was she saying?

Diana: "It's not about race. It's not about race." "Yes it is or you wouldn't be so hostile! What are you getting so mad about? What are you getting so mad about?" And there's Sue, just screaming, you know.

Another opponent of the school—Jeff, who ran a lawn mowing ser-vice—related how journalists and others drawn into the spectacle of white racism were adept at manipulating residents' expressions.

Jeff: They'd just pull strings.

JH: How would they do that?

Jeff: Well, like when you're trying to make a point and every time you make that point they twist what you say and say, "Well, you mean this, this, this." And they do that three or four times and sure enough your blood pressure starts to rise. And then sure enough, then you start going "Raaarrr!!! Cannons! Get back."

In such instances, these whites felt themselves betrayed, on the one hand, by what they assumed to be an objective media and, on the other, by their own intense feelings of frustration, which held a singu-lar significance for observers. They could not speak about charged issues concerning their neighborhood without becoming loudly emo-tional. Hence, their racialness betrayed them as well and signified in a manner that proved to be beyond their control: if whites were this upset, it must be the expression of a throbbing core of hatred rather than an inability to express the complex stakes they perceived in this conflict. Emotional discourse, though, is an index of social relations; it reveals inequalities of status and power, usually cast in gendered terms but also following the invocation of class distinctions as well.[16] Speaking with and against educated professionals who could calmly manage their sentiments as well as the appearance of their racial interests, these whites grew increasingly frustrated.[17] Dramatically captured by television and sound crews, this emotionality seemed to prove "racism" was at the core of their concerns. But considered in a broader frame, as a function of a complexly coded struggle over limited resources, their emotions alternately convey the classed contours of this contest.

Kevin, who managed an auto parts store, like other residents who spoke with reporters, expressed frustration at how long, detailed discussions of residents' concerns, sometimes lasting more than an hour, were reduced to brief sound bites that, on reflection, seemed to have been carefully manipulated to fit prefabricated story lines about racism. He related the following in a group interview that also included Diana and another opponent of the Academy, Karen.

> *Kevin:* The first time I was on TV, when I told them that I'd tear the Malcolm X sign down if they put it up there, they interviewed me for fifteen minutes and talked to me about schools, and where my kids go to school, and all of this stuff. And the only thing they showed out of that fifteen minute interview . . . I mean, by this time, the guy's got me going and then he says, "What do you think of the name Malcolm X?" And I said, "I don't like it." Then he said, "Well what are you going to do about it?" *I said,* "If they put it up there, I'll tear it down!" That's the only thing they showed!

> *Diana:* That's what they showed.

> *Kevin:* To me, they were looking for that racism, they were looking for racism. On the Sally Jessie Raphael show, they were looking for racism. And the Jerry Springer show, they were looking for racism.

> *Karen:* That's why Montel Williams didn't . . . They had Montel Williams's director out here; she flew out here to talk to us when we were going around the school, and I guess our issues were too . . .

> *Diana:* It wasn't hot enough.

> *Karen:* Yeah. It wasn't hot enough. Wasn't inflammatory enough. Because we were really concerned about our kids. And that's what we're talking about, 900 kids [and overcrowding] at Carver. Now you tell me why this school only needs 400 kids in it when Carver has 900? [Carver had only two more classrooms than the Malcolm X Academy.]

Classroom sizes, requests to the school board, informational meetings—none of these matters are very photogenic. Joni Hodder, the producer of the Montel Williams show, frankly told the *Warrendale Press and Guide* that, rather than arguments over enrollment limits, "they wanted more heat."[18] Not finding sufficient "heat," they lost all interest in the dispute. Local reporters also found residents' concerns uninteresting when they were not explicitly focused on race. Nor did they find whites' assessments of black racial interests, as represented by the curriculum, worthy of coverage. White residents were unable to turn attention to what they felt was the main issue—the "separatist" or "racist" curriculum. As Karen put it, "The [black] children ain't the issue, it's what they're teaching in there. And the fact that they want it done with taxpayer's dollars. But, that issue has never been looked into by the media. That part's just glazed over and we're just a bunch of racists complaining about nothing."

But more than an inattentive or manipulative media bothered white opponents of the Academy. They were also frustrated by the dissembling on matters of race they observed among their white neighbors. Opponents discerned an anxiety among residents about discussing race at all. Kevin admitted to being emotional but also to feeling compelled to rupture an oppressive sense of decorum that gripped his white neighbors, whether or not they supported the Academy. "That's probably why I was the one picked to go on the first TV show, because I was the one standing out there, yelling and doing all of the talking. And everybody else would talk, but when it came time for them to talk to a producer of the show or a TV camera, people weren't saying . . . they were trying to say it too nice. And my opinion was, I'm not running for political office. Somebody isn't going to like what I say no matter how nice I say it. So too bad. Maybe it's because my heart was involved in it. This is a community I've been involved in all of my life."

Kevin's sense that other whites "were trying to say it too nice" underscores the perception that a prevailing decorum determined how racial matters could be articulated and addressed; he was provoked by other whites who wouldn't speak their mind, mumbling private concerns or saying nothing rather than engaging in public debate. But in breaking this decorum, "yelling and doing all the talking," he was drawn into the media production of emotional statements, demonstrating unalloyed "racism."

Opponents insisted that their white neighbors were fearful of being labeled as "racists," a term that they avidly tracked for the contours of power its application revealed in this contest. "Racist" was singularly fixed to those perceived to be defending a white working-class neighborhood against black incursions; the ruptures of an idealized middle-class decorum—a measured calmness or rational detachment ("civility") in matters of public debate—were evident in the loud, emotionally charged protests against the school.[19] "Racist" applied to any white who either opposed the opening of the Malcolm X Academy in the old Leslie Elementary building or raised contentious questions about the school's curriculum. The significance of race was so overdetermined in this spectacle that any white in Warrendale seemed susceptible to being marked by this epithet.[20] What proved most frustrating for whites opposing the Academy was that an attention to race was largely read as "racist." There seemed to be no neutral language, short of saying nothing at all, through which racial differences and interests could be framed and discussed. In this contest, as in many such public conflicts over limited civic resources, there was no more sophisticated set of terms for evaluating nuances of these racial matters than the caustic, charged designation of "racist."

When whites countered public invocations of "racism" or their designation as "racists," they did so by challenging the terms' policing of what forms of *race-talk* were permissible. White supporters, school officials, or commentators rarely elaborated a criterion for designating people as "racists," offering little elaboration and letting the charged accusation stand as self-evident. Virginia Dominguez describes a similar discursive dynamic in accusations of "racism" between Jews and non-Jews: "Accusers assume the transparency—the referential clarity—of racism. Those implicated by the accusation typically regarded it as political name calling—too vague to have semantic-referential value, too emotionally charged not to serve as a 'call to arms' more than a valid description/interpretation. 'Racism' is offered as an ac-cusation, and taken as one."[21] Indeed, whites opposed to the Academy came to regard "racist" as a rhetorical matter, as a form of name-calling that positioned them at a distinct disadvantage in these ex-changes. They responded in a variety of ways.

The most typical response I heard was to accept the designation rhetorically, admitting to being a racist but then further insisting that was not all they were nor was it the sum of their concerns. This type of response is best characterized in a comment by Jeff: "If they want to call me a racist because I say [the Academy is] separatist, or they want to call me a bigot because I say, 'Well doesn't anyone else see what is going on? They're resegregating our children,' and putting the facts out there, let 'em. If that's what they want to label me, if that's what it means to say these things, fine. Then I'm a racist bigot. But by my definition, a racist bigot is someone who looks at somebody's skin color and deals with him accordingly. I don't do that." Such a gesture acknowledges an inability to talk over the delimited frame of reference most observers brought to this dispute, but Jeff's formulation also attempts to diffuse the emotional charge of the accusation by accept-ing it as simply a form of name-calling.[22] Other whites made a similar acknowledgment more reflectively, admitting to the possibility that racism informed their thinking and actions—but with a key proviso: that "racist" not inscribe an essentialist divide between whites and blacks. As another Academy opponent, Joyce, admitted to me, "I think we're all racists, everybody. It's like poor people display it more than others, but everybody has a bit of racism in them. Everybody." While such an acknowledgment also works rhetorically to drain "racist" of its emotional charge, Joyce's gesture was aimed more precisely at the assertion that blacks could not be racist.

From a number of sources—predominantly a two-day workshop on racism sponsored by St. Thomas Aquinas, a local church that each of the whites quoted here had attended—the Academy opponents had been presented with the assertion that blacks, because of their gener-ally disadvantaged and disempowered status nationally, could not be racists. They easily spouted the definitional stance for me: racism is equated with power; without power—institutional, political, or social—a person, and blacks generally, could simply not be racists. They coun-tered this claim by pointing to the local political dominance blacks had achieved in the city but also to the characterizations of whites by school officials and promoters of Afrocentrism associated in some manner with the Detroit Public School system. Rather than argue categorically, they referred to specific statements made by blacks in the course of this dispute. These statements ran a gamut from what might be cast as "racial" to "racist." The Academy opponents pointed to comments by callers on the talk shows charging that "we have to keep the [city] council black" or shouts at a school board meeting that "we're the majority now. We'll do what we want," each of which condensed for them the impression that blacks would insist that power operate along racial lines rather than in a "color-blind" manner. But, primarily, they pointed to statements by advocates or promoters of the Afrocentric curriculum, such as characterizations of whites as "killing machines," "devils," and "ice people," or claims that melanin actually was a basis of black cultural and intellectual superiority. Such characterizations struck these whites as "racist."

Abstractly treating the designation of people as "racist" distorts rather than illuminates this controversy. Absolute definitions of racism, while useful and provocative, run up against the problem that the significance of race is too disparate to be emphatically determined in categorical judgments. While such judgments may be effective with certain groups of whites, they undercut the basis for serious engagements by antiracists who want to enlighten such whites as those in Warrendale, a point I will elaborate on below. Alastair Bonnett criticizes antiracists' conceptualization of "white racism" for relying on "a myth of Whiteness at the centre of their discourse. This myth views 'being White' as an immutable condition with clear and distinct moral attributes. These attributes often include: being racist; not experiencing racism; being an oppressor; not experiencing oppression; silencing; not being silenced."[23] It was exactly the projection of these attributes that most frustrated the opponents of the Academy because they ignored or dismissed their volatile, confusing experiences as whites in the public schools, of being objectified as "whites" by blacks and of having a precarious class position in the tumultuous setting of Detroit. The essentialist assertion that blacks cannot be racist stresses the institutional, financial, and political dominance of whites in this country—a dominance that is mobilized to maintain racial inequality. But this emphasis requires a leveling gaze and a uniform subject position that precludes an attention to class and economic discrepancies among whites, and it posits a simplistic view of "power" as being uniformly maintained and applied. This criticism is not a reassertion of the argument that race is reducible to class; rather, it questions the tendency to dismiss class altogether as the basis for the most powerful application of antiracist discourse.

The antiracist workshop in Warrendale further strengthened the convictions of opponents to the school, in part because the dogmatic stance on racism seemed absurd to them, but also because it revealed the broad gulf between antiracist whites and those who were engaged in an emotional struggle over civic resources. The subject of antiracism came up in the course of one of several group interviews I conducted with Warrendale residents who had initially opposed the opening of the Malcolm X Academy.

> *Diana:* It was a workshop on "What is racism"? and how do you deal with it.
>
> *JH:* So what were they asking you to do?
>
> *Diana:* Just to understand why racism exists.
>
> *Joyce:* In the mission statement they came up with at the first meeting, one of the statements was "to educate ourselves on racism" so . . .
>
> *Jeff:* Well, they were trying to tell us that since we're white, we're racist.
>
> *Diana:* And black people are not racist, they're . . .
>
> *Jeff:* And black people *cannot* be racist!

Their descriptions of exchanges in the workshop over readings disseminated by the facilitators—two white women, each with lengthy local histories of activism relating to racial conflicts—seemed obviously contoured by the contrast between people mired in a losing battle and the detachment of others who are trying to enlighten them with a broader view of their predicament. They complained that facilitators would not talk about the aspects of the controversy that mattered keenly to them—such as the Afrocentric curriculum, refusing to examine its implications and ramifications, preferring instead to inclusively treat it as an innocuous expression of multiculturalism. Indeed, a more telling characterization is revealed in their divergent relations to Afrocentric discourse, as is evident in the quote from Jeff below.

Long after the Academy's opening drowned out the local issues, the school's Afrocentric curriculum remained an elusive, haunting concern for these whites—elusive, because school officials were reticent on this question; haunting, because engaging this subject led them into a disorienting, powerful assemblage of racial imagery and narratives. Afrocentrism, a molten, formative array of assertions, claims, facts, and theories, more evocative than established, confronted white residents as a bewildering perspective, challenging, threatening, and certainly racializing "whites," whether or not they contested the Academy directly.[24] The dissonance generated between the antiracist perspective and the view of whites from Warrendale in the workshop centered on how "seriously" each regarded Afrocentric discourse and whether or not they were interpellated into its subject position for "whites."

Jeff: "They gave this handout . . . They were quoting [Na'im] Akbar, and they even had a section in there on melanin . . . St. Thomas Aquinas is our own church now!"

Joyce: And after the second meeting, Jeff brought her over some stuff to read to get her better informed about what's going on with these black people. You want to talk about them . . .

Jeff: She [one of the facilitators] didn't really want to hear anything about it. I asked her, "What do you know about this curriculum that you're teaching us about, and the way we're reacting? Do you know what they're preaching?" "Yeah they've got Kwanzaa." "Do you know what Kwanzaa is?" "Yeah it's a holiday. I've been to . . . [He mimics her voice]." "DO you know what it is? It's being taught in the schools. Do you know the religious implications, and the political implication behind it? Do you know anything about Maulana Karenga, the man who invented it, Kwanzaa?" I mean I went right down the line with her. OK. Are you familiar with the libation ceremony in Kwanzaa that's similar to partaking of communion in the Roman Catholic church? And they're doing this in our schools, except that the children are drinking out of what they call a Timbiko cup, with their dead ancestors. *In school!* Now that is a religious ceremony.

When I offered that I could see the connection he was drawing, Jeff sarcastically challenged, "No. That's your Eurocentric way of thinking. That's it."

As evidenced in this exchange, white opponents of the Academy were avid consumers of Afrocentric writings and pronouncements. Since they could not get their questions about the curriculum answered by school officials, they cast a broad net, which drew in a range of claims, assertions, and charges that certainly far exceeded the tenets of the curricular program being developed by the Detroit Public Schools. From one perspective, certainly, the catholic version of Afrocentrism they compiled was interested and perhaps naive. But I think that more significantly it reflects the fact that they were susceptible to interpellation into the "white devil" subject position in this discourse. While antiracist whites can regard Afrocentric tenets as a benign, balancing addition to multiculturalism, these whites found that the discourse conveyed a deeper reality, reflecting their predicaments as "whites" in this Detroit neighborhood. Their political incapacitation in this controversy seemed to herald an onrushing of the most racially apocalyptic versions of the future preached by Afrocentrists.

Bonnett asserts that antiracists must "become aware of, and escape from, the practice of treating Whiteness as a static, ahistorical, aspatial, objective 'thing': something set outside social change, something central and permanent, something that defines the 'other' but is not itself subject to others' definitions . . . a category which is not subject to the constant process of challenge and change that have characterised the history of other 'racial' names."[25] Both figuratively—in relation to Afrocentric discourse—and literally—via the establishment of "racist" as the definitive characterization of white opposition to the Malcolm X Academy—whites in Warrendale were subject to black objectifications of their interests and anxieties. Additionally, they were subjected to antiracist discourse that also reduced their multifaceted and emotional concerns to simple expressions of racism. Bonnett charges that the "essentialising dynamic" at the heart of the antiracist project, "lead[s] towards the positioning (or self-positioning) of White people as fundamentally outside, and untouched by, the contemporary controversies of 'racial' identity politics."[26] In Warrendale, and in Detroit generally, antiracism, as a political position, seems predisposed to disregard a dramatic shift in political power and in cultural matters and would not recognize these whites as mired in fundamen-

tally "racial" predicaments—trying to regain control of their identifying features, disoriented by the disjuncture between a projected social
identity (as whites) and personal experience, feeling the inadequate fit
of stereotyped depictions.

The model of whiteness most widely promoted by antiracists posits
a generic white subject, both privileged and unconscious of the extent
or operation of that privilege. This model perhaps pertains to the vast
majority of white Americans. But its explanatory power is diminished
for whites who are engaged in race-related disputes such as the conflict over the Malcolm X Academy, and its sweeping assertions are
seriously challenged by the process of racialization that whites are
subjected to in Detroit. Bonnett, drawing on the writings of Ali Rat-
tansi and Tariq Modood, asserts that "orthodox anti-racism appears ill-
equipped to engage creatively with the fluid and complex forces of the
racialisation process" because it is unprepared to acknowledge the
contradictions, inconsistencies, and ambivalences within white and
nonwhite identities.[27] Long before Afrocentric discourse was articulated, many of these whites had endured the harsh confusion of racial
animosity and antagonism. An analysis of the dynamics of their process of racialization requires a copious collection of biographical detail, for which there is no room in this essay. But I will draw this
discussion to a close with a story told to me by Karen. She grew
up four houses away from the Herman Garden Apartments, a low-
income housing project that was overwhelmingly African American.
It is an account that does not easily fit the narratives about whiteness
spun by antiracists.

> *Karen:* Well, for me, my problem started . . . Like I said, I went
> to Herman and grew up with black people and had no
> problem! Went to Ruddimen [Elementary], still mixed,
> 75/25, 75 black, no problem. Then busing started. Some-
> how, they scooped me up, me and two of my girlfriends
> and put us on a bus with all blacks and bused us to
> Lessenger, all white. And . . . all of my friends, that had
> been my friends since first grade . . . now I was "whitey."
> 'Cause they had such an attitude going to this new school.
> All the whites in this school were afraid 'cause they had
> never been around blacks. They didn't bother me, because
> I grew up with them. But then, now, see, I was in it. I've

seen my friends change, my black friends change. It was total aggression towards the white kids: Total!

JH: As soon as they got there?

Karen: It's like *"I'm superior, I'm gonna beat your ass!"* and they were going after whitey. And then, my girlfriends, and people that I had known for years . . . I got lumped in with the new white people even though I'm on the bus everyday with the people I grew up with. I'm now white! It's like, all of the sudden they woke up: "Karen Soper's White! Beat her ass!" But I wasn't a quiet person that was going to let you beat my ass. So I fought right back with them. And then they left me alone. But then, when I started meeting white people, I started hanging around with them. It wasn't that I didn't like the black friends anymore. So black friends turned on me! I was now white. I was one of them, I was the enemy. And I'd seen it; it wasn't all in my head. Y'know, you don't go home, people stomping on you for being in your head.

JH: Had you thought about being white before that?

Karen: Well, it's like I said, we just all hung around together, and it was a peaceful coexistence. I remember one fight with a black girl in first grade. Now, a lot of the other white girls were beat up daily because they would go home crying. Well I stood up to her, and me and her had a fight, and from that day on I never got bothered again. Now, I can't say that a lot of the other whites didn't get picked on, because a lot of 'em did, for their lunch money and stuff. But for me, personally, since I stood up, I was cool. I got along with them, so I didn't get beat up. But uh . . . so I never really noticed. I knew they were black. I'm not stupid. I knew they were black. But it didn't really seem to matter; it didn't really seem to matter. But somehow when we got to the white school, all at once it mattered. I was white and they didn't want to have anything to do with me after that. Everybody went [into] their own cliques then. It wasn't groups here and groups there. It was whites here and blacks there.

Other accounts like this one, about the experiences of Warrendale whites having been racialized in the shifting demographics of schools and neighborhoods throughout Detroit, led me to consider that my subject of study was the significance of white racialness, rather than the delineation of whiteness as a generic cultural construction. By this contrast I try to bring to light the gap between what can be abstractly posited about whites in their relation to privilege and power in this country and the divergent circumstances of whites in places like War-rendale and Detroit. Karen's story is not the account of someone who was oblivious to her racial status until late in life; it is a narrative of someone who very early on was subjected to the arbitrary effects of institutional manipulations of racial difference and populations. The story offers a notable complication of the notion of white skin privilege.

Karen's story also points to some of the contributions an ethno-graphic perspective can bring to investigations of whiteness. As I noted in opening this essay, such insights derive from particular methods as well as the guiding assumptions about social reality that inform their deployment. Ethnographers approach subjects in the field with the presumption that there is a range of experience that they know more about than we do. A simple point perhaps, but it notably contrasts with objectifications of white subjects that oper-ate on a strict economy of examples to demonstrate the pervasiveness of white racism. As well, ethnographers focus on the interpretive process that subjects engage in rather than on discerning a core of personal beliefs. In this regard, I was able to approach the con-troversy in Warrendale without being burdened by the necessity of judging whether or not these whites were really racist. Instead, I could focus on discursive terrain in which these whites were positioned, gauging how this terrain was shaped through contrasts and corre-spondences with racial discourse in other sites in Detroit and in the nation at large.

This broader attention to the discursive terrain stems from the conviction informing ethnographic practice that posits place-specific dynamics as crucial to the articulation of cultural notions of identity and difference. As Begona Aretxaga relates, ethnographers regard place as "the product of relations of power and the material through which such relations are culturally articulated, challenged and repro-duced."[28] Whether or not antiracists would regard as valid these whites' claim, based on their position in the power dynamics related to the Malcolm X Academy, that black can also be "racists," it is important to recognize how this place illustrates the need to be specific, rather than abstract, about how "power" actually operates. Then, too, a goal of ethnography is to understand how people think through their experiences and circumstances. Rather than attempting to help them achieve "correct thinking" in their understandings of race, I was able to observe how Academy opponents worked to synthesize a range of information about Afrocentric studies and tenets, to reflect on both the origins of their sentiments and their objectification in the local and national media, and to strive to articulate a sense of their position on these matters that responded to historical precedents as well as to the novelty this setting presented. In this regard, I followed another conviction of ethnographic practice: that events, containing intertwined and contradictory threads of social experience, are capable of changing the way people think about their relationships and identity.[29] The significance of white racialness is not strictly determined by an essentialist core of belief oriented toward blackness as a symbolic form of otherness.

I do not want to convey the impression that ethnography, as a mode of generating social knowledge, is limited only to making claims about specific places and peoples. As I mentioned above, part of what I tracked were the correspondences and distinctions between local and national discourses on race. In this tracking I observed dynamics shaping the way whites engage in public controversies over race that I suspect are widespread, at least among whites in the economic range of middle- to working-class. In interviews with local supporters of the Academy in Warrendale, I heard numerous comments that reflect what Ruth Frankenberg has characterized as color- and power-evasive discourse.[30] Whites who championed the opening of the Academy in their neighborhood would also complain that the school "overstressed the black stuff to the normal stuff" and that "those people" have "a real bad attitude problem" or that "they're real arrogant." These whites largely did not engage in reflections over whether or not their perceptions of the Academy might stem from racist thinking, as white opponents labeled "racist" were compelled to do. I observed that, in this contest, initially whites energetically strove to determine who among them were the "racists"; once that designation had been established, they paid little attention to how the significance of race operated in their decisions and perceptions. I suggest this dynamic—of whites limiting the contagion of accusations of racism to a "hostile few" real "racists"—is active generally in public controversies over race, but I leave that to other researchers to either confirm or refute.

Antiracist activists may view the detachment ethnographers maintain as an indulgent academic extravagance, but I think it can make a contribution even to efforts that involve directly challenging and changing whites' thinking and perceptions of racial matters. The primary ethnographic skill that I try to instill in students in my methods course is the ability to simply listen well to what people are saying. That means being able to hear discourses as multiply inflected, referring to and projecting a host of competing interests and threats, audiences, and objects—none of which are easily linked back to a core psychological motivation, such as racism. Also, it is worth being able to understand both the role of place in developing nuanced inflections of discourses that seem "racial" in the abstract and the situated concerns of subjects who are not singularly driven by core impulses but, rather, are resonding to a complex, changing setting. It is also important to be able to recognize the transformative potential of events in everyday life and to be able to engage the way whites in various settings are perhaps thinking through racial perceptions as well as responding to or regurgitating cultural beliefs about racial difference. Finally, I think effective antiracist work requires an analytically sophisticated concept of class, attentive both to the influence of place—particularly in shaping the types of encounters that develop—and the role of etiquette and decorum. Whites in the upper and middle classes craft forms of decorum that keep race from being raised in "polite" conversation. Whites living closer to economic necessities not only are unable to maintain such forms of decorum, they openly reject them and act out a "loud" refusal to submit to that which they cannot fully attain. Their loudness and the emotionality from which it stems are then read—by professionals (white and black), journalists, antiracist activists, and more upscale neighbors—as signs of racism operating behind "smokescreens," as the multiple concerns of Warrendale whites were characterized. It is important to be able to ask whether or how some whites' statements are generated in a form of acting out classed assumptions about who is really a "racist."

Notes

1 As the contributors to *Off White* put it:

> We worry that in our desire to create spaces to speak, intellectually and empirically, about whiteness, we may have reified whiteness as a fixed category of experience and identity; that we have allowed it to be treated as a monolith, in the singular, as an "essential something." We despair that a terrifying academic flight toward something called white studies could eclipse the important work being done across the range of race, postcolonialism, ethnicity, and "people of color"; that research funds could shift categories; the understanding of whiteness could surface as the new intellectual fetish, leaving questions of power, privilege, and race/ethnic political minorities behind as an intellectual "fad" of the past.

Michelle Fine et al., *Off White: Readings on Race, Power, and Society* (New York: Routledge, 1997), xi–xii.

2 A fuller account of this study is provided in John Hartigan Jr., *Racial Situations: Class Predicaments of Whiteness in Detroit* (Princeton: Princeton University Press, 1999).

3 This claim, in addition to my work in Detroit, is drawn from a great number of studies on the spatial dynamics of racial identity. See Joel Streicker, "Remaking Race, Class, and Region in a Tourist Town," *Identities* 3, no. 4 (1997): 523–55; Helan Page and R. Brooke Thomas, "White Public Space and the Construction of White Privilege in U.S. Health Care: Fresh Concepts and a New Model of Analysis," *Medical Anthropology Quarterly* 8, no. 1 (March 1994): 109–16; Roger Hewitt, *White Talk Black Talk: Inter-Racial Friendship and Communication amongst Adolescents* (Cambridge: Cambridge University Press, 1986); Mark Allan Hughes, "Misspoken Truth to Power: A Geographical Perspective on the Underclass Fallacy," *Economic Geography* 65, no. 6 (July 1989): 187–207; Peter Wade, *Blackness and Race Mixture: The Dynamics of Racial Identity in Colombia* (Baltimore: Johns Hopkins University Press, 1993); Kenneth Jackson, "The Spatial Dimensions of Social Control: Race, Ethnicity, and Government Housing Policy in the United States, 1918–1968," in *Modern Industrial Cities: History, Policy, and Survival*, ed. Bruce Stave (Beverly Hills: Sage Publications, 1982), 79–128; Peter Jackson, *Maps of Meaning: An Introduction to Cultural Geography* (London: Unwin Hyman, 1989).

4 I develop this argument in more detail in "Establishing the Fact of Whiteness," *American Anthropologist* 99, no. 3 (1997): 495–505.

5 See Mary Searle-Chatterjee, "The Anthropologist Exposed: Anthropologists in Multi-Cultural and Anti-Racist Work," *Anthropology Today* 3, no. 4 (1987): 16–18; Catherine Martin, "Educating to Combat Racism: The Civic

Role of Anthropology," *Anthropology and Education Quarterly* 27, no. 2 (1996): 253–69.

6 While there is widespread acceptance for the assertion that race is culturally constructed, there has been little acknowledgment that the same holds true for class identity as well. As John Frow asserts, "There is no class essence and there are no unified class actors founded in the objectivity of a social interest; there are, however, processes of class formation, without absolute origin or telos, with definite discursive conditions, and played out through particular institutional forms and balances of power, through calculations and miscalculations, through desires and fears and fantasies." John Frow, *Cultural Studies and Cultural Value* (Oxford: Clarendon Press, 1995), 111.

7 Pierre Bourdieu points to adjectives as one of the most revealing registers for grasping the operation of class distinction; see his *Distinction: A Social Critique of the Judgment of Taste,* trans. Richard Nice (Cambridge, Mass.: Harvard University Press, 1984). The etymologies of such terms also demonstrate the enduring operation of class derogation: "mean" is related to the German term *gemein,* for common and base; "villain" derives from the Latin term for farmhands who served at a villa.

8 Stories about the controversy over the Malcolm X Academy appeared in the *New York Times* and the *San Francisco Examiner* and on National Public Radio.

9 The most consistent aspect of this controversy that linked it to other conflicts over schools was that the class dimension, while fundamental, received little attention in the media. This dimension was particularly prevalent in the Boston disputes, as Brian Sheehan has observed: "A coalition of blacks and young white professionals who favor reforms often seem to be aligned with financial and real estate interests against the social and economic displacement experienced by lower-income whites in the creation of New Boston." Sheehan, *The Boston School Integration Dispute: Social Change and Legal Maneuvers* (New York: Columbia, 1984), 2. See also Ronald Formisano, *Boston against Busing: Race, Class, and Ethnicity in the 1960s and 1970s* (Chapel Hill: University of North Carolina Press, 1991); Eleanor Wolf, *Trial and Error: The Detroit School Segregation Case* (Detroit: Wayne State University Press, 1981); Jonathan Rieder, *Canarsie: The Jews and Italians of Brooklyn against Liberalism* (Cambridge, Mass.: Harvard University Press, 1985).

10 Edward Lipuma and Sarah Meltzoff examine this type of figuring of class conflict played out through the development of and contests over land-use patterns in southern Florida, specifically how the crosscurrents of ethnicity and class delineate their design and implementation. The important connection that I see here is that Warrendale whites were enveloped in a

discursive predicament where only their class-conditioning was marked; this was accentuated by their racialness. Lipuma and Meltzoff describe second-home-owning retirees as follows: "Their style of dress (often casual but tailored clothes of natural fibers), their assured delivery and choice of words, their posture, and the respect they expect to command all indicate that they are comfortable, confident, and poised. . . . In this way, the class interests of second-home owners/retirees combine with their ideology to generate practices that are both more restrained and more nuanced than the unbridled pursuit of class-based interests, and, because they are restrained and nuanced, mask those interests." Conversely: "If second-home owners/retirees fit 'naturally' into the hearing process, fishermen could not be more ill-adapted. They lack the rhetorical style, accent, posture, and other indexes that would mark their words and views as important. The hearings . . . are geared to those with a college education. . . . Fishermen experience shame and frustration at the meetings because of their relative lack of linguistic and educational capital." Lipuma and Meltzoff "The Crosscurrents of Ethnicity and Class in the Construction of Public Policy," *American Ethnologist* 24, no. 1 (1997): 114–31, 125–26.

11 See David Wellman, *Portraits of White Racism,* 2d ed. (Cambridge: Cambridge University Press, 1993).

12 The use of the critical terms "marked" and "unmarked" becomes quite tenuous in this ethnographic setting. To talk about race in Detroit is to effect what Linda Waugh refers to as a "reversal," such that blackness is the assumed or unmarked category and whiteness is marked. The key point—often neglected by theorists of whiteness—is that all of this is relational; you cannot just refer to a category as generically marked or unmarked. White racialness can be unmarked in one domain and marked in another. As Waugh asserts, "markedness relations are understood as being relevant given particular contexts" (310). Linda Waugh, "Marked and Unmarked: A Choice between Unequals in Semiotic Structure," *Semiotica* 38, nos. 3–4 (1982): 299–318. See also David Schneider, who first applied these designations in delineating the construction of kinship in American culture, in his *American Kinship: A Cultural Account,* 2d ed. (Chicago: University of Chicago Press, 1980).

13 Warrendale, like the pre–World War II subdivisions that David Halle studies, is "typical of areas that outsiders often think of as 'working-class neighborhoods.' But those who live there are less certain. . . . Few [residents] stress occupational segregation as a defining characteristic of these areas, and they rarely refer to them as 'working class' or 'working men's' districts." See *America's Working Man: Work, Home, and Politics among Blue-Collar Property Owners* (Chicago: University of Chicago Press, 1987), 10.

14 Between 1969 and 1971 violent incidents in the schools were so numerous they were recorded hourly by Deputy Superintendent Charles Wolfe. Jeffrey Mirel, *The Rise and Fall of an Urban School System: Detroit, 1907–1981* (Ann Arbor: University of Michigan Press, 1993), 308.

15 The hosts of two shows, M'zee Nabowe's "Word Up" on WDTR and Tahira Ahmed's "African World View" on both WDTR and WCHB—participants in a panel discussion, "The Importance of Black Talk Radio," sponsored by the Malcolm X Center in January 1993—stress that what makes these shows "black" is that they present the views of "Africans in America." See also "Talking Issues in Detroit, City Tunes into Black Radio," *Detroit Free Press,* 15 February 1993.

16 Catherine Lutz, "Engendered Emotion: Gender, Power, and the Rhetoric of Emotional Control in American Discourse," in *Language and the Politics of Emotion,* ed. Catherine Lutz and Lila Abu-Lughod (Cambridge: Cambridge University Press, 1990), 69–91.

17 This perceptual formula, that extreme emotion equals racism, is widespread. Alice McIntyre provides an example of this in her analysis of "white talk," declaring certain whites' "strong, affective responses" to be "tools for resisting critique." She is frustrated by the way their "feelings of powerlessness, fear, and defensiveness shielded many of the participants from challenging the polemical nature of race talk." I hope that the example of whites in Warrendale, who also grew frustrated over their inability to disrupt "the polemical nature of race talk," conveys the possibility that strong emotion is not merely a means designed to counter the insights of those engaged in antiracist work. McIntyre, *Making Meaning of Whiteness: Exploring Racial Identity with White Teachers* (Albany: State University of New York Press, 1997), 77.

18 "Talk Show Canceled," *Warrendale Press and Guide,* 3 September 1992.

19 There is a long tradition of this intraracial positioning of working-class whites as the "real" bearers and promoters of racist sentiment. Arnold Hirsch relates an excellent example of this dynamic in Chicago conflicts over the residential color-line in the 1950s.

> Nothing would have shocked Hyde Parkers more than the assertion that they were part of a generalized "white" effort to control the process of racial succession. The imputation of a brotherhood with the ethnic, working-class rock throwers would have been more than they could bear. Yet, there was such a consensus. . . . There was certainly a wide divergence in the means deemed acceptable to manage succession, but the Hyde Park proclivity for sending building inspectors rather than debris into the homes of new black residents stemmed from the same fears that called forth crowds elsewhere. . . . Although the rhetoric of

integration was in sharp contrast to the virulent racist diatribes that
were offered in some quarters, the justifications given for actions taken
reveal the differences among the various white groups to be more in
the vehemence of language and the sophistication of the resistance
than in fundamental assumptions.
Hirsch, *The Making of the Second Ghetto: Race and Housing in Chicago,
1940–1960* (Cambridge: Cambridge University Press, 1983), 171–72.

20 Any discussion of charges of "racist" would be remiss without acknowledging its certain status as an epithet with distinct classed inscriptions.
As Ronald Formisano relates, "[T]he epithet 'racist' springs easily to the
lips of middle-class persons who live in suburbs or college towns, or who
if they live in urban retreats possess the resources enabling them to
avoid sending their children to schools that are populated with the poor,
working-class, or black." Formisano, *Boston against Busing*, xiv.

21 Virginia Dominguez, "Invoking Racism in the Public Sphere: Two Takes
on National Self-Criticism," *Identities* 1, no. 4 (1995): 325–46.

22 This is hardly a trivial matter, given the great lengths whites will go to
claim or prove they are not prejudiced. As Michael Billig observes, even
fascists strive to avoid being depicted as racists; "The Notion of 'Prejudice': Some Rhetorical and Ideological Aspects," *Text* 8, nos. 1–2 (1988):
91–110.

23 Alastair Bonnett, "Constructions of Whiteness in European and American
Anti-Racism," in *Debating Cultural Hybridity: Multi-Cultural Identities and
the Politics of Anti-Racism,* ed. Pnina Werbner and Tariq Modood (London:
Zed Books, 1997), 179–80.

24 Afrocentrism was never a fixed and ratified object in this controversy.
When opponents made reference to it, and when they suggested readings
for me, they stressed a panoply of authors, including Maulana Karenga,
Asa Hilliard, Molief Asante, and Cheikh Diop.

25 Bonnett, "Constructions of Whiteness," 177.

26 Ibid., 177.

27 Ibid., 174.

28 Begona Aretxaga, *Shattering Silence: Women, Nationalism, and Political
Subjectivity in Northern Ireland* (Princeton: Princeton University Press,
1997), 24.

29 Here I paraphrase comments by Aretxaga in *Shattering Silence.*

30 Ruth Frankenberg, *White Women, Race Matters: The Social Construction of
Whiteness* (Minneapolis: University of Minnesota Press, 1993): 142–49.

Transnational Configurations of Desire:
The Nation and its White Closets

I begin this exploration of sexualities in a transnational context with a story about "Sophia," who recently returned to the Caribbean for her Immigration and Naturalization Service interview at the American Embassy in Barbados after being undocumented in the United States since 1986. Knowing that lesbians were not allowed to have migrated to the United States before 1990 and that her application betrayed her prior so-called illegal residence in the States, she femmed up for the interview as much as conceivable to the contours of her psychic body, wearing lipstick, a different hairstyle, and ditching the ever-present baseball cap. This staging reflects a performativity of exchanges and concurrent blurrings between masculinity and femininity to present a heterosexual model of desirable and acceptable "good citizenship material." It was necessary in spite of her claim, as she puts it, that she "became a lesbian in the U.S." The irony of having to prove her pre-1990 nonlesbian status to the bureaucracy of the nation-state that is indeed the geopolitical landscape for the productive site of this very disallowed identity—namely, her postmigration lesbian identification—should not be lost here. While I want to emphasize the multivalent and often contradictory discourses that inform these processes, in this particular narrative, which claims very clear splits between heterosexuality and homosexuality, the American state attempts to contain if not erase the very identity it has enabled.[1]

Immediately after receiving her green card number and entering the United States, Sophia shaved her shoulder-length hair off, effacing any femme pretensions and viscerally replicating what would probably be called a white butch aesthetic. This moment of lesbian assertion is a "fuck you" act of defiance against a state that policed a racialized "alien" body for eleven years, demanding the invisibility of queerness in the face of her visibility as raced. At the same time, it is an act complicitous with white butch-femme aesthetics that produce and sustain figures through intersections of the nation, whiteness, and modernity,[2] producing a "most complicitous–most resistant" circuit of performativity captured by one audience: the nation. If one understands Judith Butler's "performativity of gender" as the reiterative and citational practice by which discourse produces the effects that it names, Sophia, through an imperfect repetition of the "authentic lesbian body," is at once facing both the impossibility of reproducing the original while also, and perhaps pleasurably, destabilizing it.[3]

In the face of proliferating debates about the globalization of queerness, the travels of discursive sexual regimes, and the rapid emergence of gay and lesbian organizations in the so-called Third World, what does one do with a narrative that claims "I became a lesbian after I migrated to the U.S."? (Does "becoming" signal a kind of "coming out," or a rejection of it?) It is a trajectory that absolutely refuses recourse to girlhood crushes on gym teachers, strange aunties, and other queer theory–type lesbian role models. It rejects any understood alternative sexual landscapes and may well reiterate lesbianism as solidly Western and white. And yet, the body that accompanies this narrative now, upon her return to the Caribbean, attempts to seek out other women like her, women called "Zami."[4] In this case the U.S. nation indicates the place of the "authentic" lesbian body; situating this paradigm within notions of modernity and movement, the white lesbian body; indeed, to reference the above story, the white masculine butch lesbian body. Here lesbianism and masculinity as whiteness converge at the site of the nation to produce and privilege certain narratives of desire over others.

"Circuits of Desire"[5]

This essay uses "whiteness" as a conceptual category of modernity that references yet exceeds discrete ethnic categories or markers.[6] The links between sexualities, modernity, and whiteness are particularly evident in the case of "traveling" transnational queer bodies that are interpellated through institutional discourses of the Immigration and Naturalization Service, tourism, gay and lesbian marriages, asylum laws, human rights organizations, queer liberation movements, and conceptualizations of queer diasporas.[7] This essay attempts to theorize methodological possibilities for talking about transnational sexualities and is a response to the relative marginalization of gender and sexuality in the literature on transnationalism, as well as to the whiteness of queer theory, which relies heavily on psychoanalytic models that presume the primacy of sexual difference.[8] In seeking a language that enables one to read locations across sexualities and sexualities across locations, I am attempting to negotiate the politics of desiring subjects with social theories of material analyses, interrogating different relationships between politics and pleasures, or what I call the "materialities of desire." I argue for an alternative framework of fluid sexualities that addresses hegemonic hierarchies of nameable identifiable sexualities while at the same time critiquing the privileged episteme of those identities.

Theorists of transnationalism have noted that the fundamental paradox of rapid and increased economic globalization is that as the nation-state is destabilized and national boundaries become economically porous, it must reassert hegemonies of its imagined cohesiveness and geographic boundaries in social terms. Jacqui Alexander, one of the few theorists who has examined this process in terms of sexuality, argues that "the effects of political economic international processes provoke a legitimation crisis for the state. It then moves to restore its legitimacy by recouping heterosexuality through legislation."[9] In their coedited volume *Feminist Genealogies, Colonial Legacies, Democratic Futures,* Chandra Mohanty and Alexander effectively lay out the terms within which this recuperation happens.[10] This collection is stunning if only for the mere fact that it places sexuality and its relations to gender at the *very core* of the processes that situate the demand for sameness at the nation's boundaries, challenging claims that sexuality is a bourgeois issue belonging at the bottom of a hierarchy of oppressions. Stuart Hall, however, reminded us some time ago that the nation mobilizes to recoup itself not only through sameness but within and through postmodern capitalist manipulations of "difference."[11] In this case, one may apply "difference" to mean both sexual difference and differentiation within/through sexual difference, noting that any terms of sexual citizenship are racialized, gendered, and class-inflected as well.

Thus while it is crucial to examine how, as Alexander notes, the nation "disallows the queer body,"[12] it may well be necessary to ask which nation and which queer bodies and to interrogate how nations not only produce but also sanction certain queer subjectivities over others.[13] Resituating discourses of the nation in ways that complicate a repressive-versus-productive binary can show how "sexual political subjects" use, appropriate, reject, rely on, and are even produced through, rather than simply oppose, discourses of the nation.[14] Immediate examples, ones that differ tremendously in terms of political impetus and impact, are Queer Nation's reclamation of a "queer counterpublic," Cherríe Moraga's use of national landscapes in "Queer Aztlan" and Gloria Anzaldúa's in *Borderlands*.[15] Feminist theorist Katherine Sugg asserts that in Chicana writings "lesbianism works in part to return the narrator to a complex cultural authenticity that resists white liberal feminist discourses of identity and substantiates in new ways the narrator's connection to her community and history."[16] Paula Moya among others has noted the ways in which concepts of whiteness as "contaminated privilege" function in these reclamations of lesbianism through nationhood and vice versa.[17]

Queer Diasporas

"Whiteness as contamination" is well entrenched in a historical regime of discursive belonging. Every out-and-about dyke of color in San Francisco knows that the latest hot spot for those who are "family" or "in the circle" has "gone bad" when the white dykes start showing up.[18] Along with alternative linguistic codes to signify lesbian belonging, there is an interesting originary status being claimed here, a reversal of the usual "who's invading whom" rhetoric. Whiteness functions as betrayal; particularly through politicality, feminism, and sex, whiteness is a betrayal of male "community" leadership. These paradigms of a sell-out to whiteness speak to nationalism/feminism oppositions discussed by Lisa Lowe and Inderpal Grewal.[19] But as Gloria Anzaldúa writes, "for the lesbian of color, the ultimate rebellion against her native culture is through her sexual behavior."[20]

These accusations of whiteness, contamination, and sexual betrayal of the "motherland" as well as of "culture" may result in strengthened recourses to origins, roots, and sexual "homes" that depend on, rather than reject, the nation/s. Cases in point are South Asian queer diasporic discourses that use Hindu mythology as evidence of same-sex eroticism as indigenous to Indian culture, a tactic that mobilizes ancient Hindu temple carvings, the *Kamasutra*, and other avenues of historical proof. This resistance to the whiteness of queerness through "reterritorializations" of Indian homo/sexual origins in diasporic locales are an example of what Aihwa Ong refers to as "transnational localisms," a response to a threatened or already completed violence of erasure.[21] These creations of "scenarios of origins" result in a mobilization of the Hindu Indian Nation to enter the Queer Nation.[22]

However, for many in South Asia, indeed in India itself, and those in the diaspora (due to religion, region, caste, and generational differences), Hindu India is not available as a sexual home. Hindu Indian identity is fixed into a relationship between homosexuality, whiteness, and modernity (ironically through the use of Hindu "traditions"), such that non-Hindu South Asians could never use such genealogies to claim queerness.[23] In fact, these reclamations are instead often mobilized as ammunition in reverse by Sikh and Muslim fundamentalists, and the logic goes like this: "Homosexuality is Hindu, modern, and white, not to mention Indian, and that is what we are resisting." These responses to the "demand for evidence" and accusations of betrayal parallel the links between whiteness and queerness. They privilege certain forms of queer identity, visibility, and a modernist telos of evolution captured by "coming out" and are heavily dependent on the closet as a metaphor of repression.[24]

Queer (In)visibilities?

The continuing hegemonic potential of modernist teleologies of evolution should not be underestimated. An example is a recurring scenario at the Pride Parade in San Francisco. The South Asian Gay and Lesbian organization, Trikone, marches every summer, at the back of the procession of course (the joke is that all the colored folk get stuck at the end). Inevitably, a group of ostensibly white queers will come up to our contingent and ask if there really are gays and lesbians in India. They might marvel at how we've flown all the way from India so that we can be "out and proud." Often they will ask where South Asia is. In many instances we may be subjected to a rambling combination of all three comments. All of these result from as well as produce specific erasures; of same-sex sexualities in South Asia (particularly non-Indian ones), of diasporic queers, and of visibility as a mandated function of queerness in the West, replicating discourses similar to Homi

Bhabha's "white but not quite" equation of mimicry: here, but not quite queer.

The invisibility of queers of color is reiterated through demands for evidence as predicated by strategies of visibility and other queer counterpublic spaces. One example are the tactics of Queer Nation as described by Lauren Berlant and Elizabeth Freeman.[25] Absent in this account are questions of relations to the state vis-à-vis who can and cannot afford to participate in such public visibilities, based on an "uninterrogated assumption of queer citizenship."[26] Queer Nation's strategy of reclaiming "national icons" effectively becomes a call for whiteness that reproduces the white episteme of queerness at the nation's boundaries. The irony of Queer Nation is that it is precipitated by the process that Alexander discusses: a reassertion of a heterosexual state that is due in some part to immigrant bodies that threaten the boundaries/borders of the nation. Queer Nation as an ideology will remain eternally bound to its whiteness if it cannot address how immigration functions to keep the nation-state in crisis. This crisis legitimates the rhetorical strategy of reclaiming the nation through queerness, noting that immigrants actually produce, in some part, the spaces of resistance that Queer Nation occupies.[27]

The demand to be visible, according to David Halperin, is created by a "modern regime of sexuality which says we can now choose how to be sexually free, but cannot choose whether to be sexually free."[28] Rosemary Hennessy's excellent critique of queer visibility as a function of overdetermined fetishization of class consumption also needs to be thought of within a framework of modernity and whiteness.[29] A critique of the epistemologies of queer visibility leaves the paradox of visibility intact, as demonstrated by the parade example. How does one know queers of color exist if they are not visible? If I am critiquing the demand to be visible, why am I complaining about the invisibility of queers of color? An apparent push toward visibility from predominantly middle-class South Asian diasporic as well as subcontinent queers contrasts sharply with Martin Manalansan's observation regarding working-class Filipino immigrants, for whom "visibility is dangerous."[30] (And this recalls the story of Sophia's haircut.) In such cases perhaps coming out is a narrative eclipsed by ones of immigration (for example, receiving a green card after waiting for eleven years). This is not just about immigrant/ethnic queers but also very specifically linked to class. Privileging such concerns about racialized state belongings is directly contradictory to coming out narratives that posit "out and proud" paradigms as the main prerequisite to queer liberation. Here visibility as a hegemonic discourse of queer cosmopolitanism is also linked to the role of capitalism and urban spaces in the emergence of gay identities, a process elaborated by John D'Emilio.[31]

In the ultimate quest to be free of sexuality as a space marking psychosis, neurosis, and deviance, the commodification and globalization of everything about queerness, from dildos, lipstick lesbians,[32] and sex clubs, entails that the nation is not innocent or absent in its collusion with multinational capital in the production of (elite) "queer cosmopolitan citizens." Whiteness is thus defined through inclusion in the global economy. As Anthony Burgess flippantly comments, "The best homosexuality is in America, like the best everything else, and [specifically in] California where all national tendencies achieve their most hyperbolic expression."[33] Ruth Vanita has stated that most queers in India live with "one foot in the west," further noting the regulating of global queerness through the nation.[34]

Queer Mobility?

Certain venues of Queer Studies have offered up powerful internal critiques, noting that the category "queer" is a privileged white one and that visibility and linked discourses of coming out contribute to hegemonic queernesses. The response to the whiteness of Queer Studies and its erasure of questions of the nation, race, and ethnicity has been, it seems, to both expand what queer includes, as well as to mobilize queerness. In essence there has been a call to queer queerness, stressing its fluidity and liminality, but this is itself another framework of race and class privilege. Fluidity as mobility is a privilege. This kind of oversight is not just about exclusions but more precisely about assumed inclusions. Lisa Duggan calls for a "No Promo Hetero" campaign and other political activist strategies that do not force "us" to declare "who we are."[35] These approaches become impossible when the state dictates its very offerings of belonging through determining whether one is or isn't one, in this case, gay or lesbian. The heterosexual/heterosexist nation, in its need to secure its social and geographic boundaries vis-à-vis unwelcome Others, is productive of certain "queer cosmopolitan citizens" in relation to other configurations of desire that may fall outside whiteness.

An example of this is asylum based on sexual orientation. While such asylum provides immigrants with yet another way to access residency, subjects of this legislation must be interpellated into a "citational practice."[36] As Judith Butler describes it, this is a process that "names" and also produces and privileges the effects of that naming. This practice may well flatten discursively displaced subjects into the linear subjectivity of the law, erasing, for example, bisexuality. Based on discourses of gay and lesbian human rights, asylum laws are predicated upon an erroneous modernist notion of the United States as a place free of violence for queers. Additionally, these laws mystify an often arbitrary distinction between asylees and those who are undocumented. This version of queer democracy colludes with liberal Euro-American feminism in its desire to mark a unitary, singular subject, one that can produce "evidence" of persecution in one's "native" country. This frees queers of the nation, in the ways Duggan would like, who are thus not subject to demands of disclosure of sexual identity. At the same time, it produces a double Othering of asylum seekers. Resident status becomes contingent on one's queer status. How decisions are made in these cases needs to be examined in relation to U.S. foreign policy stances; for one example, it seems that a demonized, homogenized "Islamic subject" is in particular need of salvation, whereas applicants from Mexico may have more difficulty proving a "legitimate" case. The new immigration law that went into effect on 1 April 1997 puts a one-year filing limit on these cases. In other words, immigrants now have only one year to figure out if they are gay or lesbian, if they haven't done so already, and to prove that modern queers cannot exist "back home," creating an inducement into white modernity complicit with national discourses. Such evidence assumes that gays and lesbians were "out" in their native countries in a readable way, preventing any privileging of the slippages of queer and demanding a singular, homogenized narrative of sexual activity.[37]

Another example of the national production and privileging of certain queer subjectivities over others is the debate over same-sex marriage. The irony of the same-sex marriage case in Hawaii is that while white middle-class gay men are fighting over the "right" to marry and what this might signify in terms of a supposed binary between assimilationist and progressive queer politics, what is largely overlooked are the implications of this ruling in terms of nationality. Binational couples are looking to this legislation as a subversive alternative to hetero-sexual marriage to obtain a green card. In a climate where many communities are actively seeking out and creating alternative models for coupling and co-parenting, what will become a somewhat hysteri-cal exercise in futility, should the INS ever recognize such marriages, is how exactly the INS will decide what is a "legitimate" queer mar-riage. This is something that is still confounding in terms of assessing fraudulent heterosexual marriages and results in claims of "marriage gridlock." Again, racial and class politics will play themselves out in terms of this policing—that is, European immigrants are not sus-pected of "fraudulent marriages" in the same ways as nonwhite im-migrants. Similar is the case with "domestic partnerships" in San Francisco. Trinity Ordona asks which immigrant queers wanting to register their domestic partnerships are going to own up to their "un-desirable" immigrant status?[38] But the point is more that the INS will probably never, or at least not anytime soon, recognize gay marriages as an avenue to a green card, thus limiting this option to "national queers." In this case gay marriages, as a mandate of the nation/na-tional belonging, approximates most closely what the nation wants, separating the good queers from the bad. Some queers *are* better than others. This easily replicates familiar national and racialized moraliz-ing binaries of the body: the body as a sacred site of love, intimacy, and commitment versus the body as unworthy, exploited, and the site of degeneracy.[39]

Notes on the Closet

The metaphor of the closet, which Eve Sedgwick has theorized as the "regime of the open secret,"[40] reflects Western epistemologies of pub-lic/private and secret/disclosure divides, as well as sex and desire as discourses of modernity, and presumes linear and commensurable narratives of sexuality across social spaces. The closet in its modern-ist form equates desire with speech, with agency, with consciousness. As a confessional space and an instrument of subjectivization, it is linked to freedom from repression, entrenched in power/knowledge relations.[41]

The closet as applied to the nation and other locational problem-atics that attempt to contest the nation is not any of these things. If strained, this metaphor implodes through the betrayal of the material underpinnings of its own assumptions. Gracepoore, an undocumented South Asian lesbian activist, claims that by necessity, there are "multiple possibilities for creative resistance by being simultaneously out of and inside the closet."[42] The closet here is a paradox of agency through the withholding of knowledge; and a paradox of censorship, which produces the subject it seeks to erase, speaking to the problem of the unknowability of sexuality. How does one attempt to elaborate on subject formation when objects of study are unknown, indeed unknowable, when the demand for "evidence" contradicts what José Muñoz denotes as the "ephemeral" of queerness?[43] Should one attempt to qualify the silences of closeted subalterns? Foucault's "technologies of sex" describes a process by which discourse turns sex acts into sex identities and associates those identities with corporalities.[44] This "act to identity" telos functions in vertical as well as horizontal modernities, that is, in a linear developmental historical model through time but also horizontally across geopolitical spaces. In attempting to disrupt the "queer as Western imperialism" versus "queer as liberation" binary, "indigenous" sexualities often wind up standing in for "sex acts" in a hierarchy of modernity. This configuration is one that privileges identity as consciousness, while also effacing the presence of postcolonial queers and gay and lesbian organizations in the "peripheries." Qualifying same-sex eroticism as that which signifies differently is a poststructuralist, culturally relativistic move that must be countered by carefully situated analyses of power, noting how and where an "act versus identity" split is mobilized in various globalizing discourses. These difficulties do not just exist in the so-called peripheries, but also in the metropole, as demonstrated to me in my own queer outreach work with South Asian diasporic populations, which I cannot expand upon here. If a move into queerness is indeed a "move into modernity," how does the subject exist prior to this move, or does it? Can one even speak of a "prior"? And what subject dis/formations are necessary for the "free" modern subject of modernity to sustain itself?

In closing I want to again remember Sophia, who has had her green card for six months now. These days she is talking about going to the Caribbean to do work with emerging gay and lesbian organizations, an idea that sends my own modernist trappings into horror and confused convulsions. Why would she go back after waiting so long to stay here? Or is this "return home" not quite the return I think of? My initial refusal to read her agency is complicated by her active rejection of queer modernity even as she is an agent of it. The struggles with the Derridean pharmakons of modernity and the conditional fluidities of postmodernity continue. This essay is a tribute to Sophia and the constant vexations she poses to both.

Notes

Much thanks and appreciation to those who read drafts and gave me feedback while writing this piece. They are Norma Alarcón, Marisa Belausteguigoitia, Mary Pat Brady, Inderpal Grewal, Patricia Penn Hilden, Caren Kaplan, Rachel Lee, Katherine Sugg, and Jean Walton. I am grateful to the organizers of the Making and Unmaking of Whiteness conference, especially Birgit Brander Rasmussen and Jillian Sandell. I would also like to thank Tania Hammidi and the members of the Queer Cluster at the University of California, Davis, for initiating a rigorous dialogue about this paper.

1 I present the example of Sophia as neither fact nor fiction. My intent here is to pose the problematics of how the INS regulates gender and sexuality and decides who is gay and/or lesbian, as well as to note the process of apprehending identities that cannot be contained by the narration of the law. This scenario also perhaps marks an avenue of situating and examining the debates around the readings of Judith Butler's notion of performativity, often critiqued as a problematic version of voluntaristic performance. For important discussions see Ki Namaste, "Tragic Misreadings," in *Queer Studies: A Lesbian, Gay, Bisexual and Transgender Anthology*, ed. Brett Breemyn and Mickey Eliason (New York: New York University Press, 1996), and Kath Weston, "Do Clothes Make the Woman?: Gender, Performance Theory, and Lesbian Eroticism," *Genders* 17 (1993): 1–21.

2 I want to keep the definitions of the term "modernity" in this paper in tension with each other. At some points I am predominantly referencing a temporality or periodization common to this term, and at others I am gesturing to a political condition that is understood in relation to a linear telos of progress and development. Most important, however, are the ways in which these two conceptualizations of modernity reinforce and sustain the production of certain subjects of globalization.

3 Judith Butler, *Gender Trouble: Feminism and the Subversion of Identity* (New York: Routledge, 1990), 25. These are the relationships being suggested here: while white femmeness can be rescued from its "sell-out" assumptions, the response to femmes of color is still quite often that they are being duped by their oppressive culture. In this formulation, (white) butch continues to function as the privileged marker of queerness and as such as

a form of assimilation for dykes of color. For Sophia it marks a double assimilation—into the queer butch aesthetic as well as the arrival into the U.S. nation-state.

4 While this word seems most obviously a reference to Audre Lorde's bio-mythography, *Zami: A New Spelling of My Name* (1982), I use it here more in association with the vernacular of the Caribbean, which Lorde's work popularized outside of Caribbean diasporic communities.

5 I am borrowing this phrase from the title of a special edition of *Positions* (2, no. 1 [1994]) that Yukiko Hanawa edited (1994). She uses desire to suggest the "uneasy absence of a common subject" (ix), that defies capture in the circuits of a sexual political economy defined as "both local and global at the same time" (viii).

6 Whiteness functions to mark concluding impulses of a linear modernist telos of progress and development characterized by the "arrival" of the subject often through class, educational, and income-level status. There are many examples of this; in liberal multicultural discourses, arrival is signaled by the notion of inclusion in the national body, curriculum, or canon; the model-minority discourse associated with Asian Americans is another example of the ways in which approximating "whiteness" is un-derstood through acquiring the status of the "ideal" immigrant. (Note the ways in which Asian Americans are, for example in California, considered more "white" than Latinos and Chicanos by virtue of this discourse. South Asians have also been termed "honorary" whites and in fact were not so long ago categorized as Caucasian.) I am not suggesting that an immi-grant of color is repeating whiteness simply through class aspirations but rather that, in collusion with the state, an ideal productive model citizen of the nation is understood as a white, middle-class, heterosexual, and male. Similarly, queer visibility also functions as marking a moment of "real" and definitive queer sexual subjectivity.

7 A word on the term "transnational" and how it is being used in this work. While I have started out with an example of a particular transnational act or moment, that of migration, I want to situate the transnational as a "condition," as Jean Walton has called it, one that foregrounds not only boundary crossings but also the effect of neocolonial capitalism, tourism, and globalization of material and ideological capital. I take my lead on theorizing the transnational from the introduction to *Scattered Hegemonies* by Caren Kaplan and Inderpal Grewal (1994).

8 The whiteness of queer theory could be loosely characterized as referring to the following tendencies: the Euro-American bias of queer theory, much of which lacks an analysis of ethnicity, race, nationalism, and citizenship issues while simultaneously effacing "Third World" contexts; the emer-gence of queer theory from literary and psychoanalytic epistemologies,

supposedly lending to a lack of "material" analyses and global relations; the positing of subjects that utilize queer sexuality as the only axis of subordination, excluding other interpellations of identity. Earlier writers intervening in similar problems in gay and lesbian scholarship include Gloria Anzaldúa, Cherríe Moraga, Tomás Almaguer, Cheryl Clarke, and Barbara Smith, among others. More recent critiques have been generated by Yukiko Hanawa, Martin Manalansan, Nayan Shah, and Jee Yeun Lee.

9 M. Jacqui Alexander, "Not Just (Any) *Body* Can Be a Citizen: The Politics of Law, Sexuality, and Postcoloniality in Trinidad and Tobago and the Bahamas," *Feminist Review* 48 (autumn 1994): 9.

10 Chandra Mohanty and M. Jacqui Alexander, eds., *Feminist Genealogies, Colonial Legacies, Democratic Futures* (New York: Routledge, 1997).

11 Stuart Hall, "The Local and the Global: Globalization and Ethnicity," in *Culture, Globalization, and the World System: Contemporary Conditions for the Representation of Identity,* ed. Anthony King (London: Macmillan, 1991), 29.

12 Alexander, "Not Just," 5.

13 There are many complex knots to unravel in the contemplation of what the nation, as a representational force, and the state, as a legislative apparatus convened to substantiate that force, are willing to condone and contain. On one hand, the state does not sanction visible queer identities, as in the case of the U.S. military's "don't ask, don't tell" policy, and yet, at the same time, anticipates that explicit queer subjects will avail themselves of queer asylum offerings that ultimately require assimilation into national myths of democracy and freedom. While the October 1998 killing of gay-bashing victim Matthew Shepard has generated national outrage and sorrow, referendums to allow gay marriages in Hawaii and Alaska were defeated in November. The proliferation of queer representations is not commensurate with legislative policings, and yet what is acceptable within those representations mimics certain attributes of ideal citizens of the state: white middle- and upper-class producers and consumers.

14 Yukiko Hanawa, "Introduction," *Positions: Circuits of Desire,* 2, no. 1 (1994): vii.

15 Cherríe Moraga, *The Last Generation* (Boston: South End Press, 1993), and Gloria Anzaldúa, *Borderlands/La Frontera: The New Mestiza* (San Francisco: Aunt Lute Books, 1987).

16 Katherine Sugg, " 'The Ultimate Rebellion': Sexuality and Community in Contemporary Writing," American Studies Association paper, Kansas City, November 1996.

17 Paula Moya, "Postmodernism, 'Realism,' and the Politics of Identity: Cherríe Moraga and Chicana Feminism," in *Feminist Genealogies,* ed. Mohanty and Alexander.

18 See the film directed by Cianna Stewart and Ming-Yeun S. Ma, *There Is No Name for This* (1997).

19 Lisa Lowe, "Heterogeneity, Hybridity, Multiplicity: Marking Asian American Differences," *Diasporas* 1, no. 1 (spring 1991): 24–44; and Inderpal Grewal, "Reading and Writing the South Asian Diaspora: Feminism and Nationalism in North America," in *Our Feet Walk the Sky: Women of the South Asian Diaspora*, ed. Women of South Asian Descent Collective (San Francisco: Aunt Lute Books, 1993), 226–36.

20 Anzaldúa, *Borderlands*, 19.

21 Akhil Gupta and James Ferguson, "Beyond 'Culture': Space, Identity, and the Politics of Difference," *Cultural Anthropology* 7, no. 1 (1992): 6–23.

22 Norma Alarcón, "Anzaldúa's Frontera: Inscribing Genetics," in *Displacement, Diaspora, and Geographies of Identity*, ed. Smadar Lavie and Ted Swedenbeurg (Durham: Duke University Press, 1995), 45.

23 And, in fact, the reverse often happens, in that Hindu forms of situating queerness blanket over any attempts at destabilizing such genealogies. Gayatri Gopinath, in her reading of Shyam Selvadurai's *Funny Boy* (1995), notes that despite the novel's Sri Lankan context the cultural appropriations that occur in New York around the figure of the "funny boy" often use Hindi language instead of Tamil or Sinhala. See Gayatri Gopinath, "Nostalgia, Desire, Diaspora: South Asian Sexualities in Motion," *positions* 5, no. 2 (1997). This example, to me, speaks volumes about the problems of situating queer readings. Without wanting to resurrect a binary between the "truth" of the context of this text and the falsity of the representation of it, and rather seeing this as a symptom of relevance rather than a problem per se, I think there is something to be said for the processes of queered displacement that are profoundly enabling in some instances and yet equally troublesome in other cases, raising questions about defining diasporic contexts.

24 This pessimistic reading would suggest that all attempts to renarrativize sexual genealogies are inevitably resignified through heterosexual nationalism as white and Western. In reference to India, Geeta Patel has argued that any recourse to evidence of the "past" must navigate its containment through colonial archives (Geeta Patel, Roundtable Discussion at the South Asian Studies Annual conference, Madison, WI, October, 1997). Yukiko Hanawa has similarly noted that the reach for origins through indigenous structures is already framed by colonial mythologies (Yukiko Hanawa, "The World of Suzie Wong and M. Butterfly: Race and Gender in Asian America"). *Radical History Review*, 64: (1996): 12–18. For some examples of this problem in South Asian queer diasporic contexts, see Gita Thadani, *Sakhiyani: Lesbian Desire in Ancient and Modern India*. New York: Cassell, 1996 and Rakesh Ratti, ed., *A Lotus of Another Color: An Unfolding of South Asian Gay and Lesbian Experience*. Boston: Alyson, 1993. There

are, however, moments of hope. In July 1997 at Desh Pardesh, the South Asian festival held annually in Toronto, I was surprised by my intense pleasure at watching a performance piece by Himmat Shinhat that suggested Guru Nanak, the founder of Sikhism, was "queer," in the sense that Guru Nanak wrote his devotional love poetry as female to his male traveling companion. Through a combination of spoken word, song, and metal guitar, Shinhat performed the scriptures in an intensely moving yet camp way. There is obviously more to be said about why this recuperation seemed exciting to me; what struck me most during this piece is how I, as a Sikh queer, had assumed the complete foreclosure of such strategies given the hegemonic formations of both Sikh nationalist discourses and queer Hindu discourses.

25 Lauren Berlant and Elizabeth Freeman, "Queer Nationality," in *Fear of a Queer Planet: Queer Politics and Social Theory*, ed. Michael Warner (Minneapolis: Minnesota University Press, 1993), 193–229.

26 Gayatri Gopinath, "Nostalgia," 455–77.

27 This point bears more in-depth treatment than I can give it here. The ways in which the nation tends to "shore up" its physical as well as ideological boundaries in response to labor crises blamed on the outsourcing of production processes as well as in response to a fear of a disintegrating national character due to immigration tends to focus on heteronormative discourses of "family values" and the notion of limited access to public resources and jobs. In response, queer activist strategies such as Queer Nation respond to the heterosexualizing imperatives and impulses fueling such discourses without addressing the fact of other multiple and overlapping audiences to which the state addresses its disciplinary tactics. In other words, there may be mandates for the state to carry out that actually go beyond simply maintaining sexual difference. The nation-state may well intentionally or unintentionally kill two birds with one stone—on the one hand, continually projecting immigration as well as globalization as a crisis that threatens the character of American life and, on the other, promoting heterosexual family values as a way of protecting the national body. But without linking the genealogies of these two discourses, queer activists are merely responding to symptoms and not sicknesses of the nation.

28 David Halperin, *Saint Foucault* (New York: Oxford University Press, 1995), 20.

29 Rosemary Hennessey, "Queer Visibility and Commodity Culture," *Cultural Critique* 29 (winter) (1994–95), 31–76.

30 Martin Manalansan, "In the Shadows of Stonewall: Examining Gay Transnational Politics and the Diasporic Dilemma," *GLQ: A Journal of Lesbian and Gay Studies* 2, no. 4 (1995): 434.

31 John D'Emilio, "Capitalism and Gay Identity," in *The Lesbian and Gay Studies Reader*, ed. Henry Abelove et al. (New York: Routledge, 1993), 467–78.

32 Danae Clark, "Commodity Lesbianism," in *Lesbian and Gay Studies Reader*, ed. Abelove et al., 186–201.

33 Anthony Burgess, "Notes from the Blue Coast," Saturday Review, 28 April 1979.

34 Ruth Vanita, "Do Clothes Make the Woman?: Gender, Performance Theory, and Lesbian Eroticism," *Genders* 17 (1993): 1–21.

35 Lisa Duggan, "Queering the State," *Social Text* 39 (summer 1994): 8–9.

36 Butler, *Gender Trouble*, 12.

37 While I feel these critiques are important to make in the face of relentless neoliberal globalizing forces, I also am aware that many practitioners involved in queer asylum cases are constantly faced with the problems of negotiating legal cultural hegemonies, so once again this is an ambivalent space, producing both possibilities and closures. I would like to thank Chris Nugent for pointing this out to me. Nevertheless, asylum has always been a narrative that demands difference even as it negates it. It is disturbing, for example, that so few women in comparison to men have received asylum. (See Clint Steib, "Experts Warn Time Running out for Gay Refugees," Washington Blade 20 February 1998.) This speaks not only to questions of resources, access and outreach but, I suspect, also to an erasure of female same-sex *sex* that suggests its innocuous, nonthreatening, or perhaps even assimilatable features in relation to discourses of buggery, anal sex, phallocentrism, and HIV/AIDS. It is also the case, as Heather McClure has pointed out, that women often marry for economic security and thus cannot participate "properly" in the legal definitions of queer asylum (Steib, 1998). Now with the one-year filing limit on these cases placing a temporal element to queer modernity, the question of how outreach to potential queer asylees is envisioned becomes even more important, as areas like the Chicano/Latino Mission district in San Francisco, which is populated with numerous undocumented drag queens and transgenders, are often inadvertently overlooked in favor of more "accessible" (and often wealthier) immigrants. In addition, there need to be more nuanced readings of notions of persecution in terms of bisexual and transgendered subjects, especially in how the legislation handles transsexuality. See also Heather McClure, Christopher Nugent, and Lavi Soloway, *Preparing Sexual Orientation-Based Asylum Claims*.

38 Trinity Ordona et al., 93. "In Our Own Way: A Roundtable Discussion," in *Asian American Sexualities*, ed. Russel Leong (New York: Routledge, 1996), 91–100.

39 Gayle Rubin, "Thinking Sex: Notes for a Radical Theory of the Politics of Sexuality," in *Lesbian and Gay Studies Reader,* ed. Abelove et al., 3–45.

40 Eve Kosofsky Sedgwick, "Epistemology of the Closet," in *Lesbian and Gay Studies Reader,* ed. Abelove et al., 45.

41 Michel Foucault, *The History of Sexuality: An Introduction* (New York: Vintage, 1978).

42 Gracepoore, "Three Movements in a Minor," *Trikone Magazine* 12, no. 1 (1997): 10.

43 José Muñoz, "Ephemera as Evidence: Introductory Notes to Queer Acts," *Women and Performance: A Journal of Feminist Theory* 8, no. 2 (1996), 10.

44 Foucault, *History of Sexuality.*

Vron Ware

Perfidious Albion: Whiteness and the International Imagination

There were Africans in Britain before the English came here.
—Peter Fryer[1]

Searching for a figure of speech that might convey a sense of whiteness as an interconnected global system, I remember June Jordan's brilliant evocation of the weather in her discussion of the vicissitudes and unreliability of identity politics.[2] Instead of visualizing whiteness in terms of a planetary weather system with global patterns, regional variations, and microclimates, I am inclined to approach whiteness as pollution. The weather, after all, can be good as well as bad; and although it may respond to human activity on earth, it mainly follows its own unfathomable laws. The image of pollution is more suitable because it is a product of the destructive and exploitative nature of industrial capitalism; it may be produced in one place, but its effects are not containable by cultural or political borders. It is possible to organize against the causes and effect of pollution on local, national, and international levels; but unless there is concerted effort from producers, consumers, governments and law enforcers, the measures taken will have minimal impact on the environmental devastation that is taking place day by day.

This analogy could be extended, for it fits rather well. I reach for it here because I have some questions about the internationalist aspirations of this project to "unmake" whiteness. How important is it that we recognize the parallels and differences between discourses of white supremacy produced in different countries? If, as Fredric Jameson pointed out, we can imagine the end of the world more readily than we can imagine the end of capitalism, how do we envision the end of whiteness? Or is it true, as Joel Kovel has argued, that the cure for white racism is "quite simple, really. Only get rid of imperialism, and, what comes to the same thing, see to it that people freely determine their own history"?[3]

The point about such big questions is to underline the importance of thinking about whiteness on many different scales. In some ways this is parallel to new theories of diaspora that have enabled fresh approaches to black identities and cultures across time and space. Similarly, whiteness needs to be understood as an interconnected global system, having different inflections and implications depending on where and when it has been produced. In other words, the study of whiteness requires the technologies of satellite as well as microscope in order to investigate and subvert its origins and effects on local ecologies. The politics of the geo-body are clearly crucial to this discussion, since ideologies of "race," ethnicity, and belonging are fundamentally bound up with the histories of the nation and how it is defined by competing forces. "We live in a nationalized world," asserts Geoffrey Cubitt, author of *Imagining Nations*.

> The concept of the nation is central to the dominant understandings both of political community and of personal identity . . . Notions of national distinctiveness and of international competition or comparison have become intrinsic to the ways in which we think and speak about matters as varied as economics and topography, art and climate, sport and literature, diet and human character.[4]

Writing from London, a city that preceded England, which itself bears a complex relationship to the wider terms "British Isles," "Great Britain," and "United Kingdom," I want to address some topics from this list as a way of analyzing the latest form of identity crisis that has beset this particular nation. First, I want to emphasize the importance of "international competition and comparison" without which a discussion of national anything is meaningless. My intention is to show that the struggle to define new local, national, and regional identities appropriate for the twenty-first century can serve as a paradigm for those dedicated to comprehending and subverting the mechanisms of whiteness on an international scale. This might sound like an impossible task, but it might also help to bring about new alliances and strategies that can do battle with the global aspirations of white supremacy.

It goes almost without saying that it is not a simple matter to delineate clearly between geography, ethnicity, territory, power, and national identity in any part of the world. In this essay I will be referring both to "Britishness" and "Englishness"; while these are overlapping categories it is important to understand how both have come to be contested in particularly important ways in this postcolonial era. Stuart Hall gives a lucid account of the changing definitions of Britishness and Englishness in an essay titled "New Cultures for Old":

> One only has to think of the regional, cultural, class, gender, racial, economic and linguistic differences which still persist within its boundaries, of the tensions which now accompany the idea of a "united" kingdom, and of the role of "Englishness" as the hegemonic culture in relation to the other "nations" within the kingdom—a fact which irritates many Scots, Welsh, and Northern Irish people, and which fuels nationalist sentiment and aspirations in different parts of the UK.[5]

The U.K. has to be seen as a "composite nation," and the job of the national culture is to produce a "sense of belongingness" that might unify the different elements. The role of "Englishness" is clearly crucial to the national culture as a whole as it has a "quintessential" relation to Britishness. The contingencies of imperialism brought under British jurisdiction many different ethnic groups who continue to retain an affinity with the country, either through direct settlement here or through structures such as the Commonwealth—but this does not automatically permit them to identify as English, even if they are born and brought up in the country. This next part of my argument will try to place this question of defining Englishness within a wider context of the national British culture.

To return briefly to the theme of soccer, which might be called a national obsession (encompassing all the components of the U.K.), this is one area of popular culture that demonstrates the conveniently flexible arrangement provided by a consortium of overlapping "national" identities. If, as I have indicated, the England supporters abroad are a disgrace, the behavior of Scottish fans is exemplary. When England failed to qualify for the last World Cup in 1994, the national media automatically backed the team of the Irish Republic as a substitute—which was less surprising than it might at first seem since a number of their players were born in England. After the Jamaican team failed to win any games in the 1998 tournament, some of their erst-while supporters living in Britain found themselves enthusiastically rooting for England. It might not be practical to change one's sense of national identity as easily as one might swap a T-shirt or a banner, but the international arena provided by sport demonstrates the pleasures and dangers, the significance and the irrelevance, of the strongly held feeling that one belongs to a nation.

Another important example drawn from popular culture was pro-vided by the death of Princess Diana in 1997, which has had far-reaching implications and repercussions that have not yet been fully understood. It was truly astonishing to see the flowers placed outside Kensington Palace and hear reports of the mood among the crowds who gathered to line her funeral procession. At the time it was almost impossible to understand what this all meant, particularly as the me-dia abandoned all reasoned debate in the interests of bowing to the public mood. Although muted voices were heard complaining of the fact Diana's fluctuating popularity during her lifetime had, by her untimely death, given way to nothing less than canonization, many were clearly delighted to have a new patron saint who was young, female, fashionable, and against patriarchal authority. As it happened, the country had just seen a landslide victory for a new Labour govern-ment whose leader was barely ten years older than the princess. He palpably demonstrated his own distance from his forebears when he wept on delivering his public response to her death. What more ef-fective signs could there be that Britain was poised to begin a new era in which it turned its back on tradition and presented itself as a youth-ful, forward-looking, and emotionally expressive nation?

One of the most intriguing components of this new face of Britain was the complexion of the crowd that paid tribute to Diana. One after another, journalists noted, often with incredulity, that many of the women, men, and children who flocked to lay flowers were black or Asian. It was curious that this should have been a surprise at all, but the fact that it was so widely reported compounded the sense that Britain was becoming a very different country than it had been at the time of the princess's wedding to Prince Charles in 1981. However, the mood of optimism and change experienced by many in 1997 was thoroughly dampened by events of the following year, and not just by the failure of the new government to prove itself substantially dif-ferent from the old order. The behavior of England fans during the soccer World Cup tournament in France showed that old traditions really do die hard, especially when it comes to representing the nation abroad.

In June 1998, the French police were faced with massive security problems from the day that the England team played its first game in Marseilles against Tunisia. The rioting and violence that took place as thousands of fans watched the game on a giant screen outside the packed stadium continued through the night, provoking the French police to organize mass expulsions of any English fans thought to have been involved or who were found to have a criminal record. Marseilles's regional police chief was quoted as saying: "We don't want them here, we don't want them in our city. We don't want them in France. We're going to send them away and hope they don't come back."[6] Subsequent security arrangements in other cities where England was due to play included a ban on alcohol for twenty-four hours before the match, the segregation of English fans, and a massive police presence; when the team lost to Argentina in the quarter finals, there was a huge sense of relief that the tournament could continue in the good-natured and celebratory mood that dominated elsewhere.

The predictably nationalist behavior of some English fans abroad during international soccer games invariably provokes a frenzy of self-examination in the media that provides interesting reading on questions of the national character and consciousness. Under the headline "Anglophile City Braced for Invading Hordes," one of the culprits in France, his red shirt marked with a cross of St. George, gave a typically frank response when asked why he did it: "That's a fucking stupid question. We do it because we're England, because this is what we do . . . These French would be Krauts if it wasn't for the English. We're here to represent England, you don't get respect otherwise."[7]

A columnist writing in the liberal *Guardian* sought the reason for this peculiarly English problem. Commenting on the front-page headline of a right-wing tabloid paper, which screamed "Shamed Again by the Louts," she asked, "who would want to be English?"

> Yesterday's *Daily Mail* called it "a sickening show of degenerate patriotism." So where does all this empty pride and false patriotism come from? Who stokes it up? Who poisons the air with the daft idea that to be English is best? Who pumps the bellows of belligerent nationalism? Our own right wing press, from the posh

end of the Euro-hating *Telegraph,* to the xenophobia of the *Mail,* right down to the flagrant loathing of foreigners in the *Sun.*[8]

This diagnosis is entirely correct, but it does not answer the question of why the English have been so peculiarly receptive to this propaganda, and why other nations have not had the same opportunity to be inflamed by cynical newspaper magnates. However, leaving aside these questions for the time being, it is interesting to note that on the same page as this commentary, the writer Jonathan Freedland pondered the implications of the Labour Party's elevation of a thirty-five-year-old gay Asian man to the House of Lords, the unelected second chamber of British government, under the headline: "Step Forward Waheed Alli. You Can Change Our Nation's Destiny." Freedland's concern was not, as might be first assumed, that an Asian peer in the House of Lords would help to break what he calls the "white/middle-aged/straight lock on the upper house" but that his refusal of such an honor, in effect a boycotting of the Labour system of patronage, would help to undermine a fundamentally undemocratic structure; and it would be this act of courage rather than his age, sexuality, and ethnicity that might bring about a change to the nation's destiny.

These two examples, taken from just one day in the life of a discourse of national identity, can be viewed as expressing tiny but significant elements in a new phase of struggle to shift the way in which the national collectivity imagines and represents itself. They both offer thoughtful reactions to unrelated current events but need to be seen against a background of newly charged debates on the meanings of both Britishness and Englishness and the relationship between them. I want to refer to these debates as a way of testing the concept of whiteness as a tool with which to make sense of and effectively intervene in the reimagining of a heterogeneous nation. In the course of this I hope to make some observations about the study of the making and unmaking of whiteness as a cross-cultural, internationalist exercise that seems appropriate to the broad project to which this collection is dedicated.

Prophylactic Identities

A number of different factors have now combined to revive discussion about what constitutes the national English character, what English ethnicity consists of, and, more significantly, why the English need a strong sense of national identity, now more than ever. These debates are directly linked to factors such as the devolution of Scottish, Welsh, and Northern Irish governments, the consolidation of the European Union, and the wider forces of globalization. But they are also provoked by a backlash against doctrines and practices of multiculturalism and a sense that everyone else except the English is expected to feel some pride in their ethnicity and national culture. Surveys of white youth are held up to demonstrate that their entrenched racism is partly a response to being routinely punished for asserting a cultural identity that mirrors (and stands up to) that of their peers who can claim African, Caribbean, or South Asian descent. Roger Hewitt, author of a fascinating study of school kids' speech patterns in south-east London, *White Talk Black Talk,* has carried out extensive research among white working-class youth in that area.[9] In a short film he made for use in schools, girls and boys complained bitterly of the privileges extended to their black counterparts who are allowed to wear cultural insignia without being accused of racism. This has been used as evidence by certain commentators who see the destructive anger of these disempowered and resentful young people as an inevitable consequence of misguided antiracist policies.

Ann Leslie, a journalist who served as a foreign correspondent in the former Yugoslavia in the early 1990s, and who uses this experience to argue for the psychic benefits of a strong sense of national identity, cites Hewitt's film in her advocacy of a positive reevaluation of Englishness: "If it is necessary to build up the self esteem of young blacks (which it is), that should not be at the expense of the self-esteem of young whites. English people should be proud of ourselves for our real achievements, past and present. This is not a recipe for rampant chauvinism. It is quite the opposite. It is a prophylactic against it."[10]

Leslie's conflation of white with English replicates the common-sense view that Englishness is deeply imbued with the characteristics of light skin and the nuances of "race" that float around the category. It is possible to see here how the theorization of whiteness dovetails neatly with this explanation of the dominant cultural identity—or apparent lack of it—in Britain. She writes that English people rarely had to think about their identity, since to have been born English was to have "won the first prize in the lottery of life." In an echo of Richard Dyer's famous description of the all-or-nothing quality of whiteness,

Leslie goes on to say that "we were so convinced that ours was the dominant culture that we scarcely bothered to talk of 'Englishness' itself."[11]

Winthrop Jordan has painstakingly shown the historical development of aesthetic and moral associations between light skin and northern European, specifically English, identity;[12] and Richard Dyer has recently returned to and updated this discussion of white as a skin color that works "as a category that is internally variable and unclear at the edges."[13] Dyer quotes Goethe, for instance, whose contribution to Enlightenment knowledge claims about "race" was based on the idea that light skin represented a mark of perfection in the human form. That citation is worth repeating here because it is a reminder that the apparent beauty of light skin lay in the absence of color: "We venture, however, after what has been adduced, to assert that the white man, that is, he whose surface varies from white to reddish, yellowish, brownish, in short, whose surface appears most neutral in hue and least inclines to any particular or positive color, is the most beautiful."[14] Dyer is interested in the way that this neutrality combines with the multiplicity and the "expressively dynamic" characteristic of whiteness to make it "amenable to being, within bounds, a matter of ascription—white people are who people say are white. This has a profoundly controlling effect."[15]

This last observation can be linked to the patient scholarship of historians like Alexander Saxton, David R. Roediger, Theodore W. Allen, and Grace Elizabeth Hale, whose work has done so much to unravel, explain, and challenge the making of whiteness as an economic, political, and social category in the United States. In Britain, however, a slightly different approach is required, one that examines the fluidity of its naturalizing power in relation to internal differences of class rather than "race." In the eyes of the ardent race-thinkers of the nineteenth century, the members of the Empire who had positive color in their skins were clearly not and never could be white, while the indigenous urban working class who could claim whiteness through birth were rendered subhuman by their inferior economic and social status. The representation of the East End of London as a "dark continent" is just one example of the racialized discourse of class that operated in late-nineteenth-century industrial Britain. Anna Davin's classic essay on imperialism and motherhood documented the way that working-class women were targeted by social policies to produce healthier specimens of white offspring ready to fight for their country and empire.[16] This kind of historiographical labor points to the role of the Englishwoman as a conveyor of both physical characteristics and dominant culture and shows how notions of whiteness were ascribed to the body and to the nation according to gender as well as class.

Today, post-Empire, post-decolonization, the content of Englishness, like whiteness itself, appears to be of a volatile nature, easily evaporating when put under pressure. Few people are able to define what it amounts to. In an attempt to find something distinctively English that might be worth preserving against the homogenizing forces of the European community, former Prime Minister John Major compiled a much-ridiculed list that included village cricket, warm beer, and old maids cycling to morning communion. Arch conservative Norman Tebbit fared little better with his notorious cricket test, which asserted that true Englishmen would support the national team against Indian, Pakistani, or West Indian opponents.

Leslie points out that this inability to define important ingredients of Englishness is a significant problem. To prove this she cites an interview with a group of disaffected English youth who were interviewed on this question by the *Sunday Times:* the only English achievements they could think of were the national football team and a couple of television soap operas.[17] Even the openly avowed white supremacists are not entirely clear what it is they are fighting for. A recent interview with a leading member of the far right British Nationalist Party (BNP)—whose supporters see themselves as the embattled custodians of pure English culture—revealed that the party's sense of national identity was largely defined by what it was not and who it was against. He explained to his interviewer, anthropologist Roland Littlewood, that his party's ideology now understood the question of "race" in terms of tribes and customs rather than purely biological factors. Employing the contemporary language of cultural rather than racial identity, he claimed that although an individual was assigned to a particular race by birth, people could choose to which tribe they belonged, not on the basis of genetics but of culture: "You know about African tribes; we are just the same: Celts, Saxons, Normans, Vikings and so on." How do you know which one you belong to? He admitted a certain degree of mixing and uncertainty, but said people tend to stick to their own gang, so they would know their own tribe.[18]

Here, being English seems to mean living in an enclave supported by grants for projects such as folk dancing in the church hall, eating fish and chips, and pursuing other indigenous customs that might constitute ethnic culture. Later in the same interview the BNP member claimed not to be anti-immigration but concerned about the numbers that threatened the beleaguered host community: "We want a space to celebrate cultural diversity." The litany of charges against other ethnic groups was entirely familiar, and the BNP member kept returning to the refrain: a few is all right; we just don't want to be overwhelmed.

If whiteness is synonymous with Englishness, functioning as a hidden normative code that determines who is in or out on the basis of birth *and* complexion, what is to become of the children of settlers who are born in England but who are not light-skinned and who cannot automatically assume the same privileges as those who are? Here the category of Britishness appears to be more flexible and to offer a more juridical version of national identity that is more concerned with questions of allegiance and citizenship and less closely tied to the body. This question of where the new generations of British-born black inhabitants fit in has been given a fresh slant by public festivities marking of the fiftieth anniversary of the arrival of the SS *Empire Windrush,* which carried one of the first contingents of Caribbean migrant workers to England in 1948. The stories of the *Windrush* generation and their descendants are told from the perspective of those who began life in Britain as outsiders, denied the chance to belong even as legal citizens, but who have gradually and often unwillingly begun to consider the country as their home. The historical reconstruction of their migration to and settlement in Britain, achieved through writing, photography, and television documentary, has coincided with this new phase of discourse about the parameters of English and British identities. I want to consider some aspects of contemporary debate on the content of this broader category of Britishness and to examine the prospects for a more inclusive multiethnic identity that might permanently disrupt the association of white supremacy with the future destiny of England.

Rebranding Britain

Although the idea of a national identity in crisis may not be new in the second half of the twentieth century, the concept of "branding" a country as if it were some kind of product competing on an open market is rather more surprising. Shortly after winning the general election in May 1997, the new Labour government began making noises about the need to rethink the meaning of Britishness as a way of underlining this new phase in its history. The party's phenomenal success was evidence that its transformation from "old" to "New" Labour had been entirely effective in changing its public image. Tony Blair spoke of the need to "rebrand" Britain in order to shift its image away from a fading imperial power to becoming a vigorous and above all a new, younger country. This task was picked up by the left think-tank, Demos, whose arguments were presented in a report titled *Britain: Renewing Our Identity*. Its author, Mark Leonard, emphasized Britain's place as an exciting center of movement that both attracted and organized the import and export of ideas, goods, services, people, and cultures. He represented the country as a vibrant, multicultural entity, with strong traditions of innovation, nonconformity, and fair play, and made recommendations that ranged from sending off ambassadors all over the world in order to proclaim Britain's prowess in the arts, design, and technology, consolidating Britain's position as a "clever island," to redecorating Britain's airports and tunnels so that people arriving in the country might gain a more favorable impression. The report fitted in well with the Blairite strategy to give the idea of Britishness a well-earned makeover so that the crusty images of interminable industrial and imperial decline and rapidly diminishing importance as a world power associated with seventeen years of Conservative rule give way to the notion of a youthful, exuberant, and inventive culture that is far more attractive to customers and investors in a global market.

It is easy to be cynical or at least skeptical about the Rebranding Britain project. The idea that the success of certain cultural industries prioritized and promoted by a relatively young government—under the caption "Cool Britannia"—could symbolize the revitalization of the entire economy and culture has been comprehensively dealt with, especially since the rumbles of recession could be heard in the distance. In a defense of the rebranding concept, Leonard agreed that a country cannot be marketed or sold like a product, but he explained why he was convinced that image was crucial to a nation's survival in the modern world:

> Today all modern nations manage their identities. They use logos, advertising campaigns, festivals, and trade fairs to promote a na-

tional brand. Some have been incredibly successful. Recently Ireland transformed its image from that of a rural, traditional Catholic country to an innovative "Celtic Tiger." Spain has managed to shed the shadow of Franco and redefine itself as a modern industrial nation using the *España* picture by Miró as a national logo symbolizing a bright, optimistic, young country.[19]

The mention of trade fairs is a reminder that the industrial nations have been holding lavish exhibitions to advertise their economic prowess since the Great Exhibition of 1851 and that these fairs were an integral part of molding national and nationalist identity in the nineteenth and early twentieth century well before the power of the logo was invented. Paul Greenhalgh describes how the *Rue des Nations* functioned in the 1900 *Exposition Universelle* in Paris, where one could stroll along discovering what it meant to be a German, Belgian, Swede, or Finn by looking at a combination of "cultural artifacts, industrial produce and statistical information."[20]

> More than this, each nation worked hard to project a national disposition, a character that united its peoples. The *Rue des Nations* was not only an exhibition of art or industry, it was flamboyant manifestation of nationalist activity which had grown steadily among advanced nations for much of the previous century. As with most nationalist institutions, the atmosphere hanging over the banks of the Seine was a strange one, an uneven mixture of bombast, pride, fear, insecurity and confusion.

This evocation of Disneyland, which, as many have argued, was a direct descendant of this type of trade fair, lends a further air of unreality—or perhaps what might be termed "hyperfamiliarity"—to the project of rebranding any country's national identity. On the one hand, Leonard argues that rebranding is an economic necessity, claiming that three-quarters of the world's largest companies say that national identity influences them when they buy and sell goods and services; on the other, he seems to offer a constructive political agenda when he points out that the project represents a fantastic opportunity to provide Britain with "a story that makes sense of where we have come from, reflects the best of what we are and makes a strong statement about where we are going." He believes that identity can be "worked at" so that it includes traditions of cultural openness, tolerance, and ethnic diversity along with stories of economic and political innovation and creativity. In the current climate, however much one might detest the language of marketing and image-making, it is certainly important to consider these arguments seriously and to see where else they are being made or challenged. Although these ongoing debates about historical memory and national identity have been central to anyone thinking and writing about the politics of "race" and multiculturalism, winning the argument that Britain is a multicultural, mixed society rather than an imagined community of white people who tolerate strangers is crucial to the future of democracy in the country.

This is absolutely not a new area of struggle, as anyone who has followed these debates will appreciate. But there is a different climate now, which means that the representation of these issues has particularly important implications and repercussions in the European community as well as within Britain. In the context of the electoral gains being made by the far right in France, Germany, Austria, and Belgium and the increase in neo-Nazi violence, it is even more urgent to aspire to the ideal of a national collective that finds itself at ease with its internal plurality and diversity and therefore able to contribute more effectively to the creation of a democratic, multicultural European federation.

This is one area where the issue of whiteness has to be addressed: instead of being used to advocate the purity, cleansing power, and seductiveness of the product being advertised, any illusory sense of British whiteness must be scrubbed away to reveal the rainbow colors within. Whether or not the new Labour government is prepared to put the right amount of spin on that aspect of the nation's identity remains to be seen, but these continuing debates will surely involve multifaceted attempts to come to terms with the postcolonial realities of life in Britain.

It might seem anachronistic to start talking about the White Cliffs of Dover here as a symbol of contemporary discourse; but as one of the stock visual images of England's landscape, they do crop up rather often. Composed of a myriad of microscopic creatures that we call chalk, sculpted by wind and waves over centuries, the high white cliffs have become one of the most significant features of the country's topography, long celebrated in song, stories, and pictures. Dover is situated in the extreme southeast of the country, only twenty miles from its oldest enemy, France; as Britain's most symbolic border, the cliffs have been given added layers of meaning by powerful ideologies of national belonging and exclusion that have been partly shaped by the nation's island consciousness. This was especially true in the 1940s when Hitler's army was poised to invade the country, when Churchill made his famous speech about Britain's finest hour, when so many took to their boats to prevent an attack by sea in the ill-fated Dunkirk episode. The reference to Britain's airports and tunnels made earlier was not offhand; it is now only the minority of people who actually approach the country by boat coming from the southeast. It is true that passengers in the Eurostar trains only become aware of entering the country once the train emerges from the gray concrete of the tunnel entrance and slows down to half speed. As Mark Leonard points out, the visual impact of the train tunnel for those entering and leaving the country is negligible; the experience of arriving in most airport terminals is disorienting and unmemorable. No longer do the ghostly cliffs, looming through the Channel haze, greet most visitors or welcome homecomers, and the prospect of Diana airport does not quite replace the combination of history, geology, geography, and ideology that this other entrance point supplied. However, as Stephen Daniels writes: "National identities are co-ordinated, often largely defined, by 'legends and landscapes,' by stories of golden ages, enduring traditions, heroic deeds and dramatic destinies located in ancient or promised homelands with hallowed sites and scenery."[21] The survival of the cliffs as a potent image of identity and belonging at the end of the twentieth century can be illustrated by recent examples of their appropriation in political propaganda.

Shortly before the last general election, the leader of the fascist BNP, John Tyndall, began his party political broadcast standing with the infamous rock formation in the background. His message was explicit—England for the English—as well as implicit—Wogs begin at Calais.[22] The following day saw a slightly different picture of Labour Party leader Tony Blair in a more relaxed and pensive pose, the same cliffs clearly shown in the background. This was witness to a struggle by different political parties to signal their different brands of nationalism in a way that engaged with the old brand of Britain. By choosing the cliffs as a backdrop, both politicians claimed their allegiance to a way of thinking and feeling about England that needs to be understood. In the first example, the ancient chalkface is a convenient image reflecting the archetypal purity of the nation. The BNP leader positioned himself on the clifftop, his remaining hair ruffled by the sea wind, his carefully worded broadcast failing to conceal the real agenda behind the fascist program: rights for whites, and the banishing of all those who cannot, for reasons of their skin color, belong to the island race. The choreography of the future prime minister might have represented his desire to change that particular story of Britain and to affirm the island's proximity to Europe: part of a new chapter of union with the continent with its famous sovereignty intact. Alternatively, his position could also be read as a sign that he too had the old island mentality and would resist invasion at all costs. The sign of the white cliffs deliberately and conveniently left this ambiguity open to interpretation.

The same landscape was featured in a charged racist discourse shortly after this when the National Front, rivals of the BNP, demonstrated at the arrival of Slovak gypsies claiming refugee status because of racist persecution in Czechoslovakia. The sight of this miserable bunch waving their "Go Home" banners in front of television cameras on the sea front perpetuated the illusion that Dover was where the hordes were still seeping in, expecting free housing and handouts. Not surprisingly, the mainstream media coverage of the plight of the Slovak refugees echoed the fascists' outrage in slightly muted terms, focusing on the horrified response of the authorities in Dover who were faced with providing accommodation. The fact that several families genuinely qualified for asylum several months later received still more muted coverage.

While the view of the cliffs from the land might suggest to the inhabitants a competing set of "enduring traditions" and different variations of a "golden age" worth fighting for, the view from the sea is possibly more significant. Recalling her arrival in Britain as a Guyanese colonial student in 1951, Beryl Gilroy describes how some fellow passengers broke into the patriotic song made so popular in the war, "There'll be blue birds over the White Cliffs of Dover," as they neared the English coastline. These were young men and women who had grown up in their own homeland with a sense of strong connection to Britain: "We saluted the Union Jack on Empire Day, sang 'I Vow to Thee My Country,' 'Rule Britannia,' 'The British Grenadiers,' and 'Jerusalem' with pleasure and verve."[23]

Although the majority of migrants from the former colonies en-

tered Britain at other sites, many have spoken of the conflicting emotions that they experienced on reaching the place they thought they
knew so well. Lord Kitchener, one of the most famous Calypsonians in
the Caribbean, revealed his own reactions in a documented history of
the *Windrush* voyage:

> But entering England . . . I get this kind of wonderful feeling that
> I'm going to land on the mother country, the soil of the mother
> country . . . Eventually it came up as a famous song. London is
> the place for me. How can I describe? It's just a wonderful feeling.
> You know how it is when you are a child, you hear about your
> mother country, and you know you're going to touch the soil of
> the mother country, you know what feeling is that? Imagine how I
> felt. Here's where I want to be, in London.[24]

It is precisely these kind of stories, by no means limited to the postwar
history of Britain but made especially poignant by the living voices
retelling them now, that provide new ways of imagining the nation.
The central feature of the *Windrush* season was four hour-long television documentaries exploring different aspects of the lives of migrants and their descendants from the 1940s to the present day. The
series took a chronological perspective, and each program was edited
around interviews with individuals, occasionally white as well as black,
combined with documentary footage and a single male narrative
voice. Longer versions of the interviews were transcribed in a book
edited by Mike Phillips and Trevor Phillips, *Windrush: The Inevitable
Rise of Multi-racial Britain,* which contained additional analysis and
commentary. Numerous public events were organized to take place in
the *Windrush* "season"; readings, exhibitions, concerts, and other publications and short films attempted to express and affirm the historical
links between Britain and the Caribbean and to investigate all the
different implications of black settlement in the last fifty years.

The material gathered during this unprecedented exercise provides
an extraordinary wealth of oral history that is clearly of great value to
the communities represented by it. Many of the sequences in the BBC
documentaries were harrowing to watch as individuals recalled epi-
sodes of routine discrimination, racist violence, including murder,
and callous or vindictive treatment at the hands of the police and
judiciary system. Other parts were more humorous and self-critical, as
interviewees speculated on the impact of their behavior on indigenous

culture, particularly in music and dance. However, it was also clear from watching the four hours of film that much of this history had been left out and that there was a great deal more to unearth and record, particularly while the older generations were still alive.

In a short, lively trailer advertising the BBC documentary series, young and old people of Caribbean descent announced that their presence had changed what it meant to be British. This confident assertion showed that to be black and British is no longer a contentious issue, even though it has not been easily resolved. The banners of black and white participants in the various demonstrations that marked the turning points of each decade from 1950 to the present day told their own story: Keep Britain White; If They're Black, Send Them Back; Here to Stay; Black and White Unite and Fight. The final episode in the television series celebrated the presence of black individuals in many areas of British cultural and political life that were probably unimaginable to those on the SS *Windrush* and even more so to the Britain that awaited them: a black woman peer in the House of Lords; black Members of Parliament; key players and champions representing Britain and England in the world of sport; innovative musicians, artists, media figures, and designers; and so on. It would have been hard to have been presented with this evidence and then deny that Britain had indeed been transformed by the presence and contribution of postwar Caribbean settlers. But how deep this change really is, and how different groups of people perceive and experience this shift outside the main metropolitan centers are questions that might not be answered for some time. The fact remains that the country has been offered the opportunity to listen to and reflect on the testimony of some of those who have been traditionally excluded, marginalized, and silenced.

Using the *Windrush* material as a resource, I want to flip the emphasis from the black British themselves to the view of whiteness that they both brought with them and encountered for the first time on their arrival and throughout their subsequent struggles to work and make new lives. It is important to stress that the newcomers already had a highly developed sense of what it meant to be white, absorbed during the course of contact with whites through the various histories of slavery and colonialism at home; this mirrored the expectations and associations that indigenous Britons had of blacks without necessarily having met them before. By concentrating on just some of the testimonies of the West Indian travelers regarding the early days of their arrival, I hope to suggest the value of pursuing this approach in an attempt to comprehend the principle of how whiteness operates in different locations, at different times, and within different sets of social relations.

Encountering the Color Bar

One of the most striking features of the interviews with older men and women who arrived in Britain in the 1940s and 1950s is their astonishment at seeing white people doing ordinary, menial labor. Connie Mark recalls her first impressions:

> I was blown, I was shocked, I couldn't believe what I saw. I arrived at Paddington and it was all very grey and dismal and these little white men were coming up to take our suitcases and I couldn't believe it. In fact, we travelled with a friend who stood there stunned, and I thinking all during his years as a student here he never recovered from that because it used to be one of his strongest stories. He used to say, "I couldn't believe this man coming and calling me 'sir.'"[25]

Jessica Huntley, who came to England in 1958 intending to stay for a short time and who later founded an independent publishing house and bookshop in West London, remembers her astonishment at seeing a white woman with a broom in her hand: "So in those days you used to wear the beehive, and she had a big head of hair on top and well painted, her lips was red and her eyes blue and all the rest of it, and she was sweeping the platform . . . I mean I'm only accustomed to seeing white women who's painted devils but do nothing, they don't even sweep their own home! They have six of us to do it for them."[26]

Another feature of these recollections of England in the fifties is the grayness mentioned by Connie Mark, which seemed to extend to the people themselves. Many travelers spoke about the shocking poverty that they encountered on their arrival; they simply had not expected to find so many destitute English people, as they had grown up with a sense that whiteness automatically conferred power and wealth. This realization irrevocably changed their view of England as an invincible center of empire, and the possession of light skin as a guarantor of privilege and material reward.

Other recurrent observations reflect the sheer unfriendliness of the new culture. Tryphena Anderson echoes the sentiments of many of her generation:

> Nobody tells you the truth and nobody tells you everything. When I came, I saw everybody going into their little houses, and then nobody spoke to you. That never happened in Jamaica. As long as you met somebody in the street—whether you'd met them or not—it's good morning, good evening, and hello. And you'd find you'd be saying to somebody, good morning and good evening and they never answered you, and then you felt stupid after that, so you stopped.[27]

These views of English behavior—the majority of migrants settled in England rather than in Scotland, Ireland, or Wales—were often compounded by a strong sense of homesickness for warmer, friendlier times. They were also deeply affected by the hostility meted out to them because of their appearance. Although there were many jobs available to the new migrants, they were forced to learn quickly that there were many sectors where they were not welcome. Interviewees described how the trades union movement could be effective in blocking their employment. Ben Bousquet gave an account of his early attempts to get work as a young man:

> [I]n the local places of employment—whether it be in the Post Office, whether it be in the railways, whether it be London transport, you know the places which we first went into, even to a certain extent, the hospitals—it was almost made impossible for you to get a job. And if you did get the job it became impossible, almost, to actually join the union . . . they made it that way by not approaching you, you knew that they didn't want you.[28]

Bousquet played a central role in a BBC documentary that exposed what was known as "the color bar" in the housing market. He was filmed going from house to house where there were known vacancies for working men, only to be turned away at the door with all kinds of excuses. Often landlords would place cards in the window: Room for Rent: No Irish, No Coloureds, No Dogs. As he recalled this experience in the television documentary, Bousquet was visibly distressed, even though it had happened several decades previously. The lack of rooms available for rent caused enormous hardship, forcing individuals and families to pay exorbitant rent for miserable accommodation, not al-ways owned by whites. A few fellow migrants were able to acquire property of their own to rent out to people desperate for safe housing.

Patterns of discrimination in housing and employment led inevita-bly to the development of particular areas of Caribbean settlement in cities like London, Birmingham, and Nottingham. Because of the ac-tivities of one particularly exploitative landlord, a significant number of migrants lived in an area of London known as North Kensington, which included Notting Hill and Notting Dale. The growth of teddy boy gangs throughout the 1950s had led to increasing danger on the streets for black women and men,[29] and this threat was compounded by the activities of the fascist Oswald Mosley's Union Movement. It was extraordinarily moving to hear older black women and men de-scribe their experiences of harassment on the streets where they lived and to learn about their strategies for protecting each other as they went to and from their homes after dark. Ivan Weekes described a particularly horrible incident that took place amid escalating violence from these gangs:

> I looked through the fifth floor window where I was, and there was a battle between black men, policemen, white yobbos and Teddy Boys. I mean the street was alight, except for fires and that—Molotov cocktails and so on. And blood was everywhere and it was awful. And by that time the situation had become so bad that black men used to come from surrounding areas . . . knowing the whites were going to hit this particular street, this particular night. They would come in solidarity, to fight. In other words, many black people felt, in for a penny, in for a pound.[30]

The arrival of television and the new media interest in the highly charged question of colonial immigration focused attention on this new problem of "race" and urban conflict with the result that the presence of blacks was represented as a huge problem and the main cause of the street riots that took place in London and Nottingham at this time. A journalist writing for a local London paper in 1958 is quoted at length in the *Windrush* documentary.[31] His portrayal of the hysterical agitation exhibited by apparently ordinary people—"cheerful housewives and their husbands"—who were convinced that "a gang of negroes" was set on attacking them, led by a "female brothel keeper," makes entertaining reading now but illustrates the terrifying irrationality of mob violence. The murder of Kelso Cochrane the following year, stabbed to death in the street by a group of teddy boys, brought an end to the riots and "closed the era which had ushered in a period of unprecedented change in the nature of British society."[32]

These extracts from an edited history of this wave of Caribbean migration to Britain paint a picture of unremitting bleakness and victimization. These were not the only kinds of stories to emerge, but they reveal aspects of Britain that help us to understand its current identity crisis, both at home and seen from abroad. The whiteness that shines through these stories conveys an image of people who, often under duress themselves, found it difficult to deal with strangers, particularly those who looked different and who could be prejudged in the light of "race-thinking"—deeply ingrained views about racial difference bolstered by long histories of colonialism and racial slavery. Here whiteness does not just represent a way of thinking and feeling that sets light-skinned people apart from the rest of the world, but it is also a belief system that can produce raw hatred, fear, and consequently terror, that main ingredient of white supremacy anywhere in the world. However, these are not the only stories, and the value of the *Windrush* documentaries is that they actually present a far more complex picture of transculturation, demonstrating that any view of the world in black and white is far too simplistic to be believable. Both on the screen and in print, these oral testimonies demonstrate the intimate processes of individual and collective adaptation and self-discovery. They include moving and often funny accounts of unexpected friendship, love, marriage, cooperation, and solidarity from people who may have considered themselves white but who did not subscribe to ideologies of white supremacy and who actively challenged prevailing racist practices by identifying with the migrants' struggles to make new lives for themselves. It is worth returning to the *Windrush* accounts of the 1958 riots and the subsequent murder of Kelso Cochrane in order to understand how whiteness was not necessarily synonymous with qualities of Englishness or Britishness and that the victims of race-thinking did not automatically assume that light skin color represented hostility and danger.

Mike Phillips describes the riots as a "very British affair," a comment that betrays an affectionate familiarity with the dominant culture: "During the fiercest hostilities there were white people going out of their way to reassure black people of their friendliness."[33] He goes on to cite a cutting from the *Times,* published on 2 September 1958: "Your correspondent frequently saw white and coloured children playing together. Just after a violent incident in which a coloured man was chased down the street by white youths shouting racial slogans, he saw a white man deliberately cross the street to shake hands with a coloured fruit vendor who was terrified."

The *Windrush* account of the funeral of Kelso Cochrane, a carpenter from Antigua, is perhaps a better example of the truly social history being brought to light in this period of recollection. Its value lies partly in its determination to keep Cochrane's memory alive as a sobering reminder of Britain's past, but it also provides important information about how a self-consciously mixed community was able to deal collectively with the brutalizing effects of racial terror and brutality. Rudy Braithwaite recalled the occasion:

> It was a mass funeral. People were crying all over the place. There were white folks who, from their windows, were hailing the processions when they passed. Some of the English people from around here considered Kelso Cochrane as one of theirs. It's rather interesting in that those people had no bitterness, no racist overtones. Of course, if you are in a society that is steeped with racism, you must be touched by it in some way or another. But, at the same time, those people were good people, and so they were moved.[34]

I particularly like this extract because it reveals the ways in which people learned about each other and were able to recognize similarity and connectedness in place of difference and separation. The speaker expresses a degree of surprise that so many white folks were able to transcend the racism that surrounded them, implying that this had a profound impact on the way in which the local community dealt with the grief and anger that it so visibly shared at this point. It is this kind of evidence that demonstrates in complex, uneven, and not always predictable ways, that whiteness is not reducible to skin color but refers to ways of thinking and behaving "steeped" in histories of raciology. While the distressing accounts of mob violence and random attacks provide a glimpse of the energy required to sustain and provoke the terrorizing effects of whiteness, equally important are the less sensational accounts of the responses of people who were able to resist, however, temporarily, its devastating allure. It shows the fallacy of thinking of whiteness as a category that easily contains and envelops all those deemed to belong.

Mike Phillips provides a thoughtful overview of this process of mutual discovery which, in my view, helps to explain this point about whiteness being an intrinsically leaky vessel. In a letter to Kwesi Phillips, entitled "From the past, to the present," he recalls his own boyhood growing up in London. After describing an incident when he was beaten up at school after spending an evening at a white girl's house, he writes:

> If this all sounds like nothing but the story of anger and conflict and confusion, think again. Because at the bottom of these events it is now obvious to me that there is a process of discovery going on. It's not a simple process, the sort of thing you hear being described as two lots of people meeting and getting to know each other's odd customs and strange habits. It's a lot more complicated than that. I think that the most important part of what we learned wasn't so much about unfamiliar cultures and manners, it was about ourselves. And, on the other side, I had the sense that the reactions of the English people we met were moved and shaped by the feeling about themselves which they brought to the experience.[35]

This last point actually refers to the "tormented look" in the eyes of his schoolboy attacker rather than any sense of self-criticism that it might imply. This further strengthens his point that when people from different cultural backgrounds encounter each other this is likely to precipitate a highly complex and mutual process of learning and unlearning. This is the key to thinking about the histories of multiculturalism in Britain: it argues against the dominant picture of victimized ethnic minorities struggling to integrate into a mainstream society that is uniformly suspicious and hostile; it instead invites a much more intricate view that is both holistic and attentive to local detail.

Entering Another Country

Earlier I referred to the possibility of testing the concept of whiteness as a tool with which to make sense of and effectively intervene in the

reimagining of a heterogeneous nation. Thinking cross-culturally, referring to recent work on whiteness on both sides of the Atlantic, it is
important to recognize the unique conditions of each place and to take
into account the specific histories that have produced national and
regional economies and cultures. The need to be alert to these differences applies as much to countries within Europe as it does to the
United States and other parts of the world. The fact that most of the
current scholarship on whiteness is specifically addressed to a North
American audience does not mean that it is not applicable elsewhere,
even though some examples are guilty of being insular and clearly
uninterested in making connections beyond the borders of the United
States. However, the strategies of U.S. historians of whiteness cannot
be simply transposed to a British context. Europeans who migrated or
fled to the United States were gradually and unevenly allowed to count
themselves in as white, often at great cost to their humanity and
personal integrity. This point was underlined for the wider British
public recently when Camille O. Cosby's statement was published in a
tabloid newspaper following the conviction of Ennis Cosby's mur-
derer, Mikail Markhasev, who was born in Ukraine.[36] Under the head-
ing "America Has Taught Our Son's Killer to Hate Blacks," Cosby
questioned whether Markhasev had learned to hate black people in his
native country, where the black population was near zero. "Nor was he
likely to see America's intolerable, stereotypical movies and TV programs about blacks which were not shown in the Soviet Union at the
time when he lived there." The article went on to list examples of the
way in which racism and prejudice are "omnipresent and eternalized"
in America's institutions with the result that all African Americans
"are at risk in America because of their skin color." Her point was that
Markhasev had imbibed a way of seeing blacks as part of his education
to become a white American citizen. This echoes James Baldwin's
argument, cited by David R. Roediger, that "since 'there are no white
people,'" the decision to adopt white identity was " 'absolutely a moral
choice.'" As Roediger explains: "Whiteness was a dramatic and an
American choice. At a time when immigration history missed the
drama of the European immigrant's learning of race relations in the
United States, Baldwin tellingly observed that Norwegians did not sit
around in Norway preening themselves about how wonderfully white
they were."[37]

Instead of choosing whiteness by assimilation, the British were presented with daily opportunities to make different kinds of moral choices about the kind of people they thought they were. The postwar migration of workers and their families from the former colonies involved a reckoning with ideas about "race" and history and culture derived from the past. The fact that the nation could—and still can—be imagined as an ethnically homogenous group that has been over-whelmed by peoples of different culture reflects a kind of public his-tory that has been repeatedly told from the top down. As an antidote to this, the *Windrush* generation has been offered a chance to explain what they have learned about whiteness in the course of making new lives for themselves in a strange and hostile land; the results have provided rich insights into the making of local and national identities, blurring the imagined line between what it means to be black or white in London, England, Britain, or even Europe.

In another anthology of black British writing published to mark the *Windrush* anniversary, Mike Phillips gives a wonderful account of his realization that he felt at home in England, based on his travels around the country.[38] He begins by describing his version of normal British life in the corner of London where he lives. It would be impossible, he claims, to walk a hundred yards without encountering men and women who have their origins in all corners of the world. "This appar-ent diversity—men in turbans, women wearing masks, the swishing of multi-coloured saris—has become a normal and inevitable feature of the urban landscape in Britain, and its absence becomes a fact filled with meaning."[39]

Phillips explains that it is common knowledge that as soon as one moves out of these urbanized, multicultural arenas, one enters an-other country, where the sight of a black or Asian person is so rare as to be startling. Intrigued by his own lack of knowledge about his adopted country, he decided to take a trip to Scotland, stopping in as many places as he could on the way north. He confesses his wariness at the prospect, adding that "being black in Britain confers a special vulnerability" and the fears of black people are rooted in the knowl-edge that black and Asian people can still be attacked, beaten or killed at random because of the color of their skins.[40] Here he refers specifi-cally to the murder of teenager Stephen Lawrence, who was stabbed to death in April 1993 by a gang of white youths as he waited for a bus in a London suburb. As a result of the failure of the investigating police to identify and convict Stephen's killers, the Lawrence family campaign has worked relentlessly to demand justice and to highlight the racism of the police dealing with this case. A high-profile government inquiry set up in 1998 to investigate their claims has yet to produce a final report, but during the course of giving evidence the assistant commissioner of the Metropolitan Police made a full public apology to the family for errors of judgment on the part of the authorities. Thus the vulnerability to which Phillips refers includes both the possibility of physical assault and the knowledge that racism and prejudice within the police force are likely to obstruct justice.

Nevertheless, Phillips reached a suburb of Newcastle, one of the largest cities in the far north of England, without mishap. As he was walking along, he realized that he had not seen a black or Asian person for more than half an hour. He was not so much surprised, for he knew the geography of the area, as more suddenly disoriented by the effect this had: ". . . but the sense of being the only one for miles around, a dark speck in the sea of white faces, was curiously dislocating, as if I had suddenly set foot in a foreign country, a tourist, tentatively surveying the language, the customs and the atmosphere around me."[41] His sense of normality was briefly restored when he spotted a news agent and decided that the purchase of his usual newspaper would restore his sense of reality. But the fact that the news agent was white, rather than Asian as an urban dweller might expect, threw him again and "heightened the feeling that I was in a foreign, slightly exotic place."

Despite the anxiety that he experienced at that moment, Phillips discovered as he walked on that no one paid him the slightest attention or looked at him oddly, nor did he have any reason to look over his shoulder. What had thrown him was not the hostility of white passersby but the sheer unfamiliarity of a place that he had expected to know. He compared this experience with his sense of being a stranger in the Caribbean where he was born, an outsider in the United States, a foreigner in Africa. "In comparison it was only in Britain that I could stroll through unknown territory, with the same confidence, even in the whitest pockets of the country, as if this was where I truly belonged."[42] This was a strange realization since it implied that he had in some sense stepped outside his own familiar urban world where he had relative control over his identity into a place where he expected to be "a reflected object of the white gaze." Nevertheless, he had found himself to be almost as relaxed in "a world of strange whites" as he would have been in his own London neighborhood.

Phillips interprets this discovery in the light of the history that I have been discussing above, where migrants and settlers from the Caribbean and from India, Pakistan, and Bangladesh had been struggling to establish themselves in the inner cities. He concludes:

> Nowadays moving through the "white" areas of the country what I feel is far from the anxiety of the past. Instead I have the curious sense that I am in areas which have stayed stuck in the past, and somehow failed to catch up with the look and the atmosphere of modern Britain. . . . [L]ocal conflicts may remain, but for the English the mixture of races is now a real facet of their identity, whatever color the family next door happens to be.[43]

This acceptance that Britain, encompassing England, Scotland, Wales, and Northern Ireland (and not forgetting important regional differences exacerbated by uneven economic development and industrial decline) is a multiethnic nation regardless of the concentration or dispersal of people who are visibly not white, is an example of the reimagining process that I have been discussing. But this is not just about color and visibility. Mike Phillips may not have found the comforting presence of an Asian news agent, but he might well have come across a mainstream radio station playing music by the Asian-British band Cornershop or, had he been making the same trip this year, the parodic and subversive World Cup anthem "Vindaloo." In fact, it would be extremely hard not to discern some evidence of multiculturalism even in the farthest reaches of rural England, if one was really looking for it.

Those kids interviewed by the *Sunday Times* could not think of anything that was purely English because all national cultures are in fact "irretrievably hybrid" and constantly evolving. The fatal error of the kind of approach that Leslie advocates, that favors a celebration of Englishness as a separate entity that will provide support for young whites in a multiethnic world, is that it colludes with the desire for some kind of cultural purity or essence: it seeks a return to that bond between English culture and whiteness that the last fifty years have done so much to undo. Instead of searching for "notions of national distinctiveness" among people defined by the anachronism of race and its surrogate, color, it would be far more productive and healthy to open out the definition of Englishness to include the views of relative newcomers who, like Mike Phillips and many of his generation, have realized that England is where they feel most at home.

Britain certainly is entering a new phase in its history if, to paraphrase Richard Dyer, English people are allowed to be who English people say they are. But this slow and tortuous progress toward a truly pluralist society is not happening in isolation from the rest of Europe. As I have been writing this essay, the World Cup tournament has come to a close. The victory of France over Brazil in the final round has had extraordinary repercussions that have spread far beyond the commercial world of international soccer. The fact that half the French team was composed of players whose origins reflected the multiethnic composition of the country—Senegal, Guadeloupe, Ghana, New Caledonia, Algeria, Argentina, Pays Basque, and Armenia—acted as a catalyst for the nation as a whole at a time when the racist far right Front National led by the notorious Jean-Marie Le Pen could claim 15 percent of the national vote. As one commentator pointed out, "The World Cup won't stop people voting for Le Pen, and it certainly won't put an end to the ghettoization of the suburbs. But it will affect the way the French think about themselves."[44] If this sporting event has enabled new ways of imagining the future of France, however precarious or temporary, it is also one more example of showing how whiteness might be unmade, both beyond and within the boundaries of the nation.

Notes

This essay is dedicated to the memory of Stephen Lawrence (1975–1993).

1   Peter Fryer, *Staying Power: The History of Black People in Britain* (London: Pluto Press, 1984), 1.

2   June Jordan, "Report from the Bahamas," in her *On Call* (Boston: South End Press, 1985), 46.

3   Joel Kovel, *White Racism: A Psychohistory* (New York: Columbia University Press, 1984), lv–lvi.

4   Geoffrey Cubitt, cd., *Imagining Nations* (Manchester / New York: Manchester University Press, 1998), 1.

5   Stuart Hall, "New Cultures for Old," in *A Place in the World? Place, Cultures and Globalization,* ed. Doreen Massey and Pat Jess (London: Oxford University Press, 1995), 184.

6   *The Guardian* (U.K.), 16 June 1998.

7 Ibid.

8 Polly Toynbee, "The Press Gang," *Guardian* (U.K.), 17 June 1998.

9 Roger Hewitt, *White Talk Black Talk: Inter-Racial Friendship and Communication amongst Adolescents* (London: Cambridge University Press, 1986). Hewitt's more recent work in the London borough of Greenwich was commissioned by the local council: *Routes of Racism* (London: Greenwich Council Central Race Equality Unit and Education Service, 1997).

10 Ann Leslie, "Pride, the Cure for Prejudice," in her *Mindfield: The Race Issue* (London: Camden Press, 1998), 79.

11 Ibid., 77.

12 Winthrop D. Jordan, *White over Black: American Attitudes Towards the Negro, 1550–1812* (New York: Penguin, 1966).

13 Richard Dyer, *White* (New York: Routledge, 1997), 48.

14 Johann Wolfgang von Goethe, *Theory of Colors* (Cambridge, Mass.: MIT Press, 1970), 265; cited in Dyer, *White*, 70.

15 Dyer, *White*, 48.

16 Anna Davin, "Imperialism and Motherhood," *History Workshop Journal* 5 (spring 1978), 9–65.

17 Leslie, "Pride, the Cure for Prejudice," 79.

18 Roland Littlewood, "In Search of the White Tribe," in *Mindfield*, 25–27.

19 Mark Leonard, "It's Not Just Ice-Cream," *New Statesman* (U.K.), 3 July 1998, 16.

20 Paul Greenhalgh, *Ephemeral Vistas: The Expositions Universelles, Great Exhibitions, and World's Fairs, 1851–1939* (Manchester: Manchester University Press, 1988), 112.

21 Stephen Daniels, *Fields of Vision: Landscape Imagery and National Identity in England and the United States* (Cambridge: Polity Press, 1993), 5.

22 "Wogs" is the standard British racist epithet, originating in the nineteenth century, and used to refer derogatively to anyone with "positive colour." Calais is a port on the northern coast of France, situated twenty miles from Dover across the English Channel—it therefore represents the beginning of "foreign" territory.

23 Beryl Gilroy, *Leaves in the Wind* (London: Mango Publishing, 1998), 193.

24 Mike Phillips and Trevor Phillips, *Windrush: The Irresistible Rise of Multi-Racial Britain* (London: Harper and Collins, 1998), 66.

25 Interview with Connie Mark in ibid., 126.

26 Interview with Jessica Huntley in ibid., 127–28.

27 Interview with Tryphena Anderson in ibid., 119.

28 Interview with Ben Bousquet in ibid., 119.

29 For a discussion of the origins and significance of teddy boys in 1950s Britain, see Dick Hebdige, *Subculture: The Meaning of Style* (New York: Methuen, 1979).

30 *Windrush*, 175.

31 Ibid., 176–77.

32 Ibid., 182.

33 Ibid., 182.

34 Ibid., 187.

35 Ibid., 147–48.

36 *The Mirror* (U.K.), 10 July 1998, 6.

37 David R. Roediger, *Black on White: Black Writers on What it Means to Be White* (New York: Schocken, 1998), 21.

38 Mike Phillips, "At Home in England," in Oneyekachi Wambu, ed., *Empire Windrush: Fifty Years of Writing about Black Britain* (London: Victor Gollancz, 1998), 426–31.

39 Ibid., 426.

40 Ibid., 428.

41 Ibid.

42 Ibid., 429.

43 Ibid., 431.

44 Nick Fraser, "Cup of Joy," *The Guardian* (U.K.), 15 July 1998, 2–3.

The New Liberalism in America:

Identity Politics in the "Vital Center"

"I think what I need might be," Bob Dylan sings on his 1997 album *Time Out of Mind*, "a full-length leather coat." How else to make it through middle age? Then a sardonic rhyming afterthought: "Somebody just asked me / if I'm registered to vote." Such bleak clarity is apparently now lost on Dylan's primary audience, the cohort who grew up with him. They currently occupy the political-intellectual center of the United States, home of the white male baby boomer's neoliberalism, in the form of a relatively new liberal cadre of writers and academics. This intellectual formation has done the most in recent years to make America safe for a pallid version of social democracy—they're registered to vote—while construing the realm of culture as a place that ought to be free of partisan political struggle, by which is meant the specter of so-called identity politics. If the Clintonian ruse has been to resurrect four-freedoms phraseology into a retreat from Roosevelt, the president has had a mimic chorus in this reconstructed intellectual "vital center." I will argue that an oppressive convergence of seemingly disparate cultural effects, generational ideologies, and political consequences has eventuated in a liberal discourse of class that mystifies this crucial determinant by invoking it specifically as an alternative to calls for racial, gender, and sexual liberation. In this essay I single out the foul racial nimbus, the overriding interest in white male political capital, that suffuses the "class consciousness" of boomer liberalism.

The new liberalism's trajectory is mapped in the career of someone like Joe Klein. Klein's excellent 1980 biography of Woody Guthrie makes a Carter-era rapprochement with New Deal folkishness, and inspired Bruce Springsteen himself toward summits of common-man

Americanism thereafter appropriable by the right. Klein went right more calmly, his political journalism by the mid-1980s touting a virtually reactional populism of the class-not-race variety that has finally won him a home in the precincts of James Traub, Michael Kelly, Jim Sleeper, and the rest: the *New Yorker* in the era of Tina Brown and after. Nor was Klein's roam a singular delusion. The 1990s' grand march to the center, regularly announced by Richard Rorty in such places as *Harpers* and the *New Republic* and in many ways led by *Dissent* magazine—the last hardly a surprise, given Irving Howe and Michael Harrington's explicit fondness for the Democratic Party—has been joined by all manner of erstwhile left-leaning suckers, constituting a powerful new front apparently all the more convincing for its generational profile. This formation, in fusing a new-found popular-front sensibility with a crotchety dismissal of new social movements in the name of *realpolitik,* now confronts us as the formation most in need of an antiwhite, antistatist critique. Its rise or emergence has all the seeming inevitability of a scrappy outsider speaking undeniable sense and is all the more dangerous for that. Bring out your Dems: Michael Lind, former William F. Buckley acolyte turned normative nationalist in such works as *The Next American Nation* and *Up from Conservatism;* Todd Gitlin, antiseparatist "common dreamer" in his most recent book, *The Twilight of Common Dreams;* David Hollinger, advocate of "postethnicity" in *Postethnic America;* Paul Berman, Robespierre-is-everywhere soothsayer in *A Tale of Two Utopias: The Political Journey of the Generation of 1968;* Sean Wilentz, superb if color-blind historian-cum-antimulticulturalist; Michael Tomasky, long-lost left journalist and author of *Left for Dead;* Greil Marcus, backward-looking post-Situationist conjurer of *Invisible Republic: Bob Dylan's Basement Tapes;* Michael Kazin and Maurice Isserman, lesser-evilist Clintonian historians of populism and communism, respectively; Thomas Byrne Edsall and Mary Edsall, New Democrat nostalgics and authors of the influential *Chain Reaction: The Impact of Race, Rights, and Taxes on American Politics;* Jim Sleeper, narcoleptic author of the recent attack on racial self-definition, *Liberal Racism;* Joe Klein, state romancer in *Primary Colors;* and Michael Lerner, Cornel West straight man and creator of the Clinton-beloved *Politics of Meaning.* To name only these widely published and respected writers is to survey the sensibility of a good sweep of liberal intellectual publication today, from the *New Yorker* to the *New Republic,* from the *New York Times* to the *New York Review of*

Books, from *Harpers* to *Newsweek* to the *Nation,* from *Common Knowl-edge* to *Tikkun,* from *Artforum* to *Dissent.* All of these writers, if in differing ways, lament the rise of identity politics and the decline of a public square defended on behalf of the little people, the have-nots, a true populism, common dreams—or whatever other euphemism for class can be conscripted to serve the interests of a white male cadre badly in need of a political rationale. Their achievement has been to offer a sectarian definition of "culture" as apart from the "real" sphere of political struggle and thereby to implicitly or explicitly buttress a liberal nationalism many of these writers began their careers protest-ing. And because, as I will suggest, cultural studies has done too little until very recently to develop an analysis of culture's relation to the state, the new liberalism has been able to read left intellectual work as turned off and tuned out, or, in Gitlin's corny aperçu, "marching on the English department while the right took the White House." This fact has of course only exaggerated these writers' sense of hard-won real-ism and self-importance.

You might say it began with Clintonista in 1992. Maya Angelou at the inauguration, Harvard's Robert Reich in the cabinet—the liberal braintrust was coming back to Washington. Within a month and a half, Cornel West's *Race Matters* made him a middlebrow household name and Friend of Bill. Then, in rapid succession, Clinton tapped and then capped Lani Guinier, an actual professor, for assistant at-torney general for civil rights; Henry Louis Gates Jr. became a house writer at the new *New Yorker;* and a series of books by Lind, Gitlin, Klein, and others consolidated a new "vital center." No single figure launched the new sensibility the way Arthur Schlesinger Jr.'s *The Vital Center* had codified Cold War liberalism in 1949, but the climate of opinion created by journals like the *New Yorker,* the *New Republic, Harper's,* the *New York Review of Books,* and even the *Baffler* seemed all the more autonomous and inevitable for that. (Transaction Press has duly reissued Schlesinger's *Vital Center,* and Rortyite fellow-traveler John Patrick Diggins, with an assist from Michael Lind on the vol-ume's introduction, edited the Schlesinger festschrift, *The Liberal Per-suasion: Arthur Schlesinger, Jr., and the Challenge of the American Past.*) The last few years have constituted a moment of visibility and sway for boomer liberalism—a moment during which it has as much found its voice and purpose as enunciated it. The 1995 appearances of Lind's *Next American Nation* and Gitlin's *Twilight of Common Dreams* shored up a left-liberalism perfectly situated to rush in where rightward sensationalism had run its course. Certain key public events, in the interval between the celebrated publication of *The Next American Nation* and the spring 1998 University of Virginia neoliberal symposium organized by Richard Rorty, have conspired to gel the new vital-centrism into a public, self-consciously united force with crucial ideological links and mutually informing commitments. Whiteness is their common ground. Some kind of account of the trek to what I like to think of as Rortypalooza is necessary to grasp the racial shape of the new center.

The excitement generated by the election of a new AFL-CIO leadership under John Sweeney harmonized beautifully with the emergence of the new liberal formation, which desperately sought a public political cause not allied with the radicalisms of the new social movements. The Columbia University Teach-In with the Labor Movement in October 1996, whose organizers came from the ranks of labor historians with long records of worker and union interest and involvement, managed to broker a meeting between many intellectuals (including the Rortyites) and labor leaders/rank-and-file at one rousing public event. This was an achievement in its own right and one, further, that delivered the requisite sense of promise to labor and intellectuals long fallen out in the wake of the 1948 Taft-Hartley Act, which essentially legitimated red-baiting in the unions in exchange for regular, collectively bargained standard-of-living wage increases. For the neoliberal intellectuals it was a grand new pact, since for most of them the AFL-CIO defines the limit of the labor movement in toto; not for them independent shop-floor insurgencies, unorganized workers, or radical democratic visions arising from an original perspective based on laboring cultures. The hopes all around find their way into the pages of *Audacious Democracy* (edited by Steven Fraser and Joshua B. Freeman), papers collected from the Teach-In talks and speeches. The collection attests also, though, to disturbing tendencies in the event's conception and proceedings that come in part from the organizers' allegiances. The organizing committee's co-chairs were the superb labor historians Steve Fraser and Nelson Lichtenstein, both authors of crucial books and both part of a group of scholars represented, for one instance, in the major 1989 collection *The Rise and Fall of the New Deal Order, 1930–1980* (edited by Fraser and Gary Gerstle). The almost wholly white and male authorship and focus of this collection (Elaine

Tyler May on the postwar family the lone exception), together with the book's inclusion of politically ambiguous essays by the aforementioned Thomas Byrne Edsall, Maurice Isserman, and Michael Kazin, are enough to clue you in to the secondary place accorded racial and other struggles at the Columbia Teach-In. This of course went well with the predilections of the new centrists, many of whom appeared on the Columbia panels to argue with the radicals who had in effect brought them there. The main result of this was to dull the edge of the radicals—socialists of several different stripes—while giving the liberals labor credentials to bolster their rear-guard intellectual/academic battles. Meanwhile, the Teach-In's organizing committee's white, male, boomerish profile was disheartening evidence of the unself-conscious Old-Left-meets-New front behind the Teach-In itself. This Pop Front–like approach, though dutifully attending to racism, gender inequity, and other struggles alongside the fundamental issue of labor, only revealed how added-on were the "extras" that would presumably be taken care of once the (implicitly white) working-class had won.

Certainly the Teach-In's roster, if it didn't skew the event toward the center, made publicly inescapable the conflicts between a liberal-left *realpolitik* and a more socialist left. At the opening summit, for example, Richard Rorty, speaking in the company of historians Eric Foner and Steve Fraser, early feminist (and before that, 1940s labor journalist) Betty Friedan, critical legal scholar Patricia Williams, AFL-CIO president John Sweeney, and reputed leftist Cornel West, defended labor activism and civil disobedience in the strongest terms—which, other than combating the right, is one of the most useful things a liberal can do. But then he loudly lamented the 60s flag-burning antiwar left who "began to spell 'America' with a *k*'" and thereby "did deeper and more long-lasting damage to the American left than they could ever have imagined." That got him roundly booed. Surely Rorty knew that in saying something like this he would be booed, and in that moment I respected his courage. Point is, there are real divisions here that get in the way of simplistic notions of left unity and in fact unsettled the Teach-In's idea of the left that was to help buttress the new AFL-CIO. How much better it would have been to make alliances, not with the neolibs, but with successful activist movements all over the country who might have been able to instruct the white guys on the nature of work for a strikingly recomposed labor force fighting popular struggles against the plunder of capital! Instead, vital centrists policed the left from within its company, not only writing off the student left but also, in the addresses of Todd Gitlin and others, re-fusing to consider the way blacks, Latinos, women, queers, and others have transformed utterly the very category and meaning of "the poor" or "the left" on behalf of whom they write. In fighting identity politics from the standpoint of "labor," these fellas have some thinking to do.

Two crucial developments in the time since the Columbia gathering have particularly aided boomer liberalism's credibility. The emergent cadre themselves were bolstered by the Teach-In in their haves-versus-have-nots stance. Being able to invoke a labor movement to which they felt, now, a rather intimate connection (never mind the only fledgling revival of the AFL-CIO under the less-than-salvific Sweeney) gave their perspective point, punch, and currency. Maybe it *was* time to go back to the fundamental issue of labor and class! Never mind, either, the utterly late-coming discovery of labor in most of these writers, who, as of the early 1990s, were still excoriating radical college professors in the culture wars—such as Rorty's attacks on the likes of Frank Lentric-chia, or Paul Berman on political correctness—with little concern for their now-espoused object of beauty. The "labor metaphysic" C. Wright Mills suggested the new left drop in the early 1960s has made a roaring return.

A second development, though, came along to reinflect this first one. That of course has been the labor movement's own abrupt fall from grace. With the Teamsters for a Democratic Union's Ron Carey indicted and ousted for scamming money to fund his reelection cam-paign against James Hoffa Jr. and the subsequent election of the cor-rupt Hoffa to lead the Teamsters, the labor movement has promptly lost the momentum that in some ways offered the optative glue of the new liberalism. Its writers now aloft in a sort of speculative bubble, the new cadre feels free to opine in the most authoritative fashion about matters that were not on their plate as recently as three or four years ago.

The bubble got great girth in March, surely 1998's cruelest month. The release of Rorty's *Achieving Our Country*, the March *Dissent* (with new format and carefully collected personnel), and the film *Primary Colors* combined with Rortypalooza to achieve a rare aura of syn-chronicity. Paul Berman, Louis Menand, Sean Wilentz, Michael Lind, Todd Gitlin, Mark Edmundson, and of course Rorty himself, along with a host of bit players (Eric Alterman, Carlin Romano, David Reiff, Gayatri Spivak, Mark Lilla) convoked to hail the muse of Whitmanian, Deweyan liberalism. The group's racial and class musings will be evident in a few brief notices and excerpted phrases from the three-day event. Women and people of color from across the country were, for all intents and purposes, represented in the singular person of Spivak, the conference's designated scourge. Berman proclaimed Marx's labor theory of value "wrong" and Whitman a utopian figure of "revolutionary socialism." Menand repeated the fossil line that the "contemporary left" exists only in the university. Rorty, like Menand, intimated that policy rather than theory is really what matters, quoted from *Spoon River Anthology* and urged a return to Herbert Croly's patriotic progressivism. Edmundson named religion the key preoccupation for Americans today and a prime ground on which intellectuals might reach them. Gitlin did his part to make Theodor Adorno and Max Horkheimer safe for liberalism by noting how American commodity culture, for all its deadening impact, has in its global reach become an advertisement for democracy. Lilla waxed nearly triumphant on waning left prospects ("there's not a *chance in hell* of the *Nation*'s hopes coming true"). Fareed Zakaria, second-in-command of *Foreign Affairs,* counseled against waves of "revolution" abroad (i.e., citizen-activated social change) in favor of constitutional democracy instituted from above or from outside and IMF/World Bank "economic development." And Bush's secretary of state Lawrence Eagleburger (why not?), on the final panel, was *sure* that nit-picking with China over human rights was much less effective than simply exposing them to "Western ideas." Lind and Wilentz alone offered probing readings of American party politics in the last two centuries, only in the end to either reify and eternalize case division (Lind) or too easily to proclaim it fixable (Wilentz). For her part Spivak performed well as house crank but was too firmly stationed in this role by the line-up to offer more than local, wildcat interventions from the floor on the writings of Marx (a helpful thing, when Paul Berman's around).

It was a sad and complacent spectacle for me, who had hoped for more from the independent left-liberalism of Paul Berman (once something of a C. L. R. James adherent) or Todd Gitlin. I myself blame Rorty (along with the aforementioned 1990s developments) for this conventionalizing and defanging of sometimes powerful cultural and social critics. To be sure, Rorty cannot alone be held accountable for

Berman's habit of writing off the Black Panthers as vicious thugs (for example, his review of David Horowitz's autobiography, *Radical Son,* in *Dissent*—Horowitz may actually be better than Berman on the Panthers), or indeed for the incredible arrogance of Berman's very title *A Tale of Two Utopias: The Political Journey of the Generation of 1968,* which generation apparently did not include black activists of importance. Nor is Rorty to blame for Michael Lind's anti–affirmative action stance, or Sean Wilentz's refusal to grant multicultural initiatives any space in the American cultural scene. (Mark Lilla's professed "hatred" of rap music at Rortypalooza—especially over breakfast at fine hotels in foreign lands, he related—*is* echoed in Rorty's dismissal of Ice Cube as anti-Korean in a 1994 *Dissent* debate with Andrew Ross, but even this, I freely grant, is relatively minor if utterly symptomatic.) No: Rorty has, rather, in short pieces for *Harper's,* op-eds in major newspapers, essays and reviews in *Dissent,* and public lectures all over the world, created a genealogically rich context for the emergence of the above sorts of ideas. *Achieving Our Country* only piles on, rather too thickly, to this new formation, codifying, assuming, and portending its continued existence in the face of (shadow) threats from the left.

At least Michael Lind exposes the right—Pat Robertson's lunatic anti-Semitism, William F. Buckley's mercenary ideological compromises. Rorty follows family tradition in standing fast for freedom against a terrible left specter. In the American Committee for Cultural Freedom–funded *McCarthy and the Communists* (1954), James Rorty and Moshe Decter argued McCarthy's obvious demagoguery only sought, as they put it, a way "to combat Communism responsibly." "Current membership in the Communist Party should be regarded as prima facie evidence of their unfitness to teach," they wrote, and for efficiency's sake this might well be adopted as law; as for teachers who "adhere to the Party line but cannot be shown to be Party members," routine academic processes of evaluation and administration would take care of them. Rorty *fils* peddles a much softer version of this sort of thing in his constant attacks on the "cultural left." Like so many others unsure of what to do after the demise of Communism and the abatement of the culture wars, Rorty espies an imminent derailing of left hopes by a self-involved and myopic academic set. "Leftists in the academy have permitted cultural politics to supplant real politics, and have collaborated with the Right in making cultural issues central to public debate. They are spending energy which should be directed at proposing new laws on discussing topics as remote from the country's needs as were [Henry] Adams' musings on the Virgin and the Dynamo. The academic Left has no project to propose to America, no vision of a country to be achieved by building a consensus on the need for specific reforms. Its members no longer feel the force of [William] James's and [Progressive journalist Herbert] Croly's rhetoric. The American civic religion seems to them narrow-minded and obsolete nationalism."[1]

Fighting words, of course; yet the main charges seem banal next to the rhetoric that labels the bad left permissive, traitorous, energy-wasting, and remote in the space of two sentences. Pardon me for hearing in them the keening anti-left tones of, respectively, the 1950s, 60s, 70s, and 80s played on Rorty's remarkable polemical instrument. No member of this left is actually named (save Fredric Jameson in an appendix—a minor operation), which does nothing for his argument intellectually, but, as with the anti-PC diatribes it lamely echoes, will do wonders raising the hackles of readers who know no better. The problem with the cultural left is apparently that it reads the wrong philosophers and does scholarly work (rather than public-policy advocacy). Politically it knows not whereof it speaks and talks little sense within its own academic ranks, let alone to any "public." It complains about too many injustices at once when it should stick to economic inequality. There's a lot of urgent-seeming moralizing about all this. In the end you begin to wonder why the writer spends a whole book attacking such a pathetic thing. But you also sense his disconnection from his own polemical purpose. He harangues so abstractly that you doubt he knows much about the "cultural left" he attacks; and what his "public" is supposed to make of all this when they *already* vote Democratic is up to you to figure. The overall effect is rather like that of a quaint old crank trying desperately to convince you that Whitman would have been appalled by the current state of the IRS.

With a better sense of his readership Rorty would challenge a broad public for whom his own cream-of-wheat ideas—secular humanism and the importance of labor unions—would alone be a difficult bolus to get down. He has occasionally done so, to fine effect. Is he afraid to do other, here, than present himself as a liberal martyr drowned out by noisy know-nothing leftists? If so, it's at least a legitimate worry. There's little except the huffing and puffing that you can't find in the work of, say, Robert Reich or Michael Lind. Presenting yourself as in a

political/intellectual quandary or arguing with your misguided colleagues makes liberal common wisdom at least a little more interesting. Rorty even boils down the perspectives of writers like Reich and
Lind to a few obvious liberal propositions: boosted by the kind of
national pride found in Lincoln or Whitman, intellectuals should
focus on policy rather than speculative debate, on economic inequality
rather than what Rorty calls "stigma" (race, for example), and on practical reform rather than radicalism. "The heirs of the New Left of the
1960s have created, within the academy, a cultural Left. Many members of this Left specialize in what they call the 'politics of difference'
or 'of identity' or 'of recognition.' This cultural Left thinks more about
stigma than about money, more about deep and hidden psychosexual
motivations than about shallow and evident greed. . . . The new cultural left . . . has few ties to what remains of the pre-Sixties reformist
Left. . . . This residual reformist Left thinks more about laws that need
to be passed than about a culture that needs to be changed."[2] What *isn't*
wrong with this passage? The cultural left that cares only about racial,
sexual, and gender difference descends from the white- and male-
dominated new left—the one that crumbled when women, blacks, and
queers made their own movements? This left, which reads Marx
rather than Dewey, has had nothing to say about capitalism in its
numerous trivial studies? The "cultural left" is new? (Tell it to *Partisan
Review.*) Is it a surprise that a broad, long-standing, radical tendency
isn't inspired by the pre- or post-60s reformist left? (You remember
Mr. Mills, don't you Mr. Bell?) Mostly, in the end, it seems like the
linguistic turn is over and the social-science turn has arrived. There is
indeed a good bit of the reformed sinner's tract here. Between you and
me, I never had any doubt that Nabokov was a better read than Fichte,
but I was (kind of) willing to let Rorty tell me so in *Contingency, Irony,
and Solidarity.* But *now*—we've discovered quantitative sociology will
unlock the doors of perception! What's next, Hillis Miller doing labor
history?

If only it were that good. Standing firm on the importance of policy,
economics, and reform as opposed to culture, stigma, and radicalism,
Rorty flubs all three key oppositions. First off, if you thought maybe all
the second terms might have real bearing on the first ones, forget it—
Motown had nothing to do with the Voting Rights Act, black workers
face only economic exploitation, and reform generally has nothing to
do with the push of radicalism. Rorty doesn't argue this, but his points

are made so baldly and summarily that he might as well. And yet, oddly for all its hue and cry, *Achieving Our Country* advances no policy proposals of the sort he says we all should; nor is there even ventured a notion of what counts as a policy proposal. Sometimes it's "laws" and other times assorted proclamations, but this book does nothing to dispel the sense that Rorty never advances any particularly rousing policy proposals—only the *idea* of policy-making. (His call in a December 1997 *Nation* article for universal health care, funding for Head Start, and the rest, amounting to utopian Clintonism, was proof, not exception.) He caricatures and traduces a left that has always been more involved in social justice campaigns locally or nationally than Rorty himself (even Henry Louis Gates Jr. and Martha Nussbaum took the stand in actual trials). Is a life change afoot? Rorty now believes that "the Left should put a moratorium on theory" and thus that his own celebrated work on other theorists falls short of the political mark. Maybe it hurts when Congress doesn't rally round your call for an end to the category of "ideology."

Rorty's distinctions seem to collapse under very little pressure, but that pretty much captures the enterprise. Rorty explicitly disavows sectarianism in the interest of a healthy, broad left, but the book is on the whole a liberal's rather scorching sectarian distancing move from the "heirs of the New Left." This tends to get a little confusing. Rorty begins the final lecture talking about the positive value in the 60s recognition that "economic determinism had been too simplistic." One paragraph later he's riding that way again, into a nostalgic sunset of Old Left reverie. Rorty's invocations of the "money question" have no weight because he doesn't think it important to discuss its political dimension—the nods to greed and selfishness are virtually Dickensian. Which is fine with me, of course, but hey. One infers there might be more to it than this, but Rorty makes few gestures toward any real notion of how to achieve economic redistribution, except to pass a law for it. I'm not alone, I know, in wondering where this would leave "stigmatized" working people whom labor leaders and politicians might still write out of the ranks of the deserving. Rorty tells the cultural left to open lines of communication with "the unions" but says no more—as though that would take care of it just fine. Are we talking Sweeney, Hoffa, radicalized unions, stagnant unions, leadership only, insurgent rank and file, what? And what about the 85 percent or so of nonunionized American workers? Here too the road-to-Damascus quality of the ideas is a little embarrassing—Rorty seems not to realize he's in the rear guard following the "cultural leftists" who are already there; from the back of the pack it's apparently difficult to glimpse with any clarity the political ends of the glorious means.

"Stigma," meanwhile, opens up the color-blindness that legiti-mizes the hollowness of his younger compeers. Why does he refer to oppressions other than class as stigmas? Certainly it's meant to trivial-ize rather than debate the radicals he dislikes; he undoubtedly knows no one uses the term anymore precisely because it carries the sugges-tion Rorty wants to put forward, that race, for example, is less funda-mental than other grounds of exploitation, in the end an issue of manners and private life rather than public injustice. I think the sneer backfires because it recalls Rorty's own generation of work on race—by Erving Goffman and others—which added dimension to the discus-sion but should undoubtedly be put aside the way Rorty suggests. This is not to say it's at all clear that Rorty doesn't think about race in just this limited and trivializing way. Recall the comment at the end of *Contingency, Irony, and Solidarity* where Rorty mentions "the attitude of contemporary American liberals to the unending hopelessness and misery of the lives of the young blacks in American cities": "Do we say that these people must be helped because they are our fellow human beings? We may, but it is much more persuasive, morally as well as politically, to describe them as our fellow *Americans*—to insist that it is outrageous that an *American* should live without hope." Forget the case being made, the false choice it proposes: follow the drift of the remark. Blacks exist in the book for this single moment because *they suffer;* and liberals are good liberals when they find the right language to express pity and outrage for "these people." National devotion of the paternalist sort that partially *produced* the problem will also heal it, according to Rorty. What did you think was meant by Martha and the Vandellas' national notice of "Dancing in the Street" in the classic moment of mid-60s ghetto misery? I think it *wasn't* hopeless but grateful Negroes waiting for liberals to help out; more like a nation-wide, self-conscious formation of black people feeling the lift of the social motion they'd created. Isn't it time to stop promoting the exem-plary compassion of liberal pragmatists through useful case studies of "our" suffering Negroes? For "stigma" is apparently so bad that even

when you're avoiding it you run into trouble. The avoidance as well as
the trouble signify the white identity politics barely below the surface
of this kind of new liberal program.

Indeed, Rorty dedicates *Achieving Our Country* to Irving Howe and
A. Philip Randolph; Howe earns several pages of commentary, Randolph none. This would be beneath comment if the book weren't so hot
on practice and policy of the kind Randolph effected far, far more than
Howe. Rorty, finally, is a philosopher, more comfortable talking about
Howe's intellectual self-styling than Randolph's political thought,
strategy, and action. And yet, if thought is preferred, where are, for
example, Lani Guinier, Mary Frances Berry, Patricia Williams, or
Cheryl Harris, bona fide intellectuals with actual ideas about "laws"
and voting policy? I guess the rather airless extracts from Lincoln and
Whitman on democratic ideals are more to the point. Any reason to
think this *isn't* a book of cultural leftism, divided against itself?

To pass from the senior public moralist to the boomer social and
cultural critics is to find a similar Cassandrism dressed up as tough-
minded intellectual responsibility. It ought to be said right away,
though, that the boomer work is weightier and more tenacious than
Rorty's western wind; there is at least the sense in Berman, Gitlin, and
others of struggles fought for a long time on the ground. It's just that
1968 seems to have been as traumatic for them as they say it was for
the country: the moment of black and female departures from the
ranks of the student left arrested the latter's political development at
the Chicago Democratic Convention. With Chicago '68's badge of
honor become sackcloth, these ex–new lefters now make a profile of
haranguing identity movements formed out of that moment of traumatic separation. Stanley Aronowitz has written of "when the New
Left was new"; Gitlin, Berman, and other boomer liberals offer the
least attractive picture of the new left grown old. Gitlin's *Twilight of
Common Dreams* is a convenient summation and attitudinal bell-
wether for the boomer front. Its striking accommodation of consensus visions of the national culture is all the more surreal coming
from a prominent new leftist and former SDS president. Gitlin advances what he calls a "Left universalism" that would bind up the
"profusion of identities" (gays, blacks, the Deaf) into some plausible
left unity; as Gitlin puts it, "What is a Left without a commons, even a
hypothetical one? If there is no people, but only peoples, there is no
Left." What sounds very much like a resurrected Popular Front slogan

rings strangely on the ears from a writer whose early political commitments devolved precisely upon jettisoning the Old Left. Though sympathetic to many of the changes brought about by the "new social
movements'" multiplication of difference, Gitlin has trouble seeing
why any of them should retain the autonomy that gave us those
changes or why, even theoretically, it might be important. In a very real
sense he misses their fundamental point. It is not in any way guaranteed that, after all is said and done, blacks, Chicanos, gays, lesbians,
women, the disabled, and the working class will find common cause
in some world-transforming purpose; the motive of identity-based
movements, for all their troubles of self-definition, was not to stand up
for their particular rights so that they could take their place amid the
honorable (and now expanded) left. Those movements, rather, have so
utterly transformed the idea of the left that Gitlin's common dreaming
seems merely half-asleep. As Ernesto Laclau and Chantal Mouffe argue in *Hegemony and Socialist Strategy,* the new social movements are
rarely laterally compatible in any kind of united-front way and in fact
call into question the idea that such a front won't wind up suppressing
or misrepresenting certain of the interests grouped under its um-
brella: this is Gitlin's own mistake, particularly in regard to black
struggles. Yet it is at the same time clear that any one of these movements is liable to engage a dominant social formation at one of its
weak points and spark a fire that will earn widespread solidarities. To
me it is revealing that Gitlin refuses even to consider the most widely
debated theorists of particularistic social urgency. Throughout *Common Dreams,* Gitlin reviews the wars over grade-school history books,
literary theory, academic politics, political correctness, and more—
rather like the cultural studies scholars he deplores—as though he
would rather deride the more abstruse cultural difficulties associated
with questions of local autonomy than demonstrate how that autonomy cripples the left, which would at least necessitate taking new
social struggles seriously. Instead of putting forward a revanchist idea
of cultural commonality, even if a "left" one, Gitlin contents himself
with assuming that certain black demands, for example, simply har-
monize with the aspirations of his universal left.

Thus such spectacles occur as the Todd Gitlin–Robin Kelley debate
at one of the most volatile panels of the Columbia Teach-In. Gitlin read
a stern and rather dyspeptic screed discounting group demands, such
as those of black militants, as divisive and merely local: "The fact re-

mains that African Americans constitute a minority, and no wishful thinking or census projection changes this fact. . . . Adding up abstract minorities does not automatically produce a victory for general justice. . . . American history is replete with instances of minorities submerging their particular claims, only to be forgotten, and this is always a risk. But it is much too easy to lose sight of the opposite risk, that of narrowness, and of the gains that have accrued to minorities when broad-based movements—in particular labor—have been strongest." It's a measure of Gitlin's nonrecognition of black left traditions that he can so appallingly write off blacks as a minor political bloc whose independent struggles don't result in "general justice"—quite a phrase, this last, begging the question of just what counts as "general" enough to warrant struggle (I have a notion or two). American history, I would go way out on a limb to say, is more replete with instances of submerged minorities who wound up with little or nothing than it is with the "narrowness" of black demands. (I reserve enough faith in humanity to find it difficult to believe that Gitlin *really means* to say that abolitionism, Du Bois's NAACP, Randolphism, or Kingism were "narrow" noncontributors to significant "general justice.") Having thus functionally eviscerated it, Gitlin nonetheless called for a united left front. Kelley was quick to nail the white, class-not-race-based ideal type of this front, and he proceeded to show how imaginary Gitlin's idea of the left was when the formerly white and male AFL-CIO membership, to take only one example, is now significantly female and colored and when categories such as class, race, and gender are irretrievably disrupted by their interpenetration as opposed to their simple addition. (For more of Kelley's immensely clarifying position on these matters, see chapter 4 of his book *Yo' Mama's DisFunktional!: Fighting the Culture Wars in Urban America* [1997]).

Examples abound in *Common Dreams* of Gitlin's dim view of black autonomy or self-activity. He can't even praise Martin Luther King Jr. without rushing suspiciously to embrace King's turn to the struggle of workers and the poor: "The militants of SNCC had long mocked him as 'De Lawd.' Yet he was there to mock, to oppose, to love. While King lived, he embodied the possibility of a redemptive struggle across racial lines. He journeyed to Memphis to support a strike by black garbage workers—a solidarity that had class as well as race dimensions." There are good left grounds for appreciating King's turn, but doing so as a way to write off SNCC and racial "separatism" smells a little funny. Indeed, blaming the white left's late-'60s "go-for-broke trajectory" on the advent of "black revolutionism," Gitlin speaks of this traumatic moment of black independence as though it were responsible for all manner of ugly white-ethnic reaction. (Gitlin sides with those New York Jewish teachers in the strike of 1968–69 unfortunate enough to have been "liberal" and "recently unionized" into "power and legitimacy" against the "insult" of black parents demanding more control of their children's schooling.) These are enough to remind one of the ire C. L. R. James directed toward similar Popular Front–era Communist Party sentiments (on the part of historian Herbert Aptheker and others) in the 1940s, and the parallel is not mere happenstance. As at the Columbia Teach-In, one witnesses here the odd alchemizing of the new left into the image of the old, that is, the turn from internal divisions, presented as merely cultural, to more "fundamental" matters of economic inequality fought by a united left. Gitlin often adopts the pose of the persecuted white liberal flayed for speaking sense instead of going along and getting along, and he even has Jim Sleeper's lovely habit of lampooning black middle-class discontent by contrasting it with the plight of the black poor. One poor Berkeley kid comes in for professorial sarcasm during a student strike for accelerated race-based hiring and admissions. ("In the days leading up to the strike, the organizers made little effort to explain their demands, let alone defend them," Gitlin avers.) Breaking the strike, Gitlin tells his students he'll be in the lecture hall to discuss the strike issues. Strikers come shouting into the session, Gitlin invites them to join it, and a black man yells, "We're dying out there!" Gitlin pulls a stiff one from the quiver: "I asked him, 'How is admitting more black students and hiring more black faculty going to stop the dying out there?' There was no response." Content in his ability to silence black youth and ignore connections between black death and black educational opportunity—in a single bound—Gitlin asks us to take him as an authoritative guide to left universalism. What response *is* there to this sort of thing?

As this episode suggests, there is a decidedly undialectical quality to Gitlin's argument that marks it not only as proffered within the Anglo-American academy but as kin to the baser cousin-books it seeks to subsume and transcend and in some ways does (Allan Bloom's *Closing of the American Mind*, Roger Kimball's *Tenured Radicals*, Richard Bernstein's *Dictatorship of Virtue*, Arthur Schlesinger's *Disuniting of Amer-*

ica, and so on). Gitlin's riff goes like this: look at all of these cultural excrescences and see how they're ruining the classical idea of the left! Any left sociologist worth the name, though, might think twice about why recent social struggles have taken the form of "identity"-based movements in the first place and relate them to larger questions of political economy and state formation. Surely the controversies Gitlin surveys are symptoms of some larger crisis of the state, not simply the *moral* failings of the left. In this respect cultural studies has done too little to address the problem or even idea of the state that the new liberalism has rushed to provide; in the absence of a convincing counterargument from the left, a weak left-liberal rhetoric holds sway over an increasingly corporate populism that is only in name by and for everyday people. The instructive text here is Stuart Hall et al.'s 1978 study *Policing the Crisis: Mugging, the State, and Law and Order,* a book tellingly uninfluential in recent U.S. cultural studies work. Taking as their focus Britain's media-created mugging scare of the early 1970s and with their analytical sights clearly on the seams and suturings of the state apparatuses, Hall et al. show the figure of the black mugger and the hysteria about rising crime to be a collective way of handling or managing the crisis of capitalist authority brought about by various 1960s insurrections. It seems equally clear in the present instance that identity-politics hysteria expresses a crisis of authority on the part of the American nation-state as well as the left, not only for those to whom the left never mattered and who now smell blood, but also for those to whom the canonical revolutionary white male subject is too dear to let go. If identity-based movements seem in some instances misguided or superficial, it might make sense to respond not with a moralizing version of left consensus but with a historical sense of the way left consensus has usually been a disaster for blacks, women, and many others. Instead, Gitlin's searching explanations for "the dying out there" are the "historical consequence of slavery and poverty" or the "direct result of young black men killing other young black men in the course of criminal activity." Now this is deep. (*New York Times,* come back, all is forgiven!) *Policing the Crisis* has a profounder sense of how left visionaries might respond:

> We can think of the relations of production of capitalism articulating the classes in distinct ways at each of the levels or instances of the social formation—economic, political, ideological. . . . Race is

intrinsic to the manner in which the black labouring classes are *complexly constituted* at each of those levels. . . . This gives the matter of race and *racism* a theoretical as well as a practical centrality to all the relations and practices which affect black labour. The constitution of this class fraction as a class, and the *class relations* which inscribe it, function *as race relations*. The two are inseparable. Race is the modality in which class is lived. It is also the medium in which class relations are experienced.

This account, it seems to me, points to what Gitlin would *still* find a version of "identity politics" but is in fact something subtler and more difficult to grasp (at least for Gitlin): a recognition by new social movements that their struggles, *even when parallel* to those of Gitlin's old-boys' left, in fact shape up along different axes of social existence. When fighting exploitative employers or companies, that is, black workers may well present their case as a racial one. Hence the success of black worker campaigns in North Carolina, where housekeepers at the University of North Carolina–Chapel Hill or nonunion organizing campaigns among black workers in poultry gulags or strikes at local K-Marts have made labor demands *in the form of antiracist activism:* these were successful to varying degrees because they foresook the left fundamentalism that says only "class" matters—and that only with reference to the AFL-CIO. Such campaigns meet capital-state formations or agglomerations the way they've been greeted: as particularized, super-exploitable wage labor. To whine about this as divisive, self-interested, or marginal "identity politics" seems inane when the country, at local and state levels, and notwithstanding the destruction of affirmative action, now seems less and less able to discredit worker protests fought on the ground in the name of racial justice.

What thinkers like Gitlin demonstrate, then, is not how wrong it is to bring politics into the cultural sphere but how wrong they feel a certain political understanding of culture is. The tactical evacuation of turf tussles from culture (that's *politics*) is only a political reading of culture that brings that category uncomfortably close to mystifying nationalist ideologies of American culture. In insisting on reading political strife out of culture, in other words, one begs the time-honored question of just how far a left-liberal universalism is from, as Earl Browder taught us to think of Communism in the late 1930s, "twentieth-century Americanism." It's difficult to see how a political commitment to radical equality won through conflict can be combined with a consensus approach to culture in a book devoted to staving off cultural challenges to that approach from the left. When does your left universalism simply become a hegemonic liberalism?

In his book on the 1960s, Gitlin writes feelingly about the separatist implications of Black Power's advent, which, given the cross-racial solidarity so crucial to the early new left, apparently seemed a crushing rejection of white allies, who were now told to organize in their own communities. Paul Berman still broods about this political moment in his attacks on the Panthers. Gitlin's vehement universalism, like that of several key boomer liberals, is an imaginary return to early-60s interracial brotherhood; a legitimate return, of course, though inseparable in these writers from an implied white masculinism, not to mention the naked irony that interracial brotherhood came about in the first place through the 50's and early 60's version of "identity politics"—the independent actions of African American organizers on specifically African American concerns. Gitlin's tirades against black self-activity in the present virtually parade the anger and rejection that 60s black separatism caused in this generation of white, often Jewish, male intellectuals. The pith and nerve of pain in Gitlin's accounts of the racial past and present suggest a primal scene revisited therapeutically in the hope of surcease—even while such returns yield only further attacks on autonomous black political activity, the drive-by name for which has become "identity politics."

Katha Pollitt's June 1998 *Nation* editorial reflecting on the new liberals, the Rorty conference, and Eric Alterman's account of same in an earlier *Nation* makes the crucial point about the new liberals and their own identity politics:

> All you have to do is look squarely at the world you live in and it is perfectly obvious that—as a host of scholars and activists, whom Alterman dismisses as "the racism/sexism/homophobia crowd," have documented—race and gender are crucial means through which class is structured. They are not side issues that can be solved by raising the minimum wage, although that is important, or even by unionizing more workplaces, although that is important too. Inequality in America is too solidly based on racism and sexism for it to be altered without acknowledging race and sex and

sexuality. Everybody sees this now—even John Sweeney [!] talks about gay partnership benefits as a working-class issue—except for a handful of old New Leftists, journalists and mini-pundits, white men who practice the identity politics that dare not speak its name.[3]

With the arrival of boomer liberalism, one is invited into a middlebrow discourse whose roots in white male identity are disavowed through an ironically Marxisant economic fundamentalism. The new liberals think of other kinds of exploitation and other ways of combating them as sideshow fights against prejudice—a league apart from the electorally based, elite-ruled, arena of "real" politics that demands hardheaded accommodation and reformist tinkering, spun in rhetorics and ideologies of universalism, commonality, idealism, and vision—almost by definition, given their Caucasian provenance, racially exclusive and constitutive of sex/gender dominance. The broad post–new left's return to nationalist social democracy will grace a statist bipartisan waltz into the next century. Here's hoping our better angels help us survive the boom.

Notes

1   Richard Rorty, *Achieving Our Country: Leftist Thought in Twentieth-Century America* (Cambridge: Harvard University Press, 1998), 14–15.
2   Ibid., 76–77.
3   Katha Pollitt, "Race and Gender and Class, Oh My!" *The Nation,* 8 June 1998.

How Gay Stays White and What Kind

of White It Stays

The Stereotype

When I teach college courses on queer history or queer working-class studies, I encourage students to explore the many ways that homosexuality is shaped by race, class, and gender. I know that racialized phantom figures hover over our classroom and inhabit our consciousness. I try to name these figures out loud to bring them down to earth so we can begin to resist their stranglehold on our intelligence. One by one, I recite the social categories that students have already used in our discussions—immigrant, worker, corporate executive, welfare recipient, student on financial aid, lesbian mother—and ask students first to imagine the stereotypical figure associated with the category and then to call out the figure's race, gender, class, and sexuality. As we watch each other conjure up and name these phantoms, we are stunned at how well each of us has learned by heart the same fearful chorus.

Whenever I get to the social category "gay man," the students' response is always the same: "white and well-to-do." In the United States today, the dominant image of the typical gay man is a white man who is financially better off than most everyone else.

My White Desires

Since the day I came out to my best friend in 1968, I have inhabited the social category "gay white man." As a historian, writer, and activist, I've examined the gay and the male parts of that identity, and more recently I've explored my working-class background and the Franco-

American ethnicity that is so intertwined with it. But only recently have I identified with or seriously examined my gay male whiteness.[1]

Several years ago I made the decision to put race and class at the center of my gay writing and activism. I was frustrated at how my own gay social and activist circles reproduced larger patterns of racial separation by remaining almost entirely white. And I felt abandoned as the vision of the national gay movement and media narrowed from fighting for liberation, freedom, and social justice to expressing personal pride, achieving visibility, and lobbying for individual equality within existing institutions. What emerged was too often an exclusively gay rights agenda isolated from supposedly nongay issues, such as homelessness, unemployment, welfare, universal health care, union organizing, affirmative action, and abortion rights. To gain recognition and credibility, some gay organizations and media began to aggressively promote the so-called positive image of a generic gay community that is an upscale, mostly male, and mostly white consumer market with mainstream, even traditional, values. Such a strategy derives its power from an unexamined investment in whiteness and middle-class identification. As a result, its practitioners seemed not to take seriously or even notice how their gay visibility successes at times exploited and reinforced a racialized class divide that continues to tear our nation apart, including our lesbian and gay communities.

My decision to put race and class at the center of my gay work led me as a historian to pursue the history of a multiracial maritime union that in the 1930s and 1940s fought for racial equality and the dignity of openly gay workers.[2] And my decision opened doors that enabled me as an activist to join multiracial lesbian, gay, bisexual, and transgender groups whose members have been doing antiracist work for a long time and in which gay white men are not the majority—groups that included the Lesbian, Gay, Bisexual, and Transgender Advisory Committee to the San Francisco Human Rights Commission and the editorial board of the now-defunct national lesbian and gay quarterly journal *Out/Look*.

But doing this work also created new and ongoing conflicts in my relationships with other white men. I want to figure out how to handle these conflicts as I extend my antiracist work into those areas of my life where I still find myself among gay white men—especially when we form new activist and intellectual groups that once again turn out to be white. To do this I need "to clarify something for myself," as

James Baldwin put it, when he gave his reason for writing his homo-sexual novel *Giovanni's Room* in the 1950s.[3]

I wanted to know how gay gets white, how it stays that way, and how whiteness is used both to win and attack gay rights campaigns.

I want to learn how to see my own whiteness when I am with gay white men and to understand what happens among us when one of us calls attention to our whiteness.

I want to know why I and other gay white men would want to challenge the racist structures of whiteness, what happens to us when we try, what makes me keep running away from the task, sometimes in silent despair, and what makes me want to go back to take up the task again.

I want to pursue these questions by drawing on a gay ability, developed over decades of figuring out how to "come out of the closet," to bring our hidden lives out into the open. But I want to do this without encouraging anyone to assign a greater degree of racism to gay white men, thus exposed, than to other white men more protected from exposure, and without inviting white men who are not gay to more safely see gay men's white racism rather than their own.

I want to know these things because gay white men have been among the men I have loved and will continue to love. I need them in my life and at my side as I try to make fighting racism a more central part of my work. And when students call out "white" to describe the typical gay man, and they see me standing right there in front of them, I want to figure out how, from where I am standing, I can intelligently fight the racist hierarchies that I and my students differently inhabit.

Gay Whitening Practices

Despite the stereotype, the gay male population is not as white as it appears to be in the images of gay men projected by the mainstream and gay media, or among the "out" men (including myself) who move into the public spotlight as representative gay activists, writers, commentators, and spokesmen. Gay men of color, working against the stereotype, have engaged in long, difficult struggles to gain some public recognition of their cultural heritages, political activism, and everyday existence. To educate gay white men, they've had to get our attention by interrupting our business as usual, then convince us that we don't speak for them or represent them or know enough about either their realities or our own racial assumptions and privileges. And when I and other gay white men don't educate ourselves, gay men of color have done the face-to-face work of educating us about their cultures, histories, oppression, and particular needs—the kind of personal work that tires us out when heterosexuals ask us to explain to them what it's like to be gay. Also working against their ability to put "gay" and "men of color" together in the broader white imagination are a great many other powerful *whitening practices* that daily construct, maintain, and fortify the idea that gay male means white.

How does the category "gay man" become white? What are the whitening practices that perpetuate this stereotype, often without awareness or comment by gay white men? How do these practices operate, and what racial work do they perform?

I begin by mining my own experience for clues.[4] I know that if I go where I'm surrounded by other gay white men, or if I'm having sex with a white man, it's unlikely that our race will come up in conversation. Such racially comfortable, racially familiar situations can make us mistakenly believe that there are such things as gay issues, spaces, culture, and relationships that are not "lived through" race, and that white gay life, so long as it is not named as such, is not about race.[5] These lived assumptions, and the privileges on which they are based, form a powerful camouflage woven from a web of unquestioned beliefs—that gay whiteness is unmarked and unremarkable, universal and representative, powerful and protective, a cohesive bond. The markings of this camouflage are pale—a characteristic that the wearer sees neither as entirely invisible nor as a racial "color," a shade that allows the wearer to blend into the seemingly neutral background of white worlds. When we wear this everyday camouflage into a gay political arena that white men already dominate, our activism comes wrapped in a *pale protective coloring* that we may not notice but which is clearly visible to those who don't enjoy its protection.

I start to remember specific situations in which I caught glimpses of how other gay whitening practices work.

One night, arriving at my favorite gay disco bar in San Francisco, I discovered outside a picket line of people protesting the triple-carding (requiring three photo ID's) of gay men of color at the door. This practice was a form of racial *exclusion*—policing the borders of white gay institutions to prevent people of color from entering. The management was using this discriminatory practice to keep the bar from

"turning," as it's called—a process by which a "generically gay" bar
(meaning a predominantly white bar) changes into a bar that loses
status and income (meaning gay white men with money won't go
there) because it has been "taken over" by black, Latino, or Asian gay
men. For many white owners, managers, and patrons of gay bars, only
a white gay bar can be *just* gay; a bar where men of color go is seen as
racialized. As I joined the picket line, I felt the fears of a white man
who has the privilege to choose on which side of a color line he will
stand. I wanted to support my gay brothers of color who were being
harassed at the door, yet I was afraid that the doorman might recognize me as a regular and refuse to let me back in. That night, I saw a
gay bar's doorway become a racialized border, where a battle to preserve or challenge the whiteness of the clientele inside was fought
among dozens of gay men who were either standing guard at the door,
allowed to walk through it, or shouting and marching outside. (The
protests eventually made the bar stop the triple-carding.)

I remember seeing how another gay whitening practice works
when I watched, with other members of a sexual politics study group,
an antigay video, "Gay Rights, Special Rights," produced in 1993 by
The Report, a religious right organization. This practice was the *selling*
of gay whiteness—the marketing of gays as white and wealthy to make
money and increase political capital, either to raise funds for campaigns (in both progay and antigay benefits, advertising, and direct-
mail appeals) or to gain economic power (by promoting or appealing
to a gay consumer market). The antigay video we watched used racialized class to undermine alliances between a gay rights movement
portrayed as white and movements of people of color portrayed as
heterosexual. It showed charts comparing mutually exclusive categories of "homosexuals" and "African Americans," telling us that homosexuals are wealthy, college-educated white men who vacation more
than anyone else and who demand even more "special rights and
privileges" by taking civil rights away from low-income African Americans.[6] In this zero-sum, racialized world of the religious right, gay
men are white; gay, lesbian, and bisexual people of color, along with
poor or working-class white gay men, bisexuals, and lesbians, simply
do not exist. The recently vigorous gay media promotion of the high
income, brand-loyal gay consumer market—which is typically portrayed as a population of white, well-to-do, college-educated young

men—only widens the racialized class divisions that the religious right so eagerly exploits.

During the 1993 Senate hearings on gays in the military, I saw how these and other whitening practices were used in concentrated form by another gay institution, the Campaign for Military Service (CMS).

The Campaign for Military Service was an ad hoc organization formed in Washington, D.C., by a group composed primarily of well-to-do, well-connected, professional men, including billionaires David Geffen and Barry Diller, corporate consultant and former antiwar activist David Mixner (a personal friend of Bill Clinton), and several gay and lesbian civil rights attorneys. Their mission was to work with the Clinton White House and sympathetic senators by coordinating the gay response to hearings held by the Senate Armed Services Committee, chaired by Sam Nunn. Their power was derived from their legal expertise, their access to wealthy donors, and their contacts with high-level personnel inside the White House, Senate, and Pentagon. The challenge they faced was to make strategic, pragmatic decisions in the heat of a rapidly changing national battle over what President Clinton called "our nation's policy toward homosexuals in the military."[7]

The world in and around the CMS that David Mixner describes in his memoir, *Stranger among Friends,* is a network of professionals passionately dedicated to gay rights who communicated with Washington insiders via telephone calls, memos, and meetings in the White House, the Pentagon, and private homes. Wearing the protective coloring of this predominantly white gay world, these professionals entered the similarly white and male but heterosexual world of the U.S. Senate, where their shared whiteness became a common ground on which the battle to lift the military's ban on homosexuals was fought—and lost.

The CMS used a set of arguments they called the *race analogy* to persuade senators and military officials to lift the military's antigay ban. The strategy was to get these powerful men to take antigay discrimination as seriously as they supposedly took racial discrimination, so they would lift the military ban on homosexuals as they had eliminated official policies requiring racial segregation. During the Senate hearings, the race analogy projected a set of comparisons that led to heated disputes over whether sexual orientation was analogous to race, whether sexual desire and conduct were like "skin color," or, most specifically, whether being homosexual was like being African American. (Rarely was "race" explicitly discussed as anything other than African American.) On their side, the CMS argued for a qualified analogy—what they called "haunting parallels" between "the words, rationale and rhetoric invoked in favor of racial discrimination in the past" and those used to "exclude gays in the military now." "The parallel is inexact," they cautioned, because "a person's skin color is not the same as a person's sexual identity; race is self-evident to many whereas sexual orientation is not. Moreover, the history of African Americans is not equivalent to the history of lesbian, gay and bisexual people in this country." Yet, despite these qualifications, the CMS held firm to the analogy. "The bigotry expressed is the same; the discrimination is the same."[8]

The military responded with an attack on the race analogy as self-serving, racist, and offensive. They were aided by Senator Nunn, who skillfully managed the hearings in ways that exploited the whiteness of the CMS and their witnesses to advance the military's antigay agenda. Working in their favor was the fact that, unlike the CMS, the military had high-ranking officials who were African American. The chairman of the Joint Chiefs of Staff, Gen. Colin L. Powell, who opposed lifting the ban, responded to the CMS with the argument that the antigay policy was not analogous to racial segregation because "skin color" was a "benign characteristic" while homosexuality constituted conduct that was neither benign nor condoned by most Americans.[9] Another African American Army officer, Lt. Gen. Calvin Waller, Gen. Norman Schwarzkopf's deputy commander and the highest-ranking African American officer in Operation Desert Storm, attacked the race analogy with these words: "I had no choice regarding my race when I was delivered from my mother's womb. To compare my service in America's armed forces with the integration of avowed homosexuals is personally offensive to me."[10] Antigay white senators mimicked his outrage.

During the race analogy debates, the fact that only white witnesses made the analogy, drawing connections between antigay and racial discrimination without including people of color, reduced the power of their argument and the credibility it might have gained had it been made by advocates who had experienced the racial discrimination side of the analogy.[11] But without hearing these voices, everyone in the debate could imagine homosexuals as either people who do not experience racism (the military assumption) or as people who experience discrimination only as homosexuals (the progay assumption)—two different routes that ultimately led to the same destination: the place where gay stays white, the place where the CMS chose to make its stand.

According to Mixner's memoir, the Senate Armed Services Committee "had asked CMS to suggest witnesses."[12] As gay gatekeepers to the hearings, the CMS utilized another whitening practice—*mirroring*. This is a political strategy that reflects back the whiteness of the men who run powerful institutions to persuade them to take "us" seriously, accept "us," and let "us" in because "we are just like you." From the witnesses they selected, it appears that the CMS tried to project an idealized image of the openly gay service member that mirrored the senators' racial makeup and their publicly espoused social values and sexual mores—the image of the highly competent, patriotic, sexually abstinent, young, male officer who had earned the right to serve with a proud record and therefore deserved equality. The CMS selected for the gay panel a group of articulate and courageous veterans—all white men, except for one white woman.[13] Cleverly, Senator Nunn's staff selected a panel of African American ministers opposed to lifting the ban to precede the gay white panel, so that both sides constructed and participated in a racialized dramatic conflict that reinforced the twin myths that gay is white and African Americans are antigay.

Missing was the testimony of service members whose lives bridged the hearings' false divide between black and gay—veterans who were both African American and lesbian, gay, or bisexual. In this context, a significant whitening practice at the hearings was the exclusion of Sgt. Perry Watkins as a witness. Watkins was an openly gay, African American veteran considered by many to be a military hero. Kicked out of the army as a homosexual shortly before his retirement, he successfully appealed his discharge to the Supreme Court, becoming what one attorney called "the first out gay soldier to retire from the Army with full honors."[14]

To my knowledge, there is no public record of how or why the CMS did not invite Watkins to testify.[15] (This is another privilege that comes with whiteness—the ability to make decisions that seriously affect people of color and then protect that decision-making process from public scrutiny or accountability.) Sabrina Sojourner, who recalls that she was the only African American at the CMS among the nonsupport staff, told me that she "got moved further and further from the decision-making process" because she "brought up race," including the problem of the racial dynamic set up by presenting only white witnesses to testify.[16]

There was a moment when I was personally involved with this process. As the author of *Coming Out under Fire: The History of Gay Men and Women in World War Two,* I was asked by the CMS to prepare to fly from California to Washington to testify, but my appearance was not approved by the Senate staff, who allowed no open homosexuals to testify as expert witnesses.[17] During a phone conversation with a white CMS staff member, I remember getting up the courage to ask him why Watkins wasn't a witness and was told that "Perry is a difficult personality." I didn't push my question any further, getting the message that I shouldn't ask for complicated explanations during the heat of battle and deferring to their inside-the-beltway tactical decisions, thus forfeiting an important opportunity to seriously challenge Watkins's exclusion. More instances of this painful struggle over Watkins's participation in and around the hearings must have been going on behind the scenes.[18] Watkins believed he was shut out because he was a "queeny" African American.[19]

It seems that the CMS considered Watkins to be the opposite of their ideal witness. His military story was indeed more complicated than the generic coming-out story. During his 1968 induction physical exam in Tacoma, Washington, he had openly declared his homosexuality, checking "Yes" to the written question "Do you have homosexual tendencies?" and freely describing his sexual experiences to the induction psychiatrist. But the army drafted him nevertheless because it needed him to fight in Vietnam, along with other mostly working-class African American men, who, by 1966, accounted for 20 percent of U.S. combat deaths in that war, when African Americans made up 11 percent of the U.S. population and 12.6 percent of U.S. troops in Vietnam. Journalist Randy Shilts, who later interviewed Watkins, reported that Watkins believed "the doctor probably figured Watkins would . . . go to Vietnam, get killed, and nobody would ever hear about it again."[20] So Watkins's story was not a white narrative. "If I had not been black," he told Mary Ann Humphrey in an oral history interview, "my situation would not have happened as it did. . . . Every *white* person I knew from Tacoma who was gay and had checked that box 'Yes' did not have to go into the service."[21] Watkins's story resonated more with how men of color experience antigay racism in the military than with the story so many white servicemen tell. That white narrative begins with how a gay serviceman never experienced discrimination until he discovered his homosexuality in the service and ends with his fighting an antigay discharge, without referring to how he lived this experience through his whiteness. But Watkins explicitly talked about how he lived his gay military experience through race. "People ask me," he explained, " 'How have you managed to tolerate all that discrimination you have had to deal with in the military?' My immediate answer to them was, 'Hell, I grew up black. Give me a break.' "[22] Watkins had also, while in the military, danced and sang on U.S. Army bases as the flamboyant "Simone," his drag persona; as a veteran he was HIV-positive; and in some gay venues he wore body-piercings in public.[23]

Nevertheless, Watkins's testimony at the hearings could have struck familiar chords among many Americans, including working-class and African American communities, as the experience of someone who was *real* rather than an *ideal*. His story was so compelling, in fact, that after the hearings he was the subject of two films and a segment of the television news magazine "20/20."[24] But the story of his military career—which he so openly lived through race (as an African American), sexuality (had a sex life), and gender (performed in drag)—seems to have been considered by the CMS as too contaminated for congressional testimony and too distracting for the personal media stories that were supposed to focus only on the gay right to serve.

Watkins's absence was a lost opportunity to see and hear in nationally televised Senate hearings a gay African American legal hero talk about his victory over antigay discrimination in the military and expose the racist hypocrisy of how the antigay ban was in practice suspended for African Americans during wartime. The lack of testimony from any other lesbian, gay, or bisexual veteran of color was a lost opportunity to build alliances with communities of color and to do something about the "(largely accurate) perception of the gay activist leadership in Washington as overwhelmingly white."[25] Their collective absence reinforced another powerful myth that, even in a military population that is disproportionately African American and Latino, the representative gay soldier is a white officer, and the most presentable gay face of military competence is a white face.

As the hearings progressed, some CMS activists, speaking in public forums outside the hearings, took the race analogy a step further by promoting the idea that the gay rights movement was *like* the civil rights movement. During the hearings, those who argued the race analogy had drawn parallels between racist and antigay bigotry and discrimination. But those who extended the race analogy to the civil rights movement analogy had to take several more steps. First, they had to reconceptualize the civil rights movement. They took a multiracial movement for human equality and human rights, which included many lesbian, gay, and bisexual activists, and changed it into a nongay, black movement for African American racial equality. Next, they had to imagine the gay movement as a white movement for homosexual rights rather than as a multiracial movement that grew out of and continued the work of the civil rights movement. Then they could make the analogy between these two now-separated movements—one just about race, the other just about homosexuality. The last step was to symbolically recast gay white men in the roles of African American civil rights leaders. These moves tried to correct a problem inherent in such whitening practices as excluding people of color and the wearing, mirroring, and selling of gay whiteness. Because such practices draw directly on the privileges of whiteness, they do not on their own carry much moral weight. The extended race analogy compensates for this weightlessness by first invoking the moral authority of the civil rights movement (while erasing its actual history), and then transferring that unearned moral authority to a white gay movement, without giving anything back. At its worst, the race analogy can become a form of historical erasure, political cheating, and, ultimately, a theft of cultural capital and symbolic value.

David Mixner's memoir reveals how the extended race analogy was used in and around the Campaign for Military Service. When President Clinton, at a press conference, revealed that he wouldn't rule out separating homosexuals from heterosexuals within the military, Mixner first interpreted Clinton's comments as condoning gay segregation, then began equating it with racial segregation. Mixner's account of what happened next does not include attempts to seek advice from or build alliances with people whose histories include long struggles against legal segregation. This despite solid support for lifting the ban from civil rights veterans including Coretta Scott King and Roger Wilkins, the Black Lesbian and Gay Leadership Forum, the Congressional Black Caucus (including Ron Dellums, chairman of the House Armed Services Committee and a former marine who eventually held House hearings to counter Nunn's Senate hearings), and, in public opinion polls, a majority of African Americans (in contrast to a minority of white Americans).[26] Mixner instead describes a series of decisions and actions in which he invokes scenes from the history of racial segregation and the civil rights movement and appears to be reenacting those scenes as if he were a gay (white) version of a black civil rights leader.

A telling moment was when Mixner asked his friend Troy Perry, a gay white minister who founded and heads the gay Metropolitan Community Church, to let him use the Sunday pulpit at the MCC Cathedral in Dallas as a "platform from which to speak." Covered by network television, Mixner delivered a sermon to the nation about the gay "road to freedom." In his sermon he referred to the military's antigay policy as "ancient apartheid laws" and charged that "Sam Nunn is our George Wallace" and that "[b]igotry that wears a uniform is nothing more than a uniform with a hood." He angrily warned President Clinton, cast as antigay segregationist, that "with or without you we will be free . . . we will prevail!"[27] Shortly after the sermon, Tracy Thorne, a gay white navy veteran who had courageously faced verbal abuse at the Senate hearings and who flew to Dallas to support Mixner, said out loud what had been implied by Mixner's words and actions. David Mixner "could be our Martin Luther King, no questions asked," Thorne told a reporter from a gay newspaper.[28]

Such dramatic race-analogy scenarios performed by white activists beg some serious questions. Are actual, rather than "virtual," people of color present as major actors in these scenarios, and if not, why not? What are they saying or how are they being silenced? How is their actual leadership being supported or not supported by the white people who are reenacting this racialized history? And who is the "we" in this rhetoric? Mixner's "we," for example, did not account for those Americans—including lesbian, gay, bisexual, or transgender activists from many racial backgrounds—who did not finally have or indeed need "our own George Wallace" or "our own Martin Luther King." "Martin Luther King is the Martin Luther King of the gay community," Dr. Marjorie Hill, board president of Unity Fellowship Church and former director of the New York City Mayor's Office for Lesbian and Gay Issues, has pointedly replied in response to those who were looking for King's gay equivalent. "His lesson of equality and truth and non-violence was for everyone."[29] If the gay rights movement is already part of the ongoing struggle for the dignity of all people exemplified in the activism of Dr. Martin Luther King Jr., then there is no need for gay equivalents of Dr. King, racial segregation, or the civil rights movement. If the gay rights movement is not already part of the civil rights movement, then what is it? Answering this question from a white position with the race analogy—saying that white gay leaders and martyrs are "our" versions of African American civil rights leaders and martyrs—can't fix the problem and ultimately undermines the moral authority that is its aim. This use of the race analogy ends up reinforcing the whiteness of gay political campaigns rather than doing the work and holding onto the dream that would continue the legacy of Dr. King's leadership and activism.[30]

What would the gay movement look like if gay white men who use the race analogy took it more seriously? What work would we have to do to close the perceived moral authority gap between our gay activism and the race analogy, to directly establish the kind of moral authority we seek by analogy? What if we aspired to achieve the great vision, leadership qualities, grass-roots organizing skills, and union-solidarity of Dr. Martin Luther King Jr., together with his opposition to war and his dedication to fighting with the poor and disenfranchised against the deepening race and class divisions in America and the world? How could we fight, in the words of U.S. Supreme Court Justice Harry A. Blackmun, for the "fundamental interest all individuals have in controlling the nature of their intimate associations with others," in ways that build a broad civil rights movement rather than being "like" it, in ways that enable the gay movement to grow into one of many powerful and direct ways to achieve race, gender, and class justice?[31]

These, then, are only some of the many whitening practices that structure everyday life and politics in what is often called the "gay community" and the "gay movement"—making *race analogies; mirroring* the whiteness of men who run powerful institutions as a strategy for winning credibility, acceptance, and integration; *excluding* people of color from gay institutions; *selling* gay as white to raise money, make a profit, and gain economic power; and daily wearing the *pale protective coloring* that camouflages the unquestioned assumptions and unearned privileges of gay whiteness. These practices do serious damage to real people whenever they mobilize the power and privileges of whiteness to protect and strengthen gayness—including the privileges of gay whiteness—without using that power to fight racism—including gay white racism.

Most of the time, the hard work of identifying such practices, fighting racial discrimination and exclusion, critiquing the assumptions of whiteness, and racially integrating white gay worlds has been taken up by lesbian, gay, bisexual, and transgender people of color. Freed from this enforced daily recognition of race and confrontation with racism, some prominent white men in the gay movement have been able to advance a gay rights politics that, like the right to serve in the military, they imagine to be just gay, not about race. The gay rights movement can't afford to "dissipate our energies," Andrew Sullivan, former editor of the *New Republic,* warned on the Charlie Rose television program, by getting involved in disagreements over nongay issues such as "how one deals with race . . . how we might help the underclass . . . how we might deal with sexism."[32]

But a gay rights politics that is supposedly color-blind (and sex-neutral and classless) is in fact a politics of race (and gender and class). It assumes, without ever having to say it, that gay must equal white (and male and economically secure); that is, it assumes white (and male and middle-class) as the default categories that remain once one discounts those who as gay people must continually and primarily deal with racism (and sexism and class oppression), especially within gay communities. It is the politics that remains once one makes the strategic decision, as a gay activist, to stand outside the social justice movements for race, gender, or class equality, or to not stand with disenfranchised communities, among whom are lesbian, bisexual, gay, or transgender people who depend on these movements for dignity and survival.

For those few who act like, look like, and identify with the white men who still run our nation's major institutions, for those few who can meet with them, talk to them, and be heard by them as peers, the ability to draw on the enormous power of a shared but unacknowledged whiteness, the ability never to have to bring up race, must feel like a potentially sturdy shield against antigay discrimination. I can see how bringing up explicit critiques of white privilege during high-level gay rights conversations (such as the Senate debates over gays in the military), or making it possible for people of color to set the agenda of the gay rights movement, might weaken that white shield (which relies on racial division to protect)—might even, for some white activists, threaten to "turn" the gay movement into something less gay, as gay bars "turn" when they're no longer predominantly white.

The threat of losing the white shield that protects my own gay rights raises even more difficult questions that I need to "clarify . . . for myself": What would *I* say and do about racism if someday my own whiteness helped me gain such direct access to men in the centers of power, as it almost did during the Senate hearings, when all I did was ask why Perry Watkins wasn't testifying and accept the answer I was given? What privileges would I risk losing if I persistently tried to take activists of color with me into that high-level conversation? How, and with whom, could I begin planning for that day?

Gay white men who are committed to doing antiracist activism *as* gay men have to work within and against these and other powerful whitening practices. What can we do, and how can we support each other, when we once again find ourselves involved in gay social and political worlds that are white and male?

Gay, White, Male and HIV-Negative

A few years ago, in San Francisco, a friend invited me to be part of a new political discussion group of HIV-negative gay men. Arriving at a neighbor's apartment for the group's first meeting, I once again felt the relief and pleasure of being among men like me. All of us were involved in AIDS activism. We had supported lovers, friends, and strangers with HIV and were grieving the loss of too many lives. We didn't want to take time, attention, and scarce resources away from people with AIDS, including many people of color. But we did want to find a collective, progressive voice as HIV-negative men. We wanted to find public ways to say to gay men just coming out that "We are HIV-negative men, and we want you to stay negative, have hot sex, and live long lives. We don't want you to get sick or die." We were trying to work out a politics in which HIV-negative men, who are relatively privileged as not being the primary targets of crackdowns on people who are HIV-positive, could address other HIV-negative men without trying to establish our legitimacy by positioning ourselves as victims.

When I looked around the room I saw only white men. I knew that many of them had for years been incorporating antiracist work into their gay and AIDS activism, so this seemed like a safe space to bring up the whiteness I saw. I really didn't want to hijack the purpose of the group by changing its focus from HIV to race, but this was important because I believed that not talking about our whiteness was going to hurt our work. Instead of speaking up, however, I hesitated.

Right there. That's the moment I want to look at—that moment of silence, when a flood of memories, doubts, and fears rushed into my head. What made me want to say something about our whiteness and what was keeping me silent?

My memory took me back to 1990, when I spoke on a panel of gay historians at the first Out/Write conference of lesbian and gay writers, held in San Francisco. I was happy to be presenting with two other community-based historians working outside the academy. But I was also aware—and concerned—that we were all men. When the question period began, an African American writer in the audience, a man whose name I later learned was Fundi, stood up and asked us (as I recall) how it could happen, at this late date, that a gay history panel could have only white men on it. Awkward silence. I don't trust how I remember his question or what happened next—unreliable memory and bad thinking must be characteristics of inhabiting whiteness while it's being publicly challenged. As the other panelists responded, I remember wanting to distance myself from their whiteness while my own mind went blank, and I remember feeling terrified that Fundi would address me directly and ask me to respond personally. I kept thinking, "I don't know what to say, I can't think, I want to be invisible, I want this to be over, now!"

After the panel was over I spoke privately to Fundi. Later, I resolved never to be in that situation again—never to agree to be on an all-white panel without asking ahead of time why it was white, if its whiteness was crucial to what we were presenting, and, if not, how its composition might be changed. But in addition to wanting to protect myself from public embarrassment and to do the right thing, that writer's direct challenge made me understand something more clearly: that only by seeing and naming the whiteness I'm inhabiting, and taking responsibility for it, can I begin to change it and even do something constructive with it. At that panel, I learned how motivating though terrifying it can be as a white person to be placed in such a state of heightened racial discomfort—to be challenged to see the whiteness we've created, figure out how we created it, and then think critically about how it works.[33]

In the moment of silent hesitation I experienced in my HIV-negative group, I found myself imagining for the first time, years after it happened, what it must have been like for Fundi to stand up in a predominantly white audience and ask an all-white panel of gay men about our whiteness. My friend and colleague Lisa Kahaleole Hall, who is a brilliant thinker, writer, and teacher, says that privilege is "the ability not to have to take other people's existence seriously," the "ability not to have to pay attention."[34] Until that moment I had mistakenly thought that Fundi's anger (and I am not certain that he in fact expressed any anger toward us) was only about me, about us, as white men, rather than also about him—the history, desires, and support that enabled him to speak up, and the fears he faced and risks he took by doing it. Caught up in my own fear, I had not paid close attention to the specific question he had asked us. "The problem of conventional white men," Fundi later wrote in his own account of why he had decided to take the risk of speaking up, "somehow not being able, or not knowing how, to find and extend themselves to women and people of color had to be talked through. . . . My question to the panel was this: 'What direct skills might you share with particularly the whites in the audience to help them move on their fears and better extend themselves to cultural diversity?' "[35] I'm indebted to Fundi for writing that question down, and for starting a chain of events with his question that has led to my writing this essay.

I tried to remember who else I had seen bring up whiteness. The first images that came to mind were all white lesbians and people of color. White lesbian feminists have as a movement dealt with racism in a more collective way than have gay white men. In lesbian and gay activist spaces I and other gay white men have come to rely on white lesbians and people of color to raise the issue of whiteness and challenge racism, so that this difficult task has become both gendered as lesbian work and racialized as "colored" work. These images held me back from saying anything to my HIV-negative group. "Just who am I to bring this up?" I wondered. "It's not my place to do this." Or, more painfully, "Who will these men think I think I am?" Will they think I'm trying to pretend I'm not a white man?"

Then another image flashed in my mind that also held me back. It was the caricature of the white moralist—another racialized phantom figure hovering in the room—who blames and condemns white people for our racism, guilt-trips us from either a position of deeper guilt or holier-than-thou innocence, claims to be more aware of racism than we are, and is prepared to catalog our offenses. I see on my mental screen this self-righteous caricature impersonating a person of color in an all-white group or, when people of color are present, casting them again in the role of spectators to a white performance, pushed to the sidelines from where they must angrily or patiently interrupt a white conversation to be heard at all. I understand that there is some truth to this caricature—that part of a destructive racial dynamic among white people is trying to determine who is more or less responsible for racism, more or less innocent and pure, more or less white. But I also see how the fear of becoming this caricature has been used by white people to keep each other from naming the whiteness of all-white groups we are in. During my moment of hesitation in the HIV-negative group, the fear of becoming this caricature was successfully silencing me.

I didn't want to pretend to be a white lesbian or a person of color, or to act like the self-righteous white caricature. "How do I ask that we examine our whiteness," I wondered, "without implying that I'm separating us into the good guys and bad guys and positioning myself as the really cool white guy who 'gets it' about racism?" I needed a way to speak intelligently from where I was standing without falling into any of these traps.

I decided to take a chance and say something.

"It appears to me," I began, my voice a little shaky, "that everyone here is white. If this is true, I'd like us to find some way to talk about how our whiteness may be connected to being HIV-negative, because I suspect there are some political similarities between being in each of these positions of relative privilege."

There was an awkward pause. "Are you saying," someone asked, "that we should close the group to men of color?"

"No," I said, "but if we're going to be a white group I'd like us to talk about our relationship to whiteness here."

"Should we do outreach to men of color?" someone else asked.

"No, I'm not saying that, either. It's a little late to do outreach, after the fact, inviting men of color to integrate our already white group."

The other men agreed and the discussion went on to other things. I, too, didn't really know where to take this conversation about our whiteness. By bringing it up, I was implicitly asking for their help in figuring this out. I hoped I wouldn't be the only one to bring up the subject again.

At the next month's meeting there were new members, and they all appeared to be white men. When someone reviewed for them what we had done at the last meeting, he reported that I'd suggested we not include men of color in the group. "That's not right," I corrected him. "I said that if we're going to be a white group, I'd like us to talk about our whiteness and its relation to our HIV-negative status."

I was beginning to feel a little disoriented, like I was doing something wrong. Why was I being so consistently misunderstood as divisive, as if I were saying that I didn't want men of color in the group? Had I reacted similarly when, caught up in my own fear of having to publicly justify our panel's whiteness, I had misunderstood Fundi's specific question—about how we could share our skills with other white people to help each other move beyond our fear of cultural diversity—as an accusation that we had deliberately excluded women and men of color? Was something structural going on here about how white groups respond to questions that point to our whiteness and ask what we can do with it?

Walking home from the meeting I asked a friend who'd been there if what I said had made sense. "Oh yes," he said, "it's just that it all goes without saying." Well, there it is. That *is* how it goes, how it stays white. "Without saying."

Like much of the rest of my gay life, this HIV-negative group turned out to be unintentionally white, although intentionally gay and intentionally male. It's important for me to understand exactly how that racial *unintentionality* gets *constructed*, how it's not just a coincidence. It seems that so long as white people never consciously decide to be a white group, a white organization, a white department, so long as we each individually believe that people of color are always welcome, *even though they are not there*, then we do not have to examine our whiteness because we can believe it is unintentional, it's not our *reason* for being there. That may be why I had been misunderstood to be asking for the exclusion of men of color. By naming our group as white, I had unknowingly raised the question of *racial intent*—implying that we had intended to create an all-white group by deliberately excluding men of color. If we could believe that our whiteness was purely accidental, then we could also believe that there was nothing to say about it because creating an all-white group, which is exactly what we had done, had never been anyone's intent, and therefore had no inherent meaning or purpose. By interrupting the process by which "it just goes without saying," by asking us to recognize and "talk through" our whiteness, I appeared to be saying that we already had and should continue to exclude men of color from our now very self-consciously white group.

The reality is that in our HIV-negative group, as in the panel of the Out/Write conference and in many other all-white groupings, we each did make a chain of choices, not usually conscious, to invite or accept an invitation from another white person. We made more decisions whether or not to name our whiteness when we once again found ourselves in a white group. What would it mean to make such decisions consciously and out loud, to understand why we made them, and to take responsibility for them? What if we intentionally held our identities as white men and gay men in creative tension, naming ourselves as gay *and* white, then publicly explored the possibilities for activism this tension might open up? Could investigating our whiteness offer us opportunities for reclaiming our humanity against the ways that racial hierarchies dehumanize us and disconnect us from ourselves, from each other, and from people of color? If we took on these difficult tasks, how might our gay political reality and purpose be different?[36]

When I told this story about our HIV-negative group to Barbara Smith, a colleague who is an African American lesbian writer and activist, she asked me a question that pointed to a different ending: "So why didn't you bring up the group's whiteness again?" The easy answer was that I left the group because I moved to New York City. But the more difficult answer was that I was afraid to lose the trust of these gay men whom I cared about and needed so much, afraid I would distance myself from them and be distanced by them, pushed outside the familiar circle, no longer welcomed as white and not belonging among people of color, not really gay and not anything else, either. The big fear is that if I pursue this need to examine whiteness too far, I risk losing my place among gay white men, forever—and then where would I be?

Pale, Male—and Antiracist

What would happen if we deliberately put together a white gay male group whose sole purpose was to examine our whiteness and use it to strengthen our antiracist gay activism?

In November 1995, gay historian John D'Emilio and I tried to do just that. We organized a workshop at the annual Creating Change conference of activists put on that year in Detroit by the National Gay and Lesbian Task Force. We called the workshop "Pale, Male—and Anti-Racist." At a conference of over 1,000 people (mostly white but with a large number of people of color), about thirty-five gay white men attended.[37]

We structured the workshop around three key questions: (1) How have you successfully used your whiteness to fight racism? (2) What difficulties have you faced in doing antiracist activism as a gay white man? And (3) what kind of support did you get or need or wished you had received from other gay white men?

Before we could start talking about our successes, warning lights began to flash. You could sense a high level of mistrust in the room, as if we were looking at each other and wondering, "Which kind of white guy are *you*?" One man wanted to make sure we weren't going to waste time congratulating ourselves for sharing our white privilege with people who don't have access to it or start whining about how hard it is to work with communities of color. Someone else wanted to make sure we weren't going to guilt-trip each other. Another said, "I'm so much more aware of my failures in this area, I can't even see the accomplishments."

But slowly, once all the cautions were out in the open, the success stories came out. About fighting an anti-affirmative action initiative. About starting a racism study group. About getting a university department to study why it had no teaching assistants who were students of color. About persuading a gay organization in Georgia to condemn the state's Confederate flag. "What keeps me from remembering," I wondered, "that gay white men publicly do this antiracist work? Why can't I keep their images in my mind?"

One possible answer to my question appeared in the next success story, which midway made a sharp turn away from our successes toward how gay white men can discipline each other for standing on the "wrong" side of the color line. A man from Texas, Dennis Poplin, told us about what happened to him as the only white man on the board of the San Antonio Lesbian and Gay Assembly (SALGA), a progressive, multiracial lesbian and gay alliance. When SALGA mobilized support that successfully canceled a so-called gay community conference whose planning committee was all-white—this in a city that was 65 percent Latina/Latino—a "community scandal" exploded, as he put it, "about political correctness, quotas, [and] reverse racism." A local newspaper, which was run by gay white men, started attacking SALGA. When a white reporter asked a man of color from SALGA why the group's board had no white men on it, and he replied that Dennis was on the board, the reporter said, "He's not white."[38]

Right away the men in the workshop started talking about the difficulties they'd had with other gay white men. "I find myself like not even knowing who it's safe to bring it up with," one man said. When he tries to talk about race, another said, "I'm just met with that smug, flippant, 'I'm tired of hearing about [all that].' " Others talked about fears of being attacked as too "PC."

At the "risk of opening a whole can of worms," as he put it, another man moved the discussion away from us to our relationships with white lesbians and people of color. Some men talked about how tired they were of being called "gay white men," feeling labeled then attacked for who they were and for what they tried to do or for not doing enough; about having to deal with their racism while they didn't see communities of color dealing with homophobia; and about how after years of struggling they felt like giving up. Yet here they all were at this workshop. I began to realize that all our frustrations were signs of a dilemma that comes with the privileges of whiteness: having the ability to decide whether to keep dealing with the accusations, resentments, racial categorizations, and other destructive effects of racism that divide people who are trying to take away its power; or, because the struggle is so hard, to walk away from it and do something else, using the slack our whiteness gives us to take a break from racism's direct consequences.

Bringing this dilemma into the open enabled us to confront our expectations about how the antiracist work we do should be appreciated, should be satisfying, and should bring results. One man admitted that he didn't make antiracist work a higher priority because "I [would have to face] a level of discomfort, irritation, boredom, frustration, [and] enter a lot of [areas where] I feel inept, and don't have confidence. It would require a lot of humility. All these are things that I steer away from."

Over and over the men at the workshop expressed similar feelings of frustration, using such phrases as "We tried, but . . . ," "No matter what you do, you can't seem to do anything right," and "You just can't win." These seemed to reflect a set of expectations that grew out of the advantages we have because we are American men and white and middle-class or even working-class—expectations that we *can* win, that we should know how to do it right, that if we try we will succeed.

What do we—what do I—expect to get out of doing antiracist work, anyway? If it's because we expect to be able to fix the problem, then we're not going to be very satisfied. When I talk with my friend Lisa Kahaleole Hall about these frustrations, she tells me, "Sweet pea, if racism were that easy to fix, we would have fixed it already." The challenge for me in relation to other gay white men—and in writing this essay—is to figure out how we can support each other in going exactly into those areas of whiteness where we feel we have no competence yet, no expertise, no ability to fix it, where we haven't even come up with the words we need to describe what we're trying to do. For me, it's an act of faith in the paradox that if we, together with our friends and allies, can figure out how our own whiteness works, we can use that knowledge to fight the racism that gives our whiteness such unearned power.

And whenever this struggle gets too difficult, many of us, as white men, have the option to give up in frustration and retreat into a more narrowly defined gay rights activism. That project's goal, according to gay author Bruce Bawer, one of its advocates, is "to achieve acceptance, equal rights, and full integration into the present social and political structure."[39] It's a goal that best serves the needs of men who can live our gayness through our whiteness and whose only or most important experience with discrimination is as homosexuals. James Baldwin, who wrote extensively about whiteness in America, noticed long ago the sense of entitlement embedded in a gay whiteness that experiences no other form of systematic discrimination. "[Y]ou are penalized, as it were, unjustly," he said in an interview. "I think white gay people feel cheated because they were born, in principle, into a society in which they were supposed to be safe. The anomaly of their sexuality puts them in danger, unexpectedly."[40]

The gay rights project that grows out of the shocking experience of being cheated unexpectedly by society because one is gay defines the gay political problem in its narrowest form. One solution is to get back the respect one has learned to expect as a white man. Some prominent, well-connected activists do this by educating the men who run our nation's powerful institutions, using reasoned arguments to combat their homophobia and expose discrimination as irrational—a strategy that sometimes does open doors but mostly to those who look and behave like the men in power. I have heard some of these activists express a belief that less privileged members of the "gay community" will eventually benefit from these high-level successes, but this would happen apparently without the more privileged having to do the work of fighting hierarchies that enforce race, class, and gender inequality. Their belief in a kind of "trickle-down" gay activism is based on the idea that powerful men, once enlightened, will generously allow equality to flow from the top to those near the top and then automatically trickle down to those down below. An alternative belief in "bottom-up activism" is based on the idea that, with great effort, democratic power must more slowly be built from the bottom up, and out, experimenting with more equal power relations along the way by creating links of solidarity across the divides of difference. Some gay white men explicitly reject, as nongay, this broader goal of joining activists who stand and work at the intersections of the many struggles to achieve social justice and to dismantle interlocking systems of domination. In the narrow world of exclusively gay "integrationist" activism, which its advocates privilege as the site of "practical" rather than "utopian" politics,[41] college-educated gay white men have a better chance of knowing what to say and how to be heard, what to do and how to succeed within existing institutions. Because, when antigay barriers and attitudes are broken down but no other power relations are changed, we are the ones most likely to achieve "full integration into the present social and political structure." All it takes sometimes is being the white man at the white place at the white time.

When John and I asked the workshop participants our last question—"What would you need from each other to be able to continue doing antiracist work?"—the room went silent.

When push comes to shove, I wondered, holding back a sense of isolation inside my own silence, do gay white men as *white* men (including myself) have a lasting interest in fighting racism or will we sooner or later retreat to the safety of our gay white refuges? I know that gay white men as *gay* men, just to begin thinking about relying on each other's support in an ongoing struggle against racism, have to confront how we've absorbed the antigay lies that we are all wealthy, irresponsible, and sexually obsessed individuals who can't make personal commitments, as well as the reality that we are profoundly exhausted fighting for our lives and for those we love through years of devastation from the AIDS epidemic. These challenges all make it hard enough for me to trust my own long-term commitment to antiracist work, let alone that of other gay white men.

Yet at this workshop we created the opportunity for us to see that we were not alone, to risk saying and hearing what we needed from each other in fighting racism, and to assess what support we could realistically hope to get. We wanted the opportunity to complain to another gay white man, to be held and loved when we get discouraged or feel attacked, whether justifiably or not. We wanted understanding for all the frustrations we feel fighting racism, the chance just to let them out with a gay white man who knows that it's not our racism he's supporting but the desire to see it and together figure out what to do next, so we won't give up or run away. We wanted other gay white men to take us seriously enough to call us on our racist shit in ways we could actually hear without feeling attacked. And we wanted to help each other lift at least some of the work and responsibility of supporting us from the shoulders of our friends and co-workers who are white women or people of color.

As time ran out at the workshop, I asked everyone to think about another difficult question: "Who is the gay white man who has had more experience than you in supporting other gay white men who are fighting racism, and who you can look to for advice on how to do it well?" "I think the more interesting question," one man answered, "is how many of us don't have anyone like that." We looked around at each other, wondering if any of us could name someone, until somebody said, "It's us."

Staying White

By trying to figure out what is happening with race in situations I'm in, I've embarked on a journey that I now realize is not headed toward innocence or winning or becoming not white or finally getting it right. I don't know where it leads, but I have some hopes and desires.

I want to find an antidote to the ways that whiteness numbs me, makes me not see what is right in front of me, takes away my intelligence, divides me from people I care about. I hope that, by occupying the seeming contradictions between the "antiracist" and the "gay white male" parts of myself, I can generate a creative tension that will motivate me to keep fighting. I hope to help end the exclusionary practices that make gay worlds stay so white. When I find myself in a situation that is going to stay white, I want to play a role in deciding what kind of white it's going to stay. And I want to become less invested in whiteness while staying white myself—always remembering that I can't just decide to stand outside of whiteness or exempt myself from its unearned privileges.[42] I want to be careful not to avoid its responsibilities by fleeing into narratives of how I have been oppressed as a gay man. The ways that I am gay will always be shaped by the ways that I am white.

Most of all, I want never to forget that the roots of my antiracist desires and my gay desires are intertwined. As James Baldwin's words remind me, acting on my gay desires is about not being afraid to love and therefore about having to confront this white society's terror of love—a terror that lashes out with racist and antigay violence. Following both my gay and antiracist desires is about being willing to "go the way your blood beats," as Baldwin put it, even into the heart of that terror, which, he warned, is "a tremendous danger, a tremendous responsibility."[43]

Notes

This is an expanded version of a personal essay I presented at the Making and Unmaking of Whiteness conference at the University of California at Berkeley in April 1997. I want to acknowledge that my thinking has grown out of conversations with many friends and colleagues, including Nan Alamilla Boyd, Margaret Cerullo, John D'Emilio, Arthur Dong, Marla Erlein, Jeffrey Escoffier, Charlie Fernandez, Dana Frank, Wayne Hoffman, Amber Hollibaugh, Mitchell Karp, Jonathan Ned Katz, Judith Levine, William J. Mann, David Meacham, Dennis Poplin, Susan Raffo, Eric Rofes, Gayle Rubin, Sabrina Sojourner, Barbara Smith, Nancy Stoller, Carole Vance, and Carmen Vasquez; the editors of this collection, especially Matt Wray and Irene Nexica; the participants in the "Pale, Male—and Anti-Racist" workshop at the 1995 Creating Change conference in Detroit; Lisa Kahaleole Hall and the students I joined in her San Francisco City College class on Lesbian and Gay Communities of Color; and the students in the courses I taught at the University of California at Santa Cruz, Portland State University, Stanford University, and the New School for Social Research.

1 "Caught in the Storm: AIDS and the Meaning of Natural Disaster," *Out/Look: National Lesbian and Gay Quarterly* 1 (fall 1988), 8–19; " 'Fitting In': Expanding Queer Studies beyond the *Closet* and *Coming Out*," paper presented at Contested Zone: Limitations and Possibilities of a Discourse on Lesbian and Gay Studies, Pitzer College, 6–7 April 1990, and at the Fourth Annual Lesbian, Bisexual, and Gay Studies Conference, Harvard University, 26–28 October 1990; "Intellectual Desire," paper presented at La Ville en rose: Le premier colloque Québécois d'études lesbienne et gaies (First Quebec Lesbian and Gay Studies Conference), Concordia University and the University of Quebec at Montreal, 12 November 1992, published in *GLQ: A Journal of Lesbian and Gay Studies* 3, no. 1 (February 1996): 139–57, reprinted in *Queerly Classed: Gay Men and Lesbians Write about Class,* ed. Susan Raffo (Boston: South End Press, 1997), 43–66; "Class Dismissed: Queer Storytelling Across the Economic Divide," keynote address at the Constructing Queer Cultures: Lesbian, Bisexual, Gay Studies Graduate Student Conference, Cornell University, 9 February 1995, and at the Seventeenth Gender Studies Symposium, Lewis and Clark College, 12 March 1998; "I Coulda Been a Whiny White Guy," *Gay Community News* 20 (spring 1995): 6–7, 28–30; and "Sunset Trailer Park," in *White Trash: Race and Class in America,* ed. Matt Wray and Annalee Newitz (New York: Routledge, 1997), 15–39.

2 *Dream Ships Sail Away* (forthcoming, Houghton Mifflin).

3 " 'Go the Way Your Blood Beats': An Interview with James Baldwin (1984)," Richard Goldstein, in *James Baldwin: The Legacy,* ed. Quincy Troupe (New York: Simon and Schuster/Touchstone, 1989), 176.

4 Personal essays, often assembled in published collections, have become an important written form for investigating how whiteness works, especially in individual lives. Personal essays by lesbian, gay, and bisexual authors that have influenced my own thinking and writing about whiteness have been collected in James Baldwin, *The Price of the Ticket: Collected Nonfiction, 1948–1985* (New York: St. Martin's, 1985); Cherríe Moraga and Gloria Anzaldúa, eds., *This Bridge Called My Back: Writings by Radical Women of Color* (Watertown, Mass.: Persephone Press, 1981); Cherríe Moraga, *Loving in the War Years* (Boston: South End Press, 1983); Audre Lorde,

Sister Outsider (Freedom, Calif.: Crossing Press, 1984); Elly Bulkin, Minnie Bruce Pratt, and Barbara Smith, *Yours in Struggle: Three Feminist Perspectives on Anti-Semitism and Racism* (Brooklyn: Long Haul Press, 1984); Essex Hemphill, ed., *Brother to Brother: New Writings by Black Gay Men* (Boston: Alyson, 1991); Mab Segrest, *Memoir of a Race Traitor* (Boston: South End Press, 1994); Dorothy Allison, *Skin: Talking about Sex, Class and Literature* (Ithaca, N.Y.: Firebrand, 1994); and Becky Thompson and Sangeeta Tyagi, eds., *Names We Call Home: Autobiography on Racial Identity* (New York: Routledge, 1996).

5 For discussion of how sexual identities are "lived through race and class," see Robin D. G. Kelley, *Yo' Mama's Dysfunktional!* (Boston: Beacon, 1997), 114.

6 Whiteness can grant economic advantages to gay as well as straight men, and gay male couples can sometimes earn more on two men's incomes than can straight couples or lesbian couples. But being gay can restrict a man to lower-paying jobs, and most gay white men are not wealthy; like the larger male population, they are lower-middle-class, working-class, or poor. For discussions of the difficulties of developing an accurate economic profile of the "gay community," and of how both the religious right and gay marketers promote the idea that gay men are wealthy, see Amy Gluckman and Betsy Reed, eds., *Homo Economics: Capitalism, Community, and Lesbian and Gay Life* (New York: Routledge, 1997).

7 David Mixner, *Stranger among Friends* (New York: Bantam, 1996), 291. For accounts of how the Campaign for Military Service was formed, see Mixner's memoir and Urvashi Vaid, *Virtual Equality: The Mainstreaming of Lesbian and Gay Equality* (New York: Anchor, 1995). Preceding the ad hoc formation of the Campaign for Military Service in January 1993 was the Military Freedom Project, formed in early 1989 by a group composed primarily of white feminist lesbians. Overshadowed during the Senate hearings by the predominantly male Campaign for Military Service, these activists had raised issues relating the military's antigay policy to gender, race, and class; specifically, that lesbians are discharged at a higher rate than are gay men; that lesbian-baiting is a form of sexual harassment against women; and that African American and Latino citizens, including those who are gay, bisexual, or lesbian, are disproportionately represented in the military, which offers poor and working-class youth access to a job, education, and health care that are often unavailable to them elsewhere. Vaid, *Virtual Equality*, 153–59.

8 "The Race Analogy: Fact Sheet comparing the Military's Policy of Racial Segregation in the 1940s to the Current Ban on Lesbians, Gay Men and Bisexuals," in *Briefing Book*, prepared by the Legal/Policy Department of the Campaign for Military Service, Washington, D.C. (1993).

9   Quoted from the *Legal Times*, 8 February 1993, in Mixner, *Stranger among Friends*, 286. Professor of history and civil rights veteran Roger Wilkins, responding to Powell's statement, argued that "Lots of white people don't think that being black is benign even in 1993." Mixner, *Stranger among Friends*, 286.

10 Henry Louis Gates Jr., "Blacklash?" *New Yorker*, 17 May 1993.

11 For brief discussions of how the whiteness of those making the race analogy reduced the power of their arguments, see Gates, "Blacklash?" and David Rayside, *On the Fringe: Gays and Lesbians in Politics* (Ithaca, N.Y.: Cornell University Press, 1998), 243.

12 Mixner, *Stranger among Friends*, 319.

13 The gay service members on this panel were former Staff Sgt. Thomas Pannicia, Sgt. Justin Elzie, and Col. Margarethe Cammermeyer. Margarethe Cammermeyer, with Chris Fisher, *Serving in Silence* (New York: Penguin, 1994), 299. Other former gay service members who testified at the hearings were Sgt. Tracy Thorne and PO Keith Meinhold. Active-duty lesbian, gay, or bisexual service members could not testify without being discharged from the military as homosexuals, a situation that still exists under the current "don't ask, don't tell" military policy.

14 Mary Dunlap, "Reminiscences: Honoring Our Legal Hero, Gay Sgt. Perry Watkins 1949–1996," *Gay Community News* (winter 1996): 21.

15 In his memoir, *Stranger among Friends*, Mixner makes no mention of Watkins.

16 Author's personal conversation with Sabrina Sojourner, 19 October 1998.

17 An expert witness who was white, male, and not a gay historian was allowed to introduce a brief written synopsis of historical evidence from my book.

I was one of the white men working with the CMS behind the scenes and from afar. Early in the hearings, Senator Edward Kennedy's staff asked me to compile a list of questions for him to ask during the hearings. In July, after the hearings were over and the "don't ask, don't tell" policy had been adopted, I submitted to the House Armed Services Committee written testimony, titled "Historical Overview of the Origins of the Military's Ban on Homosexuals," that critiqued the new policy and identified heterosexual masculinity, rather than the competence or behavior of homosexual service members, as the military problem requiring investigation. And I sent the CMS a copy of a paper I had given in April, "Stripping Down: Undressing the Military's Anti-Gay Policy," that used historical documents and feminist analysis to argue for investigating the military's crisis in heterosexual masculinity. In all these writings, I was trying, unsuccessfully, to get the CMS and the Senate to adopt a gender and sexuality analysis of the military policy; I used race and class analysis only to argue that the antigay policies disproportionately affected service members who were people of color and/or working-class.

18 After Watkins's death in 1996 from complications due to HIV, Mary Dunlap, a white civil rights attorney who for years had followed his appeal case, in a tribute addressed to him, called him a "generous, tireless leader" who expressed "open and emphatic criticism and unabashed indictment of the racism of those among us who so blatantly and hurtfully excluded your voice and face and words from the publicity surrounding the gaylesbitrans community's challenge to 'Don't Ask, Don't Tell' in the early 90s." Dunlap, "Reminiscences," 21.

19 Shamara Riley, "Perry Watkins, 1948–1996: A Military Trailblazer," *Outlines,* 8 May 1996.

20 Randy Shilts, *Conduct Unbecoming: Gays and Lesbians in the U.S. Military* (New York: St. Martin's, 1993), 60, 65; Mary Ann Humphrey, *My Country, My Right to Serve* (New York: HarperCollins, 1990), 248–57. Statistics are from D. Michael Shafer, "The Vietnam-Era Draft: Who Went, Who Didn't, and Why It Matters," in *The Legacy: The Vietnam War in the American Imagination,* ed. D. Michael Shafer (Boston: Beacon Press, 1990), 69.

21 Humphrey, *My Country,* 255–56.

22 Ibid.

23 Dunlap, "Reminiscences"; Shilts, *Conduct Unbecoming,* 155–56; Humphrey, *My Country,* 253–54.

24 A 1996 documentary film, "Sis: The Perry Watkins Story," was co-produced by Chiqui Cartagena and Suzanne Newman. On the "20/20" segment and a feature film on Watkins that was in preproduction, see Jim Knippenberg, "Gay Soldier Story to Be Filmed," *Cincinnati Enquirer,* 23 December 1997.

25 Rayside, *On the Fringe,* 243.

26 Keith Boykin, *One More River to Cross: Black and Gay In America* (New York: Anchor, 1996), 186–92.

27 Mixner, *Stranger among Friends,* 301–2, 308–10.

28 Garland Tillery, "Interview with Top Gun Pilot Tracy Thorne," *Our Own,* 18 May 1993.

29 Quoted from the documentary film "All God's Children," produced by Dee Mosbacher, Frances Reid, and Sylvia Rhue (Women Vision, 1996). I wish to thank Lisa Kahaleole Hall, Stephanie Smith, and Linda Alban for directing me to this quotation.

30 One way to measure how much moral authority the race analogy tries to take from the civil rights movement and transfuse it into a predominantly white gay movement is to see what moral authority remains when the race analogy is removed. David Mixner would be the David Mixner of the gay movement, the military's antigay policy would be a form of antigay bigotry,

and Sam Nunn would be "our" Sam Nunn. Or, to reverse the terms, other movements for social change would try to gain moral authority by using a "gay analogy," declaring that their movement was "like" the gay movement. These moves do not seem to carry the moral weight of the race analogy.

31 Quoted from Justice Blackmun's dissenting opinion in the U.S. Supreme Court's 1986 *Bowers v. Hardwick* decision. "Blackmun's Opinions Reflect His Evolution over the 24 Court Years," *New York Times*, 5 March 1999. I wish to thank Lisa Kahaleole Hall for the conversation we had on 24 October 1998, out of which emerged the ideas in this essay about how the civil rights movement analogy works and is used as a strategy for gaining unearned moral authority, although I am responsible for how they are presented here.

32 "Stonewall 25," *The Charlie Rose Show*, Public Broadcasting System, 24 June 1994. I wish to thank Barbara Smith for lending me her videotape copy of this program.

33 For Fundi's reports on this panel and the entire conference, see "Out/Write '90 Report, Part I: Writers Urged to Examine Their Roles, Save Their Lives," *San Diego GLN*, 16 March 1990, 7; "Out/Write Report, Part II: Ringing Voices," *San Diego GLN*, 23 March 1990, 7, 9; and "Out/Write Report, Part III: Arenas of Interaction," *San Diego GLN*, 30 March 1990, 7, 9.

34 Lisa Kahaleole Chang Hall, "Bitches in Solitude: Identity Politics and Lesbian Community," in *Sisters, Sexperts, Queers: Beyond the Lesbian Nation*, ed. Arlene Stein (New York: Plume, 1993), 223, and in personal conversation.

35 Fundi, "Out/Write Report, Part III," 7, 9.

36 I wish to thank Mitchell Karp for the long dinner conversation we had in 1996 in New York City during which we jointly forged the ideas and questions in this paragraph.

37 I have transcribed the quotations that follow from an audio tape of the workshop discussion.

38 I wish to thank Dennis Poplin for allowing me to use his name and tell this story.

39 Bruce Bawer, "Utopian Erotics," *Lambda Book Report* 7 (October 1998): 19–20.

40 Goldstein, "Go the Way," 180.

41 Bawer, "Utopian Erotics," 19–20.

42 I wish to thank Amber Hollibaugh for introducing me to this idea of "staying white" during a conversation about how a white person can be tempted to distance oneself from whiteness and escape the guilt of its privileges by identifying as a person of color. I was introduced to the idea that white privilege is unearned and difficult to escape at a workshop called

White Privilege conducted by Jona Olssen at the 1995 Black Nations/ Queer Nations Conference, sponsored by the Center for Lesbian and Gay Studies at the City University of New York. See also Peggy McIntosh, "White Privilege: Unpacking the Invisible Knapsack," *Peace and Freedom* (July/August 1989): 10–12.

43 Goldstein, "Go the Way," 177.

(E)racism: Emerging Practices
of Antiracist Organizations

Whiteness and Antiracism

The recent dramatic flurry of intellectual activities involving whiteness studies, and their coverage in popular media, disturbs Michael Eric Dyson. He fears that issues regarding racial representation and politics are being recentered on whites: "There's a suspicion among African-Americans that whiteness studies is a sneaky form of narcissism. At the very moment when African-American studies and Asian-American studies and so on are really coming into their own, you have whiteness studies shifting the focus and maybe the resources back to white people and their perspective."[1]

The highlighting of whiteness has important consequences for antiracist projects as well. Alastair Bonnett argues that whiteness has become "both the conceptual centre and the 'other' of anti-racism; the defining, normative term of anti-racist praxis and theory."[2] Bonnett critiques what he calls the "reification of whiteness" within antiracist discourse and practice. White is often treated as a fixed, objective, and ahistorical category rather than a mutable social construction. Such a perspective, he argues, "enables white people to occupy a privileged location in anti-racist debate; they are allowed the luxury of being passive observers, of being altruistically motivated, of knowing that 'their' 'racial' identity might be reviled and lambasted but never actually made slippery, torn open, or indeed, abolished."[3]

To be fair, a number of projects are explicitly concerned with deconstructing or even "abolishing" whiteness.[4] But the focus often remains on how *whites* can "unlearn" racism, reject the trappings of white racial privilege, and challenge the ideology of white supremacy. While much attention is paid to how whites can divest themselves of racial prejudices and engage in significant antiracist work, the struggles of people of color in challenging racism often remain in the shadows.

Our conceptual understanding of precisely who is the subject and object of antiracist activity is clouded by a rigid, binary understanding of race. The dominant paradigm of black/white relations (or an expanded notion of white/nonwhite relations) tends to ignore the complexity of racial politics in the contemporary period and limit the types of antiracist activities that can be imagined and realized. Yes, white racism is the dominant, hegemonic reality. But this structures relations between, and among, people of color in often enigmatic ways. This nation's historical experience cannot be interpreted, as some liberal multicultural narratives suggest, as distinct, isolated, and autonomous groups of color confronting a core white center. As George Lipsitz perceptively notes, "All racial identities are relational; communities of color are mutually constitutive of one another, not just competitive or cooperative."[5]

This is one of the themes I attempt to explore in this essay. It is based on a larger study of how people think about and engage in antiracist work. I am currently completing a project that examines how different organizations, mostly community-based groups, conceptualize contemporary racism and develop a strategic challenge to it based on that understanding.

It is particularly important to understand and evaluate current antiracist interventions given that we exist in a period where everyone across the political spectrum (with the exception of self-proclaimed white supremacists) claims to be "antiracist." That said, contemporary discourse is littered with confused and contradictory meanings regarding racism and antiracism. Bob Blauner has noted that in classroom discussions of racism white and nonwhite students tend to talk past one another.[6] Whites tend to locate racism in color consciousness and find its absence in color-blindness. In so doing, they see the affirmation of difference and racial identity among racially defined minority students as racist. Nonwhite students, by contrast, see racism as a system of power and correspondingly argue that blacks, for example, cannot be racist because they lack power. Blauner concludes that there are two "languages" of race, one in which members of racial minorities, especially blacks, see the centrality of race in history and everyday experience, and another in which whites see race as "a peripheral, nonessential reality."

The classroom, in this instance, serves as microcosm for dialogues occurring in the broader social formation. Many whites believe that the goals of the civil rights movement have been achieved, that we are now a "color-blind" society, and that we all need to "get beyond race." A lingering race consciousness, from such a perspective, only serves to create racial divisions and demonize whites as oppressors of people of color.

Such an understanding has profoundly affected the discourse of "minority rights." The notion of "color-blindness" has been strategically appropriated by conservatives seeking to dismantle the social policies designed to mitigate racial inequality. "Civil rights" initiatives and court cases are now more likely to involve issues of discrimination against whites, calling into question so-called "preferential policies" and claiming that it is whites, particularly white males, who are increasingly the victims of racism and racist practices. Challenges by whites are not framed, however, by explicit appeals for the maintenance of white skin privilege. Indeed, "whiteness" dares not speak its name. The discourse of "color-blindness" provides a way to preserve privilege, while disavowing explicit racial appeals.

In this transformed political landscape, traditional civil rights organizations have experienced a profound crisis of mission, political values, and strategic orientation. There is a pressing need to both challenge the political right's appropriation of civil rights discourse and, at the same time, to rethink the capacity of state institutions to deal with persistent forms of racial inequality. Interesting trends have emerged in response. The traditional heavy reliance on state intervention is now tempered with calls for "self-help" and appeals for private support for tackling problems of crime, unemployment, and drug abuse. Integrationist versus "separate but equal" remedies for persistent racial disparities have been revisited in a new light. The civil rights establishment increasingly confronts a puzzling dilemma—formal, legal equality has been significantly achieved, but substantive racial inequality remains and in many cases, has deepened. Given this, what would constitute an effective antiracist strategy and practice?

Concepts of Race and Racism

Part of the difficulty in sorting out what constitutes a genuine and effective antiracist intervention lies in the conceptual language of race and racism that we employ. Angela Davis says that she has become convinced that the category of race is "so laden with contradictions that it no longer works in the way it used to, at least within the context of radical theories and practices."[7] The concept of race in social science research has been subject to challenges from a number of different positions. Partially in response to the President's Initiative on Race, the American Anthropological Association engaged in a vigorous debate regarding whether the concept of race retains any meaning at all as an analytic category when biological definitions have been so thoroughly discredited.[8] In politics, the use of the "race card" has been roundly criticized from distinctive political positions. In critical assessments of the weakness of the American left, identity-based social movements have been accused of "essentializing race" and subverting the advancement of a universal political subject and unified political movement.[9]

The concept of race is problematic, but Davis has an important point to make with respect to the issues raised. "That 'race' no longer works as a focus of resistance organizing," she asserts, "does not mean that racism has become obsolete and that we should discard it as a concept."[10] Unfortunately, much like race, the term "racism" is also under critical scrutiny for its conceptual validity and analytic legitimacy. Some scholars and policy makers suggest that the term itself is subject to so many varied meanings as to render the concept useless. Some have proclaimed the "end of racism," while condoning forms of "rational discrimination."[11] In 1998 John Bunzel, a former member of the U.S. Commission on Civil Rights and current senior research fellow at Stanford's Hoover Institution, argued in a newspaper op-ed piece that the President's Advisory Board on Race should call for a halt to the use of such terms as "racism" and "racist" since they are "wielded as accusations and smear words."[12] Bunzel argues that evoking the term "racism" often breeds "bitterness and polarization, not a spirit of pragmatic reasonableness in confronting our difficult problems."

In academic and policy circles, the question of who or what is racist continues to haunt discussions. Prior to World War II, the term "racism" was not commonly used in public discourse or in the social science literature in the United States.[13] The term was originally used to characterize the ideology of white supremacy that was buttressed by biologically based theories of superiority/inferiority. In the 1950s and 1960s the emphasis of studies shifted to explore *individual* expressions of prejudice and discrimination.[14] The rise of the black power movement in the 1960s and 1970s fostered a redefinition of racism that focused on its *institutional* nature.[15]

More recent intellectual trends center on the often implicit and unconscious structures of racial privilege and racial representation in daily life and popular culture. All this suggests that more precise terms are needed to examine racial consciousness, institutional bias, inequality, patterns of segregation, and the distribution of power. Racism is expressed differently at different levels and sites of social activity, and we need to be attentive to its shifting meaning in different contexts. As David Goldberg has stated, "[T]he presumption of a single monolithic racism is being displaced by a mapping of the multifarious historical formulations of *racisms*."[16]

In *Racial Formation in the United States,* Howard Winant and I define racism through our concept of "racial projects." A racial project, from our perspective, is simultaneously an interpretation, representation, or explanation of racial dynamics and an effort to reorganize and redistribute resources along particular racial lines.[17] Employing this notion, a racial project can be said to be *racist* if it creates or reproduces structures of domination based on essentialist categories of race.[18]

Racial projects can, of course, be framed and initiated to challenge prevailing forms of discriminatory practices, inequitable social policies, and racist beliefs. In an attempt to map the landscape of antiracist interventions, a survey of groups engaged in antiracist work was conducted to examine how different organizations understand racism and develop a strategic challenge to it based on that understanding. Over 200 groups nationwide responded to a brief written survey, and in-depth case studies were done on six organizations located in New York, Los Angeles, Chicago, St. Louis, Seattle, and a regionally based group in the South.[19] The following section provides a general overview of the study and highlights some core themes that emerged from it.

Antiracist Organizations

The organizations profiled in the in-depth case studies illustrate a compelling range of interpretations of what racism is in the current period, how racism finds expression in different institutional sites, and the types of activities that can be organized to confront and contest it. There are common themes and points of convergence among these groups—and there are fundamental differences between them with respect to ideology, organization, and practice. These groups target different constituencies, and engage the state and civil society in different ways. The groups can be seen as distinctive *racial projects*.

— The Dismantling Racism Program of the National Conference in St. Louis relies on a key-actors strategy to bring about social change. Organizing dialogue workshops, the group seeks to influence the racial consciousness of influential religious, corporate, and community leaders. Individual actors, "change agents," would presumably influence their respective institutional setting and contribute to broader initiatives to improve race relations in the city of St. Louis.

— The Anti-Racism Institute of Clergy and Laity Concerned in Chicago conducts antiracist training and consulting for parochial schools, church organizations, and grassroots neighborhood groups. Its efforts are directed toward education and consciousness-raising in specific community settings. A significant accomplishment of the institute was to facilitate the racial integration of Evergreen Park, a previously all-white suburb of Chicago. In cooperation with local church leaders, the institute developed a strategy to prevent "white flight" and encourage white families to welcome black families into the community.

— The Northwest Coalition Against Malicious Harassment (NWC) based in Seattle provides assistance to local communities in a six-state region (Colorado, Idaho, Montana, Oregon, Washington, and Wyoming) to challenge expressions of organized bigotry. The NWC exposes the ideology and politics of white supremacy and the attempts of far right extremists to enter the mainstream of local party politics. In different states, the organization has helped to organize coalitions to lobby for hate crime legislation.

— The Southern Empowerment Project (SEP) operates in Tennessee, Kentucky, West Virginia, North Carolina, and South Carolina. It is an intermediary organization that conducts antiracist training for a network of community-based organizations. The SEP seeks to make an intervention in the patterns of race in the South by influencing the agenda, consciousness, and composition of its nine member organizations. At a six-week summer organizer school, SEP staff teach direct-action community organizing with an explicit focus on antiracist issues. The SEP has significantly helped all-white member organizations to diversify their staff and confront the racial dimensions of the on-going work they engage in.

— The Labor/Community Strategy Center (L/CSC) challenges corporate power and the state in an effort to reallocate and redistribute public resources. Explicitly anticapitalist in orientation, the L/CSC has challenged the environmental and mass transportation policies and practices that have inequitably affected people of color in the greater Los Angeles area. The center's most recent accomplishment was the formation of a multiracial Bus Riders Union that won a multimillion-dollar settlement from the Los Angeles Metropolitan Transit Authority to improve bus service for poor communities of color. The center framed its suit as a "civil rights" issue, noting the racial disparities in bus and rail service to various communities in the greater Los Angeles area.

— The Committee against Anti-Asian Violence (CAAAV) organizes Asian immigrants who are economically and politically vulnerable and marginalized. Many of the occupations (for example, taxi drivers, prostitutes, street vendors) are policed and/or regulated by the state, and workers live with the constant threat of state violence hovering over them. The CAAAV's intent in this setting is to develop effective organizer training and worker-based mobilization. More will be said about the CAAAV later.

The racial projects these groups articulate, develop, and put forth can be seen as responses to, and creative engagements with, the prevailing patterns of racial inequality and conflict. There is a vast spectrum of ideologies and structures that constitute what racism is—they encompass individual acts of prejudice, organized expressions of bigotry, institutional patterns of inequality in the United States, and global racial conflict. Each organization deals with racism in a specific locale and institutional setting. Each organizes its activities to confront particular manifestations of racist practice. In doing so, they help to redefine our understanding of racism and suggest what antiracist interventions are possible at the present historical moment.

Several broad themes/categories for comparison emerge from the study. The vision and practice of these groups provoke a (re)consideration of (1) our understanding of racism; (2) how racism articulates with other axes of stratification; (3) the forms of antiracist engagement; (4) the impact of global and domestic economic change on race and racism; (5) the relationship of antiracist groups to the state; and (6) the impact of the nation's changing demography and its meaning for antiracist work.

THE NATURE OF RACISM

All the groups surveyed view racism not simply as a matter of attitudes and individual prejudices but as an institutional phenomenon. Racism is seen as an ideology and practice that creates, reproduces, and maintains inequitable outcomes along racial lines. That said, there are substantial differences between the groups regarding (1) how they envision and characterize the *specific* nature of racism in the present period; (2) how they articulate the connection between racism and other forms of stratification; and (3) how they define the most effective ways to engage in antiracist activity.

Specific understandings of racism inform the practice of particular groups. The Dismantling Racism Program in St. Louis examines patterns of racial inequality with respect to jobs, housing, and access to resources at the local level, and argues that structural changes are possible by helping key actors recognize and confront racist attitudes and practices. By contrast, the Labor/Community Strategy Center in Los Angeles sees racism rooted in the class structure of society and directly confronts corporate power and the distribution of public capital. The Southern Empowerment Project is attentive to the differential impact of racism and seeks to diversify all-white organizations, while simultaneously supporting the formation and development of all-black organizations.

All the groups surveyed believe that racism, both ideologically and structurally, has changed or is changing. Things are getting worse from the Northwest Coalition's perspective. Organized bigotry has evolved as individuals and groups mute explicitly racist appeals in favor of more coded ideological themes. The results have been the mainstreaming of far right ideology, growing popular acceptance of its political themes, and increasing electoral gains by the right.

Many of the groups believe that the right has captured the moral high ground by arguing for "color-blind" policies, calling for an end to federal intervention in racial matters, and urging that we "get beyond" race. What is left intact and unexamined are the existing racial inequalities that plague various institutional sites in our society. These enduring disparities are emphasized in many of the analyses of these antiracist groups. In a difficult political context, they attempt to educate their constituencies and inform the broader public about the continuing significance of racial inequality and what can be done to mitigate it.

ARTICULATIONS

All the groups see race as articulating with other axes of stratification and difference such as class and gender. An important segment of the SEP's training workshop discusses the relationship between various "-isms" based on race, gender, class, and sexual orientation. The NWC has expanded its original mission to deal with all forms of "organized bigotry" and malicious harassment. Recently, for example, the NWC has organized against violence directed toward gays and lesbians. The CAAAV's Women Workers Project centers on the unique forms of gender, race, and class oppression that Asian immigrant prostitutes encounter from their employers, clients, and respective Asian ethnic communities.

While acknowledging the connections, groups debate the emphasis that is placed on various forms of inequality. The SEP training deals with different "-isms," but more time is spent on racism, which is highlighted in the curriculum as the most significant social division. Differences are present on the NWC's board of directors with respect to the time, energy, and resources the group will commit to challenging anti-Semitism and anti–gay/lesbian initiatives (read, in part, as "white" issues) as opposed to racist acts directed at people of color. The point is that different groups negotiate the connection between various forms of oppression in a distinctive manner, one that is shaped by the evolving ideology of the organization and types of issues they confront.

ANTIRACIST INTERVENTION
With respect to antiracist engagement, two broad strategic orientations emerge. Some groups focus on transforming the racial attitudes
of individuals and groups in hopes of affecting institutional change.
This is particularly true of organizations that have principally white
constituencies. The hope is that, in raising consciousness about race
and racial issues, the "invisible" aspects of white racial privilege will be
made explicit and visible and that whites will then strive to change the
racial environment of the settings they work in. The Dismantling
Racism Program, for example, trains people to facilitate community
workshops and develop workplace dialogue groups. The goal is for
"change agents" to influence the practices of their respective organizations in order to bring about a lessening of racial inequality and
conflict.

Other groups emphasize direct challenges to institutions in order
to disrupt the patterns of racial inequality and facilitate institutional
change. The Labor/Community Strategy Center, for example, directly
confronts institutional authority and power in hopes of redistributing
resources and improving the lives of people of color. To this end, the
self-proclaimed "think/act tank" has conducted extensive research on
the disadvantages that plague communities of color and has utilized
these findings to force significant changes in public policy with respect to air quality, toxic management, and mass transportation.

THE IMPACT OF GLOBAL AND DOMESTIC ECONOMIC CHANGE
All the groups are attentive, in varying degrees, to the impact of global
and domestic economic transformation on the nature of racism. These
changes correspondingly establish the terrain and shape the possibilities for challenging racism. From the CAAAV's perspective, the globalization of the economy and domestic restructuring have created the
demand for immigrant labor in the United States and profoundly
shaped the social experiences of immigrant workers. In filling specific
niches in the labor market, Asian immigrant workers, for example, are
subject to exploitation and violence. From this perspective, anti-Asian
racism is endemic to the vulnerable location of these workers.

The L/CSC sees racism as intimately connected to the dramatic
growth of corporate power, its ability to shape the public agenda, and
the resulting inequitable distribution of resources. Several campaigns
have focused on issues of environmental racism and the lack of access

to public services. Organizing efforts have emphasized a critique of the ability of capital to dictate the "public good" and the importance of challenging abuses that flow from the concentration of economic power.

The NWC believes that expressions of organized bigotry are rooted in the growing economic displacements that plague white rural communities in the Northwest. The group's recent public education efforts attempt to reach "economically insecure" whites who the NWC believes are susceptible to far right/white supremacist ideology. The NWC seeks to convince this population that their problems reside in broader economic changes, not in the increased presence of people of color or in a global Jewish conspiracy. In a similar manner, the Anti-Racism Institute's defense of affirmative action asks white men to blame their economic woes on the state of the economy and not on competition from people of color. In both these cases, the category of *class* is evoked to subvert a racial reading of the problems whites encounter.

While other organizations provide a more explicit race-based understanding of pressing social issues, all the groups see the changing economy as a crucial factor shaping the contemporary nature of race and racism. Economic transformations (such as capital flight, the changing labor market and its requirements) exacerbate racial problems, and many of the groups surveyed see economic processes underlying the racial issues they confront. Given this, nearly all the groups attempt to subvert or undermine the "racialization" of political, economic, and social issues. They challenge simplistic racial readings of troubles in the white popular imagination and discourse.

THE RELATIONSHIP OF ANTIRACIST GROUPS TO THE STATE

The groups surveyed in this study reveal an interesting dynamic with respect to their relationship to the state—that is, local, state, and federal governments and the attendant bureaucracies. The NWC, for example, views its connection to, and interaction with, governmental authorities as a key element of its work. Its board of directors includes gubernatorial appointees, law enforcement officers, and federal officials. Part of the NWC's charge is in helping law enforcement officers monitor and enforce malicious-harassment laws. The group also lobbies for more stringent hate crime legislation and urges public officials to denounce acts of bigotry.

Other groups have taken a more adversarial role with respect to the state. The l/csc, for example, has pressured the Los Angeles Air Quality Management District to regulate corporate pollution and challenged the Metropolitan Transit Authority regarding the allocation of public capital.

Several of the groups, by contrast, have little or no direct connection to the state and state activity. The dialogue groups initiated in St. Louis get conversations about race going, increase racial awareness, and strive to affect the quality of civic life and public engagement. For these groups, the emphasis is neither on assisting state institutions nor on making demands on them.

The point is that contemporary antiracist organizing has a varied relationship to the state. In most instances, the organizing does not rely on access to the state and state resources but takes place, instead, "outside" of the terrain of state institutions. Organizations may call upon the state to enact legislation (such as the nwc's lobbying for hate crime laws) and enforce existing regulations (for example, the l/csc's fight against corporate air polluters), but most do not seek to fundamentally transform state activity with respect to race.

CHANGING DEMOGRAPHY AND MULTIRACIAL COALITIONS

All the groups express reservations about the dominant black/white paradigm of race relations. The changing demographic makeup of the nation is evident to all these groups—even those that are located in regions where the influx and growth of Latinos and Asian Americans, among others, have not been dramatic. Though the Northwest is predominantly white, the Northwest Coalition has involved Asian American and Latino groups, as well as ones that are black and American Indian, in its organization and activities since its inception. Operating in deeply segregated cities, both Chicago's Anti-Racism Institute and St. Louis's Dismantling Racism Program have emphasized the importance of multiracial training.

But while all the groups acknowledge the importance of building multiracial coalitions, some have been more successful in pursuing this move than others. The sep recognizes the increasing presence of poor and low-wage-earning Latino immigrants in the South, but works within a black/white organizing network where specifically Latino issues and initiatives have not been considered or taken up.

The Committee against Anti-Asian Violence is unique in this field of organizations surveyed since its focus is on Asian immigrant communities. Such an emphasis is a response to the economic/political vulnerability and marginality of these communities with respect to the broader patterns of race relations. What the CAAAV's work reveals, from another perspective, is the incredible heterogeneity within presumed homogeneous and monolithic racial groups. This prompts us to question the very categories we use in our work. Multicultural organizing involves, it would seem, interrogating differences *within* groups we monolithically treat and regard as Asian American, Latino, black, and so on.

An important difference among the organizations that were profiled is the issue of who is brought together by their respective initiatives. The Dismantling Racism program, for example, principally facilitates white-on-white dialogues. The SEP's training focuses on white/black interactions, while the L/CSC's Bus Riders' Union was self-consciously a multiracial project. As the changing racial composition of the nation becomes more evident in different geographic locales, issues about engaging diverse groups and forging multiracial coalitions will become more pronounced and urgent.[20]

The next section provides a more detailed discussion of one of the groups surveyed—the Committee Against Anti-Asian Violence. The CAAAV provides a compelling illustration of how racism is (re)defined and the ways in which it is strategically challenged. The influx of Asian immigrants to the United States over the past several decades has been dramatic and has had an impact on the organization of the economy. Many immigrants have been channeled into specific sectors of the labor market where the state takes a visible role in policing their activity. The CAAAV seeks to organize among immigrant workers and in so doing offers an expansive notion of racial violence.

Racism as Hate

David Theo Goldberg makes the point that in the last decade or so, racism has been popularly conceived of as *hate*.[21] The category of "hate crimes" has been introduced in many states as a specific offense with enhanced sentencing consequences. Many colleges and universities have instituted "hate speech" codes to regulate expression and behavior both inside and outside the classroom. In 1998 Richard Machado, who sent e-mail messages to fifty-nine Asian American students and staff at the University of California at Irvine vowing to "find and kill every one of you personally," became the first person in this country to be convicted of a federal hate crime committed in cyberspace. The imposition of such regulations and codes can be seen as a response to the dramatic increase in acts of racist violence. The horrifying murder of James Byrd Jr., the forty-nine-year-old black man who was dragged to his death behind a pickup truck in 1998, is but one recent example.

The reduction of racism to hate, however, both conceptually and politically limits our understanding of racism and the ways we can challenge it. Racism has been silently transformed in the popular consciousness into acts that are abnormal, unusual, and irrational. Missing from all this are the ideologies and practices in a variety of sites in the social formation that reproduce racial inequality and domination.

Seen from this perspective, expressions of "hate" are an easy target. Goldberg argues that it is much more difficult to criminalize or otherwise to regulate racist expressions of power, not least because relations of power are so normalized and constitute "common threads of the fabric of our social formation."[22] How can a more expansive concept of racial violence be framed—one that seriously interrogates relations of power in our social formation? The work of the Committee Against Anti-Asian Violence directly takes up this question. The following section describes the CAAAV's perspective and activities. The CAAAV provides us with a different concept of anti-Asian violence—distinct, that is, from hate crimes—and allows us to consider the political possibilities and strategic orientations that flow from such a perspective.

ANTI-ASIAN VIOLENCE AND POLITICAL MOBILIZATION

Asian Americans have always been subject to racial violence, but the specific nature of racial violence and the forms of resistance to it have historically varied. The brutal murder of Vincent Chin in Detroit in 1982 inspired a wave of organizational efforts to counter random acts of anti-Asian violence. Studies of these efforts have focused on distinctive aspects. Drawing, in part, on an analysis of Detroit's American Citizens for Justice, Yen Espiritu argues that the "race lumping" characteristic of anti-Asian violence contributes to Asian panethnic consciousness in the form of "reactive solidarity."[23] Kathy Yep, in a case study analysis of three Asian/Pacific Islander community mobilizations, concludes that the socioeconomic status and identity politics of community members affected the types of responses to anti-Asian violence.[24] I want to examine the work of the Committee against Anti-Asian Violence in New York as a specific intervention that allows us to rethink the nature of racial violence.

At first glance, the CAAAV appears to be engaged in a number of seemingly disparate projects and organizing activities. These include organizing among South Asian taxi drivers, developing leadership programs for Vietnamese and Cambodian youth in the Bronx, and doing outreach with Korean women sex workers at brothels and massage parlors. But at the center of the CAAAV's work, providing coherence for its varied programs, is an expansive understanding of racism and racial violence.

The CAAAV describes itself as "a pan-Asian organization committed to combating violence and police brutality against Asian immigrants and Asian Americans in New York City."[25] The organization's activities over the nearly twelve years of its existence have dramatically evolved from addressing "hate violence" to interrogating the nature of workplace violence in the daily lives of Asian immigrant workers.

ORIGINS AND FOCUS

In response to the Vincent Chin case and other acts of random violence directed against Asian Americans, a coalition of community groups sponsored a forum called "Violence against Asians in America" on 18 October 1986 in New York City.[26] The forum was attended by 250 people and the Coalition against Anti-Asian Violence emerged from it.[27] Mini Liu, a doctor, an Organization of Asian Women member, and one of the founders of the CAAAV, later commented, "It was a radical idea for non-Asians, and some Asians as well, that Asians were affected by violence. Among the topics discussed at the forum was the issue of police brutality. There was no idea at the time that that would form the core of our later work."[28]

The focus on police brutality as a form of anti-Asian violence distinguishes the CAAAV from the activities of other anti-Asian violence groups in the country. Most of the other groups are made up of professionals—attorneys, health care providers, college professors, and politicians—who are concerned with random acts of violence directed against Asians. These groups critique the prevailing climate of racial intolerance, the rise of explicitly white-supremacist groups, and the deepening "racialization" of contemporary political issues. Activities focus on getting law enforcement agencies to develop more effective "hate crimes" policies and practices. These anti-Asian violence groups are also involved in lobbying for legislation to monitor hate crimes and subject perpetrators to stiff penalties. Eric Tang, a CAAAV staff person, is critical of most organizational approaches: "For the longest time, mainstream Asian-American organizations have used anti-Asian violence as a lobbying issue, but have failed to critically analyze the systemic roots of such violence and the particular forms it takes in newly arrived immigrant communities."[29] The CAAAV defines its mission and work in more "radical" terms. Tang states, "CAAAV takes on a lot of issues because we interpret violence broadly. There's physical violence, there's sexual violence, there's the violence of the workplace. And there's the violence of poverty itself."[30]

The organization currently defines anti-Asian violence as

— institutional racism and misconduct, especially that perpetrated by the police and government (Asian male youth, for example, are often scapegoated as criminals);
— racist discrimination, including physical harm, by private individuals whose actions are sanctioned by the culture at large;
— exploitation of immigrant labor, where Asian women are particularly at risk, manifested in dangerous working conditions and poor wages.[31]

Operating with this expanded definition, the CAAAV has carved out a series of projects to address the often "hidden" everyday reality of violence and exploitation experienced by specific Asian ethnic immigrants. Much of the activity is centered on issues of poverty and inequality and how they impact Asian immigrant working-class constituencies.

IMMIGRANT LABOR

Some 80 percent of Asian residents in New York are immigrants, and the vast majority are concentrated in low-skilled occupations in marginal industries.[37] These include working in restaurants, sewing in garment factories, driving cabs, cleaning hotel rooms, and working in massage parlors—jobs that typically offer less than the minimum wage and are often associated with unsafe work environments. The following 1995 editorial in *The CAAAV Voice* draws attention to this situation, and links it to the CAAAV's broader antiracist agenda:

> Every day there are Asian Americans in New York City who are victims of racism and anti-immigrant sentiment. When we think of Asians being victimized, we imagine teenagers stalking with baseball bats or—the more likely occurrence—men in blue with their nightsticks and guns. In reality, however, New York City Asians, especially immigrants regularly face the greatest abuse where they work—from health hazards to homicide. Racism and anti-immigrant discrimination in the labor market force Asians into dangerous jobs in marginal industries—jobs with low pay, long hours, poor working conditions, no benefits and little security. These conditions are condoned by the government, whose regulatory agencies and criminal justice system turn a blind eye to abusive practices or participate in the abuse themselves.[33]

The CAAAV has identified the Asian immigrant working class as its main constituency, and the organization's evolving concerns have highlighted the workplace as a site of exploitation and potential violence for immigrant workers. Broadly defining and dividing its work into the core areas of advocacy, community organizing, leadership development, community education, and coalition building, the CAAAV has developed a number of semi-autonomous projects[34] to serve Asian immigrant communities. One of the first projects was the Lease Drivers Coalition. Its on-going task is to organize primarily South Asian immigrant cab drivers to challenge a racist and exploitative taxi industry in New York.

Another program area is the Youth Leadership Project, which is geared toward developing youth leadership in low-income and refugee Asian communities. Summer programs have been developed over the past two years to involve Asian youth in workshops and campaigns around housing and welfare reform. Youths have conducted door-to-door campaigns around issues such as tenant rights and securing social service benefits.

One of the CAAAV's most recent initiatives is the Women Workers Project, which is an attempt to organize Asian women sex workers in the city. Many immigrant women with limited language and job skills are often driven to engage in sex work because of the absence of other economically viable options. They have little say in the conditions of their existence and are often subject to physical violence. The project is attempting to promote safe working conditions, health care, and fair wages for these women.

Interestingly, these program areas were developed by the CAAAV to reach different Asian ethnic constituencies. The Lease Drivers Coalition was conceived as a way of organizing the South Asian community. The Youth Leadership Program is an attempt to reach Southeast Asian youth, while the Women Workers Project is an attempt to organize Korean women. Issues are defined, framed, and organized in reference to the pressing needs of specific communities.

This is important since different ethnic communities, and classes within them, are subject to a unique constellation of factors that account for their location in the broader social formation, how they experience it, and the problems they encounter. Mindful that distinct Asian ethnic groups are affected by racism, economic exploitation, and state violence in different ways, the CAAAV has defined program areas that target the needs and concerns of specific communities. The CAAAV's approach and activities serve to disrupt the notion of a fixed, uniform, and homogeneous Asian American community. In many respects the CAAAV is a "coalition" of distinct groups and interests.

CHANGES

The CAAAV has developed a unique approach to antiracist organizing. It is one that has evolved over the years from a response to "hate violence" to the initiation of projects that confront the daily violence that Asian immigrants encounter in the workplace. Central to the CAAAV's expansive definition of anti-Asian violence has been an analysis of the economy and the state. Asian immigrant workers find themselves in marginal positions in the labor market that subject them to exploitative conditions. The state "polices" immigrant populations and subjects workers to its enforcement, but it fails to "protect" them. Youths are criminalized, sex workers are subject to raids and arrest, and taxi drivers are regulated by the police. In this respect, the CAAAV uniquely challenges the role of state-sanctioned violence on Asian American communities.

Having started and organized several program areas targeting specific Asian ethnic communities, the CAAAV is currently in a period of consolidation and transformation. The organization is attempting to restructure itself to serve as a center to train organizers, to develop community organizing methodologies, and to frame and advance antiracist strategies. Its goal is to build and sustain movements in Asian ethnic communities to deal with distinct forms of institutional inequality and violence. This is animated by the desire to build the capacity of different Asian ethnic communities to effectively organize and mobilize around issues on their own behalf.

In the midst of these changes, the CAAAV maintains an unwavering commitment to challenging the patterns of violence directed against and experienced by Asian American communities. This concern constitutes the heart and soul of the organization and informs all of its antiracist work.

ADDRESSING RACIALIZED POWER

The reduction of racism to forms of "hate," discussed at the start of this section, severely limits our ability to comprehend the dimensions of racialized power. Racial violence is regarded in popular opinion as an irrational act—a "crime of passion." The ways that racial violence is perpetrated by the state and by the organization of the economy are rendered invisible and not subject to interrogation.

The CAAAV provides a very different and more expansive concept of racial violence: one that grapples with what Lisa Lowe names as the *"contradictions* of Asian immigration" that have "placed Asians 'within' the U.S. nation-state, its workplaces, and its markets, yet linguistically, culturally, and racially marked Asians as 'foreign' and 'outside' the national polity."[35] From this perspective, anti-Asian violence is far more pervasive than individual random acts of hate, and the strategies to challenge and prevent it are far more complex.

Power, Conflict, and the Promise of "Interracial Justice"

The issue of racialized power raises a host of important political questions. One crucial lesson that emerged from this study of antiracist organizations was the urgent political necessity to rethink race and the possibilities for alliances among groups of color. This is not to absolve whites of the responsibility to challenge racism, but it is an attempt to decenter whiteness in relation to communities of color. Some multicultural narratives, for example, position groups of color vis-à-vis a core white culture. Groups of color are rarely, if ever, treated as dynamic referents for each other. To do so, however, would help to significantly destabilize the rigid bipolar model of race. It would suggest a profound rethinking of what it means to do antiracist work. This final section explores this issue and its implications.

In February 1998 the President's Initiative on Race came to the San Francisco Bay Area—San Jose to be exact—for a dialogue on race and poverty. In opening remarks, Judith Winston, the executive director of the initiative, said, "California is becoming transformed into one of America's truly multicultural societies. If we want to make the future brighter, we need to understand how to make this multiracial, multiethnic society work better."[36] Unfortunately, the community dialogue that followed subsequently degenerated into a shouting match between various racially defined groups. It seems we have a *long* way to go before we "understand how to make this multiracial, multiethnic society work better."

California, a state that should be offering the rest of the nation positive lessons about the transition to a multiracial society, sadly provides examples of ill-conceived political reaction. In this regard, it is important to think about the divisive impact of California's Proposition 187 and Proposition 209. Proposition 187 directed the suspension of social services to "illegal alien" populations, while Proposition 209, the so-called Civil Rights Initiative, prohibited all forms of affirmative action by the state of California. There were some interesting parallels between them. In both cases, the focus was on the state and the allocation and deployment of public resources. And both initiatives could be viewed as a distinct form of symbolic politics—one in which perception of the problem was crucial. In an analysis of Proposition 187, Kitty Calavita argues that supporters did not subscribe to some of the main policy components of the initiative, but voted for the measure nonetheless.[37] Supporters did not want to throw "illegal" aliens out of the schools or provoke a public health crisis—but they did want to send a political message to check immigration.

Part of the "success" of these initiatives was their ability to exploit conflicts and tensions between (and within) racial minority communities. Political interests were not framed in reference to whiteness; the issues were not presented in white versus nonwhite terms. In the campaign for Proposition 187, African American "interests" were framed as counter to that of Latino, and to a lesser extent Asian, immigrants. From one vantage point, it was argued that immigrants were siphoning off social services and resources that could be utilized to help impoverished segments of the African American community. In debates regarding Proposition 209 on affirmative action, Asian American "interests" were defined in opposition to those of blacks and Latinos. Drawing on admissions controversies in higher education, neoconservatives argued, for example, that race-based affirmative action victimized Asian Americans as much as, perhaps more than, it did whites.[38]

Political issues are frequently racially coded and framed in a manner that uncritically assumes a zero-sum game of race relations. In this zero-sum game, group members are seen as "naturally" segregated and fundamentally antagonistic toward each other. One group's gain is perceived to be another group's loss. Herein lies the possibilities for open conflict.

We are going to see more of this type of conflict as issues compel racial interests to be defined in ways that cut across different communities of color. Clearly a new antiracist politics needs to be articulated with respect to the impending "fire next time." Two conceptual critiques need to be advanced in this revisioning of antiracist politics. One involves the concept of race, and the other centers on our understanding of power.

Much of the existing political discourse employs an essentialist understanding of race—one that sees races as fixed and given, discrete and homogeneous. By contrast, what is needed is a politics that takes seriously the processes of racialization and increasing heterogeneity within a presumed racial group. Our collective understanding of who blacks, Latinos, and Asians are has been significantly destabilized by the dramatic influx and growth of "new" groups—Laotians, Guatemalans, Haitians, and Sudanese among others. Adding to the mix are questions of ethnicity, class, gender, and sexuality that render a category such as Asian American or Latino quite problematic constructs depending on the context.[39] What is needed is a politics that is attentive to these differences and to their meaning for race-based struggles.

A new antiracist politics needs to revisit the question "Who has the power?" Many of the groups surveyed define racism as "prejudice plus power," and employing this formula they correspondingly argue that people of color cannot be racist since they lack power. But things are not that simple or straightforward. In the post–civil rights era, some racial minority groups have carved out a degree of power in select urban areas—particularly with respect to administering social services and distributing economic resources. This has led, in cities like Oakland and Miami, to conflicts between blacks and Latinos over educational programs, minority business opportunities, and political power.

Going deeper than this, it is important to see that power is not a "thing"—it is a complex field of relationships, including coercive ones and the ability to produce ideas. Power involves the ability to resist as well as to rule; it involves challenging large-scale institutions as well as the meaning-systems we encounter in everyday life. In this sense, racialized minorities do have at least some power, and it is debilitating in the long run for a subordinate and oppressed group to think of itself as powerless.

A starting point for dialogue among racial minorities is to acknowledge the historical and contemporary differences in power that different groups possess. Groups are positioned in unequal ways in a racially stratified society. In a recent study of perceived group competition in Los Angeles, sociologists Lawrence Bobo and Vincent Hutchings found, among other things, that whites felt least threatened by blacks and most threatened by Asians, while Asians felt a greater threat from blacks than Latinos.[40] These findings underscore how different racial groups serve as dynamic referents for each other and how they possess a particular understanding of their location in a racial hierarchy. Such distinct perceptions of "group position" are related to, and implicated in, the organization of power.

Acknowledging differences in power between groups, whether real or imagined, has profound implications for the possibilities of coalition building. In a recent essay, law professor Eric Yamamoto recounts the campaign in 1993 among churches within the Hawaii Conference of the United Church of Christ for an Asian American apology to Native Hawaiians and for multimillion dollar reparations.[41] At issue was how other Asian Americans, particularly Japanese and Chinese Americans, have been complicit in the exploitation and oppression of Native Hawaiians.

Drawing on this case, Yamamoto advances a concept of "interracial justice"—one that is attentive to the historical and contemporary differences in power that different groups possess. Interracial justice reflects a commitment to antisubordination among nonwhite racial groups:

> It entails a hard acknowledgment of the ways in which racial groups have harmed and continue to harm one another, sometimes though forms of oppression, along with affirmative efforts to redress past harms with continuing effects. More specifically, interracial justice is comprised of two related dimensions. One dimension is conceptual . . . it involves a recognition of situated racial group power. . . . The second dimension is practical. It involves messy, shifting, continual and often localized processes of interracial healing.[42]

Such efforts are not meant to divert attention away from the prevailing reality of white racism. Groups of color labor under a social system that has been historically structured by white supremacy and continues in the present to reinforce white privilege. But the hegemonic racial order has not treated all nonwhite groups in a similar manner. Tomás Almaguer in his study of white supremacy in nineteenth-century California notes that different racial/ethnic groups encountered a "differential racialization."[43] Nonwhite groups were envisioned, socially constructed, and positioned in relation to each other by white elites. This has consequences for group position and how political interests get defined.

A focus on "interracial justice" should not be read as minimizing or erasing the class and ethnic heterogeneity of the racial categories that we so glibly refer to as "black," "Latino," "Asian," and so on. The emphasis here, however, is on racial minority groups to acknowledge "differences" and begin to transform "power over" one another into "power to" coexist, cooperate, and work together politically.

All the groups surveyed are grappling with the issue of relations between communities of color and its meaning for their on-going work. Even those whose primary constituencies are white and/or black are attentive to the changing racial composition of the nation and believe that the dominant black/white paradigm of race is in need of revision. This acknowledgment, however, has seldom translated into practical activities tailored to address the processes of differential racialization. But the promise of "interracial justice" remains.

Antiracism in a Post–Civil Rights Era

In many respects, the current political climate is a dismal one. Racial inequalities are downplayed or ignored; race-based policies such as affirmative action are being questioned or dismantled; and "color-blindness" is touted as the only effective antiracist position. Amid this landscape, the racial projects the surveyed organizations articulate, develop, and put forth can be seen as both responses to and creative engagements with the prevailing patterns of racial inequality and discourse. The vision and practice of these groups have been framed, whether consciously or not, in dialogue with the civil rights movement, and this engagement has shaped, to a large degree, certain points of convergence with the civil rights agenda. That said, these organizations should be regarded as new interventions—ones that are responding to the changing meaning of race in political discourse and institutional life.

Most of the emerging practices of these organizations are moving away from the civil rights community's engagement with litigation and the strict pursuit of legal and legislative reforms. These groups operate in distinctive spaces—transforming popular consciousness in community-based settings, organizing workers in marginal sectors of the economy, and challenging white supremacist groups in predominantly white, rural communities. Their presence, organizational form, and practice suggest that antiracist work has entered a new phase, one that embraces a vision of social justice that extends beyond formal legal guarantees of racial equality and equal opportunity. This vision of social justice argues that "equality under the law" is not enough. What is required is a hard look at how racial meanings and practices are suffused into patterns of both everyday and institutional life and how they indelibly shape individual consciousness, collective identities, corporate actions, and government policies. The complexity of racism requires an equally complex response and antiracist challenge.

Of significant note is the development of explicitly antiracist organizations centered on, and lead by, people of color. Many of the 200 organizations the study initially surveyed were run by whites whose principal constituencies were white. These groups were involved in prejudice-reduction work among whites or facilitating dialogue among them regarding race and racism. Even in groups that encouraged dialogue and collective activities between different racial groups, the focus was often on whites with the goal of substantively transforming *white attitudes* toward people of color.

This focus is in many ways understandable, given racial realities in the United States. As Joe Feagin and Hernán Vera convincingly argue, racism in the United States is *white racism,* a "socially organized set of attitudes, ideas, and practices that deny African Americans and other people of color the dignity, opportunities, freedoms, and rewards that this nation offers white Americans."[44] But racism cannot be simply challenged by whites becoming racially conscious, unlearning racism, and/or aggressively denying the privileges of whiteness. Antiracist work needs to move in several different directions—ones that decenter the focus on whiteness. Different communities of color need to confront divisions and conflicts between them, and coalitions and alliances need to be built among all racial groups, with people of color in leading roles. The movement for racial justice will demand the participation of all groups and a commitment to thoroughly interrogate the dimensions of racialized power. Such an interrogation of power needs to be attentive to how different groups have been positioned in the racial hierarchy and how such locations affect the framing of political interests. This will prove to be quite a challenge.

The organizations profiled in the study remind us of the continuing significance of race and the persistence of racism in different sites of our social order. In the present political moment, such a reminder is of crucial importance. The political right trumpets the emergence of a color-blind society and proudly proclaims the "end of racism." Even within progressive circles, Angela Davis notes, "charges of racism are often viewed as old and tired arguments." But, she continues, "there is a sense in which the term "racism" still maintains its ability to ruffle people's feathers. There is a persistently piercing character about the term 'racism' that is one sign of the perseverance of power relations based on race."[45]

It is those relations of power that we need to discern, deconstruct, and challenge. This is a crucial lesson that has emerged from this study of antiracist organizations. In distinct ways, they have illustrated the need not only to acknowledge racism but also to actively work toward its abolition.

Notes

This essay relies on a study of antiracist organizations titled "Confronting the New Racisms: Anti-Racist Organizing in the Post–Civil Rights Era," funded by the C. S. Mott Foundation. The study was carried out by the Applied Research Center in Oakland, California. Researchers on the project were Gary Delgado, Rebecca Gordon, and myself. An earlier version of this essay was presented at the 93d Annual Meeting of the American Sociological Association, 21–25 August 1998 in San Francisco.

1 Quoted in Margaret Talbot, "Getting Credit for Being White," *New York Times Magazine,* 30 November 1997, 118.
2 Alastair Bonnett, "Constructions of Whiteness in European and American Anti-Racism," in *Debating Cultural Hybridity: Multi-Cultural Identities and the Politics of Anti-Racism,* ed. Pnina Werbner and Tariq Modood (London and Atlantic Highlands, N.J.: Zed Books, 1997), 181.
3 Ibid., 178.
4 See, for example, Noel Ignatiev and John Garvey, *Race Traitor* (New York and London: Routledge, 1996).
5 George Lipsitz, *The Possessive Investment in Whiteness: How White People Profit from Identity Politics* (Philadelphia: Temple University Press, 1998), 210.
6 Bob Blauner, "Talking Past Each Other: Black and White Languages of Race," in *Race and Ethnic Conflict: Contending Views on Prejudice, Discrimination, and Ethnoviolence,* ed. Fred L. Pincus and Howard J. Ehrlich (Boulder, Colo.: Westview, 1994).
7 Angela Y. Davis, "Gender, Class, and Multiculturalism: Rethinking 'Race' Politics," in *Mapping Multiculturalism,* ed. Avery F. Gordon and Christopher Newfield (Minneapolis: University of Minnesota Press, 1996), 43.
8 *Anthropology Newsletter* 38, no. 7 (October 1997); 38, no. 9 (December 1997); 39, no. 2 (February 1998); 39, no. 3 (March 1998); 39, no. 5 (May 1998); and 39, no. 6 (September 1998).
9 Todd Gitlin, *The Twilight of Common Dreams: Why America is Wracked by Culture Wars* (New York: Metropolitan Books, 1995).
10 Davis, "Gender, Class," p. 44.
11 For example, Dinesh D'Souza, *The End of Racism* (New York: Free Press, 1995).
12 John H. Bunzel, "Words That Smear, Like 'Racism,' Provoke Polarization," *San Francisco Sunday Examiner and Chronicle,* 26 July 1998.
13 The term may have first surfaced in Magnus Hirschfeld, *Racism* (London: Victor Gollancz, 1938).
14 T. W. Adorno et al., *The Authoritarian Personality* (New York: Harper, 1950);

Gordon W. Allport, *The Nature of Prejudice* (Cambridge, Mass.: Addison-Wesley, 1954).

15 Louis L. Knowles and Kenneth Prewitt, eds., *Institutional Racism in America* (Englewood Cliffs, N.J.: Prentice-Hall, 1970); Robert Blauner, *Racial Oppression in America* (New York: Harper and Row, 1972).

16 David Theo Goldberg, ed., *Anatomy of Racism* (Minneapolis: University of Minnesota Press, 1990), xiii.

17 Michael Omi and Howard Winant, *Racial Formation in the United States: From the 1960s to the 1990s* (New York and London: Routledge, 1994), 56.

18 Ibid., 71.

19 Michael Omi, Gary Delgado, and Rebecca Gordon, "Confronting the New Racisms: Anti-Racist Organizing in the Post-Civil Rights Era," executive summary prepared by the Applied Research Center for the C. S. Mott Foundation (January 2000).

20 The implications of this will be discussed below in the discussion on "interracial justice."

21 David Theo Goldberg, "Hate, or Power?" chap. 2 of *Racial Subjects: Writing on Race in America* (Routledge, 1997).

22 Ibid., 23.

23 Yen Le Espiritu, "Reactive Solidarity: Anti-Asian Violence," chap. 6 of *Asian American Panethnicity: Bridging Institutions and Identities* (Philadelphia: Temple University Press, 1992).

24 Kathy Yep, "The Power of Collective Voice," *Asian American Policy Review* 4 (1994): 33–63.

25 Committee Against Anti-Asian Violence brochure 1996.

26 Members of this coalition included the Asian American Legal Defense and Education Fund, the Coalition of Labor Union Women (New York), the Japanese American Citizens League (New York), the Khmer Association in the U.S., Korean Americans for Social Concern, Korean American Women for Action, the Organization of Asian Women, the Organization of Chinese Americans (New York), and the Young Korean American Service & Education Center.

27 Note that the organization's name was originally the *Coalition* Against Anti-Asian Violence reflecting its emergence from these sponsoring members. Its name was changed to the *Committee* Against Anti-Asian Violence in 1988.

28 Interview with Mini Liu, 4 October 1996, New York. Liu notes that a forum panelist, Sook Nam Choo, spoke about coalitional work around police brutality against Koreans in Queens.

29 Interview with Eric Tang, 4 October 1996, New York.

30 Ibid.

31 CAAAV brochure (1996). With respect to Asian American women it is

interesting to note that this focus on gender is very recent. Though the organization grew out of the efforts of the Organization of Asian Women, their initial activity had no specific gender analysis.

32 "From Tenants to Taxi Drivers—CAAAV Organizes in Immigrant Communities," *CAAAV Voice* 4, no. 2 (fall 1992): 5.

33 Editorial, *CAAAV Voice* 7, no. 1 (spring 1995): 1.

34 The projects are semi-autonomous in that they have their own specific organizers, distinct constituencies, and are not subsumed under the organizational dictates of the CAAAV as a whole.

35 Lisa Lowe, *Immigrant Acts: On Asian American Cultural Politics* (Durham: Duke University Press, 1996), 8.

36 Louis Freedberg, "State's Diversity Adds Color to Talks: Race Panel Comes to San Jose." *San Francisco Chronicle,* 10 February 1998.

37 Kitty Calavita, "The New Politics of Immigration: 'Balanced-Budget Conservatism' and the Symbolism of Proposition 187," *Social Problems* 43, no. 3 (August 1996): 284–305.

38 Michael Omi and Dana Y. Takagi, "Situating Asian Americans in the Political Discourse of Affirmative Action" *Representations,* no. 55 (summer 1996): 155–62.

39 Lisa Lowe, "Heterogeneity, Hybridity, Multiplicity: Asian American Differences," chap. 3 of *Immigrant Acts,* 60–83.

40 Lawrence Bobo and Vincent Hutchings, "Perceptions of Racial Group Competition: Extending Blumer's Theory of Group Position to a Multiracial Social Context," *American Sociological Review* 61, no. 6 (December 1996): 951–72.

41 Eric Y. Yamamoto, "Rethinking Alliances: Agency, Responsibility and Interracial Justice," *UCLA Asian Pacific American Law Journal* 3, no. 1 (fall 1995): 33–74.

42 Ibid., 34–35.

43 Tomás Almaguer, *Racial Fault Lines: The Historical Origins of White Supremacy in California* (Berkeley and Los Angeles: University of California Press, 1994), 4–7.

44 Joe R. Feagin and Hernán Vera, *White Racism* (New York and London: Routledge, 1995), 7.

45 Davis, "Gender, Class," 44.

William Aal

Moving from Guilt to Action: Antiracist Organizing and the Concept of "Whiteness" for Activism and the Academy

As an antiracist organizer and trainer over the last twenty years, I have grasped at any tools that might make my work easier and more effective. Many of us who work at the grassroots level against racism do so because we see it as the fundamental problem underlying and linking other forms of oppression and social injustice in the United States. None of us were born antiracist organizers; we became such as we saw devastating effects that racism has on people of color, on the humanity of white people, and on the moral and spiritual fabric of society. Like others grappling with the pervasive and seemingly intractable problem of racism in this country, I have studied history, Marxism and other forms of political economy, social psychology, sociology—anything that might help one to understand how our society got organized the way it is and what it will take to change it.

I became an "expert" at being racist from having been born and raised "white" in a country that is structured along racist lines. At the same time, because I am a beneficiary of this system, the impact of racism is almost entirely invisible to me. In order to get real insight into the dynamics, it has been necessary for me to read history and analysis by people of color to get the view from "outside." In order to survive each day, whether there is a white person in the room or not, they have to deal with the consequences of a world ordered by white skin privilege. They are the experts on whiteness and its impact on themselves, "white" people, and the United States as a whole.

In the work that I and other trainers and organizers do, it is invaluable to define the concept of white identity as privilege. Many people self-identified as white experience themselves as beyond history and without community. Their culture is one of consumption—of ideas, art, and spirituality, as well as of material objects. When trying to encourage "white" people to help eliminate racism, it is helpful to encourage them to remember that by fighting racism we act to restore our own humanity and culture as well. We welcome the academic study of whiteness as a way to reclaim history, yet many of us are uneasy with this trend as well. This essay grew out of a concern that "whiteness" as an academic subject of study can easily slip from being the examination of an important social/political category to becoming just another career path. People often start out with a commitment to serve, but the process of professionalization takes them away from the community. This is a pitfall that is systemic to U.S. work culture. I see the same dynamic in the dichotomy between diversity training and anti-oppression organizing. As a "diversity trainer," it is also easy to end up making a career of working in the corporate sector and becoming disassociated from the oppressed communities. In fact, there is a whole generation of people coming through various university programs in multicultural work or "cross-cultural" training or similar fields who are looking for work as trainers or organizers and yet have had very little experience as activists.

I felt very ambivalent about writing for an academic book when first approached. I didn't want my work to become more fodder for the academic paper mill. On other the hand, I have wanted to make a contribution to the antiracist movement in this country by challenging academics to produce materials useful to the struggle for justice and to actively engage—because we could really use a hand!

One lesson I have learned over the years is that in order to eradicate racism activists and organizers need to start working with those who benefit from racist structures and who play the biggest part in maintaining them. So it makes sense for me to use this opportunity to address academics who are overwhelmingly white and are certainly among those who benefit from and maintain the status quo. Therefore, they can play an important part in bringing about change.

There are intellectual projects that could take all of us further. What we need in the movement is a better understanding of how "whiteness" as a set of overlapping identities, structures, and power relations keeps the United States divided along the lines of race, class, and gender. We need to know more about how we got into the predica-ment in which most of the "white" people in the United States either are unaware of the impacts that their daily lives have on "others," both inside the United States and around the world, or don't care. We need to reclaim our history through an antiracist lens, especially remem-bering and learning from those of our ancestors who have stood for justice.[1] And we also need to contribute to the process of creating new ways of being together across lines of difference in classrooms, con-ferences, and the community.

The stories we tell need to be deep, to promote critical thinking, and be both accessible and relevant for people outside the academy. I long for someone to engage with the thinking of Antonio Gramsci, Stuart Hall, bell hooks, Cornel West, Edward Said, Roberto Unger, and oth-ers in ways that relate these cultural and intellectual struggles with everyday life. The work of these intellectuals makes an enormous contribution toward revealing the fact that the structures of injustice are not natural phenomena ("the way the world has and will always be") but were created by humans in specific historical contexts and therefore *can be changed.* By helping us understand the formative contexts of daily life and the institutional arrangements that maintain oppression, engaged academics could help foster new ways of think-ing about our social/political problems.

Stories from a Few Antiracist Whites

To clarify my own thinking, I decided to talk with a few other trainer/activists around the United States about what the idea of whiteness means to them and what they would want from the study of white-ness. I talked with three people who have been doing antiracist work for many years. Two of them have Ph.D.'s and work in academic settings, though they both have taken decidedly nontraditional paths. Each of us is committed to a form of social justice that includes look-ing at the intersecting axes of class, gender, and race. We take it as a given that without racial justice, there can be no gender justice and vice versa. At the same time, each of us understands that racism is at the center of much of what it means to be white in America. We understand that our worldview, our sense of what is ours without asking and our knowledge of what we are not supposed to talk about, is structured by our white identities. I asked them three or four questions about their motivations for doing the work, their vision for the future, what they thought about "white studies," and what they would want from such an endeavor. When I mentioned the ambivalence I myself felt about the field, they acknowledged similar feelings. We all have learned a lot from academics and at the same time have been outraged by some of the dynamics described later in this article. These conversations challenge academics to turn some of their own tools of critical analysis on their own work: to examine how they make choices about what to focus on, whose interests the research they are doing serves, and to whom they are accountable.

Mark Scanlon Green is an academic who has also done a lot of antiracist organizing and brings a gender analysis to his thinking about race. His Ph.D. dissertation was on the subject of white males and diversity work. He now works in a private academic setting, working principally with students of color. Mark took up antiracist work, coming out of a complex personal/family history, his identity as a gay man, and a political commitment to change from the age of fourteen. "My choice to focus on white men is personal and political," he says.

> As a white man who has become actively involved in the diversity movement, I have wondered how it is that I have chosen to challenge the system that assigns me higher status and more power than it does to people of color and white women. If all the unearned privilege I have is a boon to my personal and professional development, why would I, or for that matter, any other man in his right mind, choose to work to eliminate its influence? . . . I have also realized, however, that over the years, many of my political "fellow travelers" were every bit as racist, sexist, and heterosexist as the larger society they claimed they wanted to change. And since racism is at the heart of the American experience, without dealing with it, we can't move forwards with a progressive social agenda. If the Rosetta Stone is found that decodes the process by which some white men, who are at the pinnacle of social status and power, actively engage themselves in changing the system, significant social change becomes possible.

Eventually he ended up feeling attacked from several fronts in the "diversity" arena. He says, "It is much harder for a white man to be out front as a trainer." White people didn't accept his leadership, and people of color didn't trust a white person doing "diversity training." Mark gave up active organizing with white people since he couldn't see social change occurring from doing "diversity work." He doesn't see himself as an activist anymore. He has chosen as his life work to be supportive of people of color getting access to higher education and puts the majority of his academic commitment in that direction, mentoring students from nontraditional backgrounds. He is committed to "academic excellence" not only to help students get access but also to insist that they grab that access, make it theirs in whatever way makes sense to them, and to shine in their competence.

His vision of a world that has dealt with racism is one based on equal access to resources—educational, economic, and political. It has to do with principles of justice as opposed to "equality." He wants academics looking at whiteness to be focused on eliminating the barriers to access within the academy that white people keep putting in front of people of color. The challenge is to make space for people of color on a truly equal footing; liberalism, individualism, and tokenism need to be combated.

Sharon Howell, raised poor, was the first in her family to go to college. She is now an academic as well. A lifelong antiracist, she has been a member and a leader of a non-Marxist revolutionary organization that was dedicated to creating a revolution with people of color in the lead. She works at a large midwestern university and is a leader in her community as an antiracist and antihomophobic organizer. She currently leads the major grassroots effort to rebuild Detroit. Along with Margo Adair, she is a founding member of Tools for Change, a consulting group that conducts workshops around antiracism and economic justice in work settings and for political groups.

Sharon would rather do anything else than have to deal with racism. There are more interesting things to do in the world, she says, like reconstruct Detroit so that it is a city that sustains all its people. But, according to her, racism gets in the way of that project. Detroit was destroyed because of racism. And now the majority of people left in the city are people who can't afford to leave, so—white, black, Arab, Asian, or Latino—they have common ground to stand on. Much of Detroit looks like a war zone. Whole blocks of houses have been bulldozed to the ground because absentee landlords abandoned their properties as economic values went down. There is little blue-collar work left in Detroit proper and its surrounding suburban areas, as the big auto makers have moved toward automation and outsourcing overseas and to other, nonunionized parts of the city. So the racial question has now more clearly than ever become one of class. The folks at the bottom have to deal with each other in order to survive. Yet race still is a "wedge issue" that is used to divide people.

So, for Sharon, it is necessary to deal with racism at all levels, interpersonally, within organizational structures and in "civil" society. Interpersonal racism, the kind that keeps white people and people of color from being able to trust each other because of white people's conscious or unconscious identification with the white power structure, needs to be dealt with to build long-lasting relations of solidarity. A former member of the National Organization for an American Revolution (NOAR), a revolutionary organization dedicated to the revolutionary leadership of African Americans and other people of color, she and her writing partner and political comrade Margo Adair started doing organizational consulting with groups committed to progressive social change in the mid-1980s. They, like Mark, realized that the relationships of oppression that exist in the dominant society are reproduced within those groups. Their analysis of organizational culture as an outgrowth of European American (white) middle-class patriarchal culture led them to look at how patterns of power govern access to resources and structure relations in groups committed to ecological or social justice.

They developed the concept of internalized privilege to help explain why people in positions of power usually don't see how their actions impact others and move through the world with a sense of entitlement. They also put forward the idea of "wonderbreading" which is what assimilation does. In order to make it into the category of "white" and receive its privileges, people were forced to give up their loyalty to their own traditions, language, community, and principles. In this framework, "white" is solely an identity of privilege. Value is no longer placed on community, place, or history but, instead, on access to power and commodities. Business decisions are based on purely economic rationality, without taking into account these other dimensions. Communities are reduced to individuals and families to reproductive units. Culture becomes devoid of richness. Understanding these dynamics reveals what white people have to gain by ridding society of racism. Sharon sees it as important to help people of European descent see how their identification with white privilege keeps them from moving toward racial justice and how their guilt over that compounds the problem even more.

Her vision of a society based on principles of justice has led to work on Detroit Summer, a multigenerational project dedicated to rebuilding the most devastated parts of Detroit. Each summer, youth from Detroit and all around the country work with neighborhood people cleaning up parks, reconstructing homes, and re-creating a vital community. Leadership development and the study of Detroit's history and culture are integral parts of the project. Sharon sees this work as part of her life commitment. Her request to other academics is that they engage in projects of social justice that will inform their writings about social movements and help deepen their commitment to eliminate racism.

Marian Meck Root grew up in "Middle America," in the mainstream Lutheran church. At an early age, she realized the spiritual void left by people's refusal to deal with racism. She is a theologian in a major East Coast city and is part of a feminist theological center that keeps antiracism at the heart of its work.

She and her co-workers are grappling with the spiritual void left by racism, asking the question "How did this happen that we as a (white) people and as individuals are so spiritually afraid and weak?" She believes that when white people begin to address this question, they will begin to unearth some clues about ending racism. It is a project that can't be undertaken individually but, rather, communally. It is one according to her that can't be approached merely from the rational, linear patriarchal side. "It requires going against . . . the dominant culture especially of the academy which projects its own fears onto the feminine."

In her exploration of the concept of whiteness she defines white "to mean those of us who have had enough European ancestry to benefit from having white skin and who have been raised to assume that our culture is generic or universal and to act out of a sense of racial and/or cultural superiority even when we deny or cannot see ourselves doing that." She talks about spirituality as in some sense acknowledging mystery and giving up the illusion of control. Pointing out that white folks are very attached to control and domination, she draws the conclusion that we have a hard time with mystery and hence spirituality.

For Marian, Europeans haven't always been this way; it is a historical development of recent vintage. It helps explain our yearnings for spirituality and some of our racist appropriation of other people's spiritual traditions.

While acknowledging the yearning, she notes that spirituality has much to do with ancestors and that white Americans have distanced themselves, literally, from theirs. "We don't know ourselves because we don't know where we come from." Looking back on thousands of years of European history, she sees a progressive disintegration of tribal life, that is, life connected to the land and to ancestors. Without romanticizing tribal existence, she states that there was a felt relationship between the spiritual and the material, between intuition and rational ways of knowing. She calls for a reconnection of mind and body and spirit as well as for a reintegration of our communities. In order carry out this project, we as white people have to forgive our ancestors and ourselves, and we have to hope for forgiveness by people of color without having the right to expect it.

What Marian wants from "whiteness studies" is a critique of Western rational thinking and individualism. This critique would help overcome the dualist splits between mind and body, individual and community, spirit and idea. The critique would embody a way forward to a healing transformation.

As for myself, I am an owner of a small house painting business and work with environmental and economic justice organizations. I am a former member of NOAR, along with Sharon, and am also an associate of Tools for Change. I work on coalition-building with people of color around issues of ecological and economic justice.

I came to an antiracist sensibility when I was ten or eleven. I grew up in a lower-middle-class, single-parent, Jewish family in upstate New York. We lived in a mixed ethnic neighborhood. I saw how much easier our lives were as a "white" family than those of my "black" friends and their families in similar economic circumstances. In the 1950s and early 1960s, we were able to see our cash-poor life as merely a temporary setback on the way to a fully middle-class life. Help from her parents alleviated my mother's temporary unemployment, and she knew that with her college education she would eventually be able to get a better job in the expanding civil service economy. My African American neighbors would have to wait a generation for members of their family to get access to education before being able to obtain that kind of work—and even then economic life would be precarious at best. Experiencing that difference had a profound impact on how I interpreted the success stories that my upper-middle-class Jewish and white Christian friends were given by their families. It made it impossible for me to accept the myths of individual progress or the metaphors of assimilation or the "melting pot" that were the basis of white American cultural hegemony.

As the Vietnam War unfolded, I began to see the links between racism at home and U.S. imperialism around the world. It became clear to me that the reasons racism and its related manifestations of sexism and homophobia were still present in the United States was because "white" people, and "white" men especially, were not willing to give up the position and power that they (we) gained by our white skin privilege. Of course, at the time I didn't have an analysis, only a feeling that something was wrong.

When I first became involved in the movement for racial justice in the 1960s, the social project seemed clear: to eliminate racism as an underlying ordering of public space and to create opportunities for women and men of color to enter into business, academic, and religious spheres on an "equal basis." We started with a basic understanding that racism is rooted in unfounded negative attitudes about people of color (prejudice) tied with the power to oppress them (institutional bias). All that was needed was to "change people's attitudes" and to make sure that policies in educational institutions, restaurants, residences, and banks provided equal access to resources.

In college in the early 1970s, I was exhilarated by the development of the various identity movements, as they allowed people who had been locked out of society to express their humanity to the society at large and begin to claim power for themselves. At the same time, as I watched the tendency of people in those movements to claim their piece of the American pie, I became confused. For me it was the very existence of that pie that required the United States to maintain the race, class, and gender divides, that kept some people rich while the majority remained poor. I also saw something like the pain that "wonderbreading" engendered for my parents' generation affect some African American friends of mine when they started going to college. They lost intimate contact with their childhood friends and sometimes with their families, as they chose to "make it" in academia or the business world. In short, I began to see the limitations of the concept of "equality" since in fact "equality" really meant "play by the rules of the game and don't question the status quo." It didn't allow for the transformation of the social context to include all the experiences and values that are embodied by those who have been locked out. In short, people were being welcomed to join a society whose rules were set by the oppressors.

Since identity politics by itself didn't call for the total transformation of society, only for either a piece of the pie or for carving out autonomous spaces for blacks, Latinos, women, gays, lesbians, or other disadvantaged people, it began to feel in the 1980s that we would have a fractured society that wasn't necessarily a more just one. With my membership in NOAR, I was able to see the power of being in an organization dedicated to the leadership of African American people for the whole country. I was challenged to be a leader in this context and to think collaboratively with people very different from myself. What NOAR was unable to incorporate into its practice was a deep understanding of the subjective side of reality, social power, and cultural differences. Despite our political unity, which included an understanding of racism as the underlying contradiction of the United States, we were still unable to deal with racism and internalized it within our own ranks.

I joined Tools for Change because, as a group, we grapple with these kinds of issues and help organizations deal effectively with them. Central to our work is a focus on the subjective side of politics, which includes the particularities of culture differences, the importance of the sacred, and the dynamics of both formal and informal power. We try to encourage people and organizations to become visionary. Without vision, we find ourselves re-creating the same patterns of life. In this context, I am attempting to develop an organizational development model of "opening the imagination to change," which incorporates vision, addresses issues of power, and encourages critical thinking. In this way I hope to be able to help organizations deal with race and class hierarchies by rethinking their mission and re-visioning the way they do their work. I would like to challenge academics to do the same. It would be an exciting program that turned its critical gaze inward to try to create a real space for people of color.

My own vision for racial justice involves a society that goes beyond celebrating difference, actually embodying cultural differences and gender and gender orientation differences—in short embracing all of its contradictions and highlighting them. People would no longer have to assimilate to make it; equal access would be a given.

Whiteness and Activism

Whiteness as a conceptual framework in a political context first emerged out of a need to confront some of the limitations of antiracist organizing. At the same time, whiteness has been part of the U.S. sensibility since the country's founding. Many groups and strata of "white" people have been conscious of their whiteness and protective of their privileges. The whole process of "assimilation" was one of immigrants coming to the United States and struggling to become "white" in order to access the legitimacy and resources associated with that status. But by the late 1950s white skin privilege was no longer morally unquestioned in public discourse, and by the mid-1960s its legal status was challenged. By the mid-1970s, at least within the movements for social justice, it wasn't supposed to exist. Yet racism has kept its hold on the fabric of our society and in the structures of even those organizations committed to social justice. The rhetoric of antiracism present in these organizations often has actually acted as a buffer against challenges to racism. People have a self-image of being antiracist, yet the middle-class norms that preclude them from admitting mistakes or showing ignorance make it nearly impossible for them to address these issues. When antiracism is addressed, conversations become focused on intentions rather than the impact.

After years of antiracist organizing, we have learned that white people can't ask people of color to do "our" work for us. Many organizers reluctantly came to the conclusion that the issue was white people's inability or lack of will to examine our own privilege. We were reluctant because we didn't want to deal with other white people—we distrusted them, as we distrusted ourselves. Many of us had come to hate our own whiteness as we learned of the legacy of racism. Not trusting other white folks, we felt better being in the company of people of color. We did not want to come to grips with our own history. Some of us felt that we didn't even have a culture. But, in order to eradicate racism, we realized that we had to start working with those who benefit from racist structures and who play the largest part in maintaining them.

Those of us who do antiracist organizing and training have found that white people have developed a lot of avoidance and defense strategies. I see every day how much investment white folks have in holding onto their power. Recently, this was brought home to me again. After a major success in grassroots organizing against the World Trade Organization meeting in late 1999 in Seattle, where a huge coalition of labor, environmental, human rights activists, and community people took to the streets, a lot of money started flowing to continue the organizing. Many of the groups that organized around this event took part in evaluations of the work. Jointly we critiqued our movement around the lack of diversity. Just after the evaluation, one part of the coalition, a mostly white student group was offered money for organizing at the University of Washington campus, which is also mostly white. They never even consulted with a partner youth of color group that had been organizing very effectively on this issue over a longer period. When challenged, the white group said they had never even thought about it. They had merely seen it as an opportunity to do the work. They would have done outreach to youth of color, but they never thought to share resources with or to take leadership from an already existing group. To date, I am not aware of steps taken to approach the youth of color group.

We have seen how white people, especially those who are better educated, are very good at using antiracist language to allow themselves to feel good about themselves without actually having to change. What we have had to develop are some ways to help white people understand what a high price they pay for their privileged position—so that ultimately they can see that the reason to work for justice is also to free themselves.

We have found in our antiracist work that the first hurdle to get around is a paralysis of guilt and defensiveness. Most white people know very well their skin color is tied to social privileges—so they feel guilty and at the same time don't feel personally invested in change. They don't understand very well the historical nature of our racist social structure, and so they find it very hard to imagine real change and what that might look like. Noel Ignatiev's *How the Irish Became White* is an example of academic work that can help "regular white folks" understand whiteness in the context of their own history. It helps them begin to see their own place in all of this. Although it is often very painful, using the concept of whiteness has been helpful in workshops as a tool for breaking through many patterns that hold back white people from organizing together to eliminate racism.

One of the first things I do in antiracist workshops is to ask people about their family backgrounds, to help them get in touch with their own history. From there, we can begin to ask questions like "What strengths do you draw from your family history?" and "What did you and/or your family have to give up to be white?" For people to really become invested in change, they need to get a sense of the violence they do to themselves and others in order to live in this kind of society. They need to get in contact with the grief from which they spend so much time and energy dissociating. When white people understand how much energy they expend to create the kind of amnesia that is a necessary part of whiteness, they can begin to see whiteness as a crippling condition that makes it very hard to imagine what a racially just society could be about. At this point, the transformation for justice is as much for "us" as for some distant and impersonal "them."

At the same time, in order to understand the depth and subtleties of the way racism works in the United States, people need to understand history and be able to make critical analyses of the power dynamics they encounter. By looking at the way that class and race intersect, participants can begin to see the way in which these dynamics hold each other in place. They are introduced to the concepts of position (what social strata you come from), stand (whom you are accountable to), bias (whose interests do your attitudes serve), and impact (who benefits and who loses from your actions). Understanding the difference between impact and intention can help people sort out very thorny situations and can help us move from guilt into action. In these workshops, I appeal to the heart and the imagination and the head. Our own history and our own grief—that is the heart. Understanding the historical nature of whiteness—that is what helps us imagine alternatives. Developing a critical analysis of the power structure and what can be done to change it—that is the head.

White Studies in the Academy

Many academics have become engaged in the study of whiteness as a part of their political work to fight racism in the academy as well as outside, and they courageously pursue their work in the face of great opposition from more established disciplines. Yet the realities of the academic environment soon become painfully evident. There is little support for new faculty, especially in the social sciences and humanities. There is an attack on Ethnic and Women's Studies and related disciplines, and academic institutions as a whole are less and less open to new types of knowledge.

Marian Root, in her piece "The Heart Cannot Express Its Goodness," invokes James Baldwin's statement that the price of whiteness and membership in the privileged ranks is the loss of community. Both Root and Sharon Howell note that this loss of community forces us to be "self-reliant or perish." Capitalism relies on individualism and competition. The university as a middle-class institution both reinforces and reproduces these values. It is organized by and rewards middle-class values like individualism and competitiveness. Collective work is generally not rewarded or even recognized—yet fighting racism has to be more than anything a collective project. Of course, those who can afford individualism are exactly those who have power. Individualism is taught in most U.S. schools from first grade on; it is embedded in the grading system and entrance requirements for undergraduate and graduate programs. Try to imagine a collective Ph.D.!

I do appreciate that this book is an exception to the rule, due to its having a collective editorial board. And, as I have said before, there are many who enter academia out of a sense of responsibility to communities of color. Unfortunately, there are structural forces at work that make it difficult for such academics to stay connected with those communities.

I have a picture in mind. It is not a photograph of academic reality but, rather, a painting, a view from an outsider's eyes. Academics are forced by the requirements of academic life to search for "new" intellectual terrain to explore and stake out.[2] Identity studies seem to follow a life cycle: as time goes on, important political projects begin to attract people who are looking to find a new niche in which to build their careers. At first, the terrain seems "virginal" and untouched (pick your favorite gender-laden term). So the explorer moves around the new territory, poking into people's history, sociology, psychology, and biology, overturning loose stones and pulling up plants. The explorer seeks to unveil knowledge, and the one who is there first creates a claim on large areas of the terrain. The knowledge belongs to the explorer who "discovers" it. Of course, in culture and social studies, the terrain involves human beings; the "new" knowledge is about their lives, their cultures, and their dreams. The academic in general has no sense of accountability to those who are the "subjects" or "objects" of investigation.

As new investigators arrive, they scour around for new and unusual parts of the territory, perhaps a unique species or perhaps a hidden corner. They compete for control over the territory by writing in a manner that uses the most abstract prose. Papers are written in a language so difficult to access that most of us lose patience. After an appropriate tour de force, perhaps the author gains access to scarce academic resources, a temporary teaching post; perhaps if he or she is lucky, the fabled tenure-track position. The people or group studied has not benefited from any of this process, although later they might get thanked in the credits. Sometimes they find their privacy violated and see sacred aspects of their culture now displayed in books and articles, to be read by anonymous strangers who know little, if anything, about the context in which those mysteries were created. Then there is the worst-case scenario: they find that they no longer have control of an aspect of their lives that previously they had had. Instead, they find an insidious slippage into dependency has been initiated by the whole process. This critique is not new. For example, the field of anthropology has long challenged researchers and applied anthropologists to do relevant and accountable work.[3] Obviously, this particular trajectory has nothing to do with a struggle for social justice or with those of us who try to organize against racism.

Part of the explanation has to do with how academics do their work. The prevailing view of academic work comes from the dominant ideology of empirical science: first discover a phenomenon, then analyze it, and then use it to support your argument (in this case for change). From my experience, this model of advocacy is ineffective either as a way to effect change within organizations or as a way to bring people into movements. No critique by itself has ever sustained transformation over time on either a personal or a group level. Creating a new society requires vision, passion, and commitment. Scholarship that engages reason, the imagination, and the heart and that empowers the community can help that process. Vine Deloria Jr., bell hooks, Stuart Hall, and Howard Zinn are role models for those who wish to follow this path.

Useful scholarship would help us connect ourselves to the historical and social complexes that we refer to when we speak of whiteness.

But doing scholarship in the service of antiracism also means that scholars need to pay attention to the language in which they communicate their thoughts and their findings. Unlike academics, antiracist organizers cannot afford to distance themselves from the community, nor can we afford to slip into a language that alienates and excludes. There is no antiracist organizing without connection to the community. So that is one thing academics who are truly interested in whiteness in terms of antiracist work might try to think about: are they writing for tenure committees alone, or are they writing for all of us?

I look forward to an academy that values community, collaboration, and justice as much as rigor, creativity, and novelty. I have been inspired by the words of Roberto Unger in his *Politics:*

> In this work, true satisfaction can be found only in an activity that enables people to fight back, individually or collectively against the established settings of our lives—to resist these settings or even to re-make them. Those who have been converted to this idea of a transformative vocation cannot easily return to the notion of work as an honorable calling within a fixed scheme of social roles and hierarchies, nor can they remain content within a purely instrumental view of labor as a source of material benefits with which to support themselves and their families.[4]

What would a transformative vocation be? What kinds of life and career choices would need to be made? And what kind of institutional structures could we create that would allow activists the time and resources to reflect on their work and academics to engage fully in the practical effort to make society a just and open space? This is a challenge for activists and scholars alike.

Notes

1 Mab Segrest's *Memoirs of a Race Traitor* (Boston: South End Press, 1994), Lillian Smith's *Killers of the Dream* (New York: Norton, 1978), and Linda Stout's *Bridging the Class Divide and Other Lessons for Grassroots Organizing* (Boston: Beacon, 1996) are all written by southern "white" women committed to racial justice. Each in her own way examines the experience of racism in the South and gauges the effects of racism and sexism on her own life and society. All talk about the possibility and impact of standing in resistance to white supremacy. See also Noel Ignatiev, *How the Irish Be-*

came White (New York: Routledge, 1995), and Howard Zinn, *A People's History of the United States* (New York: Harper and Row, 1980).

2 The Portuguese word *explorador* has two meanings: to explore and to exploit. Sometimes I wonder whether the English word should carry both connotations.

3 See Dell H. Hymes, ed., *Reinventing Anthropology* (Ann Arbor: University of Michigan Press, 1999).

4 Roberto Mangabeira Unger, *Politics, a Work in Constructive Social Theory, Volume 1* (Cambridge: Cambridge University Press, 1987), 13.

Bibliography

Adair, Margo, and Sharon Howell. 1990. *Breaking Old Patterns, Weaving New Ties*. San Francisco: Tools For Change Press.

——. 1987. *The Subjective Side of Politics*. San Francisco: Tools For Change Press.

Adorno, T. W. et al. 1950. *The Authoritarian Personality*. New York: Harper.

Ahmad, Aijaz. 1992. *In Theory: Classes, Nations, Literatures*. New York: Verso.

Alarcón, Norma. 1995. "Anzaldúa's Frontera: Inscribing Genetics." In *Displacement, Diaspora, and Geographies of Identity*, eds. Smadar Lavie and Ted Swedenbeurg. Durham, N.C.: Duke University Press.

Alexander, M. Jacqui. 1994. "Not Just (Any)*Body* Can Be a Citizen: The Politics of Law, Sexuality, and Postcoloniality in Trinidad and Tobago and the Bahamas." *Feminist Review* 48 (autumn): 5–23.

Alexander, M. Jacqui, and Chandra Talpade Mohanty, eds. 1997. *Feminist Genealogies, Colonial Legacies, Democratic Futures*. New York: Routledge.

Allen, Robert. 1970. *Black Awakening in Capitalist America: An Analytic History*. New York: Anchor.

Allen, Theodore W. 1997. *The Invention of the White Race*. 2 vols. New York: Verso.

All God's Children. 1996. Produced by Dee Mosbacher, Francis Reid, and Sylvia Rhue. Women Vision.

Allison, Dorothy. 1994. *Skin: Talking about Sex, Class, and Literature*. Ithaca, N.Y.: Firebrand.

Allport, Gordon W. 1954. *The Nature of Prejudice*. Cambridge, MA.: Addison-Wesley.

Almaguer, Tomás. 1994. *Racial Fault Lines: The Historical Origins of White Supremacy in California*. Berkeley: University of California Press.

Altman, Dennis. 1996. "On Global Queering." *Australian Humanities Review* 2 (July–August).

American Sociological Association. 2000. *95th Annual Meetings of American Sociological Association*. Program.

Anner, John, ed. 1996. *Beyond Identity Politics: Emerging Social Justice Movements in Communities of Color*. Boston: South End Press.

Anonymous. 1996. *Primary Colors: A Novel of Politics.* New York: Random House.

"Anti-Gay Use of Research Angers Boston Doctor." 1992. *San Francisco Chronicle,* 4 August.

Anzaldúa, Gloria. 1987. *Borderlands/La Frontera: The New Mestiza.* San Francisco: Aunt Lute Books.

Appiah, Kwame Anthony. 1992. *In My Father's House: Africa in the Philosophy of Culture.* New York: Oxford University Press.

Apple, Michael. 1999. Foreword in *White Reign: Learning and Deploying Whiteness in America,* eds. Joe L. Kincheloe, et al. New York: St. Martin's Press.

Aretxaga, Begona. 1997. *Shattering Silence: Women, Nationalism, and Political Subjectivity in Northern Ireland.* Princeton, N.J.: Princeton University Press.

Bailey, Frederick G. 1960. *Tribe, Caste, and Nation: A Study of Political Activity and Political Change in Highland Orissa.* Manchester, England: Manchester University Press.

Baldwin, James. 1985. "White Man's Guilt." In *The Price of the Ticket.* New York: St. Martin's Press.

———. 1961. *Nobody Knows My Name: More Notes of a Native Son.* New York: Dell.

Bawer, Bruce. 1998. "Utopian Erotics." *Lambda Book Report* 7 (October): 19–20.

Berman, Paul. 1996. *A Tale of Two Utopias: The Political Journey of the Generation of 1968.* New York: Norton.

Berlant, Lauren, and Elizabeth Freeman. 1993. "Queer Nationality." In *Fear of Queer Planet: Queer Politics and Social Theory,* ed. Michael Warner. Minneapolis: Minnesota University Press.

Berry, Wendell. 1989. *The Hidden Wound.* San Francisco: North Point Press.

Bérubé, Allan. Forthcoming. *Dream Ships Sail Away.* New York: Houghton Mifflin.

———. 1997. "Intellectual Desire." In *Queerly Classed: Gay Men & Lesbians Write about Class,* ed. Susan Raffo. Boston: South End Press.

———. 1997. "Sunset Trailer Park." In *White Trash: Race and Class in America,* eds. Matt Wray and Annalee Newitz. New York: Routledge.

———. 1995 and 1998. "Class Dismissed: Queer Storytelling Across the Economic Divide." Keynote address at Constructing Queer Cultures: Lesbian, Bisexual, Gay Studies Graduate Student Conference, Cornell University, 9 February and at 17th Gender Studies Symposium, Lewis and Clark College, 12 March.

———. 1995. "I Coulda Been A Whiny White Guy." *Gay Community News* 20 (spring): 6–7.

———. 1990. " 'Fitting In': Expanding Queer Studies beyond the *Closet* and *Coming Out.*" Paper presented at Contested Zone: Limitations and Possibilities of a Discourse on Lesbian and Gay Studies, Pitzer College, 6–7 April and at the Fourth Annual Lesbian, Bisexual, and Gay Studies Conference, Harvard University, October 26–28.

———. 1988. "Caught in the Storm: AIDS and the Meaning of Natural Disaster." *Out/Look: National Lesbian and Gay Quarterly* 1 (fall): 8–19.

Billig, Michael. 1988. "The Notion of 'Prejudice': Some Rhetorical and Ideological Aspects." *Text* 8, nos. 1–2: 91–110.

Bittles, A. H., and D. F. Roberts, eds. 1992. *Minority Populations: Genetics, Demography and Health.* London: Macmillan.

Blackburn, Robin. 1997. *The Making of New World Slavery: From the Baroque to the Modern, 1492–1800.* New York: Verso.

———. 1988. *The Overthrow of Colonial Slavery, 1776–1848.* New York: Verso.

"Blackmun's Opinions Reflect His Evolution Over the 24 Court Years." 1999. *New York Times,* 5 March.

Blauner, Bob. 1994. "Talking Past Each Other: Black and White Languages of Race." In *Race and Ethnic Conflict: Contending Views on Prejudice, Discrimination, and Ethnoviolence,* eds. Fred L. Pincus and Howard J. Ehrlich. Boulder, Colo.: Westview Press.

———. 1989. *Black Lives, White Lives: Three Decades of Race Relations in America.* Berkeley: University of California Press.

———. 1972. *Racial Oppression in America.* New York: Harper and Row.

Bloom, Allan David. 1987. *The Closing of the American Mind: How Higher Education Has Failed Democracy and Impoverished the Souls of Today's Students.* New York: Simon and Schuster.

Blumer, Herbert. 1958. "Race Prejudice as a Sense of Group Position." *Pacific Sociological Review* 1 (spring): 3–7.

Blumer, Herbert, and Troy Duster. 1980. "Theories of Race and Social Action." In *Sociological Theories: Race and Colonialism.* Paris: UNESCO.

Bobo, Lawrence, and Vincent Hutchings. 1996. "Perceptions of Racial Group Competition: Extending Blumer's Theory of Group Position to a Multiracial Social Context." *American Sociological Review* 61, no. 6 (December): 951–72.

Bogg, James. 1970. *Racism and the Class Struggle: Further Pages from a Negro Worker's Notebook.* New York: Monthly Review Press.

———. 1963. *The American Revolution: Pages from a Negro Worker's Notebook.* New York: Monthly Review Press.

Bonilla-Silva, Eduardo. 2000. "Poor Whites Are Not the Only 'Racists' in America: An Analysis of the Racial Views of Upper Class Whites in Detroit." Paper presented at the 95th Annual Meetings of the American Sociological Association, Washington, D.C., 13 August.

Bonnett, Alastair. 1997. "Constructions of Whiteness in European and American Anti-Racism." In *Debating Cultural Hybridity: Multi-Cultural Identities and the Politics of Anti-Racism,* eds. Pnina Werbner and Tariq Modood. London: Zed Books.

Bourdieu, Pierre. 1984. *Distinction: A Social Critique of the Judgment of Taste,* trans. Richard Nice. Cambridge, M.A.: Harvard University Press.

Boykin, Keith. 1996. *One More River to Cross: Black and Gay in America.* New York: Anchor.

Bradshaw, John. 1988. *Bradshaw On: The Family.* Deerfield Beach, Florida: Health Communications, 1988, 7–8.

Bulkin, Elly, Minnie Bruce Pratt, and Barbara Smith, eds. 1984. *Yours in Struggle: Three Feminist Perspectives on Anti-Semitism and Racism.* Brooklyn: Long Haul Press.

Bunzel, John H. 1998. "Words That Smear, Like 'Racism,' Provoke Polarization." *San Francisco Sunday Examiner and Chronicle,* 26 July.

Butler, Judith. 1990. *Gender Trouble: Feminism and the Subversion of Identity.* New York: Routledge.

Calavita, Kitty. 1996. "The New Politics of Immigration: 'Balanced-Budget Conservatism' and the Symbolism of Proposition 187." *Social Problems* 43, no. 3 (August): 284–305.

Cammermeyer, Margarethe, with Chris Fisher. 1994. *Serving in Silence.* New York: Penguin.

Campbell, James, and James Oakes. 1997. "The Invention of Race: Rereading White over Black." In *Critical White Studies: Looking Behind the Mirror,* eds. Richard Delgado and Jean Stefancic. Philadelphia: Temple University Press.

Carson, Clayborne. 1981. *In Struggle: SNCC and the Black Awakening of the 1960s.* Cambridge, MA.: Harvard University Press.

Chambers, Ross. 1997. "The Unexamined." In *Whiteness: A Critical Reader,* ed. Mike Hill. New York: New York University Press.

Charles, Abrams. 1966. "The Housing Problem and the Negro." In *The Negro American,* eds. T. Parsons and K. Clark. Boston: Houghton Mifflin.

Chavez, Linda. 1998. *The Color Bind: California's Battle over Affirmative Action.* Berkeley: University of California Press.

Chesnut, Mary. 1980 [1949]. *Diary from Dixie,* ed. Ben Ames Williams. Cambridge, MA.: Harvard University Press.

Chinmayananda, Swami. 1993. *Atma Bodha.* Bombay: Central Chinmaya Mission Trust.

Chung, Christy, and Aly Kim, Zoon Nguyen, Trinity Ordona, with Arlene Stein. 1996. "In Our Own Way: A Roundtable Discussion." In *Asian American Sexualities: Dimensions of the Gay and Lesbian Experience,* ed. Russell Leong. New York: Routledge.

Clark, Danae. 1993. "Commodity Lesbianism." In *The Lesbian and Gay Studies Reader,* ed. Henry Abelove et al. New York: Routledge.

Cohen, Phil. 1997. "Labouring under Whiteness." In *Displacing Whiteness: Es-*

says in *Social and Cultural Criticism*, ed. Ruth Frankenberg. Durham, N.C.: Duke University Press.

Collins, Randall. 1987. "Interaction Ritual Chains, Power, and Property: The Micro-Macro Connection as an Empirically Based Sociological Problem." In *The Micro-Macro Link*, ed. Jeffrey Alexander et al. Berkeley: University of California Press.

Conley, Dalton. 1999. *Being Black, Living in the Red: Race, Wealth, and Social Policy in America*. Berkeley: University of California Press.

Cubitt, Geoffrey, ed. 1998. *Imagining Nations*. Manchester, England: Manchester University Press.

Daniels, Stephen. 1993. *Fields of Vision: Landscape Imagery and National Identity in England and the United States*. Cambridge: Polity Press.

Davin, Anna. 1978. "Imperialism and Motherhood." *History Workshop Journal* 5 (spring): 9–65.

Davis, Angela Y. 1996. "Gender, Class, and Multiculturalism: Rethinking 'Race' Politics." In *Mapping Multiculturalism*, eds. Avery F. Gordon and Christopher Newfield. Minneapolis: University of Minnesota Press.

Davis, David Brion. 1984. *Slavery and Human Progress*. Oxford: Oxford University Press.

de Beauvoir, Simone. 1953. *The Second Sex*. trans. H. M. Parshley. New York: Vintage.

Delgado, Richard, and Jean Stefancic, eds. 1997. *Critical White Studies: Looking Behind the Mirror*. Philadelphia: Temple University Press.

DeLoria, Vine, Jr. 1995. *Red Earth, White Lies: Native Americans and the Myth of Scientific Fact*. New York: Scribners.

——. 1994. *God is Red: A Native View of Religion*. 2nd ed. Golden, CO: North American Press.

——. 1988. *The Metaphysics of Modern Existence*. New York: Harper and Row.

D'Emilio, John. 1993. "Capitalism and Gay Identity." In *The Lesbian and Gay Studies Reader*, ed. Henry Abelove et al. New York: Routledge.

Department of Personnel and Administrative Reforms, Government of Karnataka. 1987. *Brochure on Reservation for Scheduled Castes, Scheduled Tribes, and other Categories of Backward Classes in Services and Posts*. Bangalore, India: Department of Personnel and Administrative Reforms, Government of Karnataka.

Diggins, John Patrick, ed. 1997. *The Liberal Persuasion: Arthur Schlesinger Jr. and the Challenge of the American Past*. Princeton, N.J.: Princeton University Press.

Dikotter, Frank. 1992. *The Discourse of Race in Modern China*. Palo Alto, CA: Stanford University Press.

Dominguez, Virginia, 1995. "Invoking Racism in the Public Sphere: Two Takes on National Self-Criticism." *Identities* 1, no. 4: 325–46.

Douglass, Frederick. 1982. *The Narrative of the Life of Frederick Douglass, an American Slave*, ed. Houston Baker Jr. New York: Penguin.

D'Souza, Dinesh. 1995. *The End of Racism*. New York: Free Press.

Du Bois, W. E. B. 1996. *The Souls of Black Folk*. New York: Penguin.

——. 1995 [1920]. "The Conservation of Races." In *W. E. B. Du Bois: A Reader*, ed. David Levering Lewis. New York: Holt.

——. 1995 [1920]. "The Souls of White Folk." In *W. E. B. Du Bois: A Reader*, ed. David Levering Lewis. New York: Holt.

——. 1977 [1935]. *Black Reconstruction in America: An Essay toward a History of the Part Which Black Folk Played in the Attempt to Reconstruct Democracy in America, 1860–1880*. New York: Atheneum.

——. 1965. *The World and Africa: An Inquiry into the Part Which Africa Has Played in World History*. New York: International Publishers.

Duggan, Lisa. 1994. "Queering the State." *Social Text* 39 (summer): 8–9.

Dunlap, Mary. 1996. "Reminiscences: Honoring Our Legal Hero, Gay Sgt. Perry Watkins, 1949–1996." *Gay Community News* (winter): 21.

Duster, Troy. 1996. "Individual Fairness, Group Preferences, and the California Strategy." *Representations* 55 (summer): 41–58.

——. 1995. "Postindustrialism and Youth Unemployment: African Americans as Harbingers." In *Poverty, Inequality, and the Future of Social Policy*, ed. Katherine McFate et al. New York: Sage.

——. 1990. *Backdoor to Eugenics*. New York: Routledge.

Dyer, Richard. 1997. *White*. New York: Routledge.

——. 1988. "White." *Screen* 29, no. 4 (autumn): 44–64.

Edsall, Thomas Byrne, and Mary Edsall. 1992. *Chain Reaction: The Impact of Race, Rights, and Taxes on American Politics*. Rev. ed. New York: Norton.

Erdrich, Louise. 1993 [1984]. *Love Medicine*. New and expanded version. New York: Holt.

Eichstedt, Jennifer. 2000. "White Identities in the Struggle for Racial Justice." Paper presented at the 95th Annual Meetings of the American Sociological Association, Washington, D.C., 14 August.

Espiritu, Yen Le. 1992. "Reactive Solidarity: Anti-Asian Violence." In *Asian American Panethnicity: Bridging Institutions and Identities*, ed. Yen Le Espiritu. Philadelphia: Temple University Press.

Feagin, Joe R., and Hernán Vera. 1995. *White Racism*. New York: Routledge.

Fine, Michelle, Lois Weis, Linda C. Powell, and L. Mun Wong, eds. 1997. *Off White: Readings on Race, Power, and Society*. New York: Routledge.

Fishkin, Shelly Fisher. 1995. "Interrogating 'Whiteness,' Complicating 'Blackness': Remapping American Culture." *American Quarterly* 47, no. 3: 428–66.

Foley, Neil. 1997. *The White Scourge: Mexicans, Blacks, and Poor Whites in Texas Cotton Culture*. Berkeley: University of California Press.

Fordham, Signathia. 1996. *Blacked Out: Dilemmas of Race, Identity, and Success at Capital High*. Chicago: University of Chicago Press.

Forgotten Fires. 1998. Director Michael Chandler.

Formisano, Ronald. 1991. *Boston against Busing: Race, Class, and Ethnicity in the 1960s and 1970s*. Chapel Hill: University of North Carolina Press.

Foucault, Michel. 1978. *The History of Sexuality: An Introduction*. New York: Vintage.

Frankenberg, Ruth. 2000. "Contexts and Attachments: Reflections on the Psyche of Whiteness." Paper presented at the 95th Annual Meetings of the American Sociological Association, Washington, D.C., 14 August.

——. 1996. "'When We Are Capable of Stopping. We Begin to See': Being White, Seeing Whiteness." In *Names We Call Home: Autobiography On Racial Identity*, eds. Becky Thompson and Sangeeta Tyagi. New York: Routledge.

——. 1994. "Whiteness and Americanness." In *Race*, eds. Steven Gregory and Roger Sanjek. New Brunswick, N.J.: Rutgers University Press.

——. 1993. *White Women, Race Matters: The Social Construction of Whiteness*. Minneapolis: University of Minnesota Press.

——, ed. 1997. *Displacing Whiteness: Essays in Social and Cultural Criticism*. Durham, N.C.: Duke University Press.

Frankenberg, Ruth, and Matt Wray. 1998. "White Studies." On *A Higher Education*, KCSM TV, 6 May.

Frankenberg, Ruth, and Lata Mani. 1993. "Crosscurrents, Crosstalk: Race, 'Postcoloniality,' and the Politics of Location." *Cultural Studies* 7, no. 2 (May): 292–310.

Fraser, Nick. 1998. "Cup of Joy." *The Guardian* (U.K.), 15 July.

Fraser, Steven, and Joshua B. Freeman, eds. 1997. *Audacious Democracy: Labor, Intellectuals, and the Social Reconstruction of America*. Boston: Houghton Mifflin.

Fredrickson, George M. 1995. *Black Liberation: A Comparative History of Black Ideologies in the United States and South Africa*. New York: Oxford University Press.

——. 1981. *White Supremacy: A Comparative Study in American and South African History*. Oxford: Oxford University Press.

Freedberg, Louis. "State's Diversity Adds Color to Talks: Race Panel Comes to San Jose." *San Francisco Chronicle*, 10 February 1998.

Freud, Sigmund. 1989. *Civilization and Its Discontents*, trans. and ed. James Strachey. New York: Norton.

——. 1965. *New Introductory Lectures on Psychoanalysis*, trans. James Strachey. New York: Penguin.

"From Tenants to Taxi Drivers: CAAV Organizes in Immigrant Communities." 1992. *CAAAV Voice* 4 no. 2, Fall, 5.

Frow, John. 1995. *Cultural Studies and Cultural Value.* Oxford: Clarendon Press.

Fryer, Peter. 1984. *Staying Power: The History of Black People in Britain.* London: Pluto Press.

Fundi. 1990. "Out/Write '90 Report, Part I: Writers Urged to Examine Their Roles, Save Their Lives." *San Diego GLN*, 16 March.

———. 1990. "Out/Write Report, Part II: Ringing Voices." *San Diego GLN*, 23 March.

———. 1990. "Out/Write Report, Part III: Arenas of Interaction." *San Diego GLN*, 30 March.

Gallagher, Charles A. 2000. "White Stories: Race Relations According to the Dominant Group." Paper presented at the 95th Annual Meetings of the American Sociological Association, Washington, D.C., 13 August.

Garrow, David. 1981. *The FBI and Martin Luther King, Jr.: From "Solo" to Memphis.* New York: Norton.

Gates, Henry Louis, Jr. 1993. "Blacklash?" *New Yorker,* 17 May, 42–44.

Gilroy, Beryl. 1998. *Leaves in the Wind.* London: Mango Publishing.

Gilroy, Paul. 1987. *There Ain't No Black in the Union Jack.* London: Hutchinson.

Gitlin, Todd. 1995. *The Twilight of Common Dreams: Why America Is Wracked by Culture Wars.* New York: Holt.

Glazer, Nathan. 1998. *We Are All Multiculturalists Now.* Cambridge, MA: Harvard University Press.

———. 1978. *Affirmative Discrimination: Ethnic Inequality and Public Policy.* 2d ed. New York: Basic.

Gluckman, Amy, and Betsy Reed, eds. 1997. *Homo Economics: Capitalism, Community, and Lesbian and Gay Life.* New York: Routledge.

Goethe, Johann Wolfgang von. 1970 [1840]. *Theory of Colors.* Cambridge, MA: MIT Press.

Goldberg, David Theo. 1997. "Hate, or Power?" In *Racial Subjects: Writing on Race in America,* ed. David Theo Goldberg. New York: Routledge.

———. 1993. *Racist Culture: Philosophy and the Politics of Meaning.* Oxford: Blackwell.

———, ed. 1990. *Anatomy of Racism.* Minneapolis: University of Minnesota Press.

Goldstein, Richard. 1989. " 'Go the Way Your Blood Beats': An Interview with James Baldwin (1984)." In *James Baldwin: The Legacy,* ed. Quincy Troupe. New York: Simon and Schuster.

Gopinath, Gayatri. 1997. "Nostalgia, Desire, Diaspora: South Asian Sexualities in Motion." *positions* 5, no. 2: 455–77.

Gordon, Milton M. 1964. *Assimilation in American Life: The Role of Race, Religion, and National Origins.* New York: Oxford University Press.

Gossett, Thomas F. 1963. *Race: The History of an Idea in America.* New York: Schocken.

Gracepoore. 1997. "Three Movements in a Minor." *Trikone Magazine* 12, no. 1: 10.

Grant, Madison. 1916. *The Passing of a Great Race, or The Racial History of European History.* New York: Scribners.

Greenhalgh, Paul. 1988. *Ephemeral Vistas: The Expositions Universelles, Great Exhibitions, and World's Fairs, 1851–1939.* Manchester, England: Manchester University Press.

Grewal, Inderpal. 1993. "Reading and Writing the South Asian Diaspora: Feminism and Nationalism in North America." In *Our Feet Walk the Sky: Women of the South Asian Diaspora,* ed. Women of South Asian Descent Collective. San Francisco: Aunt Lute Books.

Grossberg, Lawrence. 1992. *We Gotta Get Out of This Place: Popular Conservatism and Postmodern Culture.* New York: Routledge.

Gundel, Max. 1926. "Einige Beobachtungen bei der Rassenbiologischen Durchforschung Schleswig-Holsteins." *Klinische Wochenschrift* 5: 1186.

Gupta, Akhil, and James Ferguson. 1992. "Beyond 'Culture': Space, Identity, and the Politics of Difference." *Cultural Anthropology* 7, no. 1 (1992): 6–23.

Hacker, Andrew. 1992. *Two Nations: Black and White, Separate, Hostile, Unequal.* New York: Scribners.

Hale, Grace Elizabeth. 1998. *Making Whiteness: The Culture of Segregation in the South, 1890–1940.* New York: Pantheon.

Hall, Lisa Kahaleole Chang. 1993. "Bitches in Solitude: Identity Politics and Lesbian Community." In *Sisters, Sexperts, Queers: Beyond the Lesbian Nation,* ed. Arlene Stein. New York: Plume.

Hall, Stuart. 1995. "New Cultures for Old." In *A Place in the World? Place, Cultures, and Globalization,* eds. Doreen Massey and Pat Jess. London: Oxford University Press.

——. 1991. "The Local and the Global: Globalization and Ethnicity." In *Culture, Globalization, and the World System: Contemporary Conditions for the Representation of Identity,* ed. Anthony D. King. London: Macmillan.

——. 1980. "Race, Articulation, and Societies Structured in Dominance." In *Sociological Theories, Race, and Colonialism.* Paris: UNESCO Press.

Halle, David. 1987. *America's Working Man: Work, Home, and Politics among Blue-Collar Property Owners.* Chicago: University of Chicago Press.

Halperin, David. 1995. *Saint Foucault.* New York: Oxford University Press.

Hamilton, Annette. 1997. "Primal Dream: Masculinism, Sin, and Salvation in Thailand's Sex Trade." In *Sites of Desire, Economies of Pleasure: Sexualities in Asia and the Pacific,* eds. Lenore Manderson and Margaret Jolly. Chicago: University of Chicago Press.

Hanawa, Yukiko. 1994. Introduction to *Positions: Circuits of Desire* 2, no. 1.

Hanawa, Yukiko. "The World of Suzie Wong and M. Butterfly: Race and Gender in Asian America." *Radical History Review* 64: 12–18.

Harding, Vincent. 1981. *There Is a River: The Black Struggle for Freedom in America*. New York: Vintage.

Harris, Cheryl. 1993. "Whiteness as Property." *Harvard Law Review* 106, no. 8 (June): 1709–91.

Harris-Warrick, Ronald M., and Eve Marder. 1991. "Modulation of Neural Networks for Behavior." *Annual Review of Neuroscience* 14: 39–57.

Hartigan, John, Jr. 1999. *Racial Situations: Class Predicaments of Whiteness in Detroit*. Princeton, N.J.: Princeton University Press.

———. 1997. "Establishing the Fact of Whiteness." *American Anthropologist* 99, no. 3: 495–505.

Heath, Shirley Brice. 1983. *Ways with Words: Language, Life, and Work in Communities and Classrooms*. Cambridge: Cambridge University Press.

Hebdige, Dick. 1979. *Subculture: The Meaning of Style*. New York: Methuen.

Hegel, G. W. F. 1967. *The Phenomenology of Mind*, trans. J. B. Baillie. New York: Harper and Row.

Hemphill, Essex, ed. 1991. *Brother to Brother: New Writings by Black Gay Men*. Boston: Alyson.

Hennessy, Rosemary. 1994–1995. "Queer Visibility and Commodity Culture." *Cultural Critique* 29: 31–76.

Herrnstein, Richard J., and Charles Murray. 1994. *The Bell Curve: Intelligence and Class Structure in American Life*. New York: Free Press.

Hewitt, Roger. 1986. *White Talk, Black Talk: Inter-Racial Friendship and Communication among Adolescents*. Cambridge: Cambridge University Press.

Hewitt, Roger. 1997. *Routes of Racism*. London: Greenwich Council Central Race Equality Unit and Education Service.

Hill, Mike, ed. 1997. *Whiteness: A Critical Reader*. New York: New York University Press.

Hirsch, Arnold. 1983. *Making the Second Ghetto: Race and Housing in Chicago, 1940–1960*. Cambridge: Cambridge University Press.

Hirschfeld, Magnus. 1938. *Racism*. London: Victor Gollanzc.

Hollinger, David A. 1995. *Postethnic America: Beyond Multiculturalism*. New York: Basic Books.

hooks, bell. 1995. *Killing Rage/Ending Racism*. New York: Holt.

———. 1992. "Eating the Other." In *Black Looks: Race and Representation*. Boston: South End Press.

Horowitz, David. 1997. *Radical Son: A Generational Odyssey*. New York: Free Press.

Horsman, Reginald. 1981. *Race and Manifest Destiny: The Origins of American Racial Anglo-Saxonism*. Cambridge, MA: Harvard University Press.

Hughes, Henry. 1981. "Treatise on Sociology." In *The Ideology of Slavery: Proslavery Thought in the Antebellum South, 1830–1860*, ed. Drew Gilpin Faust. Baton Rouge: Louisiana State University Press.

Hughes, Mark Allan. 1989. "Misspoken Truth to Power: A Geographical Perspective on the Underclass Fallacy." *Economic Geography* 65, no. 6 (July): 187–207.

Humphrey, Mary Ann. 1990. *My Country, My Right to Serve.* New York: HarperCollins.

Hurtado, Aida. 1996. *The Color of Privilege: Three Blasphemies on Race and Feminism.* Ann Arbor: University of Michigan Press.

Hymes, Dell H., ed. 1999. *Reinventing Anthropology.* Ann Arbor: University of Michigan Press.

Ignatiev, Noel. 1995. *How the Irish Became White.* New York: Routledge.

Ignatiev, Noel, and John Garvey, eds. 1996. *Race Traitor.* New York: Routledge.

Jackson, Kenneth. 1982. "The Spatial Dimensions of Social Control: Race, Ethnicity, and Government Housing Policy in the United States, 1918–1968." In *Modern Industrial Cities: History, Policy, and Survival,* ed. Bruce Stave, 79–128. Beverly Hills: Sage Publications.

Jackson, Peter. 1989. *Maps of Meaning: An Introduction to Cultural Geography.* London: Unwin Hyman.

James, C. L. R. 1989. *The Black Jacobins: Toussaint L'Ouverture and the San Domingo Revolution.* Rev. 2d ed. New York: Vintage.

Jensen, Arthur R. 1969. "How Much Can We Boost IQ and Scholastic Achievement?" *Harvard Educational Review* 39: 1–123.

Jordan, June. 1985. *On Call: Political Essays.* Boston: South End Press.

Jordan, Winthrop D. 1968. *White over Black: American Attitudes toward the Negro, 1550–1812.* Baltimore: Penguin.

Kadi, Joanna. 1996. *Thinking Class: Sketches from a Cultural Worker.* Boston: South End Press.

Kallen, Horace. 1924. *Culture and Democracy in America.* New York: Boni and Liveright.

Kaplan, Caren, and Inderpal Grewal. 1994. *Scattered Hegemonies.* Minneapolis: University of Minnesota Press.

Katz, Judy. 1978. *White Awareness: A Handbook for Anti-Racism Training.* Norman: University of Oklahoma Press.

Katz, Solomon H. 1995. "Is Race a Legitimate Concept for Science?" In *The AAPA Revised Statement on Race: A Brief Analysis and Commentary.* Philadelphia: University of Pennsylvania.

Kaufman, Cynthia. 1997. " 'The Making and Unmaking of Whiteness': a conference report." *Socialist Review* (autumn) [incorrectly published as vol. 26, nos. 3 and 4 (1996)]: 195–201.

Kaufmann, Felix. 1958. *Methodology of the Social Sciences.* New York: Humanities Press.

Kelley, Robin D. G. 1997. *Yo' Mama's Dysfunktional! Fighting the Culture Wars in Urban America.* Boston: Beacon.

Kimball, Roger. 1990. *Tenured Radicals: How Politics Has Corrupted Our Higher Education*. New York: Harper and Row.

Kinchloe, Joe L., Shirley R. Steinberg, Nelson M. Rodriguez, Ronald Chennault, eds. 1998. *White Reign: Deploying Whiteness in America*. New York: St. Martin's Press.

Kingston, Maxine Hong. 1981. *China Men*. New York: Ballantine.

———. 1976. *The Woman Warrior*. New York: Vintage.

Kivel, Paul. 1995. *Uprooting Racism: How White People Can Work for Racial Justice*. Philadelphia: New Society Publishers.

Klein, Joe. 1980. *Woodie Guthrie: A Life*. New York: Knopf.

Knippenberg, Jim. 1997. "Gay Soldier Story to be Filmed." *Cincinnati Enquirer*, 23 December.

Knowles, Louis L., and Kenneth Prewitt, eds. 1970. *Institutional Racism in America*. Englewood Cliffs, N.J.: Prentice-Hall.

Kochman, Thomas. 1981. *Black and White Styles in Conflict*. Chicago: University of Chicago Press.

Kovel, Joel. 1984. *White Racism: A Psychohistory*. New York: Columbia University Press.

Kozol, Jonathan. 1991. *Savage Inequalities: Children in America's Schools*. New York: Crown.

Kreiger, Nancy, et al. 1993. "Racism, Sexism, and Social Class: Implications for Studies of Health, Disease, and Well-being." *American Journal of Preventive Medicine*, 9, no. 6-suppl.: 82–122.

Kung, Hans. 1979. *Freud and the Problem of God*. New Haven: Yale University Press.

Legal/Policy Department of the Campaign for Military Service. 1993. "The Race Analogy: Fact Sheet Comparing the Military's Policy of Racial Segregation in the 1940s to the Current Ban on Lesbians, Gay Men and Bisexuals." In *Briefing Book*, Washington, D.C.: Legal/Policy Department of the Campaign for Military Service.

Leonard, Mark. 1998. "It's Not Just Ice-Cream." *New Statesman* (U.K.), 3 July.

Lerner, Michael. 1996. *The Politics of Meaning: Restoring Hope and Possibility in an Age of Cynicism*. New York: Addison-Wesley.

Lewis, Amanda E. 2000. "Some Are More Equal than Others: Whiteness and Colorblind Ideology at the Dawn of the 21st century." Paper presented at the 95th Annual Meetings of the American Sociological Association, Washington, D.C., 13 August.

Leslie, Ann. 1998. "Pride, the Cure for Prejudice." In *Mindfield: The Race Issue*, ed. Ann Leslie. London: Camden Press.

Levine, Rhonda F. 2000. "What White Men Think about Race." Paper presented at the 95th Annual Meetings of the American Sociological Association, Washington, D.C., 14 August.

Lind, Michael. 1996. *Up from Conservatism: Why the Right Is Wrong for America.* New York: Free Press.

——. 1995. *The Next American Nation: The New Nationalism and the Fourth American Revolution.* New York: Free Press.

Lipsitz, George. 1998. *The Possessive Investment in Whiteness: How White People Profit from Identity Politics.* Philadelphia: Temple University Press.

Lipuma, Edward and Sarah Keene Meltzoff. 1997. "The Crosscurrents of Ethnicity and Class in the Construction of Public Policy." *American Ethnologist* 24, no. 1 (February): 114–31.

Littlewood, Roland. 1998. "In Search of the White Tribe." In *Mindfield: The Race Issue,* ed. Ann Leslie. London: Camden Press.

López, Ian F. Haney. 1996. *White by Law: The Legal Construction of Race.* New York: New York University Press.

Lorde, Audre. 1984. *Sister Outsider.* Freedom, CA: Crossing Press.

——. 1982. *Zami: A New Spelling of My Name.* Watertown, MA: Persephone Press.

Lott, Eric. 1993. *Love and Theft: Blackface Minstrelsy and the American Working Class.* New York: Oxford University Press.

Lowe, Lisa. 1996. *Immigrant Acts: On Asian American Cultural Politics.* Durham, N.C.: Duke University Press.

——. 1991. "Heterogeneity, Hybridity, Multiplicity: Marking Asian American Differences." *Diasporas* 1, no. 1 (spring): 24–44.

Luhmann, Niklas. 1979. *Trust and Power: Two Works.* Trans. Gianfranco Poggi. New York: Chichester.

Lutz, Catherine. 1990. "Engendered Emotion: Gender, Power, and the Rhetoric of Emotional Control in American Discourse." In *Language and the Politics of Emotion,* eds. Catherine Lutz and Lila Abu-Lughod. Cambridge: Cambridge University Press.

Mailer, Norman. 1957. *The White Negro.* San Francisco: City Lights.

Malcolm Chapman, ed. 1993. *Social and Biological Aspects of Ethnicity.* New York: Oxford University Press.

Malcom X. 1986. *The End of White World Supremacy: Four Speeches.* New York: Seaver Books.

Manalansan, Martin. 1995. "In the Shadows of Stonewall: Examining Gay Transnational Politics and the Diasporic Dilemma." *GLQ: A Journal of Lesbian and Gay Studies* 2, no. 4: 425–38.

Mani, Lata. 1998. *Contentious Traditions: The Debate on Sati in Colonial India.* Berkeley: University of California Press.

Marcus, Greil. 1997. *Invisible Republic: Bob Dylan's Basement Tapes.* New York: Holt.

Marcuse, Herbert. 1966. *Eros and Civilization: A Philosophical Inquiry into Freud.* Boston: Beacon Press.

Martin, Catherine. 1996. "Educating to Combat Racism: The Civic Role of Anthropology." *Anthropology and Education Quarterly* 27, no. 2: 253–69.

Massey, Douglas, and Nancy Denton. 1993. *American Apartheid: Segregation and the Making of the Underclass.* Cambridge: MA: Harvard University Press.

———. 1988. "Residential Segregation of Blacks, Hispanics, and Asians by Socio-economic Status and Generation." *Social Science Quarterly* 69: 797–817.

———. 1987. "Trends in the Residential Segregation of Blacks, Hispanics, and Asians." *American Sociological Review* 52: 802–25.

Masson, Jeffrey. 1992. *The Assault on Truth: Freud's Suppression of the Seduction Theory.* New York: Farrar, Straus and Giroux.

Masters, Edward Lee. 1921. *The Spoon River Anthology.* New York: Macmillan.

McCarthy, Cameron, and Warren Crichlow, eds. 1993. *Race, Identity, and Representation in Education.* New York: Routledge.

McClintock, Anne. 1995. *Imperial Leather: Race, Gender, and Sexuality in the Colonial Conquest.* New York: Routledge.

McClure, Heather, Christopher Nugent, and Lavi Soloway. 1997. *Preparing Sexual Orientation-Based Asylum Claims: A Handbook for Advocates and Asylum Seekers.* Chicago: The Heartland Alliance for Human Needs and Human Rights.

McCunn, Ruthanne Lum. 1981. *Thousand Pieces of Gold: A Biographical Novel.* San Francisco: Design Enterprises of San Francisco.

McDermott, Monica. 2000. "Whiteness as Perceived Stigma: Identity Construction among Disadvantaged Whites." Paper presented at the 95th Annual Meetings of the American Sociological Association, Washington, D.C., 13 August.

McIntosh, Peggy. 1989. "White Privilege: Unpacking the Invisible Knapsack." *Peace and Freedom* (July/August): 10–12.

McIntyre, Alice. 1997. *Making Meaning of Whiteness: Exploring Racial Identity with White Teachers.* Albany: State University of New York Press.

Mercer, Kobena. 1994. *Welcome to the Jungle.* New York: Routledge.

Michaels, Walter Benn. 1998. "Autobiography of an Ex-White Man." *Transition* 73, no. 7, 1: 122–43.

———. 1996. "Posthistoricism: The End of the End of History." *Transition* 70, no. 6, 2: 4–19.

———. 1992. "Race Into Culture: A Critical Genealogy of Cultural Identity." *Critical Inquiry* 18, no. 4 (summer): 655–81.

Miles, Robert. 1989. *Racism.* New York: Routledge.

Mirel, Jeffrey. 1993. *The Rise and Fall of an Urban School System: Detroit, 1907–1981.* Ann Arbor: University of Michigan Press.

Mixner, David. 1996. *Stranger among Friends.* New York: Bantam.

Mohanty, Chandra, and M. Jacqui Alexander, eds. 1997. *Feminist Genealogies, Colonial Legacies, Democratic Futures.* New York: Routledge.

Molnar, Stephen. 1992. *Human Variation: Races, Types, and Ethnic Groups.* 3d ed. Englewood Cliffs, N.J.: Prentice Hall.

Moraga Cherríe. 1993. *The Last Generation.* Boston: South End Press.

———. 1983. *Loving in the War Years.* Boston: South End Press.

Moraga, Cherríe and Gloria Anzaldúa, eds. 1981. *This Bridge Called My Back: Writings by Radical Women of Color.* Watertown, MA: Persephone Press.

Morgan, Edmund. 1975. *American Slavery, American Freedom: The Ordeal of Colonial Virginia* New York: Norton.

Morrison, Toni. 1992. *Playing in the Dark: Whiteness and the Literary Imagination.* Cambridge, MA: Harvard University Press.

Moya, Paula. 1997. "Postmodernism, 'Realism,' and the Politics of Identity: Cherríe Moraga and Chicana Feminism." In *Feminist Genealogies, Colonial Legacies, Democratic Futures,* eds. Chandra Mohanty and M. Jacqui Alexander. New York: Routledge.

Moyana, Toby Tafirenyika. 1989. *Education, Liberation, and the Creative Act.* Harare, Zimbabwe: Zimbabwe Publishing House.

Muñoz, José. 1996. "Ephemera as Evidence: Introductory Notes to Queer Acts." *Women and Performance: A Journal of Feminist Theory* 8, no. 2: 10.

Namaste, Ki. 1996. "Tragic Misreadings." In *Queer Studies: A Lesbian, Gay, Bisexual and Transgender Anthology,* eds. Brett Breemyn and Mickey Eliason. New York: New York University Press.

Newitz, Annalee, and Matt Wray. 1998. "White Studies." On *A Higher Education,* KCSM TV, 6 May.

Nexica, Irene and Birgit Rasmussen, Matt Wray, Kellie Stoddart, Pamela Perry, Eric Klinenberg, and Jillian Sandell. 1997. "A Conference Report: The Making and Unmaking of Whiteness." *Bad Subjects* 33.

Novick, Michael. 1995. *White Lies, White Power: The Fight Against White Supremacy and Reactionary Violence.* Monroe, ME: Common Courage Press.

O'Reilly, Kenneth. 1995. *Nixon's Piano: Presidents and Racial Politics from Washington to Clinton.* New York: Free Press.

Oliver, Melvin L., and Thomas M. Shapiro. 1995. *Black Wealth/White Wealth: A New Perspective on Racial Inequality.* New York: Routledge.

Omi, Michael, Gary Delgado, and Rebecca Gordon. 2000. *Confronting the New Racisms: Anti-Racist Organizing in the Post-Civil Rights Era.* Executive summary prepared by the Applied Research Center for the C. S. Mott Foundation.

Omi, Michael and Dana Y. Takagi. 1996. "Situating Asian Americans in the Political Discourse of Affirmative Action." *Representations,* 55 (Summer 1996): 155–62.

Omi, Michael and Howard Winant. 1994. *Racial Formation in the United States: From the 1960s to the 1990s,* 2nd ed. New York: Routledge.

Ortiz, Fernando. 1995 [1947]. *Cuban Counterpoint: Tobacco and Sugar*, trans. Harriet de Onis. Durham, N.C.: Duke University Press.

Page, Helan, and R. Brooke Thomas. 1994. "White Public Space and the Construction of White Privilege in U.S. Health Care: Fresh Concepts and a New Model of Analysis." *Medical Anthropology Quarterly* 8, no. 1 (March): 109–16.

Park, Robert E. 1950. *The Collected Papers of Robert E. Park*, ed. Everett Hughes. Glencoe, IL: Free Press.

Patel, Geeta. 1997. Roundtable discussion at the South Asia Studies Annual Conference. Madison, Wisconsin, October.

Perry, Pamela. 1998. "Beginning to See the White." Ph.D. diss. University of California, Berkeley.

Phillips, Mike. 1998. "At Home in England." In *Empire Windrush: Fifty Years of Writing about Black Britain*, ed. Oneyekachi Wambu. London: Victor Gollancz.

Phillips, Mike, and Trevor Phillips. 1998. *Windrush: The Irresistible Rise of Multi-Racial Britain*. London: HarperCollins.

Plotke, David. N.d. "Democratic Breakup." Manuscript.

Podhoretz, Norman. 1997. "My Negro Problem—and Ours." In *The Essential Neoconservative Reader*, eds. Mark Gerson and James Q. Wilson. New York: Addison-Wesley.

Polednak, Anthony P. 1969. *Racial and Ethnic Differences in Disease*. New York: Oxford University Press.

Pollit, Katha. 1998. "Race and Gender and Class, Oh My!" *The Nation* 8 June.

Post, Robert, and Michael Rogin, eds. 1998. *Race and Representation: Affirmative Action*. New York: Zone Books.

Purohit, B. D., and S. D. Purohit. 1990. *Handbook of Reservation for Scheduled Castes and Scheduled Tribes, on the Matters Concerning Employment, Education, and Election*. New Delhi: Jainsons Publications.

Quadagno, Jill. 1994. *The Color of Welfare*. New York: Oxford University Press.

Rapping, Elayne. 1996. *The Culture of Recovery: Making Sense of the Self-Help Movement in Women's Lives*. Boston: Beacon Press.

Ratti, Rakesh, ed. 1993. *A Lotus of Another Color: An Unfolding of the South Asian Gay and Lesbian Experience*. Boston: Alyson.

Rayside, David. 1998. *On the Fringe: Gays and Lesbians in Politics*. Ithaca, N.Y.: Cornell University.

Razack, Sherene H. 1998. *Looking White People in the Eye: Gender, Race, and Culture in Courtrooms and Classrooms*. Toronto: University of Toronto Press.

Rich, Adrienne. 1979. *On Lies, Secrets, and Silence: Selected Prose*. New York: Norton.

Rieder, Jonathan. 1985. *Canarsie: The Jews and Italians of Brooklyn against Liberalism*. Cambridge, MA: Harvard University Press.

Riley, Shamara. 1996. "Perry Watkins, 1948–1996: A Military Trailblazer." *Outlines* 8 May.

Roediger, David R. 1998. *Black on White: Black Writers on What It Means to be White*. New York: Schocken Books.

———. 1994. *Toward the Abolition of Whiteness: Essays on Race, Politics, and Working Class History*. New York: Verso.

———. 1991. *The Wages of Whiteness: Race and the Making of the American Working Class*. New York: Verso.

Root, Marion. 1997. "The Heart Cannot Express Its Goodness." *Brown Papers* 5 (February).

Rorty, Richard. 1998. *Achieving Our Country: Leftist Thought in Twentieth-Century America*. Cambridge, MA: Harvard University Press.

Rubin, Gayle. 1993. "Thinking Sex: Notes for a Radical Theory of the Politics of Sexuality." In *The Lesbian and Gay Studies Reader*, eds. Henry Abelove et al. New York: Routledge.

Rustin, Bayard. 1964. "From Protest to Politics." *Commentary* 39 (February) 25–31.

Saldívar, José David. 1997. *Border Matters: Remapping American Cultural Studies*. Berkeley: University of California Press.

Sartwell, Crispin. 1998. *Act Like You Know: African-American Autobiography and White Identity*. Chicago: University of Chicago Press.

Saxton, Alexander. 1990. *The Rise and Fall of the White Republic: Class Politics and Mass Culture in Nineteenth-Century America*. New York: Verso.

Schein, Louisa. 1994. "The Consumption of Color and the Politics of White Skin in Post-Mao China." *Social Text* 41 (winter): 141–64.

Schlesinger, Arthur, Jr. 1998 [1949]. *The Vital Center: The Politics of Freedom*. New Brunswick, N.J.: Transaction Publishers.

Schneider, David. 1980. *American Kinship: A Cultural Account*. 2d ed. Chicago: University of Chicago Press.

Schrag, Peter. 1998. *Paradise Lost: California's Experience, America's Future*. New York: New Press.

Schusterov, G. A. 1927. "Isohaemoagglutinierende Eigenschaften des Menschlichen Blutes nach den Ergebnissen einer Untersuchung an Straflingen des Reformatoriums (Arbeitshauses) zu Omsk." *Moskovskii Meditsinksii Jurnal* 1: 1–6.

Schutz, Alfred. 1973. "Common Sense and Scientific Interpretation of Human Action." In *Collected Papers I: The Problem of Social Reality*, ed. Maurice Natanson. The Hague: Martinus Nijhoff.

Scott, Ellen K. Forthcoming. "From Race Cognizance to Racism Cognizance: Dilemmas in Anti-Racist Activism. In *Feminism and Anti-Racism: International Struggles for Justice*, ed. by Kathleen Blee and France Winddance Twine. New York: New York University Press.

——. 1997. "Feminists Working Across Racial Divides: The Politics of Race in a Battered Women's Shelter and a Rape Crisis Center." Ph.D. diss., University of California, Davis.

——. 1998. "Creating Partnerships for Change: Alliances and Betrayals in the Racial Politics of Two Feminist Organizations." *Gender and Society* 12, no. 4: 400–423.

Searle-Chatterjee, Mary. 1987. "The Anthropologist Exposed: Anthropologists in Multi-Cultural and Anti-Racist Work." *Anthropology Today* 3, no. 4: 16–18.

Sedgwick, Eve Kosofsky. 1993. "Epistemology of the Closet." In *The Lesbian and Gay Studies Reader*, ed. Henry Abelove et al. New York: Routledge.

Segrest, Mab. 1994. *Memoir of a Race Traitor.* Boston: South End Press.

——. 1985. *My Mama's Dead Squirrel: Lesbian Essays on Southern Culture.* Ithaca, N.Y.: Firebrand Books.

Selvadurai, Shyam. 1994. *Funny Boy.* New York: Harvest Press.

Shafer, D. Michael, ed. 1990. "The Vietnam-Era Draft: Who Went, Who Didn't, and Why It Matters." In *The Legacy: The Vietnam War in the American Imagination.* Boston: Beacon Press.

Sheehan, Brian. 1984. *The Boston School Integration Dispute: Social Change and Legal Maneuvers.* New York: Columbia University Press.

Shilts, Randy. 1993. *Conduct Unbecoming: Gays and Lesbians in the U.S. Military.* New York: St. Martin's Press.

Shipman, Pat. 1994. *The Evolution of Racism: Human Differences and the Use and Abuse of Science.* New York: Simon and Schuster.

Sis: The Perry Watkins Story. 1996. Produced by Chiqui Cartagena and Suzanne Newman.

Sleeper, Jim. 1997. *Liberal Racism.* New York: Viking.

Smith, Lillian. 1978. *Killers of the Dream.* New York: Norton.

Smith, Rogers M. 1997. *Civic Ideals: Conflicting Visions of Citizenship in U.S. History.* New Haven, CT: Yale University Press.

Sniderman, Paul M., and Thomas Piazza. 1993. *The Scar of Race.* Cambridge, MA: Harvard University Press.

Sojourners Magazine, ed. 1988. *America's Original Sin: A Study Guide on White Racism.* Washington, D.C.: Sojourners Magazine.

Solomos, John, and John Wrench, eds. 1993. *Racism and Migration in Western Europe.* Providence, R.I.: Berg.

Spillers, Hortense. 1987. "Mama's Baby, Papa's Maybe: An American Grammar Book." *Diacritics* (summer): 65–81.

Spivak, Gayatri Chakravorty. 1995. In *In Other Worlds: Essays in Cultural Politics.* New York: Routledge.

Steib, Clint. 1998. "Experts Warn Time Running out for Gay Refugees." *Washington Blade,* 20 February.

Steinberg, Stephen. 1995. *Turning Back: The Retreat from Racial Justice in American Thought and Policy.* Boston: Beacon Press.

Stoler, Ann Laura. 1995. *Race and the Education of Desire: Foucault's History of Sexuality and the Colonial Order of Things.* Durham, N.C.: Duke University Press.

"Stonewall 25." 1994. *The Charlie Rose Show.* Public Broadcasting System 24 June.

Stout, Linda. 1996. *Bridging the Class Divide and Other Lessons for Grassroots Organizing.* Boston: Beacon Press.

Streicker, Joe. 1997. "Remaking Race, Class, and Region in a Tourist Town." *Identities* 3, no. 4: 523–55.

Sugg, Katherine. 1996. "'The Ultimate Rebellion': Sexuality and Community in Contemporary Writing." Paper presented at American Studies Association meeting, Kansas City, MO: November.

Takaki, Ronald T. 1989. *Strangers from a Different Shore: A History of Asian Americans.* Boston: Little, Brown.

Talbot, Margaret. 1997. "Getting Credit for Being White." *New York Times Magazine,* 30 November, 118.

"Talking Issues in Detroit, City Tunes into Black Radio." 1993. *Detroit Free Press,* 15 February.

"Talk Show Canceled." 1992. *Warrendale Press and Guide,* 3 September.

Tapper, Melbourne. 1999. *In the Blood: Sickle Cell Anemia and the Politics of Race.* Philadelphia: University of Pennsylvania Press.

Thadani, Giti. 1996. *Sakhiyani: Lesbian Desire in Ancient and Modern India.* New York: Cassell.

There Is No Name for This. 1997. Film directed by Cianna Stewart and Ming-Yeun S. Ma.

Thompson, Becky. 2001. *A Promise and a Way of Life: White Anti-Racist Activism.* Minneapolis: University of Minnesota Press.

Thompson, Becky, and Sangeeta Tyagi, eds. 1996. *Names We Call Home: Autobiography on Racial Identity.* New York: Routledge.

Tillery, Garland. 1993. "Interview with Top Gun Pilot Tracy Thorne." *Our Own,* 18 May.

Tomasky, Michael. 1996. *The Life, Death, and Possible Resurrection of Progressive Politics in America.* New York: Free Press.

Tonry, Michael. 1995. *Malign Neglect: Race, Crime, and Punishment in America.* New York: Oxford University Press.

Torgovnick, Marianna. 1991. *Gone Primitive: Savage Intellects, Modern Lives.* Chicago: University of Chicago Press.

Toynbee, Polly. 1998. "The Press Gang." *The Guardian* (U.K.), 17 June.

Traub, James. 1998. "Nathan Glazer Changes His Mind, Again." *New York Times Magazine,* 28 June, 23–25.

"Two Boys Found Guilty in Arkansas School Shooting." 1998. *Reuters Limited,* 12 August.

Unger, Roberto Mangabeira. 1987. *Politics, A Work in Constructive Social Theory.* Vol. 1. Cambridge: Cambridge University Press.

Vaid, Urvashi. 1995. *Virtual Equality: The Mainstreaming of Lesbian and Gay Equality.* New York: Anchor Books.

Van Dyke, Nella K., and Sarah Soule. 2000. "Explaining Variation in Levels of Patriot and Militia Mobilization." Paper presented at 95th Annual Meetings of the American Sociological Association, Washington, D.C., August 16.

Vanita, Ruth. 1996. "The Straight Path to Salvation; or, The Unspeakable in the Decolonized Indian Academy." Paper presented at MLA meetings, Washington, D.C., December.

Wacquant, Loïc J. D. 1997. "For an Analytics of Racial Domination." *Social Theory and Political Power* 11: 221–34.

Wade, Peter. 1993. *Blackness and Race Mixture: The Dynamics of Racial Identity in Colombia.* Baltimore, MD: Johns Hopkins University Press.

Ware, Vron, and Les Back. Forthcoming. *The Trouble with Whiteness.* Chicago: University of Chicago Press.

Waters, Mary. 1990. *Ethnic Options: Choosing Identities in America.* Berkeley: University of California Press.

Waugh, Linda. 1982. "Marked and Unmarked: A Choice between Unequals in Semiotic Structure." *Semiotica* 38, nos. 3–4: 299–318.

Wellman, David T. 1997. "Minstrel Shows, Affirmative Action Talk, and Angry White Men: Making Racial Otherness in the 1990s." In *Displacing Whiteness: Essays in Social and Cultural Criticism,* ed. Ruth Frankenberg. Durham, N.C.: Duke University Press.

———. 1993. *Portraits of White Racism.* 2d ed. Cambridge: Cambridge University Press.

West, Cornel. 1993. *Race Matters.* Boston: Beacon Press.

Weston, Kath. "Do Clothes Make the Woman? Gender, Performance Theory, and Lesbian Eroticism." *Genders* 17: 1–21.

Wiegman, Robyn. 1999. "Whiteness Studies and the Paradox of Particularity." *boundary 2* 25, no. 3 (fall): 115–50.

Wieviorka, Michel. 1997. "Is It So Difficult to be Anti-Racist?" In *Debating Cultural Hybridity: Multi-Cultural Identities and the Politics of Anti-Racism,* eds. Pnina Werber and Tariq Modood. London: Zed Books.

Wildman, Stephanie M. 1996. *Privilege Revealed: How Invisible Preference Undermines America.* New York: New York University Press.

Willett, Cynthia. 1998. "The master-slave dialectic; Hegel versus Douglass." In *Subjugation and Bondage: Critical Essays on Slavery and Social Philosophy,* ed. Tommy L. Lott. Lanham: Rohman & Littlefield, 151–70.

Wilson, William Julius. 1992. "The Right Message." *New York Times,* 17 March, A23.

——. 1980. *The Declining Significance of Race: Blacks and Changing American Institutions.* 2d ed. Chicago: University of Chicago Press.

Wilson, James Q., and Richard Herrnstein. 1985. *Crime and Human Nature.* New York: Simon and Schuster.

Winant, Howard. 1997. "Behind Blue Eyes: Whiteness and Contemporary U.S. Racial Politics." *New Left Review* 225 (Sept.–Oct.): 73–88.

——. 1997. "Racial Dualism at Century's End." In *The House That Race Built,* ed. Wahneema Lubiano. New York: Pantheon Books.

——. 1994. *Racial Conditions: Politics, Theory, Comparisons.* Minneapolis: University of Minnesota Press.

Wolf, Eleanor. 1981. *Trial and Error: The Detroit School Segregation Case.* Detroit, MI: Wayne State University Press.

Wray, Matt, and Annalee Newitz, eds. 1997. *White Trash: Race and Class in America.* New York: Routledge.

Wray, Matt. Forthcoming. "Angry White Men: Figuring Whiteness and Masculinity in Affirmative Action Debates." In *What, Then, Is White?,* eds. Noel Ignatiev and Jacqueline Mimms. New York: Oxford University Press.

Yamamoto, Eric Y. 1995. "Rethinking Alliances: Agency, Responsibility and Interracial Justice." *UCLA Asian Pacific American Law Journal* 3, no. 1 (fall): 33–74.

Yep, Kathy. 1994. "The Power of Collective Voice." *Asian American Policy Review* 4: 33–63.

Young, Robert. 1995. *Colonial Desire: Hybridity in Theory, Culture, and Race.* New York: Routledge.

Zinn, Howard. 1980. *A People's History of the United States.* New York: Harper and Row.

Zolberg, Aristide. 1989. "The Next Waves: Migration Theory for a Changing World." *International Migration Review* 23, no. 3: 403–30.

Zweigenhaft, Richard L. 2000. "Are There Blacks in the White Establishment? Another Look." Paper presented at the 95th Annual Meetings of the American Sociological Association, Washington, D.C., 14 August.

Contributors

WILLIAM AAL is an activist and popular educator who for the past twenty years has brought an antiracist perspective into struggles for economic, gender, and environmental justice. He is a member of the Seattle Global Economy Working Group, the Washington Biotechnology Action Council, and the Economic Literacy Action Network, and is a cofounder of the Urban Action School. He does training, organizational development and consulting as an associate of Tools for Change (website: www.toolsforchange.org). He resides in Seattle, Washington.

ALLAN BÉRUBÉ is an independent scholar, a member of the National Writers Union, and a founder of the San Francisco Lesbian and Gay History Project. Since 1978 he has written, lectured, and presented slide shows on U.S. lesbian, gay, and transgender history. He is author of the award-winning book *Coming Out under Fire: The History of Gay Men and Women in World War Two* (Free Press, 1990). He co-wrote the 1994 Peabody Award–winning documentary film based on his book. He has taught lesbian and gay history courses at the University of California at Santa Cruz, Stanford University, Portland State University, and the New School for Social Research. In 1994 he was awarded a Rockefeller fellowship at the Center for Lesbian and Gay Studies at CUNY, and in 1996 he was awarded a prestigious MacArthur fellowship. He is currently writing a history of gay work and activism among the crew members of the great ocean liners from the Great Depression to the Cold War, titled *Shipping Out* (Houghton Mifflin, forthcoming).

DALTON CONLEY is currently associate professor of sociology and director of the Center for Advanced Social Science Research at New York University. Prior to joining the ranks of NYU, he was a faculty member of the Departments of Sociology and African American Studies at Yale University. He is the author of *Being Black, Living in the Red: Race, Wealth, and Social Policy in America* (University of California Press, 1999), and *Honky* (University of California Press, 2000), a memoir of growing up white in a predominantly minority urban-housing project. Conley has written extensively on issues of race and socioeconomic status and is currently working on a project that examines how siblings from the same family of origin end up in different class positions as adults. Conley is a recipient of a Robert Wood Johnson Foundation Investigator Award.

TROY DUSTER is a Chancellor's Professor of Sociology at the University of California, Berkeley, and is also on the faculty of the Institute for the History and Production of Knowledge and the Department of Sociology at New York University.

RUTH FRANKENBERG is an associate professor of American studies at the University of California, Davis. Her works on whiteness include *White Women, Race Matters: The Social Construction of Whiteness* (University of Minnesota Press, 1993) and *Displacing Whiteness: Essays in Social and Cultural Criticism* (Duke University Press, 1997), which she edited. Her current work includes an ethnography in progress, "A Quiet Revolution: Spiritual Practices in the Contemporary United States."

JOHN HARTIGAN, JR. currently teaches in the Americo Paredes Center for Cultural Studies in the Department of Anthropology at the University of Texas, Austin. His published works include articles in *Social Research, Cultural Studies,* and *American Anthropologist,* and *Racial Situations: Class Predicaments of Whiteness in Detroit* (Princeton University Press, 1999).

ERIC LOTT teaches American studies at the University of Virginia. He is the author of *Love and Theft: Blackface Minstrelsy and the American Working Class* (Oxford University Press, 1993) and the forthcoming *Darkness USA: The Cultural Contradictions of American Racism.*

MICHAEL OMI is a professor of comparative ethnic studies at the University of California, Berkeley. He is the author (with Howard Winant) of *Racial Formation in the United States* (2d edition, Routledge, 1994), and articles on Asian Americans and race relations, right-wing political movements, and race and popular culture. He is currently completing a study of the emerging practices of antiracist organizations in the United States. In 1990 he was the recipient of UC Berkeley's Distinguished Teaching Award.

JASBIR KAUR PUAR is assistant professor of women's studies and geography at Rutgers University. She wrote her Ph.D. dissertation on transnational sexualities and Trinidad in the department of comparative ethnic studies, University of California, Berkeley. She has published several articles on South Asian diasporic cultural politics in *Q&A: Queer in Asian America* (ed. Eng and Hom, Temple University Press, 1997), *New Frontiers in Women's Studies* (ed. Maynard and Purvis, Taylor and Francis, 1996), and *Socialist Review.*

MAB SEGREST is a writer, organizer, and teacher who lives in Durham, North Carolina. Her book *Memoir of a Race Traitor* (1994) won the Lambda Editor's Choice and was named an Outstanding Book on Human Rights in North America. She is currently coordinator of the Urban-Rural Mission (USA). This essay will be in her next collection, *Born to Belonging*, forthcoming from Rutgers University Press.

VRON WARE is a writer, photographer, and teacher who has one foot in London and the other in Connecticut. She was editor of the antifascist journal *Searchlight* in the early 1980s. *Beyond the Pale: White Women, Racism and History* was published by Verso in 1992, and *The Trouble with Whiteness*, her new collection of polemical essays about whiteness, culture, and politics (with Les Back) is forthcoming from the University of Chicago Press.

HOWARD WINANT is a professor of sociology at Temple University. He is the author of *Racial Conditions: Politics, Theory, Comparisons* (1994) and the co-author (with Michael Omi) of *Racial Formation in the United States: From the 1960s to the 1990s* (2d ed., Routledge, 1994). He has also written a book on economic policy, *Stalemate: Political Economic Origins of Supply-Side Policy* (Praeger, 1988) and *The World Is a Ghetto: Race and Democracy Since World War II* (New York: Basic Books, 2001). His work on race examines the continuing centrality of racial identity and racial inequality. His current research concerns the contested meaning and evolving political dynamics of race in selected European, African, and American countries.

Editors

BIRGIT BRANDER RASMUSSEN is a doctoral candidate in the department of comparative ethnic studies at the University of California, Berkeley, and a Danish Research Academy fellow. She specializes in comparative ethnic literatures and is writing her dissertation on colonial semiosis—the meeting of heterogeneous textual practices—in early and contemporary American literatures. She has translated Danish immigrant poetry for the Longfellow Institute Series in American Languages and Literatures at Harvard. She has published short stories and is a contributor to KVINDFO, a web magazine on gender and culture.

ERIC KLINENBERG is Assistant Professor of Sociology at Northwestern University, a faculty fellow at the Institute for Policy Research, and an individual projects fellow of the Open Society Institute. His forthcoming book, a social autopsy of the 1995 Chicago heat wave and an account of emergent forms of urban danger and deprivation, will be published by the University of Chicago Press in 2002. He has published articles in *Theory and Society, Body and Society, Ethnography, Le Monde Diplomatique,* and *Actes de la Recherche en Sciènces Sociales.*

IRENE J. NEXICA is a writer whose latest work analyzes popular music and its intersections with mainstream and academic theories of gender, ethnicity, nationality, class, and sexuality, particularly in the United States and Britain. She also researches fandom and the ways that communities converge and interact. She is currently focusing on the Spice Girls, boy bands, and other "teen" music marketed to listeners of all ages.

MATT WRAY received his doctorate from the department of comparative ethnic studies at the University of California, Berkeley, and is currently Assistant Professor of Sociology at the University of Nevada, Las Vegas. His forthcoming book on historical representations of poor rural whites in the United States will be published by Duke University Press. His articles have appeared in the *Minnesota Review* and *Social Justice*. He is coeditor of *White Trash: Race and Class in America* (Routledge, 1997) and *Bad Subjects: Political Education for Everyday Life* (New York University Press, 1998).

Index

Aal, William, 13, 17

Abolitionism, 106–8, 228

Affirmative action: economic status and, 275–76; education and, 83, 286; ethnicity and, 4, 89; legislation, 4–7, 20 nn.12, 14, 106; South Africa and, 125–26

AFL-CIO, 217–18, 228, 231

African Americans: Asian Americans and, 131, 286; assimilation and, 302–3; civil rights movement, 4, 5, 102–3; economic status of, 127–28, 129; homosexuality and, 240–41; Latinos and, 286–87; in the military, 240–44, 261 n.7; whiteness and, 2, 27–28, 31–33, 34 n.22, 77–81, 249. *See also* Race and racism

Afrocentric curriculum, 142–47, 151, 153–57, 160

AIDS activism, 243, 248–53, 258

Alexander, M. Jacqui, 13, 169, 172

Allen, Theodore, 13, 191

Almaguer, Tomàs, 288

Alterman, Eric, 220, 232

American Anthropological Association, 269

American Federation of Labor, 119

American Sociological Association, 86–92

Angelou, Maya, 216

Anti-Racism Institute of Clergy and Laity Concerned (Chicago), 271, 277

Antiracist activism: civil rights movement, 91, 102–5, 244–45, 263 n.30, 268–70, 289; diversity training, 295–96, 301–2; in the gay community, 235, 248, 254–56, 259, 297–98; organizations, 49–51, 271–77, 289–90; whiteness and, 83, 153–57, 160–61, 254–56, 266–67, 305–6. *See also* Race and racism

Anti-semitism, 221, 276

Anzaldúa, Gloria, 170

Apartheid, 122, 124–25, 127, 133 n.1

Aronowitz, Stanley, 226

Asian Americans: African Americans and, 131, 286; Committee against Anti-Asian Violence (CAAAV), 272, 277–81; economic status of, 281–82; education and, 35–36; Organization of Asian Women, 280; violence against, 279–81, 283–84; whiteness of, 21 n.22, 89, 178 n.6

Assimilation, 302–7

Baldwin, James, 207, 236, 259, 307

Berman, Paul, 215, 219–21, 226, 232

Bernier, François, 26, 31, 33

Bérubé, Allan, 13, 16, 242, 262 n.17

Bhabha, Homi, 171–72

Biology and genetics, 8, 42 n.11, 101, 104, 115–17, 121–22, 133 n.2, 192

Black Lesbian and Gay Leadership Forum, 244

Black Panthers, 232

Black Power, 232

Blair, Tony, 194, 197–98

Blumer, Herbert, 101, 104

Bonnett, Alistair, 153, 156, 266

Borders: of race, 8–9, 26, 34–35, 40–41, 102, 131–32, 237–38; of sexuality, 167–74, 182 n.37

Bradshaw, John, 63–65

Britain: Caribbean immigrants in, 198–200, 203–4, 208; cultural identity of youth in, 190–92, 210–11; national identity, 193–95, 198–200, 203–6; reimaging of, 192–96; working class in, 191–92

British Nationalist Party (BNP), 192–93, 197–98

Butler, Judith, 168, 174, 177 n.3

California, 4–7, 19 n.10, 130–31, 136 n.30, 285–86

California Civil Rights Initiative, 4–7, 19 n.10, 285–86

Campaign for Military Service (CMS), 239–42, 244

Capitalism, 59, 62, 169, 218–19, 272, 307

Carribean/West Indians, 199–200, 203–4, 208, 209

Caste system (India), 126–28, 136 n.26

Census, United States, 9, 129

Chesnut, Mary Boykin, 54–55, 67

Civil Rights Act (1964), 105

Civil rights movement, 91, 102–5, 244–45, 263 n.30, 268–70, 289

Class: gender and, 172–73, 232, 247, 302; middle class, 6, 25, 34; poverty and, 219; race and, 36–37, 83, 122, 141–42, 145, 228, 238, 302; working class, 122, 191–92, 217

Cold War era, 98–100, 216

Colonialism, 13, 74–75, 81, 98–99, 192

Color blindness, 90–91, 103, 225, 247, 267–68, 289–90

Columbia University Teach-In (1996), 217–20, 227–28, 229

Committee against Anti-Asian Violence (CAAAV), 272, 277–84

Communism, 221, 229, 231

Congressional Black Caucus, 245

Conley, Dalton, 14, 15

Connerly, Ward, 5, 6–7, 84

Crenshaw, Kimberlé, 104

Culture: African Americans and white, 28, 31–33; and cultural disfunction, 65–67; globalization and, 185, 220; of the Left, 222–23; multiculturalism, 130–31, 190, 194–96, 206, 210, 221, 285; of whiteness, 10–11, 28, 299–301; youth and, 11, 190–92, 210–11

Davis, Angela, 269, 290

De Beauvoir, Simone, 56

D'Emilio, John, 173, 254

Democratic Party, 215, 226

Detroit Summer, 300

Diana, Princess of Wales, 187–88

Discrimination: affirmative action and, 4–7, 20 nn.12, 14, 83, 89, 106, 125–26, 275–76, 286; and African Americans in the military, 239–44, 261 n.7; apartheid, 122, 124–25, 127, 133 n.1; in education, 11–12, 34–35; in employment, 202–3, 273; and gays and lesbians in the military, 179 n.13, 239–45, 261 n.7, 262 nn.13, 17; in housing, 11, 27, 117–20, 131, 135 n.17, 202–3; police departments and, 124, 208–9; racial profiling as, 114, 134 n.3

Dismantling Racism Program of the

National Conference (St. Louis), 271, 273, 275, 277, 278

Douglass, Frederick, 52–53, 65–67

Du Bois, W. E. B., 45–46, 51, 55, 88, 99, 104, 108, 228

Duggan, Lisa, 173, 174

Durkheim, Emile, 104

Duster, Troy, 15

Dyer, Richard, 190–91, 211

Economic status: of African Americans, 127–28, 129; of Asian Americans, 281–82; national identity and, 194–96; New Deal, 118–19; of poor whites, 89–90, 275–76; wages and, 127–29, 217; whiteness and, 201–2, 244, 247, 261 n.6, 302; of working class in Britain, 191–92. See also Labor; Working class

Edmundson, Mark, 219, 220

Education: Afrocentric curriculum, 142–47, 151, 153–57, 160; Asian Americans and, 35–36; discrimination in, 11–12, 34–36; legislation and, 4, 5, 6–7, 19 n.10, 20 n.15; minority student achievement, 4–7; the New Left in the university, 220–22; public schools, 34–35, 142–46, 149–50, 229

Erdich, Louise, 80

Espiritu, Yen, 279

Ethnicity, 2, 4, 35–40, 89, 192–94, 198–200

Ethnography, 140–41, 159–60

Fabian, Johannes, 144

Family dysfunction, 63–67

Feagin, Joe, 290

Feminism, 18 n.6, 63, 174

Foner, Eric, 218

Foucault, Michel, 101, 176

Frankenberg, Ruth, 14, 160, 270

Fraser, Steve, 217, 218

Freire, Paulo, 67

Freud, Sigmund, 56–59, 63, 69 n.25

Friedan, Betty, 218

Gates, Henry Louis, 216, 224

Gay men: AIDS activism and, 243, 247–53, 258; antiracist activism and, 248, 254–56, 297–98; gay rights movement and, 244–45, 263 n.30; in the military, 179 n.13, 239–45, 261 n.7, 262 nn.13, 17; whiteness of, 235–41, 244, 246–50, 261 n.6

Gilroy, Paul, 72

Gitlin, Todd, 215, 216, 219–20, 226–27, 229–32

Glazer, Nathan, 103

Globalization: American culture and, 220; and asylum, 174, 182 n.37; of homosexuality, 168–69, 173; identity and, 185–86, 194–95; racism and, 99, 109 n.4

Goethe, Johann Wolfgang von, 191

Goffman, Erving, 224

Goldberg, David, 270, 278–79

Gramsci, Antonio, 100, 101, 296

Green, Mark Scanlon, 297

Greenhalgh, Paul, 195

Grewal, Inderpal, 170

Grossberg, Lawrence, 59–60

Guinier, Lani, 216, 226

Hale, Grace Elizabeth, 191

Hall, Lisa Kahaleole, 250, 256

Hall, Stuart, 75, 169, 186, 230, 296, 308

Harris, Cheryl, 6, 80, 104, 226

Hartigan, John, Jr., 15

Hate crimes, 278–79, 281, 283–84

Hegel, Georg Wilhelm Friedrich, 55–56

Hennessy, Rosemary, 172
Herrnstein, Richard, 121
Hewitt, Roger, 190
Hill, Marjorie, 245–46
Hinduism, 171, 180 n.23
Hoffa, James, Jr., 219, 224
Homophobia, 45, 49, 83, 257
Homosexuality: African Americans and, 240–41; AIDS activism and, 243, 247–53, 258; antiracist activism and, 235, 248, 254–56, 259, 297–98; Black Lesbian and Gay Leadership Forum, 244; coming out, 175–76; gay rights movement, 244–45, 263 n.30; gays and lesbians in the military, 179 n.13, 239–45, 261 n.7, 262 nn.13, 17; globalization of, 167–70, 168–69, 173; homophobia and, 45, 49, 83, 257; and marketing of gay whiteness, 238–39, 244, 246, 261 n.6; and marriage and domestic partnerships, 174–75; national identity and, 170–73; Queer Nation, 170, 172, 181 n.27; Queer Studies, 173; Queer theory, 169, 178 n.8; race and, 168–69, 236–37, 239–44, 247, 250, 255, 257–58; San Antonio Lesbian Gay Assembly (SALGA), 255; Trikone (South Asian Gay and Lesbian Organization), 171–72; whiteness of, 168–73, 178 n.6, 181 n.27, 235–41, 244, 246–50, 254–58, 261 n.6. See also Queerness
hooks, bell, 10–11, 12, 22 n.34, 44–45, 296, 308
Horkheimer, Max, 220
Housing, 11, 27, 117–20, 131, 135 n.17, 202–3
Howe, Irving, 215, 226
Hughes, Henry, 53, 55, 59
Hughes, Langston, 2

Identity: black, 66, 185, 187, 227; Britain, 185–86, 189–95, 197–200, 210–11; politics, 1, 184, 216–19, 227, 230–32, 302–3; racial, 38–39, 52–53, 104, 111 n.25, 115, 117; re-imaging of, 194–97, 198–200; sexual, 170–73, 176, 179 n.13, 227, 232; sports and, 186–89, 192, 211. See also Gay men; Lesbians; Race and racism; Whiteness
Ignatiev, Noel, 124, 305–6
Immigrants and immigration: Asian American, 21 n.22, 35–36, 89, 131, 178 n.6, 272, 277–86; assimilation of, 302–4; in Britain, 193–95, 198–200; from the Carribean, 199–200, 203–4, 207–8, 209; legislation against, 4–7, 285–86; sexual identity and, 167–69, 172, 174–75, 177 n.1, 182 n.37; violence against, 203–6
India, 78, 126–28, 170–72

James, C. L. R., 62, 229
Jameson, Fredric, 184, 222
Jim Crow, 48, 122
Johnson, Lyndon, 105
Jordan, June, 184
Jordan, Winthrop, 191

Kazin, Michael, 215, 218
Kelley, Robin, 227–28
Kelly, Michael, 215
Kimball, Roger, 229
King, Martin Luther, Jr., 5, 103, 105, 228–29, 245–46
Kingston, Maxine Hong, 80

Labor: antiracist activism and, 231, 275–76; blacks in, 118, 223; discrimination in, 202–3, 273; immigrants and, 202–3; in South Africa, 125–

26; unions and, 119, 202–3, 217–19, 223–24, 228, 231, 235; wages, 127–29, 217; women and, 118, 228, 280, 282–83

Labor/Community Strategy Center (L/CSC), 272, 275, 277

Laclau, Ernesto, 227

Latinos: affirmative action and, 4, 89; and African Americans, 286–87; in the military, 261 n.7; and poverty, 219, 277; racial identity of, 38

The Left, 106, 220–28, 230

Legislation: Civil Rights Act (1964), 105; Jim Crow, 48, 122; National Housing Acts (1934 & 1949), 119, 120; Proposition 187, 4, 285–86; Proposition 209, 4–7, 19 n.10, 285–86; Taft-Hartley Act (1948), 217; Wagner Act (1935), 118–19

Leonard, Mark, 194, 195, 197

Lesbians, 167–70, 238, 247, 250, 261 n.7

Leslie, Ann, 190–91, 192

Liberalism, 103–6, 214–21, 225–26, 232–33

Lind, Michael, 215, 216, 219–23

Lipsitz, George, 5, 267

Lott, Eric, 16

Lowe, Lisa, 170, 284

Making and Unmaking of Whiteness conference, 3–4, 84, 130

Malcolm X Academy (Detroit), 142–46, 149–50

Marcuse, Herbert, 58, 59, 67

Marketing: of gay whiteness, 238–39, 244, 246, 261 n.6; of national identity, 194–97, 198–200

Marxism, 220, 223

Media images of race, 143–50, 163 n.10, 165 n.17, 203–4

Menand, Louis, 219, 220

Michaels, Walter Benn, 104, 106, 108

Military service: African Americans in, 240–44, 261 n.7; Campaign for Military Service (CMS), 239–42, 244; gays and lesbians in, 179 n.13, 239–45, 261 n.7, 262 nn.13, 17; Latinos in, 261 n.7; Military Freedom Project, 261 n.7

Mills, C. Wright, 219

Mixner, David, 239, 241, 244–45, 261 n.7, 263 n.30

Mohanty, Chandra, 13, 169

Moraga, Cherríe, 8, 170

Morrison, Toni, 2, 97

Mouffe, Chantal, 227

Multiculturalism, 130–31, 190, 194–96, 206, 210, 221, 285

Myrdal, Gunnar, 99

National Front, 198, 211

National Housing Acts (1934 & 1949), 119, 120

National Organization for an American Revolution (NOAR), 299, 301, 303

Native Americans, 80, 130

Native Hawaiians, 287

Neighborhoods, 27–32, 120, 144, 146

Neoconservatism, 102–3, 105

New Deal, 118–19, 214

North Carolinians Against Racist and Religious Violence, 50

Northwest Coalition Against Malicious Harassment (NWC), 271, 274, 276, 277

Nunn, Sam, 239, 240, 245, 263 n.30

Nussbaum, Martha, 224

Omi, Michael, 16, 98

Ong, Aihwa, 171

Organization of Asian Women, 280

Perry, Pamela, 131
Phillips, Mike, 199, 204–6, 208–10
Police departments, 124, 208–9, 276, 280–81
Populism, 215, 216
Poverty, 218–19, 229, 277
President's Initiative on Race, 285
Proposition 187, 4, 285–86
Proposition 209, 4–7, 19 n.10, 285–86
Puar, Jasbir Kaur, 16
Public schools, 34–35, 142–46, 149, 150

Quadagno, Jill, 118
Queerness: Queer Nation, 170, 172, 181 n.27; Queer Studies, 173; Queer theory, 169, 178 n.8. *See also* Homosexuality

Race and racism: academic studies of, 269–70; Afrocentric curriculum, 142–47, 151, 153–57, 160; antiracist activism, 278–82; Asian Americans, 278–82; biology and genetics of, 8, 42 n.11, 101, 104, 115–17, 121–22, 133 n.2, 192; black/white dualism in United States, 11, 130–31, 277; class and, 141–42, 145, 228, 232, 238, 302; colonialism and, 74–75, 98–99; color blindness, 90–91, 103, 247, 267–68, 289–90; ethnicity and, 35–38; family dysfunction and, 63–67; gay and lesbian community and, 168, 236–37, 239–44, 247, 250, 257–58; hate crimes, 278–79, 281, 283–84; immigrants and immigration, 99, 204–5; invisibility of whiteness, 73–82, 91, 164 n.12; media images of, 143–50, 163 n.10, 165 n.17, 203–4; in the military, 240–44, 261 n.7; political

views on, 102–6, 214–19; racial identity, 38–39, 52–53, 104, 111 n.25, 115, 117; working class and, 36–37, 45–46, 141–42. *See also* Whiteness
Racial formation theory, 100–101, 109 n.7, 111 n.25
Randolph, A. Philip, 226, 228
Rapping, Elaine, 62, 70 n.31
Reich, Robert, 216, 222, 223
Religion, 171, 220, 300–301
Roediger, David, 2, 77–80, 107, 124, 132, 191, 207
Roosevelt, Franklin D., 118
Root, Marian, 300, 307
Rorty, Richard, 215, 217–19, 220–23, 224, 226

Said, Edward, 296
San Antonio Lesbian Gay Assembly (SALGA), 255
Saxton, Alexander, 191
Schlesinger, Arthur, 216, 229–30
Schuyler, George S., 80
Sedgwick, Eve, 175
Segrest, Mab, 14, 15
Slavery, 45–46, 51–56, 59–60, 63–67, 130
Sleeper, Jim, 215, 229
Smith, Barbara, 253
SNCC (Student Nonviolent Coordinating Committee), 228–29
South Africa, 124–26, 127, 129
Southern Empowerment Project (SEP), 272, 274, 278
Spivak, Gayatri, 220
Sugg, Katherine, 170
Sweeney, John, 217, 218, 224

Taft-Hartley Act (1948), 217
Takaki, Ron, 131
Teamsters for a Democratic Union, 219

Third World, 78, 102, 168
Tools for Change, 298, 301, 303
Transnationalism, 168–69, 174, 178
    n.8, 182 n.37
Trikone (South Asian Gay and Lesbian
    Organization), 171–72
Twelve-Step Program, 60–63, 67, 70
    n.31

UNESCO Statement on Race (1995),
    115, 116
Unger, Roberto, 296
Unions, 119, 202–3, 217–19, 223–24,
    228, 231, 235

Violence: against Asian Americans,
    279–81, 283–84; black men and,
    230; in Britain, 203–6, 208; hate
    crimes, 278–79, 281, 283–84;
    homophobia and, 45, 49, 83, 257;
    police departments and, 124, 208–
    9, 276, 280–81; white supremacy
    and, 12, 43–44, 49–55; women and,
    51–55, 78–79
Voting rights, 5, 106, 118, 223

Wagner Act (1935), 118–19
Ware, Vron, 16
Waters, Mary, 37–38
Watkins, Perry, 241, 242–43, 248, 263
    n.18
Wellman, David, 85
West, Cornel, 215, 216, 218, 296
Whiteness: academic studies of, 18
    n.6, 82–84, 86–92, 295–97, 301,
    306–9; African Americans and, 2,
    27–28, 31–33, 34 n.22, 77–81, 249·
    AIDS activism and, 243, 247–53,
    258; antiracism and, 13, 83, 152 ,7,
    160–61, 254 ,   ^Am cans
    and, 21 n.22, 89, 178 n.6; assimila-
    tion, 207–8, 299–307; black (Brit-

ish) views of, 200–202; contested
    meanings of, 7–11, 76, 81, 85, 106–
    8, 111 n.25, 131–32; culture of, 10–
    11, 28, 299–301; ethnicity, 38–40;
    of gays and lesbians, 170–73, 178
    n.6, 181 n.27, 235–41, 244–50, 254–
    58, 261 n.6; globalization of, 184–
    86; invisibility of, 73–82, 91, 164
    n.12; neoconservatism and, 102–3,
    105; passing for white, 104, 115, 117;
    reimaging of, 196–98, 300–301;
    slavery and, 45–46, 51–56, 59–60,
    63–67, 130; and white supremacy,
    12, 43–44, 49–55, 98–103, 184, 271,
    276
Wilentz, Sean, 215, 219, 220, 221
Williams, Patricia, 218, 226
Winant, Howard, 15, 270
Windrush, 199–200, 203–4, 208
Women: affirmative action and, 5–6;
    Asian American, 282–83; in British
    working class, 191–92; feminism,
    18 n.6, 174; and identity politics,
    226, 227; and labor, 118, 228, 280,
    282–83; lesbians, 167–70, 238,
    247, 250, 261 n.7; and poverty, 219;
    and union membership, 228; vio-
    lence toward, 51–55, 78–79;
    women's studies, 2, 18 n .
Working class: A -` .. Americans in,
    282; in ʒritain, 191–92; men in, 6,
    276; .acism in, 36–37, 144; stereo-
    typ es of, 141–42, 165 n.19, 238;
    · /hites in, 45–46, 89–90, 141–42,
    161–62, 165 n.19
World Trade Organization, 305

Yamamoto, Eric, 287–88
Yep, Kathy, 279–80
Youth, 11, 190–92, 210–11, 282

Zinn, Howard, 308

Library of Congress Cataloging-in-Publication Data

The making and unmaking of whiteness / edited
by Birgit Brander Rasmussen, et al.

p.   cm.

Papers from a conference held at the University of
California at Berkeley in 1997.

Includes bibliographical references and index.

ISBN 0-8223-2730-9 (cloth : alk. paper) —
ISBN 0-8223-2740-6 (pbk : alk. paper)

1. Whites—United States—Race identity—Congresses.

2. Race awareness—United States—Congresses.

3. Racism—United States—Congresses.

4. United States—Race relations—Congresses.

5. United States—Social conditions—Congresses.

6. Social classes—United States—Congresses.

I. Brander Rasmussen, Birgit

E184.A1 M2627 2001

305.8'034073—dc21   2001028688